Register Now for Online Access to Your Book!

S0-DNN-679

SPRINGER PUBLISHING COMPANY
CONNECT™

INCLUDES A STUDENT TOOLBOX

Your print purchase of *The Social Work Field Placement,* **includes online access to the contents of your book**—increasing accessibility, portability, and searchability!

Access today at:

http://connect.springerpub.com/content/book/978-0-8261-7553-3 or scan the QR code at the right with your smartphone and enter the access code below.

FRWS99AH

Scan here for quick access.

SPC

SPRINGER PUBLISHING COMPANY
View all our products at springerpub.com

John Poulin, PhD, MSW, is a professor emeritus and adjunct professor at Widener University's Center for Social Work Education in Chester, Pennsylvania, currently teaching the foundation field seminar in Widener's online MSW program. In 2016, he retired from Widener University, where he taught generalist practice, research, and policy courses for 32 years. Dr. Poulin received a BA from the University of Southern Maine, an MSW from the University of Michigan, and a PhD from the University of Chicago's School of Social Service Administration. As a former director of Widener's BSW program, he founded its MSW program and served as the dean and director for 13 years. He also served for 10 years as the executive director of Social Work Consultation Services (SWCS), an innovative community-based field placement agency developed by the school of social work in collaboration with local community human services organizations. SWCS provides a wide range of free social work services to low-income community residents as well as free capacity-building services to underresourced community-based human services organizations. SWCS has served as a field placement site for hundreds of BSW and MSW students. Dr. Poulin has published numerous journal articles and book chapters and three editions of a generalist social work practice textbook. He also has to his credit many national and international conference presentations.

Selina Matis, PhD, LCSW, a lifelong resident of southwestern Pennsylvania, is a social work faculty member at California University of Pennsylvania, where she earned her MSW. She received her doctoral degree in social work from Widener University. In addition, she has a BS in elementary education and an MS in school psychology, both from California University. Clinically, she has worked primarily in the mental health arena supporting children and their families in a variety of settings. Her research interests include resilience, mental well-being, trauma, burnout, and self-care. Educationally, Dr. Matis has taught at both BSW and MSW levels in a variety of subject areas, including research, policy, human behavior in the social environment, and program evaluation. She has experience supporting students through the field process in a variety of ways, including as a field coordinator, field faculty liaison, and MSW supervisor. Dr. Matis has published and presented on a variety of topics, including resilience, trauma-informed social work, working with families, helping students succeed, and the social work competencies.

Heather Witt, PhD, MEd, LMSW, is a licensed social worker and associate professor at Boise State University's School of Social Work in Boise, Idaho. Dr. Witt received a BS in psychology from Boise State University and an MSW and MEd and PhD from Widener University. Currently, she teaches human behavior in the social environment, research, and macro subjects in the BSW and MSW programs. As a clinical social worker, Dr. Witt has experience providing individual, group, family, and couples therapy to children, adolescents, adults, and older adults regarding a variety of issues, including sexual abuse, infertility, grief and loss, depression, anxiety, sexual dysfunction, and others. She has also provided psychoeducational sex education groups for families. She has worked as a practitioner and in administration in community health and nonprofit education settings. Dr. Witt's research publication and presentation topics include infertility, body image, eating disorders, gender differences, humility, trauma-informed approaches in the classroom, and cross-cultural research on body image, fear of intimacy, psychological well-being, and sexual anxiety among Chinese individuals. She has authored multiple research articles on these topics and a Special Topics chapter on infertility in *Sexuality Concepts for Social Workers and Human Service Professionals*.

The Social Work Field Placement

A Competency-Based Approach

John Poulin, PhD, MSW
Selina Matis, PhD, LCSW
Heather Witt, PhD, MEd, LMSW

SPRINGER PUBLISHING COMPANY

Springer Publishing Company, LLC
11 West 42nd Street
New York, NY 10036
www.springerpub.com

Acquisitions Editor: Kate Dimock
Compositor: Graphic World

ISBN: 978-0-8261-7552-6
ebook ISBN: 978-0-8261-7553-3
DOI: 10.1891/9780826175533

Student Supplements are available from Springerpub.com/fieldwrk
Student Toolbox: 978-0-8261-7556-4

Instructor's Materials: Qualified instructors may request supplements by emailing
textbook@springerpub.com:
Instructor's Manual: 978-0-8261-7554-0
Instructor's PowerPoints: 978-0-8261-7555-7

20 21 22 23 24 / 7 6 5 4 3

The author and the publisher of this Work have made every effort to use sources believed to be reliable to provide information that is accurate and compatible with the standards generally accepted at the time of publication. The author and publisher shall not be liable for any special, consequential, or exemplary damages resulting, in whole or in part, from the readers' use of, or reliance on, the information contained in this book. The publisher has no responsibility for the persistence or accuracy of URLs for external or third-party Internet websites referred to in this publication and does not guarantee that any content on such websites is, or will remain, accurate or appropriate.

Library of Congress Cataloging-in-Publication Data

Names: Poulin, John E., author. ǀ Matis, Selina, author. ǀ Witt, Heather,
  author.
Title: The social work field placement : a competency-based approach /
  John Poulin, Selina Matis, Heather Witt.
Description: New York, NY : Springer Publishing Company, LLC, [2019] ǀ
  Includes bibliographical references and index.
Identifiers: LCCN 2018023942 (print) ǀ LCCN 2018030149 (ebook) ǀ ISBN
  9780826175533 ǀ ISBN 9780826175526 (pbk.) ǀ ISBN 9780826175533 (ebk.)
Subjects: LCSH: Social work education. ǀ Social service—Fieldwork.
Classification: LCC HV11 (ebook) ǀ LCC HV11 .P66 2019 (print) ǀ DDC
  361.3071/55--dc23
LC record available at https://lccn.loc.gov/2018023942

Contact us to receive discount rates on bulk purchases.
We can also customize our books to meet your needs.
For more information please contact: sales@springerpub.com

Publisher's Note: New and used products purchased from third-party sellers are not guaranteed for quality, authenticity, or access to any included digital components.

Printed in the United States of America.

Social workers and social work students are fighting for the rights of women, sexual minorities, racial and ethnic minorities, immigrants, refugees, and all other oppressed people in the United States and throughout the world. They combat social and economic injustice daily and are on the front lines in the struggle for equality and social justice in these troubling times. It is to these committed advocates that we dedicate this book.

Contents

Additional Contributors

Marina Barnett, DSW, is currently an associate professor in Widener University's Center for Social Work Education. Dr. Barnett teaches social welfare policy, organizational practice and grant writing, and community organization at the BSW, MSW, and PhD levels. Dr. Barnett has served in the Philadelphia and Chester communities as a consultant to numerous community-based organizations and government offices. Her research interests include geographic information system (GIS) mapping of community assets and using community empowerment approaches to train community residents to understand and conduct research in their own communities.

Stephen Kauffman, PhD, is a professor at Widener University's Center for Social Work Education, where he has taught community practice, program evaluation, research, and policy since 1991. Since receiving his PhD from Bryn Mawr College and his MSW from Washington University in St. Louis, his research and practice have focused on citizen participation and community and organizational responses to global problems, such as environmental decay, poverty (in all its dimensions), and education.

With this focus, major research projects have included program evaluations of U.S Department of Justice violence prevention programs, U.S. Department of Health and Human Services housing programs, 21st century community learning centers, lead abatement, and teenage pregnancy prevention. The programs (and evaluations) have received funding from U.S. Department of Justice, U.S. Department of Housing and Urban Development, the state of Pennsylvania, and several private foundations.

Most recently, his work has targeted the relationship between universities and their surrounding environments. He has published in *Social Work, Journal of Social Work Education, Journal of Community Practice, Journal of Baccalaureate Social Work,* and elsewhere.

Preface

GOAL OF THE BOOK

This book is designed to help BSW and MSW students enrolled in foundation field placements and field seminars structure their field placement learning around the nine Council on Social Work Education (CSWE) profession social work competencies defined in the 2015 Educational Policy and Accreditation Standards (EPAS). Our goal is to ensure that foundation field placement students integrate course learning related to the social work competencies with their field placement learning experiences in a purposeful, reflective, and integrated manner.

In our opinion, social work field education is facing three related challenges in relation to the mandated professional competencies and students' field placement experiences. The first is the disconnect between social work education's emphasis on the competencies and the practice of social work in the field. Unlike social work education, agency-based social work practice is not organized around the CSWE competencies. Thus, social work field placement students are faced with two competing pressures: their social work programs' focus on professional competencies development and their field placements' focus on the tasks and skills related to the delivery of services and adherence to the agency's model of practice. This book helps structure students' field learning to ensure that competency development is addressed throughout the field experience. It focuses the field experience and learning opportunities on the social work competencies. Each chapter is directly linked to a professional competency with substantive content on the competency, field reflection questions, critical thinking questions, a detailed case example illustrating one or more competencies with discussion questions, and electronic competency resource links to websites and videos.

A second challenge is that most field instructors are not well versed on competency-based education and the 2015 EPAS emphasis on professional competencies. This leads to a lack of direct emphasis in student supervision related to the students' competency development. It is natural for supervisors to focus their supervision on the students' field tasks, work with clients, use of self, and administrative issues. However, including or framing supervision around the nine professional competencies does not happen organically with most field instructors. This book addresses this challenge by providing students with a toolbox that includes a competency field log intended to ensure that their field supervision includes discussions of their experiences and progress on each of the nine professional competencies. The student toolbox also contains an instrument to assess their field supervision as a way to increase the students' and field instructors' awareness of the administrative, educational, and supportive components of supervision to help ensure that all three are covered in the supervisory processes. As noted earlier, students' competency development around the educational component is often not addressed in field supervision. The Field Supervision Inventory and the Competency Reflection Logs provided in the student toolbox help ensure that the students' experiences and progress related to the professional social work competencies are directly addressed in their field supervision. As an additional supplement to the field instructors' training and education on the 2015 EPAS, all purchasers of the print edition of this book are able to download an ebook version at no additional cost.

A third challenge facing field education in social work is that the EPAS 2015 mandates that at least one of a social work program's assessment measures be based on demonstration of the competency in real or simulated practice situations. Students' field placements meet the "real" practice situation criteria and are often used for one of the required outcome measures for each competency. Typically, the field instructor is tasked with completing the student's evaluation, which is tied in some way to the professional competencies. The challenge is obtaining meaningful data on competency assessment. This becomes problematic when competency development has not been incorporated into the ongoing supervisory process. When this happens, supervisors do not have the data needed to make accurate and valid assessments. The evaluation tends to be based on overall impressions without supporting data. This, in our opinion, raises serious questions about the validity of the data used for one of the mandated two measures.

This book helps address this challenge. The competency field log used to help structure field learning and supervision centered on competency development is also an excellent tool for a competency-based assessment conducted by the field instructors. The competency field log documents the students' experiences, affective reactions, and critical thinking on each competency throughout the field placement. It becomes the data on which the field instructors can base their assessment in completing the schools' field assessment tool. When used this way, the field instructor has the students' documentation and reflections from their field experiences related to each competency to help in evaluating student progress. This helps ensure that the field instructor's evaluation is data driven and not just based on an overall impression. We believe that the use of the competency log will help field instructors differentiate the students on each competency based on actual experiences related to each competency. This will not happen if experiences related to each competency during the internship are not processed and discussed in supervision during the field placement and if a record of those experiences is not part of the students' field evaluation.

Thus, the goal of this book is threefold. First, it helps structure students' field learning on the social work competencies. Second, it helps educate social work field instructors on the social work competencies mandated by CSWE. Third, it helps provide valid data to social work programs on their students' mastery of the nine social work competencies if they use the student field evaluation by their field instructors as one of their required two program outcome measures.

DISTINGUISHING FEATURES/LEARNING TOOLS

In this book, we cover topics students need for successful field experiences and tie these topics to the professional social work competencies. The chapter topics and associated competencies are shown as follows:

Chapter Title	Chapter Topics	EPAS Competency
Chapter 1: The Social Work Field Placement	Field placement process, expectations, roles and expectations, professional expectations, safety, time management, and values and ethics	Competency 1: Demonstrate Ethical and Professional Behavior
Chapter 2: Evaluating Your Professional Competencies	Accreditation, EPAS 2015, social work competencies, holistic competency, cognitive and affective processes, assessing professional competence, competency reflection log, learning contracts, goals and objectives, and evaluation	Competency 9: Evaluate Practice With Individuals, Families, Groups, Organizations, and Communities
Chapter 3: Using Supervision to Guide Professional Development and Behavior	Learning styles, types of supervision, student/supervisor match, trust, risk taking, vulnerability, assessing the supervisory relationship and problem-solving supervision issues	Competency 1: Demonstrate Ethical and Professional Behavior
Chapter 4: Using Reflection and Self-Regulation to Promote Well-Being Through Self-Care	Well-being, burnout, vicarious trauma, compassion fatigue, self-care activities, and support networks	Competency 1: Demonstrate Ethical and Professional Behavior
Chapter 5: Building Relationships and Interprofessional Collaboration	Helping relationships, elaboration skills, empathetic skills, trust building, collaboration, interprofessional collaboration, building professional relationships, role and responsibilities, working on a team, and collaboration and benefits	Competency 6: Engage With Individuals, Families, Groups, Organizations, and Communities
Chapter 6: Demonstrating Professional Behavior in Oral, Written, and Electronic Communications	Oral communication, professional speaking, jargon and acronyms, written communication, case notes, process recordings, biopsychosocial assessments, electronic communication, social media, email, ethical use of technology, and HIPAA	Competency 1: Demonstrate Ethical and Professional Behavior
Chapter 7: Engaging Diversity and Difference in Practice	Social work values and ethics, diversity and bias, culture, competence, cultural competence, standards for cultural competence, empathy and humility, and forms of oppression	Competency 2: Engage Diversity and Difference in Practice

(continued)

Chapter Title	Chapter Topics	EPAS Competency
Chapter 8: Advancing Human Rights and Social Justice in Your Field Placement	Theories and frameworks for social justice, types and sources of power, social identities, social locations, social constructions, social processes, conflict, implications for field and strategies for change	Competency 3: Advance Human Rights and Social, Economic, and Environmental Justice
Chapter 9: Engaging in Research to Inform and Improve Practice, Policy, and Service Delivery in Your Field Placement	Research and evaluation, NASW's *Code of Ethics*, micro evaluations, client logs, behavioral observations, rating scales, goal attainment scales, standardized measures, designing the evaluation, single-subject designs, needs assessments, organizational evaluations, process evaluation, outcome evaluation, logic models, and using research to inform practice decisions	Competency 4: Engage in Practice-Informed Research and Research-Informed Practice
Chapter 10: Engaging in Policy Practice in Your Field Placement	NASW's *Code of Ethics*, policy practice, organizational policies, accessing policies, updating and disseminating policies, social welfare policies, advocacy, promoting social justice, engaging in advocacy efforts, and empowering clients to advocate for themselves	Competency 5: Engage in Policy Practice
Chapter 11: Micro Assessment: Individuals, Families, and Groups	Critical thinking, strengths perspective, principles of strength-based assessment, assessing individuals, assessing client strengths, assessing families, assessing groups, and microsystem assessment tools	Competency 7: Assess Individuals, Families, Groups, Organizations, and Communities
Chapter 12: Mezzo Assessment: Organizations and Communities	Assessing organizations, organizational identity, understanding your organization, internal organizational considerations, organizational environmental considerations, organizational assessment, organizational assessment tools, assessing communities, community needs assessments, and asset assessment	Competency 7: Assess Individuals, Families, Groups, Organizations, and Communities
Chapter 13: Micro Interventions: Individuals, Families, and Groups	Definition of generalist practice, types of generalist social work interventions, micro-level interventions, goals, intervention plans, individual and family interventions and group interventions	Competency 8: Intervene With Individuals, Families, Groups, Organizations, and Communities
Chapter 14: Mezzo Interventions: Organizations and Communities	Role of organizations and communities in generalist practice, NASW's *Code of Ethics*, mezzo generalist practice, planning and program development, SWOT analysis, program development and grant writing, community development, coalition building, and community education and training	Competency 8: Intervene With Individuals, Families, Groups, Organizations, and Communities

NASW, National Association of Social Workers

In addition to providing substantive content related to the nine social work competencies, this book has a number of field reflection questions in each chapter to help students connect the chapter content with their own field experiences.

Another key feature is that each chapter has multiple critical thinking questions to help students think about the chapter competency and the interrelationships among the competencies. We believe that helping students see the connections among the competencies is critical to developing holistic competency. Our critical thinking questions help students see the interrelationships and their intersections.

Each chapter also has a detailed case example that illustrates the chapter competency and other professional competencies. These case examples bring to life the application of social work competencies in actual case situations. The case examples provide students with an opportunity to reflect on a case situation and describe how they would respond. Each case example is designed to engage the students' critical thinking and decision-making skills in relation to the identified social work competency.

Another key feature of this book is the Student Toolbox located on Springer Publishing Company's website (springerpub.com/fieldwrk) and the numerous website and video links located at the end of each chapter. The Student Toolbox provides students with electronic access to all of the tools discussed in the book. These tools, especially the Competency Reflection Logs and Field Supervision Inventory, will help students have a successful competency-focused field placement experience. The Student Toolbox also has a number of micro- and mezzo-assessment tools that will aid students in their social work practice experiences. The Student Toolbox, combined with each chapter's website and video links, provide students with a wealth of supplemental resources to enhance their field placement learning opportunities.

This book has a number of instructor resources. There are PowerPoint presentations for each chapter. The presentations cover the key points in each chapter and provide a structured guide for presenting the chapter content to the students. An Instructor's Manual covers each chapter with a field reflection assignment and grading rubric, a peer-to-peer or small-group discussion assignment and grading rubric, and a written chapter competency assignment and grading rubric. The three types of assignments (reflection, discussion, and competency) are all applicable for use in site-based, hybrid, and online course formats. **Qualified instructors can access these materials by sending an email to textbook@springerpub.com.**

CHAPTER COVERAGE OF PROFESSIONAL COMPETENCIES

Chapter	Competency								
	C1 Values	C2 Diversity	C3 Justice	C4 Research	C5 Policy	C6 Engagement	C7 Assessment	C8 Intervention	C9 Evaluation
Chapter 1	√	•	•	•	•				
Chapter 2	•	•	•	•	•	•	•	•	√
Chapter 3	√					•			•
Chapter 4	√					•			•
Chapter 5	•	•				√			
Chapter 6	√					•	•		
Chapter 7	•	√	•			•	•	•	
Chapter 8	•	•	√			•	•		
Chapter 9	•			√					•
Chapter 10	•		•	•	√		•	•	•
Chapter 11	•	•	•				√		
Chapter 12	•		•	•	•		√		•
Chapter 13	•	•						√	
Chapter 14	•	•		•				√	

√ primary coverage; • secondary coverage.

The Social Work Field Placement

CASE VIGNETTE

Jan is a first-year MSW student with a field placement in a public child welfare agency. She is assigned to a unit that provides case management services for adolescents in foster care, their birth parents, and their foster parents. In her internship, Jan monitors clients' service plans, provides supportive counseling for adolescents, helps link clients to other services and resources, and advocates for clients who need help from various systems and organizations.

Jan is pleased with her field placement because she is getting experience in working with individual clients and families. However, she is concerned about the services being provided to one of her families. The family clearly needs parenting classes, but they are not eligible because of program requirements about prior participation. Jan feels that not providing parenting programing is an ethical concern and a violation of the National Association of Social Work (NASW) Code of Ethics regarding services to clients. Although Jan feels that she is facing an ethical dilemma, she is unsure what she can do to change the rules or get the families the needed services.

Jan decides to talk to Mary, her field instructor, about her concerns. Mary helps Jan realize that generalist social work practice includes macropractice activities as well as her microactivities with the children and their families. Together they formulate a plan in which Jan advocates for her clients' participation in the parenting program and for a change in the program requirements. Both activities enable Jan to address her ethical concerns and to develop her competence as a generalist social worker.

Why was it important for Jan to talk with her field instructor about how she was feeling? How should field students handle ethical concerns that occur at their placement?

LEARNING OBJECTIVES

This chapter provides an introduction to your field placement and the expectations for social work interns. It also helps you understand your field placement agency and its major functions as well as provides safety guidelines. The chapter's content on values and ethics, ethical decision making, and ethical behavior is directly related to social work

(continued)

LEARNING OBJECTIVES *(continued)*

Competency 1: Demonstrate Ethical and Professional Behavior. By the end of this chapter, you will be able to

- Describe the process of field education.
- Identify and define the roles of the field coordinator, field faculty liaison, field supervisor, and task supervisor.
- Conduct an assessment of your field placement agency's major functions.
- Describe the NASW safety guidelines.
- Identify five steps in de-escalating an angry/hostile client.
- Identify the value base of the profession and its ethical principles.
- Apply frameworks for ethical decision making.
- Recognize professional and ethical social work behaviors.

WELCOME TO FIELD PLACEMENT

Let us be among the first to congratulate you on reaching this important milestone in your social work education. Welcome to field placement! You are about to embark on the adventure that is field education, social work's signature pedagogy. Many professions require internships of sorts, but "field" is unique to social work and has a long-standing history tied to the profession's early days. When apprenticeships were used to teach early charity workers how to support clients. During the field experience, you will have the opportunity to integrate your course content and experiences and apply that understanding to your social work practice at your field placement. The hours you spent reading, studying, in lectures, and completing assignments have all sought to prepare you for this point. In field, you will work closely with and be supervised by a professional social worker in providing services to individuals, families, groups, and communities in need. All senior BSW students and first-year MSW students are required by the Council on Social Work Education's (CSWE) Commission on Accreditation (COA) to have a generalist field placement in which they are exposed to generalist social work practice.

Field Reflection Questions

What are your expectations of field?

What do you hope to gain during your placement experience?

THE FIELD PLACEMENT PROCESS

There are several stages in the field placement process. The first step in the field process is one that you have most likely already completed—the field placement setup. Searching for a compatible field site is very important because you will be spending so much time there over the next few months. Typically, field personnel seek to match students with available placements or students are tasked with identifying potential field placement sites. Most often an interview at the potential field placement site is required. This interview is very much like a job interview. You should come prepared with a resume, an understanding of the agency's mission and service programs, and questions about supervision and potential assignments. During this process, it is equally important that you, as the student, interview the agency as well. You need to ask yourself the following: Is this a good fit for me? Will I get the support I need? Do I feel a sense of connection with the agency and my potential field instructor?

After interviewing at a potential field site (or two), when there is a mutually agreed-upon placement, a checklist of requirements will need to be completed. This checklist often depends on the agency and its requirements of students. Common items required by agencies include such things as background checks (criminal, child abuse, FBI), meeting with the human resources department to complete necessary paperwork and liability insurance forms, as well as any other tests or trainings required prior to the start of your placement.

After you have completed all of the preplacement requirements, it is important to be clear on your schedule. You should speak with your field instructor to confirm your first day and the schedule you will have. Everyone involved should be clear on the schedule, including when you will be meeting for supervision each week.

At the start of the semester, you will begin your field placement and your accompanying field course. Soon after the start of your placement, you will need to develop a learning plan, sometimes referred to as learning contract, with your field supervisor. Your institution will have a format for this document. The purpose of this plan is to develop mutually agreed-upon goals and related activities that will guide your learning and mastery of the professional competencies. It ensures that you receive the learning opportunities that are required of you by the CSWE related to the educational policy and accreditation standards (EPAS)—which we discuss in more detail in Chapter 2.

Throughout the semester, you will be meeting weekly with your field course, and there will be required assignments and discussions to explore and reflect upon the learning that is occurring in your field placement. You will have evaluations to be completed at the midpoint and the end of the semester. There will also be site visits throughout the semester, during which your field faculty contact will meet with you and your field supervisor at your field site to review your placement. The last stage of the process is the closure of the field placement. We explore this process more in the later chapters.

EXPECTATIONS AND REALITY

Your field placement experience is an exciting time because it is most likely something that you have not done before. When approaching something new, it is important to be clear on what it is and what it is not. Your field placement is:

- An educational opportunity in a real-world setting to engage with individuals, families, groups, organizations, and communities.

- A time to incorporate all that you have learned in your social work courses in a supervised setting.

- A time to grow your social work self.

Your field placement is not:

- The same as a full-time job (although it may look a lot like a typical job position, the focus of field should be on the educational experience you are having).

- Simply a required number of hours that you must complete at an agency (the time you spend in the field must be meaningful and directed toward meeting the goals that you have outlined in your learning plan).

Field Reflection Questions

What are the three ways that you can demonstrate professionalism in your field placement?

Can you identify one area of growth you hope to focus on in your field experience?

We recommend that you familiarize yourself at the very start of the field experience with your institution's field placement manual. This manual will outline all of the policies and procedures required of you at your institution.

ROLES AND RESPONSIBILITIES

You will be working with many people during your field experience, some more directly than others, but everyone is working together to help you succeed and develop into the best social worker you can be. It is important to be clear on the roles of each person you will be working with during your field placement so that you understand how he or she is available to support you. But first let us review your role as a field placement student.

SOCIAL WORK INTERN

As a student, in what is probably your first social work field placement, your primary responsibility is to adopt a learner role. You are there to learn the practice of social work. This is done through gaining social work practice experiences at your placement, reflection upon your experiences, and discussion of your experiences with your field instructor. Be open to learning. *You are not expected to know everything.* You are expected to ask questions and adopt a position of not knowing. This is often hard for students who want to do well and show their field instructors and professional colleagues that they are competent and capable. Nevertheless, adopting the learner role is critical to a successful field placement and professional growth. Relax and accept that you are not expected to know everything. You are there to learn about social work practice. Ask questions, reflect upon your experiences with your field instructor, and be open to constructive feedback.

FIELD COORDINATOR

This person is an employee of the institution where you are enrolled, and his or her primary responsibility is to coordinate placements for social work students. The field coordinator works year-round to identify potential placements and cultivate relationships with agencies that host social work students. The field coordinator will help you throughout the preplacement setup process.

FIELD FACULTY LIAISON

This person is also an employee of the institution. And his or her primary responsibility is to support your learning throughout the semester. You will most likely be meeting with your field faculty liaison weekly in class (or online) to provide updates regarding your placement. Any institutional assignments or requirements (e.g., your learning plan and evaluations) will be submitted to your liaison. Visits to your field site will also be conducted by your liaison. In almost all cases, this person is the direct connection between what is happening in your field placement and the institution. If there is a problem in field, your faculty liaison is there to support you and mediate if necessary. Ultimately, your faculty liaison is an advocate for you and your educational experience in field.

FIELD INSTRUCTOR/SUPERVISOR

This is the social worker who will support you throughout your placement. You will meet with your field instructor every week for supervision (more about this in Chapter 3). Your field instructor is most likely an employee of the agency where you are completing your field placement; however, there are instances when that is not the case. When the field instructor is not an employee of the agency, you will also have a task supervisor.

TASK SUPERVISOR

This is the person who is responsible for overseeing your day-to-day tasks while you are at your field placement. Not all placements require a task supervisor. Some reasons that you may have a task supervisor include that the task supervisor does not have a social work degree or that the field instructor's job responsibilities require that this person is not on-site to the degree necessary to support you.

SOCIAL WORK PEERS

Your fellow classmates who are going through the field process with you are an excellent resource and support during your own field experience. When you meet during your field seminar classes, your peers can often offer insights and suggestions that may provide a fresh perspective on issues you are facing in the field. Do not underestimate the value of having this network of fellow social workers!

UNDERSTANDING YOUR FIELD PLACEMENT AGENCY

A successful field placement experience does not happen automatically, but rather requires intentional effort and commitment on your part. One of your first tasks is to assess the lay of the land and find out everything you can about the agency and how it operates. A good starting place is the agency's **vision and mission** statements (a more detailed discussion of vision and mission statements can be found in Chapter 12). Mission and vision statements capture the essence of the organization's beliefs and values. A vision statement explains the overall goal of the organization looking into the future, whereas the mission statement outlines the present plan to realize the vision (McQueary, 2014). Both the vision and mission statements can usually be found on an organization's website. They are also often found in an organization's promotional literature and/or in its policy manuals. Not all organizations will have a vision statement, but almost all will have a mission statement. Become familiar with your field placement's vision and mission statements. Reviewing them will give you a clear idea of your agency's essential reason for existence or core purpose. Doing so will also give you insight into the values on which your agency's programs and services are built.

Another important aspect of your field placement agency related to its mission is its **organizational auspices**. One level of distinction is whether it is a **governmental agency**. Governmental agencies are operated and funded by municipal, county, state, or federal governmental bodies. Such agencies are mandated to provide specific types of services to specified client populations. These types of services are usually mandated by public laws and/or governmental regulations. If your field placement is with a government agency or service, we recommend that you review the legislation that has mandated its services and that you research how its programs and services are funded.

If your field placement is not a governmental agency, then the distinction is whether it is a **not-for-profit or for-profit organization**. For-profit organizations are structured like any business and are in the business of providing social services to make money. In recent years, there has been a growth in for-profit organizations in the human services field (Schmid, 2008). They are often funded by government contracts, insurance reimbursement, and/or clients paying for the services received. If you are placed in a for-profit organization, find out how its programs and services are funded. Also, be very cognizant of how making a profit impacts the delivery of services and client-based decisions.

If your field placement agency is a nonprofit organization, then a common distinction is whether it is a **sectarian or nonsectarian organization**. Sectarian agencies have a religious affiliation, whereas nonsectarian organizations do not. The mission, as well as programs and services, of sectarian agencies are often driven by religious doctrine and beliefs. Staff and interns of sectarian agencies are often required to agree with the beliefs of the sponsoring religious organization. If your field placement is with a sectarian organization, it is very important that you are aware of and understand how its religious beliefs and practices impact client services and what you can and cannot do in your work within the agency and with clients. It is again important to understand how the agency's programs and services are funded and what, if any, constraints the funding sources place on the provision of its services.

It is also important for you to become familiar with all of your agency's **programs and services**. Just becoming knowledgeable about the program or unit where you are located is insufficient. It is critical that you have a clear understanding of *all* of the agency's programs and services. Review each program's goals, eligibility criteria, target population, and services offered. This will help you in serving your clients and in understanding how your field placement agency functions. How, and in what ways, do the agency's programs and services support its vision and mission? How are the different programs and services funded?

One way to see how all of the components of your field placement agency fit together is to review the agency's **organizational structure**. Often there is an organizational chart that lays this structure out visually. It will show you where the different programs are located in the organizational structure and who reports to whom. Be clear on how your program or service fits into the organizational structure and how it fits into the administrative structure of the agency. Knowing the chain of command can help your successfully negotiate your field placement experience.

Finally, we recommend that you keep your eyes and ears open to gain a sense of your field placement agency's **organizational climate or culture**. Pay attention to how the administration communicates and interacts with the staff, how staff communicate and interact with each other, staff morale, and the general feel of working in the agency. Are the communication and interactions formal and hierarchical? Do the members interact in a friendly and supportive way? Do the staff have lunch together or do they eat alone? Are supervisors accessible and available for questions? Answers to these types of questions and understanding of the organizational culture will help you adapt your style to what is acceptable within your field placement agency. Misreading or not understanding the organizational culture increases the chances that questions about your adjustment and/or performance will be raised. Remember that everyone there is employed by the agency and knows the formal and informal functioning of the agency and what is expected. You are a new nonpaid intern. You do not know how the agency functions, but from the beginning you will be expected to behave according to the formal and informal norms of the agency. So, until you get it figured out, play it safe and stick to the learner role and ask.

PROFESSIONAL EXPECTATIONS

In field, you should always present yourself as a professional. Being a professional is a multidimensional task that envelops all aspects of what you do in the field. There are a variety of ways that you can demonstrate that you are a professional. Arriving on time and being prepared is a simple way to demonstrate professional commitment. If you are sick and cannot make it to the agency, it is your responsibility to reach out to your field supervisor and let him or her know. Dependability is an important aspect of professionalism.

Acting with integrity and follow-through is another important aspect of the professional expectations that come along with field. If you are asked to complete a task during your field placement, do your best to complete it. With that being said, if you are unsure of what you are to do or have a question, it is absolutely okay to ask your field supervisor. Remember, field is a learning experience; no one expects you to have all of the answers on day 1. This is a process where you will be able to grow over time.

> ### Field Reflection Questions
>
> In what ways does technology impact your social work practice in your field placement?
>
> How can the use of technology in your field placement result in the use of unethical behaviors?

Professionalism can also be demonstrated through how you present yourself. Is your dress appropriate for the setting you are in? Depending on where you are placed, there is a wide range of acceptable attire for social workers. No matter how formal or casual the attire, your attire should be clean, neat, and respectable. Although ripped jeans and cropped tops may be in style, they may not be appropriate when working in the field. If you have questions regarding what professional attire is appropriate in your placement, ask your field supervisor.

How you dress is one way that you present yourself; another way is through your verbal and nonverbal communication. In field, you are going to be meeting and interacting with many individuals. It is important to make good first impressions, and one way to do that is by using good communication skills. When meeting individuals, remember the power of eye contact and a handshake. Engage in conversations with those who are with you and pay attention. Turn off or silence your cell phone when in meetings or when you are with clients.

SAFETY

Understanding and following best practices regarding your personal safety is an important social work skill (a safety checklist that you can use in your field placement is available in Student Resources at www.springerpub.com). Social work can be a dangerous profession. Social workers interact with persons with severe mental health issues, abusive people, people with poor impulse control, substance abusers, and other potentially violent clients. Therefore, it is very important that you become knowledgeable about the safety procedures of your field placement agency and with safety best practices for your work with clients at your agency and in the community.

Ideally, your field placement agency will have an orientation for its interns that will include a review of the agency's policies and procedures related to safety. Regardless of whether such an orientation is provided, we recommend that you discuss safety procedures with your field instructor in supervision early on in your internship. Your field instructor is usually your best source for developing your safety awareness and knowledge of how to best ensure your safety when interacting with your clients. Also, always include safety on your supervision agenda when you have upcoming interactions with potentially dangerous clients and when you are scheduled to meet with clients in the community or in their own homes. Be proactive. It is your responsibility to know your agency's policies and procedures, to know your clients and potential safety threats, to know the community and potentially dangerous areas and/or times, to develop your best-practice safety skills, and to discuss safety with your field instructor prior to meeting with potentially dangerous clients in the agency or in the field.

We recognize that many social work students are reluctant to address safety proactively. Often students feel that bringing up safety issues makes them look judgmental or unsuited for social work. This is a misperception. According to NASW (2013a), it is your right to report safety concerns and you should not fear retaliation, blame, or questioning of your competence from your supervisor or colleagues. As a social work intern, your job includes developing your assessment (Competency 7) and intervention skills (Competency 8). Both assessing and intervening with clients have safety components and are important skills for effective social work practice with clients. To avoid stereotyping particular groups of people and to promote your safety, you should practice safety assessment and risk reduction with all clients and in all settings (NASW, 2013a).

SAFETY GUIDELINES

An NASW (2013a) task force of leading social work professionals developed comprehensive safety guidelines for social workers. We recommend that you download these guidelines for reference during your social work practicum (see the NASW links in the Website Links section). The following discussion briefly summarizes the guidelines that pertain to your work with clients. Guidelines related to agency policies and procedures are not reviewed here. However, we encourage you to review them on your own and, if needed, to advocate for the development of agency policies and practices that enhance social worker safety.

NASW's (2013a) safety guidelines have four standards that focus on worker behavior: (a) use of mobile phones, (b) office safety, (c) risk assessment for field visits, and (d) transporting clients. Exhibit 1.1 shows the recommended procedures for each of the four safety standards.

Field Reflection Question

How well do your field placement agency's safety policies and procedures correspond to those recommended by the NASW?

Become knowledgeable of the recommendations listed earlier and review them periodically throughout your field placement. Do not become complacent when it comes to safety. Following NASW safety guidelines should become a routine part of your social work practice. The NASW guidelines, however, do not cover how to handle angry clients and de-escalate potentially threatening situations. The NASW (2013b) publication on managing

EXHIBIT 1.1

NASW Safety Guidelines

Standard	Practice Recommendations
Office safety	• Use meeting spaces that allow for an easy exit in potentially violent situations. • Have another person present when meeting with a potentially abusive or aggressive client. • Restrict access to objects that may be used as weapons.
Use of mobile phones	• Keep your mobile phone fully charged and carry a phone charger. • Be familiar with cell phone coverage in areas you visit. • Make sure you know how to use your mobile phone before going in to the field. • Keep emergency contacts on speed dial. • Keep GPS-enabled mobile phone applications activated while in the field. • Agree on and use "code" words to convey threats to your supervisor or colleagues. • Send text message of acknowledgment of circumstances. • Use your mobile phone discreetly, so as not to inadvertently escalate a potentially volatile situation or become a possible target for a robbery.

Risk assessment for field visits	Prior to each field visit, conduct a risk assessment that includes:
	• Environmental factors
	  • Do you have the exact address?
	  • Does the neighborhood pose a risk for violence?
	  • Is the scheduled time more risky than other times?
	  • Were there any events within the past 48 hours that might increase risk?
	  • Does the area have reduced mobile phone reception?
	  • Will identification of the agency increase risk?
	  • Are there groups or individuals in the path to the visit?

(continued)

EXHIBIT
1.1

NASW Safety Guidelines (*continued*)

Standard	Practice Recommendations

	• Client's living space
	  • Does access require use of elevators or stairs?
	  • Are common spaces well lighted and clean?
	  • Are exits easily accessible?
	  • Who is likely to be at home during the visit?
	  • Is anyone engaged in criminal or dangerous activities?
	  • Is there a risk of disease, infection, or pests in the home?
	  • Is the family known to have weapons in the home?
	• Proposed work activities
	  • Will you be engaged in a high-risk activity?
	• Risk because of the client's condition
	  • Does the client have a substance abuse problem, particularly with alcohol?
	  • Does the client have a mental health problem?
	  • Does the client have a history of violence or threatening behavior?
	  • Does the client have a communicable disease?
	• Worker vulnerability
	  • Will you be alone?
	  • Are there any visible physical conditions that may increase your vulnerability?
	  • Are you inexperienced?
	  • Do you appear timid or vulnerable?
	  • Will your attire increase your vulnerability?
	  • Are there any accessories that will increase your vulnerability?
	  • Is there anything in your appearance that will attract attention?

NASW, National Association of Social Work.

angry clients has identified five strategies for de-escalating threatening interactions with clients. The first is to stay calm. Role-model a calm composure. Do not lean forward, make only minimal arm or hand movements, take deep calming breaths, and ask your client to remain calm. The second recommendation is to listen. Allow your client to vent and be heard. Third, remind your client that you are there to help. Emphasize why you are there and why you are working together. The fourth NASW recommendation is to empathize with your client and his or her feelings. Using empathy, communicate that you understand and help the client feel heard. Finally, establish and maintain boundaries. Remind your client that you are respectful in your communication and that you expect the same in return. Indicate that you want to hear your client's concerns, but you need him or her to adhere to certain rules of

Field Reflection Question

What do you need to do to strengthen your ability to de-escalate an angry client?

communication, such as speaking in a calm voice and not using profanity (NASW, 2013b). If your field placement orientation did not cover de-escalation of hostile/angry clients, we strongly recommend that you and your field instructor discuss it in supervision.

TIME MANAGEMENT

While you are enrolled in field, you are going to be very busy. To be successful, you must be able to manage your time effectively. The field experience needs to be a priority; however, you will still need to balance other aspects of your life (e.g., work, family, other courses you may be taking). Managing your time effectively will help guard across stressors such as burnout that we discuss later in this chapter.

There are many resources available online to help you manage your time; some of them are listed in the Website Links section. You may want to set up a planner, either with paper and pen or electronically. The planner can serve as a great way to see everything you need to do and help you find the time to do it. It always helps to keep you on task. Of course, a planner is a good tool only if you actually use it. If a planner does not work for you, that is okay—figure out what does work for you and use that.

A first important step in time management is understanding what you are managing. A good place to start is by taking an inventory of the demands in your life. This inventory should be complete and capture all aspects of your life, personal and professional. Once you have a list of the demands that are present in your life, evaluate all of those items. During your field placement, you are going to be quite busy; if there are any items on your demand inventory that you can take off the list, that may be something you would want to consider. Conversely, there will be some things that you cannot (nor would you want to) remove from the list. Consider how you can effectively and efficiently divide your time among these things. It may require support from friends and family, which is totally fine. It is okay to ask for help. It is also okay to set healthy boundaries and limits regarding your schedule. This may require you to turn down invitations and say no to things at times. This is okay to do as well; respecting your time and setting healthy limits is an excellent self-care strategy that we explore later in this book.

> **Field Reflection Question**
>
> What are the three strategies you can use to manage your time successfully while you are participating in field?

Once you know which demands you face, it is important to set priorities and develop a schedule that works for you. It is okay to try out a schedule and tweak it if it does not work for you. By learning to value your time and manage it effectively, you are learning a vital skill that will serve you well throughout your social work career.

SOCIAL WORK VALUES AND ETHICS

The practice of social work is based on a number of value positions and principles that guide the work with clients irrespective of the approach used, the presenting client problem, the client population, or the setting in which services are provided. These values and principles apply to all forms of social work practice.

CORE SOCIAL WORK VALUES

Social work is a value-based profession (Beckett & Maynard, 2005; Reamer, 1990). Values provide the basis for professional social work practice (Congress & McAuliffe, 2006; Gumpert & Black, 2006). They guide the actions we take and our evaluations of what is "good" (DuBois & Miley, 2014). Social work has a rich tradition of principles and beliefs. The heart of these is reflected in the NASW's (2017) *Code of Ethics*, which identifies core social work values, associated ethical principles, and ethical standards. The core professional values are the following: service to others, social justice, dignity and worth of the person, and importance of human relationships, integrity, and competence. These values and their associated ethical principles all play a critical role in generalist social work practice.

Service

The first ethical principle is that *"social workers' primary goal is to help people in need and to address social problems."* Service to others is placed above self-interest. Volunteering to serve others and address social problems is a commitment that all social workers are charged with accepting. Social work is a service profession dedicated to providing help to individuals, families, and groups in need, and to improving community and social conditions. The focus is on helping others directly by enhancing their capacities to resolve problems and indirectly by linking clients with resources, improving service delivery systems, and developing social programs and policies.

Social Justice

The second ethical principle is that *"social workers challenge social injustice."* Social justice has long been valued in social work. Concern with social justice and inequality in the profession goes back to the advocacy efforts of Jane Addams and the settlement house movement of the early 1900s. The *Code of Ethics* states that challenging social injustice is an ethical principle of the profession:

> Social workers pursue social change, particularly with and on behalf of vulnerable and oppressed individuals and groups of people. Social workers' social change efforts are focused primarily on issues of poverty, unemployment, discrimination, and other forms of social injustice. Social workers strive to ensure access to needed information, services, and resources; equality of opportunity; and meaningful participation in decision making for all people. (NASW, 2017, Ethical Principles, Social Justice, para. 2)

Social workers traditionally work with people who are victims of discrimination and prejudice. Many of our clients are unemployed or underemployed, have limited access to resources, received inadequate education and training, and are among the most disadvantaged members of society. They often face prejudicial attitudes and are identified as lesser persons (DuBois & Miley, 2014). Social injustice is manifested in discrimination on the basis of race, gender, social class, sexual orientation, age, and disability. Prejudicial attitudes provide justification for social structures that provide fewer prospects—fewer opportunities, fewer possibilities, and fewer resources—for those persons with lower status (DuBois & Miley, 2014).

Social workers' commitment to social justice is based on concern about the negative effects of discrimination and prejudice on disadvantaged populations. We often work with clients who have been denied basic rights and opportunities. We are called on to challenge social injustice and to increase the opportunities, possibilities, and resources of our clients. We have an ethical responsibility to address the social, physical, and economic needs of our clients as well as their psychological needs. The 2015 EPAS expanded the concept of social justice to include economic and environmental justice (CSWE, 2015).

Dignity and Worth of the Person

The third ethical principle is that *"social workers respect the inherent dignity and worth of the person."* This entails treating our clients in a caring and respectful fashion, and being mindful of individual differences and cultural and ethnic diversity. The underlying assumption of this value is that all human beings have intrinsic worth, irrespective of their past or present behavior, beliefs, lifestyle, race, or status in life (Hepworth, Rooney, Rooney, & Strom-Gottfried, 2017). As a social worker, you are expected to treat your clients with respect and dignity. They deserve respect by virtue of their humanness. This does not mean that you have to agree with your clients' life choices or decisions. It *does* mean that you should strive to affirm their dignity and self-worth. Not doing so can have profound negative effects on the helping process, and doing nothing could potentially cause harm.

Before clients are willing to risk and trust, they need to feel accepted and valued. Doing so is even more important when clients' problematic behaviors involve moral, social, or legal infractions. A client whose behavior has violated social and cultural norms is not likely to engage in a collaborative helping relationship with a professional who communicates disapproval and condemnation.

Closely associated with respect for the individual is a nonjudgmental attitude. As a social worker, you must not place blame on the client through either your attitude or your behavior. Focus on understanding your clients and their difficulties and on helping them find solutions or alternative ways of behaving. If you blame them for their difficulties and assign pejorative labels, most will become defensive and unwilling to trust you. The more you understand the life experiences of your clients, no matter how personally distressing their behaviors or beliefs may be, the more likely it is that you will be able to accept them as human beings (Hepworth et al., 2017).

Many of our clients' behaviors conflict with our personal values and beliefs. More often than not, there will be a clash of values between you and your clients. These differences should be viewed as a normal part of generalist social work practice. Expect them and accept them. There are going to be differences; in fact, there are going to be major differences. If you focus on your values and assign blame to clients for adopting behaviors or attitudes with which you disagree, you will not be able to help them.

Adopting a nonjudgmental attitude is a prerequisite for developing effective working relationships (Poulin, 2010). The challenge is to maintain your own values without imposing them on others and without judging those whose behaviors and beliefs are in conflict with your own belief system. To accomplish this, you need to be open to others and treat everyone with respect and dignity. This is difficult when you have negative feelings about a client. You are human, and you will have negative feelings about some clients. Pretending that you do not have these feelings will not work; clients will sense insincerity and negative reactions. The best approach is to try to understand each client, and to communicate that understanding in a caring and nonjudgmental manner. Clients are not seeking your approval; they are seeking your help. They need to feel that they have been heard and that you understand them and their situations. They need to feel that you care and that you want to work with them. Communicating care and concern facilitates the helping process. If clients perceive you as judging and blaming them, they are not likely to accept help from you.

Importance of Human Relationships

The fourth ethical principle is that *"social workers recognize the central importance of human relationships."* The *Code of Ethics* states that "social workers seek to strengthen relationships among people in a purposeful effort to promote, restore, maintain, and enhance the well-being of individuals, families, social groups, organizations, and communities" (NASW, 2017). Focusing on the relationship issues of clients is common in generalist social work. Many clients need help in improving their human relationships and interpersonal interactions.

Historically, the helping relationship has been given a central role in the helping process (Perlman, 1979). The *Code of Ethics* states that "social workers engage people as partners in the helping process" (NASW, 2017). The term "relationship" implies that there is a reciprocal interactive process between two people. In social work, the helping relationship is a partnership. Both you and the client have input and make decisions together; you are joint participants. Social workers do not solve problems for their clients, but rather work with clients and help them solve their own problems.

Beginning social workers often feel that unless they are doing something specific and concrete for their clients, they are not being helpful. You will be tempted to do things for clients, using your skills and abilities to get the task done, and then hand over the results to clients. Doing so will make you feel useful and productive. But avoid the temptation, because it is a trap. More often than not, clients will not appreciate your generous efforts on their behalf. By doing work for them, you will put them in a dependent position, highlighting their inability to manage their lives. No one likes feeling incompetent and dependent. Rather than making your clients dependent on you, empower them. Help them help themselves. Help them do whatever they need to do to manage their own lives as best they can. Ultimately, your clients must become confident and learn to do tasks for themselves.

In summary, the helping relationship in social work is a collaborative partnership. Social workers do not work for clients; rather, they work with clients.

Integrity

The fifth ethical principle is that *"social workers behave in a trustworthy manner."* You have probably heard the sentiment that honesty is the best policy; in the social work profession, we value honesty very much. Social workers should demonstrate integrity at all times through honesty, sincerity, and responsibility. This is the key to developing trust and a positive helping relationship. Be open and honest. It is okay to admit that you do not know or are unsure about something. If that happens, let your clients know that you will find out, and then follow through and get back to your clients with the information.

Field Reflection Questions

How can you demonstrate the six core values of social work during your field placement?

Which values and ethical principles are most challenging for you?

Competence

The sixth ethical principle is that *"social workers practice within their areas of competence and develop and enhance their professional expertise."* Social workers are to practice within their areas of training and seek ongoing supervision, education, and support on a regular basis. As a social work intern, your primary learning objective for your field placement is to become a competent generalist social worker. This is done by demonstrating proficiency through your practice experiences as they relate to the nine professional competencies defined by the CSWE (2015). The development of competence is a lifelong undertaking that involves critical thinking, reflection, and ongoing professional development.

ETHICAL STANDARDS

The core social work values and ethical principles embody the ideals to which all social workers should aspire. The *Code of Ethics* sets specific standards and explains how the core values and principles influence the actions of professional social workers. The standards spell out social workers' ethical responsibilities to clients, to colleagues, in practice settings, as professionals, to the social work profession, and to the broader society (NASW, 2017). They are detailed, comprehensive guidelines for social work professionals. The *Code of Ethics* (NASW, 2017) also identifies the six areas of professional behavior: responsibilities to clients, to colleagues, to practice settings, as professionals, to the profession, and to the broader society. Each area of responsibility includes a number of subareas. For example, ethical responsibilities to clients cover 16 subareas, such as commitment to clients, self-determination, informed consent, and competence. Exhibit 1.2 outlines the six areas of professional responsibilities as well as the associated subareas. A detailed discussion of each ethical standard in the six areas of professional behavior areas may be found in the *Code of Ethics* (NASW, 2017).

As a social work intern, it is important that you become very familiar with the areas of professional responsibility. A thorough knowledge of the NASW *Code of Ethics* early in your field placement experience will help ensure that you engage in ethical practice and help you avoid unethical behavior. It is your responsibility as a professional social worker to be familiar with the *Code of Ethics* and follow it in your professional practice.

ETHICAL DILEMMAS

Social workers frequently have ethical obligations to several parties at the same time. For example, we have ethical obligations to both our clients and our employing organizations. This creates the potential for conflict, or ethical dilemmas. An ethical dilemma occurs when one or more social work values are in conflict. In these situations, you are forced to choose between two competing values or undesirable courses of action. Because we have ethical responsibilities to our clients, our colleagues, our practice settings, the profession, and the broader society, value conflicts and ethical dilemmas occur often within and between the six areas of professional responsibilities outlined in Exhibit 1.2.

Resolving ethical dilemmas is never easy or straightforward. Rarely is there a clear-cut right or wrong choice. The choice is between two seeming "rights"; the task is to determine which "right" is more so given the circumstances.

Outline of Ethical Standards

SOCIAL WORKERS' ETHICAL RESPONSIBILITIES TO CLIENTS		
Commitment to clients	Self-determination	Informed consent
Competence	Cultural awareness	Conflicts of interest
Privacy and confidentiality	Access to records	Sexual relationships
Physical contact	Sexual harassment	Derogatory language
Payment for services	Decision-making capacity	Referral for services
Termination of services		
SOCIAL WORKERS' ETHICAL RESPONSIBILITIES TO COLLEAGUES		
Respect	Confidentiality	Interdisciplinary collaboration
Disputes with colleagues	Consultation	Sexual relationships
Sexual harassment	Impairment of colleagues	Incompetence of colleagues
Unethical conduct of colleagues		
SOCIAL WORKERS' ETHICAL RESPONSIBILITIES IN PRACTICE SETTINGS		
Supervision and consultation	Education and training	Performance evaluation
Client records	Billing	Client transfer
Administration	Staff development	Commitments to employers
Labor–management disputes		
SOCIAL WORKERS' ETHICAL RESPONSIBILITIES AS PROFESSIONALS		
Competence	Discrimination	Private conduct
Impairment	Misrepresentation	Solicitations
Acknowledging credit	Dishonesty, fraud, and deception	
SOCIAL WORKERS' ETHICAL RESPONSIBILITIES TO THE SOCIAL WORK PROFESSION		
Integrity of the profession	Evaluation and research	
SOCIAL WORKERS' ETHICAL RESPONSIBILITIES TO THE BROADER SOCIETY		
Public participation	Public emergencies	Social and political action

The first step in addressing ethical dilemmas is to refer to the *Code of Ethics* for clarification of the standards of practice. The *Code*, however, does not offer bases for choosing between two or more conflicting standards. A number of guidelines have been developed to help individuals resolve ethical dilemmas. A hierarchy of value assumptions is the basis for decision making; the hierarchy developed by Reamer (1990) is shown in the following list.

ETHICAL GUIDELINES

1. The rights to life, health, well-being, and necessities of life are superordinate and take precedence over rights to confidentiality and opportunities for additive "goods" such as wealth, education, and recreation.

2. An individual's basic right to well-being takes precedence over another person's right to privacy, freedom, or self-determination.

3. People's right to self-determination takes precedence over their right to basic well-being, provided they are competent to make informed and voluntary decisions with consideration of relevant knowledge and so long as the consequences of their decisions do not threaten the well-being of others.

4. People's rights to well-being may override laws, policies, and arrangements of organizations.

The first guideline proposes that a person's right to health and well-being takes precedence over the right of confidentiality. If you had to choose between protecting a person's health and well-being and violating a client's confidentiality, you would choose health and well-being. For example, the right of neglected and abused children to protection takes precedence over their parents' rights to confidentiality.

The second guideline proposes that a person's right to health and well-being takes precedence over another person's right to privacy, freedom, or self-determination. When you must choose between protecting a person's freedom and protecting another person from harm, the choice is to protect the person from harm. For example, if a client reveals plans to seek physical revenge on his or her former spouse, you should warn the former spouse.

The third guideline states that a person's right to self-determination takes precedence over his or her own right to well-being. That is, an individual's self-determination supersedes that person's well-being. The principle promotes freedom to choose and possibly fail or make mistakes. It protects the right of people to carry out actions that do not appear to be in their own best interests, as long as they are competent to make informed and voluntary decisions. However, the first guideline takes precedence if the individual's decision might result in death or serious harm. For example, you must take action to protect a client who is at risk of committing suicide.

The final guideline proposes that the right to well-being may override agency policies and procedural rules. Social workers are obligated to follow the policies and procedures of social work agencies, voluntary associations, and organizations. When agency policy has a negative effect on a client's well-being, however, violating the policy or procedure may be justified.

The guidelines described earlier—or any other guidelines—will not always provide clear-cut courses of action. They will, however, help you prioritize values to help clarify your thinking about an ethical issue. Resolving ethical dilemmas almost always entails making value judgments and subjective interpretations. For example, the third guideline states that a person's right to self-determination takes precedence over his or her right to basic well-being, provided he or she is competent to make an informed decision. A social worker may have to apply this guideline to a person who is mentally ill and homeless, who prefers to remain on the street, and who has little or no interest in participating in a treatment program. Does this person have the right to refuse treatment as well as the right to live wherever he or she wants? The complicating factor in this situation is determining the person's competence and the degree of physical or mental harm that is likely to ensue. Can a person who is mentally ill, delusional, and exhibiting psychotic behavior make informed decisions? At what point does refusing shelter or treatment create a serious risk of physical and mental harm? Clearly, the answers to these questions are subjective and open to value judgments.

In attempting to resolve ethical dilemmas, always invoke the concept of shared responsibility and decision making. Do not make the decision on your own; enlist others in the process. Get your supervisor's or administrator's advice and approval before you take action on an ethical dilemma. Case Example 1.1 illustrates the difficult decisions involved in resolving ethical dilemmas.

CASE EXAMPLE 1.1: AN ETHICAL DILEMMA

Jill is a first-year MSW student who has been placed in an after-school program for emotionally disturbed children. The program is run by a comprehensive mental health agency that offers a wide range of services for children and adults. The agency is a subsidiary of a larger organization that owns and operates a number of inpatient and outpatient mental health facilities. The after-school program has two full-time social workers, a case aide, a half-time supervisor, and a quarter-time program administrator.

Approximately 20 children with emotional and behavioral problems are provided with on-site services 5 days a week and with in-home services once a week. Because of a technicality, the program lost its primary source of funding and was slated to close. Jill found out about the pending closing of the program from her supervisor. She was told not to tell the other staff or the children. The program administrator had decided that it was best for the children, their parents, and the staff not to know in advance about the closing.

Jill was concerned about the children's need to have enough time to deal with their feelings about leaving the program and about the parents' needs to have time to make other arrangements for the treatment and after-school care of their children. She also wondered how the lack of process about closing the program would affect the staff and their morale. Jill believed that the well-being of the children was being subjugated to the perceived needs of the agency. She suspected that the agency administrator felt that telling the children and their parents would upset them and that the children would act out more than usual during the time remaining in the program.

She also suspected that the agency administrator wanted to avoid having the parents put pressure on the agency to continue the program. It appeared to her that the closing policy was designed to protect the agency from disruption at the expense of the children and their parents.

Jill is faced with an ethical dilemma. She has been told by her supervisor to follow an agency policy that she believes is not in the best interests of her clients.

1. *What are Jill's options?*

2. *Is it advisable for her to apply guideline 4 and disregard agency policy?*

3. *What might be the consequences of such an action?*

4. *How should she attempt to resolve her dilemma?*

SUMMARY

In this chapter, we explored the process of field placement as well as expectations of what field is and is not. Roles and responsibilities of the field coordinator, field faculty liaison, field supervisor, task supervisor, and peers were reviewed. Professionalism is essential in field. Standards for the social work profession, including social work competencies, EPAS, and the *Code of Ethics* all contribute to the field experience. Time management was also underscored as an important consideration as you begin your journey into field.

CRITICAL THINKING QUESTIONS

Competency 1 focuses on ethical and professional behavior. You are expected to understand the value base of the profession and its ethical standards. You need to understand frameworks of ethical decision making and how to apply principles of critical thinking to those frameworks in practice, research, and policy arenas. You are also expected to understand how your personal values impact your work with clients and the distinction between personal and professional values. The following discussion questions focus on ethical dilemmas:

1. Sara is a new field student at the county child protective services organization. During her second week of field placement, her supervisor begins assigning clients to her caseload. Sara reviews the list of clients with whom she is to make contact and notices she knows one of the names. A client whom her supervisor had assigned to her is next-door neighbor. What should Sara do? Why? What is the ethical concern?

2. Joanie is a field student at a hospital. While she is working in the emergency room, a patient who has been exhibiting suicidal and homicidal ideation is admitted and social work is called for a consult. Joanie has never worked with a client like this before and does not feel confident in her skills to assess for safety. What should Joanie do? Why? What is the ethical concern?

3. How do your personal values align with the core values of the profession? How are they similar? How are they different?

4. What should you do if your personal values conflict with the core social work values?

5. How do social workers' personal values impact their work with clients? What would you do if you have clients who behave in ways that go against your personal values and beliefs?

COMPETENCY 1: DEMONSTRATE ETHICAL AND PROFESSIONAL BEHAVIOR

Social workers understand the value base of the profession and its ethical standards, as well as relevant laws and regulations that may impact practice at the micro, mezzo, and macro levels. They understand frameworks of ethical decision making and how to apply principles of critical thinking to those frameworks in the practice, research, and policy arenas. Social workers recognize personal values and the distinction between personal and professional values. In addition, they understand how their personal experiences and affective reactions influence their professional judgment and behavior. Social workers understand the profession's history, its mission, and the roles and responsibilities of the profession. They appreciate the role of other professions when engaged in interprofessional teams. Social workers recognize the importance of lifelong learning and are committed to continually updating their skills to ensure they are relevant and effective. They also understand emerging forms of technology and the ethical use of technology in social work practice. Social workers:

- Make ethical decisions by applying the standards of the NASW's *Code of Ethics*, relevant laws and regulations, models for ethical decision making, ethical conduct of research, and additional codes of ethics as appropriate to context.
- Use reflection and self-regulation to manage personal values and maintain professionalism in practice situations.
- Demonstrate professional demeanor in behavior; appearance; and oral, written, and electronic communication.
- Use technology ethically and appropriately to facilitate practice outcomes.
- Use supervision and consultation to guide professional judgment and behavior.

CASE SUMMARY—"I AM PRAYING FOR MY SON"

PRACTICE SETTING DESCRIPTION

Topsham Rehabilitation and Healthcare Center in Virginia is a 134-bed long-term geriatric home and short-term rehabilitation unit. The building in which the facility is currently housed is much older than many of the long-term care facilities in the area, as it used to be part of a prison in the 1950s. The facility consists of five hallways: Three are long-term residential semiprivate and four-bed ward rooms, one hall is specifically for short-term residents filled with private and semiprivate rooms, and the final hall has a mixture of both short- and long-term private and semiprivate rooms. A large majority of the clientele in the facility come from lower- to middle-class socioeconomic homes. Because of the geographic location of Topsham Rehab and Health, the majority of residents come from factory or service industry jobs. The facility has an activities department, which facilitates various programs each day, as well as a complete kitchen and dietary staff, regulating and addressing the dietary needs of the individual patients. There is also a Physical, Occupational, and Speech Therapy department, which works 7 days a week for both restorative care for long-term residents and daily rehabilitation for short-term residents. On staff, there is a licensed social worker, an MSW student intern, and a social services assistant. There are three main courtyards in which the residents and patients may congregate, as well as large gathering spaces for activities and meals.

IDENTIFYING DATA

Ruth is a 75-year-old Caucasian female who is a very strict Catholic. Her religious views help define her beliefs and values. She moved into the facility about 2.5 years ago when her son decided that she should not be living alone. She ambulates in a wheelchair but is independent with all of her own activities of daily living. She also has mild dementia, which is the reason she was not eligible for an independent living facility.

Ruth was previously married and has one adult son. He lives in Florida and is homosexual. Her son is a pilot and is in a long-term relationship with a man he met while working at one of the airports. Ruth is in California. where she still owns a home. Her son decided that she should not live by herself, and placed her in Topsham Rehab and Health. Ruth is a college graduate and worked as an assistant at a law firm for many years. Although she was able to hold down a job in her later years, she had a very difficult time as a younger woman. Her husband was physically abusive to her and emotionally abusive to her son. She stayed with her husband until his death from a heart attack 20 years ago. Ruth was diagnosed with major depressive disorder and anxiety at a relatively young age. Her mental health issues and abusive relationship with her husband have contributed to her strained relationship with her son.

PRESENTING PROBLEM

Ruth expects that because of her status as her son's mother, he should take care of her and be involved in her life. He does not feel this way, although he does talk to her by phone on a regular basis. Ruth's relationship with her son is strained and a cause of concern for her. She feels that it is her place to give motherly advice to her son and expects him to behave and act in a certain way; when he does not, she attempts to make him feel guilty. Because of her strong Catholic beliefs, there have been many arguments regarding her son's homosexuality. Her frustration over her son and his "lifestyle" seems to be contributing to Ruth's increased depression and anxiety over the past 6 months.

ASSESSMENT

Ruth is a very bright woman who comes from a relatively affluent background. Her son speaks to Ruth on a regular basis, and they have a lot in common. The main strain in that relationship is his sexual orientation. Ruth uses humor as a coping mechanism, and because of her fun-loving nature, she is very well liked in the facility. This gives her a support system within the facility that she does not otherwise receive from her son. Although Ruth's spirituality can be a strength to get her through the day and to find a sense of purpose, her unwillingness to accept her son as a gay man and her rejection of his life partner creates a huge barrier to having the kind of relationship she desires with her son. By refusing to accept her son's homosexuality and his relationship with his life partner, she is causing her son to distance himself from her. Instead, she refuses to bend and believes that if she preaches to him and prays for him enough, he will become heterosexual.

CASE PROCESS SUMMARY

In working with Ruth, I have focused on helping her improve her relationship with her son and her understanding of why her placement at Topsham Rehab and Health is appropriate given her age and beginning stages of dementia. When we started working together, I asked Ruth what she would like to achieve in our work together. She stated that she wanted to understand why her son decided that Topsham Rehab and Health was the best place for her and how to achieve a better relationship with her son. Recently, there has been a lot of hostility from Ruth regarding her son. When I attempt to challenge her or to get her to look at the situation from a different perspective, she shuts down or becomes very aggressive. Because of this, I realize how difficult it can be for a woman with her set of beliefs to grasp why her son is not married with children.

While working with Ruth, I have realized how difficult it can be to not be judgmental and impose my values and personal beliefs on how I approach our work. First, it is very difficult for me to accept that because of her strong religious beliefs, she cannot seem to accept that her son is homosexual. I grew up in a family that did not have strong spiritual ties, but was very geared toward humanism and compassion for diversity, so I have a difficult time relating to those who use their beliefs to belittle or berate others.

Alex, MSW Intern

DISCUSSION QUESTIONS

- In this case summary, identify a potential ethical issue facing Alex in her individual work with Ruth. Discuss why it is an ethical issue referencing the NASW's *Code of Ethics* and the CSWE's *Competency on Ethics and Professional Behavior.* Describe at least three steps Alex needs to take to minimize the potential ethical issue.

- In this case summary, identify at least one mezzo-level and one macro-level ethical issue. Discuss why each is an ethical issue by referencing the NASW's *Code of Ethics* and the CSWE's *Competency on Ethics and Professional Behavior.* Describe how each ethical issue could potentially impact Alex's work with Ruth and what steps Alex could take to address the potential ethical issues.

- In your field placement, describe an experience you have had that is similar to the ethical issues facing Alex. Discuss what you did to address the potential ethical issue. Discuss your effectiveness in dealing with the issue and what you would do differently when it comes up again.

ELECTRONIC COMPETENCY RESOURCES

WEBSITE LINKS

NASW: Guidelines for Social Worker Safety
www.socialworkers.org/LinkClick.aspx?fileticket=6OEdoMjcNC0%3D&portalid=0

NASW: *Code of Ethics* (electronic download—English or Spanish)
www.socialworkers.org/About/Ethics/Code-of-Ethics/Code-of-Ethics-English

Toolkit: "Time Management: Beat Work Overload. Be More Effective. Achieve More" (n.d.)
www.mindtools.com/pages/main/newMN_HTE.htm

Article: "Time Management Tips for Social Workers Struggling to Maintain Control" by Stephen Boylan (2010)
www.communitycare.co.uk/2014/01/10/time-management-tips-social-workers-struggling -maintain-control

Article: "Why I'm so Busy" by Addison Cooper (n.d.)
www.socialworker.com/extras/social-work-month-2015/why-so-busy

VIDEO LINKS

Short lecture on NASW's *Code of Ethics*
www.youtube.com/watch?v=26N6p9O9HcU

The Placement Experience (3-minute clip of a student discussing Field)
www.youtube.com/watch?v=XYr1scwc2ZI

Professional Ethics and Values in Contemporary Social Work Practice
www.youtube.com/watch?v=lImSqcEDOGs

Social Work Ethical Dilemmas
www.youtube.com/watch?v=xnLvGuHv9zk

REFERENCES

Beckett, C., & Maynard, A. (2005). *Values and ethics in social work*. London, UK: Sage.

Congress, E., & McAuliffe, D. (2006). Social work ethics: Professional codes in Australia and the United States. *International Social Work, 49*, 151–164. doi:10.1177/0020872806061211

Council on Social Work Education. (2015). Educational policy and accreditation standards for baccalaureate and master's social work programs. Retrieved from https://www.cswe.org/getattachment/Accreditation/Accreditation-Process/2015-EPAS/2015EPAS_Web_FINAL.pdf.aspx

DuBois, B., & Miley, K. K. (2014). *Social work: An empowering profession* (8th ed.). Boston, MA: Pearson.

Gumpert, J., & Black, P. (2006). Ethical issues in group work: What are they? How are they managed? *Social Work with Groups, 29*(4), 61–74. doi:10.1300/J009v29n04_05

Hepworth, D. H., Rooney, R. H., Rooney, G. D., & Strom-Gottfried, K. (2017). *Direct social work practice: Theory and skills* (10th ed.). Belmont, CA: Cengage.

McQueary, A. (2014). 10 effective nonprofit mission and vision pages. Retrieved from https://wiredimpact.com/blog/10-effective-nonprofit-mission-vision-pages

National Association of Social Workers. (2013a). *Guidelines for social work safety in the workplace*. Silver Spring, MD: Author. Retrieved from https://www.socialworkers.org/LinkClick.aspx?fileticket=6OEdoMjcNC0%3D&portalid=0

National Association of Social Workers. (2013b). *Managing clients who present with anger*. Silver Spring, MD: Author. Retrieved from https://www.socialworkers.org/assets/secured/documents/practice/managingangerinclients.pdf

National Association of Social Workers. (2017). *Code of ethics*. Silver Spring, MD: Author. Retrieved from https://www.socialworkers.org/About/Ethics/Code-of-Ethics/Code-of-Ethics-English

Perlman, H. H. (1979). *Relationship: The heart of helping people*. Chicago, IL: University of Chicago Press.

Poulin, J. (2010). *Strengths-based generalist practice: A collaborative approach* (3rd ed.). Belmont, CA: Cengage.

Reamer, F. G. (1990). *Ethical dilemmas in social service* (2nd ed.). New York, NY: Columbia University Press.

Schmid, H. (2008). The role of nonprofit human service organizations in providing social services: A prefatory essay. Retrieved from doi:10.1300/J147v28n03_01

Evaluating Your Professional Competencies

Ron, who is a first-year MSW student, has a field placement at an area agency on aging. He had worked at a social services agency as a case manager for 3 years before he began his graduate studies. In this field placement, he oversees the delivery and coordination of the various services being provided to elderly clients. As part of his field placement duties, Ron visits his clients in their homes and completes a comprehensive assessment, from which he develops a case management and evaluation plan. Although he has been a case manager in the past, he is excited about providing social work services to a different client population in a different service system with the opportunity to learn new skills.

Ron, however, is unsure how his performance as a social work intern will be evaluated. He has learned that he must develop a learning contract in collaboration with his field instructor and that the learning contract needs to focus on practice experiences related to professional competencies. He has also learned that at the end of the semester he will be evaluated on his proficiency on nine professional competencies. Ron realizes that a successful field placement is a requirement for staying in the MSW program and critical to his career goals. He wants to be sure that his learning contract and associated field placement experiences provide opportunities to address all the professional competencies and that his semester evaluation accurately reflects his learning and competency attainment.

How can Ron evaluate his professional practice regarding the nine competencies? How can Ron know whether he has successfully met the requirements for the competency?

The focus of this chapter is on assessing your mastery of the professional competencies in your field placement. The competency associated with this chapter is Competency 9: Evaluate practice with individuals, families, groups, organizations, and communities. This competency is much broader than the focus of this chapter. Content related to this competency is typically found your social work practice courses and your research courses and is covered in Chapter 9. Although the focus

(continued)

© Springer Publishing Company DOI: 10.1891/9780826175533.0002

LEARNING OBJECTIVES *(continued)*

here is more narrowly defined than the competency itself, it is nevertheless very much related to your evaluation of your practice with clients. By the end of this chapter, you will be able to

- Identify the nine social work professional competencies and the role they play in social work education and accreditation.
- Describe the dimensions associated with the social work competencies.
- Conceptualize holistic competency and the interrelationships of social work competencies.
- Conduct competency self-assessments and reflections on your client interactions or field placement experiences.
- Create a field placement learning contract with identified goals, objectives, activities, and data sources for evaluation.
- Understand the role your learning contract plays in your field placement experience.
- Understand the connection between a field reflection log, your learning contract, supervision, and evaluation of your progress on the social work competencies.

ACCREDITATION AND PROFESSIONAL COMPETENCIES

The accrediting body for social work education programs in the United States is the Council on Social Work Education's (CSWE's) Commission on Accreditation (COA). The CSWE's Commission on Educational Policy (COEP) creates educational policy for social work education and COA creates accreditation standards. The educational policy and accreditation standards together form the Educational Policy and Accreditation Standards (EPAS) that guide the accreditation of baccalaureate- and master's-level social work educational programs (Poulin & Matis, 2015).

SOCIAL WORK COMPETENCIES: EPAS 2015

Each of the nine professional competencies describes the knowledge, values, skills, and cognitive and affective processes that make up the competency at the generalist level of practice, followed by a set of behaviors that integrate these components. These behaviors represent examples of observable components of the competencies, whereas the preceding statements represent the underlying content and processes that inform the behaviors (CSWE, 2015).

Competency 1: Demonstrate Ethical and Professional Behavior

Social workers understand the value base of the profession and its ethical standards, as well as relevant laws and regulations that may impact their practice at the micro, mezzo, and macro levels. They understand the frameworks of ethical decision making and know how to apply principles of critical thinking to those frameworks in the practice, research, and policy arenas. Social workers recognize personal values and the distinction between personal and professional values. They also understand how their personal experiences and affective reactions influence their professional judgment and behavior. Social workers understand the profession's history, mission, and roles and responsibilities. They also understand the role of other professions when engaged in interprofessional teams. Social workers recognize the importance of lifelong learning and are committed to continually updating their skills to ensure they are relevant and effective. They also understand emerging forms of technology and the ethical use of technology in social work practice. Social workers:

- Make ethical decisions by applying the standards of the National Association of Social Workers' (NASW) *Code of Ethics*, relevant laws and regulations, models for ethical decision making, models for ethical conduct of research, and additional codes of ethics as appropriate to the particular context.

- Use refection and self-regulation to manage personal values and maintain professionalism in practice situations.

- Demonstrate a professional demeanor through their behavior; appearance; and oral, written, and electronic communications.

- Use technology ethically and appropriately to facilitate practice outcomes.

- Use supervision and consultation to guide professional judgment and behavior.

Competency 2: Engage Diversity and Difference in Practice

Social workers understand how diversity and difference characterize and shape the human experience and are critical to the formation of identity. The dimensions of diversity are understood as the intersectionality of multiple factors including, but not limited to, age, class, color, culture, disability and ability, ethnicity, gender, gender identity and expression, immigration status, marital status, political ideology, race, religion and spirituality, sex, sexual orientation, and tribal sovereign status. Social workers understand that, as a consequence of differences in such factors, a person's life experiences may include oppression, poverty, marginalization, and alienation or, alternatively, privilege, power, and acclaim. They also understand the forms and mechanisms of oppression and discrimination and recognize the extent to which a culture's structures and values, including social, economic, political, and cultural exclusions, may oppress, marginalize, alienate, or create privilege and power. Social workers:

- Apply and communicate understanding of the importance of diversity and difference in shaping life experiences in their practice at the micro, mezzo, and macro levels.

- Present themselves as learners and engage clients and constituencies as experts in their own experiences.

- Apply self-awareness and self-regulation to manage the influence of personal biases and values in working with diverse clients and constituencies.

Competency 3: Advance Human Rights and Social, Economic, and Environmental Justice

Social workers understand that every person, regardless of position in society, has fundamental human rights, such as freedom, safety, privacy, an adequate standard of living, health care, and education. They understand the global interconnections of oppression and human rights violations and are knowledgeable about theories of human need and social justice and strategies to promote social and economic justice and human rights. Social workers understand strategies designed to eliminate oppressive structural barriers to ensure that social goods, rights, and responsibilities are distributed equitably and that civil, political, environmental, economic, social, and cultural human rights are protected. Social workers:

- Apply their understanding of social, economic, and environmental justice to advocate for human rights at the individual and system levels.

- Engage in practices that advance social, economic, and environmental justice.

Competency 4: Engage in Practice-Informed Research and Research-Informed Practice

Social workers understand quantitative and qualitative research methods and their respective roles in advancing the science of social work and in evaluating their practice. They know the principles of logic, scientific inquiry, and culturally informed and ethical approaches to building knowledge. Social workers understand that evidence that informs practice derives from multidisciplinary sources and multiple ways of knowing. They also understand the processes for translating research findings into effective practice. Social workers:

- Use practice experience and theory to inform scientific inquiry and research.

- Apply critical thinking to engage in analysis of quantitative and qualitative research methods and research findings.

- Use and translate research evidence to inform and improve practice, policy, and service delivery.

Competency 5: Engage in Policy Practice

Social workers understand that human rights and social justice, as well as social welfare and services, are mediated by policy and its implementation at the federal, state, and local levels. They understand the history and current structures of social policies and services, the role of policy in service delivery, and the role of practice in policy development. Social workers understand their role in policy development and implementation within their practice settings at the micro, mezzo, and macro levels and they actively engage in policy practice to effect change within those settings. They recognize and understand the historical, social, cultural, economic, organizational, environmental, and global influences that affect social policy. They are also knowledgeable about policy formulation, analysis, implementation, and evaluation. Social workers:

- Identify social policies at the local, state, and federal levels that impact well-being, service delivery, and access to social services.

- Assess how social welfare and economic policies affect the delivery of and access to social services.

- Apply critical thinking to analyze, formulate, and advocate for policies that advance human rights and social, economic, and environmental justice.

Competency 6: Engage With Individuals, Families, Groups, Organizations, and Communities

Social workers understand that engagement is an ongoing component of the dynamic and interactive process of social work practice with, and on behalf of, diverse individuals, families, groups, organizations, and communities. They value the importance of human relationships. Social workers understand theories of human behavior and the social environment, and critically evaluate and apply this knowledge to facilitate engagement with clients and constituencies, including individuals, families, groups, organizations, and communities. They understand strategies to engage diverse clients and constituencies to advance practice effectiveness. Social workers understand how their personal experiences and affective reactions may impact their ability to effectively engage with diverse clients and constituencies. They value principles of relationship building and interprofessional collaboration to facilitate engagement with clients, constituencies, and other professionals as appropriate. Social workers:

- Apply knowledge of human behavior and the social environment, person-in-environment, and other multidisciplinary theoretical frameworks to engage with clients and constituencies.

- Use empathy, reflection, and interpersonal skills to effectively engage diverse clients and constituencies.

Competency 7: Assess Individuals, Families, Groups, Organizations, and Communities

Social workers understand that assessment is an ongoing component of the dynamic and interactive process of social work practice with, and on behalf of, diverse individuals, families, groups, organizations, and communities. They understand theories of human behavior and the social environment, and critically evaluate and apply this knowledge in the assessment of diverse clients and constituencies, including individuals, families, groups, organizations, and communities. Social workers understand the methods of assessment that are used with diverse clients and constituencies to advance practice effectiveness. They recognize the implications of the larger practice context in the assessment process and value the importance of interprofessional collaboration in this process. Social workers understand how their personal experiences and affective reactions may affect their assessment and decision making. Social workers:

- Collect and organize data, and apply critical thinking to interpret information from clients and constituencies.

- Apply knowledge of human behavior and the social environment, person-in-environment, and other multidisciplinary theoretical frameworks in the analysis of assessment data from clients and constituencies.

- Develop mutually agreed-on intervention goals and objectives on the basis of their critical assessment of strengths, needs, and challenges within clients and constituencies.

- Select appropriate intervention strategies on the basis of the assessment, research knowledge, and values and preferences of clients and constituencies.

Competency 8: Intervene With Individuals, Families, Groups, Organizations, and Communities

Social workers understand that intervention is an ongoing component of the dynamic and interactive process of social work practice with, and on behalf of, diverse individuals, families, groups, organizations, and communities. They are knowledgeable about evidence-informed interventions to achieve the goals of clients and constituencies, including individuals, families, groups, organizations, and communities. Social workers understand theories of human behavior and the social environment, and they critically evaluate and apply this knowledge to effectively intervene with clients and constituencies. They understand methods of identifying, analyzing, and implementing evidence-informed interventions to achieve client and constituency goals. Social workers value the importance of interprofessional teamwork and communication in interventions, recognizing that beneficial outcomes may require interdisciplinary, interprofessional, and interorganizational collaboration. Social workers:

● Critically choose and implement interventions to achieve practice goals and enhance capacities of clients and constituencies.

● Apply knowledge of human behavior and the social environment, person-in-environment, and other multidisciplinary theoretical frameworks in interventions with clients and constituencies.

● Use interprofessional collaboration as appropriate to achieve beneficial practice outcomes.

● Negotiate, mediate, and advocate with and on behalf of diverse clients and constituencies.

● Facilitate effective transitions and endings that advance mutually agreed-on goals.

Competency 9: Evaluate Practice With Individuals, Families, Groups, Organizations, and Communities

Social workers understand that evaluation is an ongoing component of the dynamic and interactive process of social work practice with, and on behalf of, diverse individuals, families, groups, organizations and communities. They recognize the importance of evaluating processes and outcomes to advance practice, policy, and service delivery effectiveness. Social workers understand theories of human behavior and the social environment, and they critically evaluate and apply this knowledge in evaluating outcomes. They understand qualitative and quantitative methods for evaluating outcomes and practice effectiveness. Social workers:

Field Reflection Questions

Which social work competencies will be covered in your field placement activities organically as part of your internship duties?

For which social work competencies will you have to make special efforts to ensure you have related learning opportunities?

● Select and use appropriate methods for evaluation of outcomes.

● Apply knowledge of human behavior and the social environment, person-in-environment, and other multidisciplinary theoretical frameworks in the evaluation of outcomes.

- Critically analyze, monitor, and evaluate intervention and program processes and outcomes.

- Apply evaluation findings to improve practice effectiveness at the micro, mezzo, and macro levels (CSWE, 2015).

HOLISTIC COMPETENCY

McKnight (2013) proposes that competence is an "ongoing ability" to "integrate knowledge, skills, judgment, and professional attributes in order to practice safely and ethically" within one's professional scope (p. 460). The CSWE (2015, p. 6) defines holistic competence as the demonstration of knowledge, values, skills, and cognitive and affective processes that include the social worker's critical thinking, affective reactions, and exercise of judgment in regard to unique practice situations.

KNOWLEDGE

The knowledge dimension comprises your mastery of the substantive content of the competency. Social work curricula are constructed to provide students with course work that includes readings, assignments, and discussions that educate students on the current knowledge related to each competency. Students also increase their competency knowledge through their own research on the topics that constitute the underlying content and processes of each competency. A prerequisite of one's ability to demonstrate competence is a solid understanding and knowledge of the literature that supports the competency.

VALUES

The values dimension is less clear than the knowledge dimension. Although Competency 1 is about values and professional behavior, the other eight competencies have social work values dimensions as well. The values dimensions can have knowledge (social work values) as well as skill (ethical behavior and decision making) components. Understanding the values and ethics associated with the application of the different social work competencies in unique practice situations is a fundamental aspect of ethical decision making and professional social work competence.

SKILLS

The skills dimension refers to your ability to apply social work knowledge and values in your social work practice. Numerous skills are associated with each professional competency. Your field placement experience will provide you with an opportunity to apply, refine, and learn social work skills in practice situations. Your skill is your ability to apply social work theories, concepts, and techniques in your practice with clients or client systems.

COGNITIVE AND AFFECTIVE PROCESSES

This dimension has three associated subdimensions—critical thinking, affective reactions, and professional judgment. Critical thinking is the open-minded search for understanding. It is a process focused on answering the *why* question. This process includes "providing evidence, examining the implications of the evidence, recognizing any potential contradictions and examining alternative explanations" (Heron, 2006, p. 221). The CSWE (2015) defines critical thinking as an intellectual, disciplined process of conceptualizing, analyzing, evaluating, and synthesizing multiple sources of information generated by observation, reaction, and reasoning. Critical thinking is a crucial component of professional competence because it ensures that your social work practice is reasoned and thoughtful, and not merely the rote application of social work techniques. Affective reaction, by contrast, generally refers to the affective component of social work practice with clients (Rubaltelli & Slovic, 2008). It is the worker's emotional response to the client's presentation and situation, and is tied to empathy and other affective processes. Affective reaction has relevance for social work competency, in that effective social work practice requires cognitive and affective understanding of the client as well as one's own feelings, emotions, and reactions (Poulin & Matis, 2015).

Professional judgment is about decision making in social work practice. A key issue debated in relation to decision making in this setting is the extent to which social workers use analytical versus intuitive reasoning styles (Collins & Daly, 2011). Thus, professional judgment is reasoned decision making on the basis of evidence, knowledge, analytical reasoning, and practice wisdom. It is a process of examining all facets of the case and making a reasoned decision supported by both objective and subjective evidence. Exercising informed professional judgment is a critical component of professional social work competence (Poulin & Matis, 2015).

Field Reflection Questions

How do you plan to incorporate cognitive and affective processes in your social work practice at your field placement?

How can you help structure your field placement supervision to ensure that you address your competencies in a multidimensional way?

The nine social work competencies and the associated dimensions are the interrelated components of professional social work practice. The competencies are interconnected; they do not stand alone. Holistic competency is social work practice using multiple professional competencies in each practice activity or client interaction.

Figure 2.1 shows a conceptualization of the various interrelationships among the nine professional social work competencies. The competencies in the outer ring of the circle are those that apply broadly to all practice situations. Ethical behavior, diversity, and social justice competency are fundamental components of effective social work practice at all levels (Poulin & Matis, 2015). The competencies in middle ring of the figure are the two areas of social work practice that are not client based. That is, policy practice and research competence are informed by the competencies of diversity, social justice, and ethical behavior and, in turn, inform social work practice with clients and constituencies. The competencies in the inner circle of the figure are those related to social work practice with individuals, families, groups, organizations, and communities. Diversity, social justice, ethical behavior, policy practice, and research competencies all inform the practice competencies of engagement, assessment, intervention, and evaluation with different clients and constituencies (Poulin & Matis, 2015).

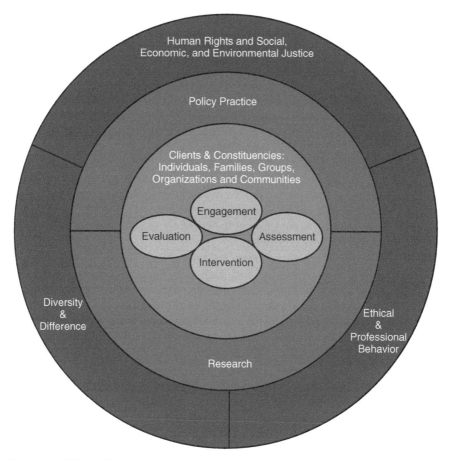

FIGURE 2.1 Social work competencies.

Poulin, J., & Matis, S. (2015). Social work competencies and multidimensional assessment. *Journal of Baccalaureate Social Work, 20,* 117–135. doi:10.18084/1084-7219.20.1.117

ASSESSING YOUR PROFESSIONAL COMPETENCE

Competency is a complex concept that focuses on your ability to do, not just on what you know (Bogo, Rawlings, Katz, & Logie, 2014). It involves "both performance *and* the knowledge, values, critical thinking, affective reactions, and exercise of judgment that inform performance" (CSWE, 2015, p. 6). Your social work program will evaluate your performance in your field placement and most likely your competency attainment. Most social work programs use some type of field placement measure of their students' mastery of the nine professional competencies. Nevertheless, we believe that an important part of one's professional development is ongoing and continuous self-assessment. Social work professionals must continually engage in a process of reflection and self-assessment as part of their ethical practice in providing the best possible services to their clients. Social work students in field placement must also engage in a process of reflection and self-assessment. Reflection and self-assessment is a critical component of learning and your professional development. The Competency Reflection Log (CRL) presented in this book is designed to help you with the task of self-reflection and assessment of your development for each of the nine professional competencies. We suggest that you main-tain an ongoing log for each competency. When you have a client interaction or field placement experience related to a professional competency, you should record it in the appropriate CRL and briefly reflect upon that experience. You can then use your reflec-tion during the supervision by your field instructor to enhance your learning related to the competency. This ongoing qualitative assessment of your progress on each com-petency will help keep the focus of your learning on the professional competencies. It will also give you a record and information that you can bring to your field placement evaluation meeting with your field instructor.

In conducting your reflections and self-assessments, we suggest you focus on three levels of competence—knowledge, behavioral, and meta. The three levels are hierarchical, with meta being the highest level of competence. Achieving competence at a lower level is a prerequisite for achieving a higher level of competence.

We are calling the lowest level knowledge competence. Mastery of a body of knowl-edge related to each social work competency is a prerequisite to being able to demonstrate competency in the world of practice (Poulin & Matis, 2015). The social work competencies developed by the CSWE are complex, and each competency contains content covering numerous substantive areas. Before completing an entry into a competency log, we sug-gest you always review the substantive content of the competency, identify the content areas that apply to the experience you are recording, and conduct an honest self-assess-ment of your understanding of the relevant body of knowledge. Identifying what you do not know is as important as understanding what you do know. If you find gaps in your knowledge base, discuss this issue with your field instructor, who perhaps can recom-mend readings and/or resources to strengthen your knowledge base relevant to your field placement and the client population with whom you work.

The second level of practice competence is behavioral competence. This is the ability to apply knowledge and skills to a practice situation (Poulin & Matis, 2015). We believe that achieving cognitive and behavioral competence for each social work competency is the basic level of social work practice competence. Achieving this level of professional competency is a realistic goal for students in a generalist field placement. Your self-assess-ment of your behavioral competence requires you to specify observable practice behav-iors. The EPAS 2015 lists example practice behaviors for each competency. In addition, there are many other practice behaviors associated with each competency. In completing your competency logs, identify and describe the practice behaviors you used in the client interaction or field experience. The description should be specific and observable. The next step is to reflect on how it went, what worked, why it worked, what did not work, why, what you would do differently next time, and any questions you have. Again, the ben-efits of completing the competency logs are that doing so increases your self-awareness of your progress and learning related to the competencies, and the reflections can be used in supervision to further your learning and skill development.

The third and highest level of practice competence is metacompetence (Bogo, 2016). This level of competence entails a demonstration of competence that is "informed by knowl-edge, values, affective reaction, critical thinking, and professional judgement in regard to unique practice situations" (CSWE, 2015, p. 6). Students achieving this level of competence are able to integrate knowledge and skills associated with different competencies, apply critical thinking and reflection, and apply their skills in unique practice situations. The key components of metacompetence are internal processing components of critical thinking, reflection, and affective processes. Thus, your self-assessment on your CRL also includes reflection upon your critical thinking, affective reaction, and professional judgment related to your client interaction or field experience. Simply put, you need to reflect upon the internal processing you used. What was the thinking behind your practice behavior?

In summary, your CRLs should include the following item: a brief description of the client interaction or field experience, reflection upon your competency knowledge related to the interaction, identification of the practice behaviors used, reflection upon the effectiveness of your practice behaviors, and reflection upon your internal processing. Your descriptions and reflections should be brief summaries of the key points. The purpose is to help focus your field placement experience on your learning related to the social work competencies. Exhibit 2.1 is a sample CRL for Competency 1: Demonstrate Ethical and Professional Behavior

■ SAMPLE CRL—COMPETENCY 1: DEMONSTRATE ETHICAL AND PROFESSIONAL BEHAVIOR

The CRL is designed to help you stay focused on your mastery of each social work professional competency throughout your field placement experience (electronic templates of the CRLs for each of the nine social work competencies can be found in Student Resources at www.springerpub.com). Completing your CRLs should be an ongoing and dynamic process of recording and reflecting upon your progress in mastering the social work competencies. To be an effective tool, each CRL must be reviewed and updated as needed, on at least a biweekly basis. We also recommend that you review your CRLs with your field instructor on a biweekly basis. Exhibit 2.1 is a sample CRL entry for the ethical and professional behavior competency (CSWE, 2015).

■ THE LEARNING CONTRACT

The learning contract is an essential component of your field placement learning experience. Its purpose is to guide your learning and make it purposeful. Learning contracts usually specify activities or learning opportunities related to the social work competencies. They may also specify learning goals associated with the various learning activities and some sort of assessment rubric. However, learning contract formats vary from program to program. Therefore, this section reviews the core components related to your learning that more than likely will be included in your school's field placement learning contract.

As a student in a generalist field placement, you must be proactive to ensure that you have opportunities to master the social work competencies and develop the skills needed to be ready for your specialization field placement or for generalist practice. Being proactive in your first couple of weeks at your field placement is not an easy task. Nevertheless, it is important. Targeted and focused learning will not happen automatically. Thus, you need a plan that creates learning opportunities related to the professional social work competencies and your individual learning needs. The learning contract is this plan, which shapes and directs your field placement experience.

Student field placements are a major component of social work education. BSW students must complete a minimum of 400 field hours and MSW students must complete a minimum of 900 field hours (CSWE, 2015). Completing the field placement requirements entails a huge investment of time, effort, and energy. Not all field placements are equal: There is great variation in terms of the quality of supervision and types of learning experiences. Many

EXHIBIT 2.1

Sample Competency Reflection Log: Competency 1—Demonstrate Ethical and Professional Behavior

Describe the client interaction or field experience and provide a brief context for the interaction.	Reflect upon your substantive competency knowledge related to the client interaction or field experience.	Identify the practice behaviors you used and reflect upon your affective reaction and effectiveness.	Reflect upon the internal processing (critical thinking and affective reaction) you used to make your practice decisions during the client interaction or field experience.
Date: 9/21/18			
A new participant who joined my substance abuse treatment group is someone I know personally from my neighborhood.	I am knowledgeable about the NASW *Code of Ethics* generally but not fully knowledgeable about all of the ethical standards. I understand the standard on privacy and confidentiality pretty well, but I am not as clear about the standard on conflicts of interest.	I used two practice behaviors: (a) make an ethical decision by following the ethical standard on privacy and confidentiality; and (b) use supervision to guide professional judgments. I think I was effective with the first practice behavior because I did not acknowledge knowing the new member. By doing so, I maintained her privacy. I felt (affective reaction) that violating her privacy would be inappropriate and that she would acknowledge me if that is what she wanted (self-determination). Discussing the situation with my supervisor was also effective. I got additional clarification on how to handle similar situations in the future and clarification of the conflicts of interest standard related to dual relationships. We developed a strategy for future group meetings with the new participant.	When I realized I knew the new participant, I immediately knew that I had to make a decision about acknowledging our relationship. I reviewed in my mind the NASW *Code of Ethics* and was pretty confident that I had to respect her privacy, because acknowledging her could be embarrassing and I did not know her preferences. On the basis of that, I made the decision to not acknowledge that we knew each other. I feel this was the correct decision because she did not acknowledge me and my supervisor supported my decision.
Date:			
Describe client interaction or field experience.	Reflect upon your substantive knowledge of competency.	Identify the practice behaviors you used and reflect upon your affective reaction and effectiveness.	Reflect upon your internal processing related to your practice decisions.

field settings provide excellent learning opportunities; others, less so. A number of factors can affect your field placement experience—for example, the match between your learning style and your field instructor's teaching style, the quality of your supervision, your relationship with your field instructors, and the organizational culture and support. Some of these factors are outside your control. One area in which you do have control is framing your learning contract and negotiating the activities and learning opportunities that will contribute toward your professional development.

Having a negative field placement experience can negatively impact your perceptions of the profession, as well as your interest and commitment to social work as a career (Kanno & Koeske, 2010). The field placement experience is critical to your learning and development as a social work professional. A key to having an excellent field placement learning experience is developing an individualized learning contract that identifies learning opportunities tied directly to the social work competencies and your individual learning needs. To be effective, your learning contract needs to be an ongoing component of your field placement experience. It is not something that is completed and then ignored or forgotten. Instead, the learning contract must be reviewed regularly and your progress evaluated; if learning opportunities related to all of the social work competencies have not emerged naturally, then you must explore with your field instructor creative ways to make that happen. It is your responsibility to monitor your learning contract and make sure you have learning opportunities for each social work competency. Many of the competencies will be covered organically during your field placement activities; others might not. For those not covered, you will need to brainstorm with your field instructor about ways to include them. Professional competence requires competence in all nine areas, not just with some of the competencies.

DEVELOPING YOUR LEARNING CONTRACT

Most social work programs require a field placement learning contract. Your school has a format and template that you must follow. Regardless of the template for your school's learning contract, there is a process you should follow. The first step is to review the social work competencies and become very familiar with the core professional social work competencies. The social work competencies have been defined by the profession as the baseline for effective generalist social work practice. Your job as a social work student is to graduate as a competent social work professional. Your field placements are where you have the opportunity to engage in social work practice and associated activities related to the nine social work competencies. Thus, before developing your learning contract, you need to have a clear understanding of what is expected of you as a professional social worker.

Having reviewed the professional competencies, your next step is to complete a self-assessment of your knowledge, skills, strengths, and challenges related to each competency. Ask yourself where you are in terms of your professional development and identify specific areas that need strengthening. Be honest with yourself. Your goal is not to show what you know, but rather to identify areas that need further development. For each competency, develop two or three specific learning goals related to the competency. Your goals should be specific and based on your self-assessment. We recommend at least one knowledge goal, one behavioral goal, and one metagoal.

Having completed your competency self-assessment and identified potential learning goals, you are now ready to meet with your field instructor to identify field

Field Reflection Questions

After completing a draft of your learning contract, to what extent are your goals, objectives, and tasks truly yours and how well do they represent your learning needs?

After competing your learning contract, which steps will you take to make it an active part of your field learning?

placement activities and learning opportunities related to each competency. The key is to identify activities that will provide learning opportunities related to the nine social work competencies and to the personal goals and challenges you have identified. Be comprehensive and identify as many activities as possible. This will help you and your field instructor design a field placement experience that proactively addresses your learning needs related to your professional growth and development. This is very different from just going to your field placement and letting whatever happens happen. Your field placement should be a structured learning experience. A comprehensive learning contract creates the structure and places the focus on your learning and professional development.

DEVELOPING GOALS AND OBJECTIVES

Learning goals are derived directly from your self-assessment. They should focus on areas you want to strengthen and what you hope to accomplish in your field placement learning process. The challenges you identified in your self-assessment are essentially opportunities for growth related to each competency. Your learning goals are positive statements about what you hope to accomplish in your field learning (Poulin, 2010).

PURPOSE OF GOALS

Goals serve multiple purposes. General goals are less effective than clear and specific goals. When goals are vague and very general, work is characterized by frequent shifts in direction and focus (Poulin, 2010). Thus, one of the major purposes of goals is to set the direction for the work. Specific goals ensure that you and your field instructor are in agreement about your learning. With vague and general goals, you and your field instructor may have different expectations or interpretations about what you hope to accomplish.

Goals help facilitate the specification of your learning activities. They help determine appropriate tasks and activities that will be undertaken to help you make progress on your goals and competencies. Without clear and specific goals and objectives, it is difficult to determine whether progress is being made and whether a desired end has been attained.

GOALS AND OBJECTIVES

Goals are positive statements about desired ends. In fairly broad terms, they describe the hoped-for end result of your field learning. Goal statements do not need to be measurable—they are global statements of a desired positive outcome.

Objectives are subgoals that lead to the achievement of the long-term goal. They are the *measurable* intermediate steps that, when accomplished, help you achieve your goal. They need to be feasible. Try to select objectives that are realistic and obtainable. Whenever possible, write objectives in positive language. State what will be accomplished rather than what will be eliminated. Use words that describe specific behaviors. Describe what you will actually do (or think or feel) to achieve the objective (Poulin, 2010). In summary, effective objectives should be steps toward goals that are realistic and attainable, observable and measurable, and stated in positive terms that emphasize outcomes.

EVALUATION OF YOUR FIELD PERFORMANCE

The evaluation of your field performance is done by your field instructor. Typically, your field instructor conducts your end-of-the-semester evaluation, and your grade for the semester is submitted by your faculty field liaison. Your field instructor will evaluate you using an instrument provided by your school. Field evaluation instruments vary from school to school. What they all have in common are items rating your performance on the nine social work competencies. Some will be simple rating scales asking your field instructor for a single overall rating on each competency. Others might ask your field instructor to rate you on the practice behaviors included in the competency descriptions. Qualitative assessments might be used singly or in combination with rating scales. Regardless of the evaluation method or instrument used by your school, the bottom line is that your field instructor, in collaboration with you, will complete your performance evaluation, which determines whether you pass the field course. Therefore, it is incumbent on you to make sure your field instructor has the data necessary to make an informed evaluation of your performance. To make sure this happens, you have to be proactive. Just assuming that your field instructor will remember what you did and how well you did in your various tasks and activities related to each competency is risky.

Field Reflection Questions

In your field placement, how will you evaluate your knowledge related to each competency?

What are your skills?

Discuss your critical thinking and professional judgments.

How can you help structure your field placement supervision to ensure that you address your competencies multidimensionally?

Agency practice is very demanding these days. Being a field instructor is an added demanding responsibility to an already busy schedule. Your field instructor is there to provide guidance and constructive feedback. He or she will tend to view your performance in terms of your assigned tasks and agency needs. Viewing your performance in terms of the social work competencies requires a different lens and perspective. To facilitate your learning and to ensure an accurate competency-based evaluation, you, as the student intern, need to organize and provide data on your performance to your field instructor. There are several ways this can be accomplished.

In developing your learning contract, be sure to build into the evaluation component sources of data for your field instructor's evaluation. Some potential sources of data for your field instructor are (a) observation of your interactions with clients and/or colleagues, (b) your reflection notes, (c) review of your written work, and (d) insights gained through your participation in supervision sessions. Regardless of the data source, one common thread is that the data need to be reviewed, discussed, and processed with your field instructor during supervision and then a summary with reflections entered in the appropriate CRL. To help ensure that competency conversations take place in supervision, include them on your weekly supervision agendas. Remember that it is your responsibility to help structure your supervision to include processing your field experiences and client interactions related to the social work competencies.

We believe that the CRL is an excellent way to make this happen. For example, build into your learning contract the field instructor's observations of your interactions with clients and/or staff. Make sure the observations get scheduled and take place. Reflect upon the interaction in your CRL. Put the observed interaction on your supervision agenda and process it with your field instructor in supervision. Then add a postsupervision summary and reflection entry into your CRL summarizing the feedback you received from your field instructor and any additional thoughts you have about your performance related to your knowledge, behavior, and internal processing related to the social work competency. This should happen after every supervisory session in which you process and review any of your data sources. Your CRLs for each competency will then become data that you can bring to your semester evaluation. These data will include your field instructor's observations and feedback, as well as your reflections and self-assessment of your progress on the competency being reviewed. If you are conscientious and make entries into your CRLs throughout the semester, you will bring a wealth of data to your performance evaluation. Your data combined with your field instructor's personal insights will increase the chances of a valid and helpful evaluation dramatically. This process requires work on your part, but we believe the end result in terms of structuring your learning, receiving constructive feedback, and furthering your professional development is well worth the extra effort.

With this approach, you are responsible for organizing the data for your performance evaluation and making it available in an assessable manner for review by your field instructor. Your field instructor is responsible for analyzing your data, incorporating his or her insights on the basis of observation and interactions with you, and making a professional assessment of your performance on each social work competency. The evaluation instruments used to document your performance will most likely be provided by the school. Regardless of the type of instrument used or the format used by your school, your CRL data will provide the kind of information needed for your field instructor to complete a comprehensive data-driven evaluation.

Your learning contract and your CRLs are two tools that will help focus your field learning on the social work competencies—the key components of the performance evaluation required by your school. They will also help you bridge the gap between agency and school expectations that are, more often than not, different. Your school's focus is on the professional competencies, whereas your field placement's focus tends to be on service delivery and following agency procedures. Both are important for a successful field placement experience. Our point is that you have to take responsibility for ensuring that the school's focus and the points on which you will be evaluated are built into your field practicum experience.

Exhibit 2.2 is a sample learning contract for a first-year MSW student's generalist field placement. The sample learning contract includes a brief agency description, goals, objectives, data sources, and identified placement activities for two competencies. Each example has only one goal per competency. Your field placement learning contract will likely have more than one goal for each of the nine competencies. It could also include due dates for the various tasks as well as contact information on yourself, your placement agency, your field instructor, field liaison, and possibly other types of information.

EXHIBIT
2.2

Sample Learning Contract

BRIEF DESCRIPTION OF AGENCY SETTING
The community agency is a safe space for women and children escaping violence. The program provides temporary emergency assistance with other difficulties such as budgeting, credit complications, legal questions and obstacles, and meditation. The agency has 32 beds within 10 different rooms. The residents have access to laundry facilities, computers with Internet access, a full kitchen, a dining a room, television room, and public transportation. There is a children's program that offers homework assistance and summer camp as well as other activities. The crisis hotline is also operated from within the agency and is staffed 24 hours a day. Crisis hotline advocates provide support, safety planning, and referrals.

COMPETENCY 1: DEMONSTRATE ETHICAL AND PROFESSIONAL BEHAVIOR
Social workers understand the value base of the profession and its ethical standards, as well as relevant laws and regulations that may impact practice at the micro, mezzo, and macro levels. They understand frameworks of ethical decision making and know how to apply principles of critical thinking to those frameworks in the practice, research, and policy arenas. Social workers recognize personal values and the distinction between personal and professional values. They also understand how their personal experiences and affective reactions influence their professional judgment and behavior. Social workers understand the profession's history, its mission, and the roles and responsibilities of the profession. They understand the role of other professions when engaged in interprofessional teams. Social workers recognize the importance of lifelong learning and are committed to continually updating their skills to ensure they are relevant and effective. In addition, they understand emerging forms of technology and the ethical use of technology in social work practice. Social workers:

- Make ethical decisions by applying the standards of the NASW's *Code of Ethics*, relevant laws and regulations, models for ethical decision making, models for ethical conduct of research, and additional codes of ethics as appropriate to context.
- Use reflection and self-regulation to manage personal values and maintain professionalism in practice situations.
- Demonstrate professional demeanor in behavior; appearance; and oral, written, and electronic communications.
- Use technology ethically and appropriately to facilitate practice outcomes.
- Use supervision and consultation to guide professional judgment and behavior.

Goal: To become proficient in my ability to apply the NASW's *Code of Ethics* in my social work practice with my clients.
    Objective 1 (knowledge): I will demonstrate my knowledge of the NASW's ethical standards by bring potential ethical conflicts I encounter in my work with clients to my supervision with my field instructor.
    Objective 1 data source: CRL summaries and reflection notes on discussions of ethical conflicts in supervision and summary of feedback received from the field instructor.

(continued)

**EXHIBIT
2.2**

Sample Learning Contract (*continued*)

Objective 2 (behavior): I will apply ethical guidelines, in consultation with my field instructor, to effectively resolve ethical dilemmas I encounter in my work with clients.
Objective 2 data source: CRL summaries and reflection notes on my field instructor's observations and feedback on my ability to apply ethical guidelines in resolving an ethical dilemma with a client.
Objective 3 (behavior): I will demonstrate professional behavior in implementing ethical dilemma resolutions.
Objective 3 data source: CRL summaries and reflection notes on my field instructor's observations and feedback on my ability to demonstrate professional behavior in resolving an ethical dilemma with a client.
Objective 4 (meta): I will engage in self-reflection to help me effectively manage my personal values and value conflicts with my clients.
Objective 4 data source: CRL summaries and reflection notes on supervisory sessions where we discussed my use of self-reflection related to managing personal values and value conflicts.

ACTIVITIES/TASKS
I will discuss ethical standards and ethical dilemmas with my field instructor.
I will discuss my personal values and value conflicts with my supervisor to help guide my professional judgment and behaviors.
I will attend an agency training session on Health Insurance Portability and Accountability Act (HIPPA) requirements.
I will read the NASW's *Code of Ethics*.
I will read agency guidelines on professional behavior; appearance; and oral, written, and electronic communications.
I will complete biopsychosocial intake assessments with my assigned clients.
I will apply NASW's ethical standards in my interactions with clients.

COMPETENCY 9: EVALUATE PRACTICE WITH INDIVIDUALS, FAMILIES, GROUPS, ORGANIZATIONS, AND COMMUNITIES
Social workers understand that evaluation is an ongoing component of the dynamic and interactive process of social work practice with, and on behalf of, diverse individuals, families, groups, organizations, and communities. They recognize the importance of evaluating processes and outcomes to advance practice, policy, and service delivery effectiveness. Social workers understand theories of human behavior and the social environment, and critically evaluate and apply this knowledge in evaluating outcomes. They understand qualitative and quantitative methods for evaluating outcomes and practice effectiveness. Social workers:

• Select and use appropriate methods for evaluation of outcomes.
• Apply knowledge of human behavior and the social environment, person-in-environment, and other multidisciplinary theoretical frameworks in the evaluation of outcomes.
• Critically analyze, monitor, and evaluate intervention and program processes and outcomes.

(*continued*)

EXHIBIT
2.2

Sample Learning Contract (*continued*)

- Apply evaluation findings to improve practice effectiveness at the micro, mezzo, and macro levels.

Goal: To become proficient in using qualitative methods to evaluate my practice effectiveness.

Objective 1 (knowledge): I will demonstrate my knowledge of qualitative assessment by documenting my efforts to qualitatively assess my practice effectiveness in my CRLs and by discussing my practice effectiveness in supervision with my field instructor.

Objective 1 data source: CRL summaries, reflection notes, and supervisory feedback on discussions of qualitative assessment methods received from the field instructor.

Objective 2 (behavior): I will use qualitative evaluation methods to improve my practice effectiveness with my clients.

Objective 2 data source: CRL summaries and reflection notes on my field instructor's observations and feedback on using qualitative assessments to improve my practice effectiveness.

Objective 3 (meta): I will engage in ongoing self-reflection and critical thinking to improve practice effectiveness.

Objective 3 data source: CRL summaries and reflection notes on supervisory sessions where we discussed my use of critical thinking and self-reflection improved practice effectiveness.

ACTIVITIES/TASKS

I will discuss qualitative assessment methods with my field instructor.

I will use supervision with my field instructor to process my self-reflections related to assessing and improving my practice effectiveness.

I will seek out training on practice evaluation and qualitative methods of assessment.

I will review various qualitative assessment methods covered in my research courses.

I will engage in ongoing self-reflection when completing biopsychosocial intake assessments with my assigned clients.

I will continually implement practice effectiveness assessments in my interactions with my clients.

CRL, Competency Reflection Log.

SUMMARY

This chapter has focused on the social work competencies and assessing your professional competence. We reviewed the knowledge, behavioral, and metadimensions of holistic competency and their subdimensions—knowledge, values, skills, and cognitive and affective processes. A CRL was introduced to help you document your competencies related to your client interactions and field experiences.

This chapter also reviewed your field placement learning contract, including its role and purpose in helping you structure and guide your field learning experiences.

We reviewed goals, objectives, specifying field activities/tasks, and evaluating your field performance. We strongly encouraged you to create a thoughtful and meaningful learning contract that is an ongoing component of your field placement experience. To be of value, your learning contract must be an active, living document. The remainder of this chapter focuses on discussion and critical thinking questions, as well as providing a detailed case summary related to Competency 9 with additional critical thinking and reflection questions.

CRITICAL THINKING QUESTIONS

Competency 2 focuses on diversity and difference. This competency impacts and intersects with all of the other eight social work competencies. As a social worker, you are expected to understand how diversity and differences characterize and shape the human experience. The dimensions of diversity are understood as the intersectionality of multiple factors. You are expected to understand that, as a consequence of differences, a person's life experiences may include oppression, poverty, marginalization, and alienation or, alternatively, privilege, power, and acclaim (CSWE, 2015). Competency 3 focuses on social, economic, and environmental justice. You are expected to understand that every person, regardless of his or her position in society, has fundamental human rights such as freedom, safety, privacy, an adequate standard of living, health care, and education. You need to understand strategies designed to eliminate oppressive structural barriers to ensure that social goods, rights, and responsibilities are distributed equitably and that civil, political, environmental, economic, social, and cultural human rights are protected (CSWE, 2015). The following critical thinking questions focus on the intersections between Competencies 2 (diversity), 3 (justice), and 9 (evaluation):

1. Identify at least one social justice issue associated with assessing your professional competence. Describe the issue and discuss why it is a social justice issue impacting your work with vulnerable populations.

2. Discuss two ways you can make your learning contract reflect cultural humility (see Chapter 7 for a definition of cultural humility). Identify one behavioral objective and one meta-objective to include in your field placement learning contract related to the competency on diversity and difference. Discuss the challenges you face in achieving the identified learning objectives.

3. In thinking about your field placement and the clients whom you will serve, describe your knowledge of your clients' diversity and cultural backgrounds. Discuss how you would assess your knowledge and skill level in terms of your cultural competency when working with client population. Describe what you would do to increase your practice effectiveness.

4. In your work with a client in your field placement, identify a social, economic, or environmental justice issue that is connected to your competency in evaluating your practice effectiveness. Describe the issue and discuss how it affects your competency to use qualitative or quantitative methods of evaluation. Discuss strategies you would use to strengthen your social justice competencies.

5. In your work with a client in your field placement, describe your self-reflections and affective reactions that have influenced your professional decision making.

What have you used to assess social, economic, or environmental justice issues impacting your client as well as your own practice effectiveness? If you have difficulty identifying a justice connection, discuss reasons why this may be the case.

COMPETENCY 9: EVALUATE PRACTICE WITH INDIVIDUALS, FAMILIES, GROUPS, ORGANIZATIONS, AND COMMUNITIES

Social workers understand that evaluation is an ongoing component of the dynamic and interactive process of social work practice with, and on behalf of, diverse individuals, families, groups, organizations, and communities. They recognize the importance of evaluating processes and outcomes to advance practice, policy, and service delivery effectiveness. Social workers understand theories of human behavior and the social environment, and critically evaluate and apply this knowledge in evaluating outcomes. They understand qualitative and quantitative methods for evaluating outcomes and practice effectiveness. Social workers:

- Select and use appropriate methods for evaluation of outcomes.

- Apply knowledge of human behavior and the social environment, person-in-environment, and other multidisciplinary theoretical frameworks in the evaluation of outcomes.

- Critically analyze, monitor, and evaluate intervention and program processes and outcomes.

- Apply evaluation findings to improve practice effectiveness at the micro, mezzo, and macro levels.

CASE SUMMARY—"AGAINST MY VALUES"

PRACTICE SETTING DESCRIPTION

Transitions is a group home run by a nonprofit social services agency that contracts with the county's public children and family services agency to provide housing and social work services to female teenagers who are aging out of foster care. A wide range of counseling, life skills, case management, and educational services are offered to prepare the participants for independent living. Transitions serves eight teenagers age 15 to 19 at any one time, and the average stay for those who complete the program is about 2 years. All of the teenagers have been in long-term foster care, and most have lived in a number of foster homes while growing up.

The group home has a BSW-level social worker who serves as the house parent and is in charge of running the house. There are three case aides—one during the day and two during the evening hours. Social workers based at the parent agency are assigned to provide counseling services, and run life skills groups and educational programming for the participants. As a first-year MSW student, I am completing my generalist field placement at Transitions. My primary roles as an intern are to provide case management and mentoring services to three of the teenagers residing in the group home. My field instructor is the social worker assigned to provide counseling services to the Transitions residents.

IDENTIFYING DATA

Mary is a 17-year-old African American female who has been in foster care since the age of 5. She was placed in care because of parental neglect. Her mother was addicted to heroin and would leave Mary and her younger sister unsupervised for hours at time. There was also suspicion of abuse by one of her mother's numerous paramours. During Mary's 12 years in foster care, her mother's parental rights were terminated but Mary was never adopted. She lived in six different foster homes before she was placed in the Transitions group home when she was 15 years old. Mary struggled in school, and had frequent suspensions for behavior issues and truancy. Although she was at grade level for her age, academically she was performing well below her grade level. Mary dropped out of high school when she turned 16 years of age.

Mary has not had contact with her mother since her termination of parental rights when Mary was 8 years old. She had occasional visits with her younger sister but has not had any contact with her for the past 5 years. Mary's relationhips with five of her former foster parents are strained or nonexistent. She maintains phone contact and occasionally visits her first foster mother. Mary has few friends and has trouble getting along with her peers. She is not close to any of the other group home residents.

The Transitions house parent, the case aides, and some of the social workers view Mary as hostile and manipulative. They give her a wide berth and tend to not confront her if she is angry or acts out. They make no real effort to engage with her, develop relationships, or encourage her participation in the life skills or educational groups. The social worker, my field instructor, who is assigned to Mary, meets with her occasionally, but he reports that she is essentially unwilling to engage in a counseling relationship. Mary is one of my three assigned internship clients. My field instructor has asked me to try to develop a relationship with Mary, and help her engage in the services offered by the program. He warned me that this will be a challenge, but he is hopeful that she can be reached.

PRESENTING PROBLEM

Mary has been in the group home for 2 years and is scheduled to transition to independent living in 1 year. She is a high school dropout with poor academic skills. She has shown little to no progress in strengthening her basic life skills and has not made any progress in terms of obtaining the educational resources she needs to improve the skills she would need for most types of minimum wage jobs.

In the group home, Mary is basically allowed to reside there but not to participate in the services offered. She does not have a positive relationship with any of the staff or group home residents. Most of the time, Mary displays indifferent or negative attitudes and responds angrily or is dismissive to any efforts to engage with her. At the most fundamental level, the presenting problem is that Mary is not prepared for independent living and she is not participating in the life skills, educational services, or counseling services that are designed to strengthen her ability to successfully make the transition out of foster care. In addition, Mary's poor interpersonal and relationship skills will hinder her transition to independent living.

ASSESSMENT

It appears that the staff are willing to tolerate Mary's hostile behavior and isolation rather than engage in any type of confrontation with her. I believe that Mary is tolerated and allowed to stay in the group home because there are no other options for her. Her social worker and my field instructor, however, has not given up on Mary: He has hope that she can be reached and engaged in a helping relationship.

Mary had a difficult early childhood with a neglectful parent. In all probability, Mary did not form a secure attachment with her mother. Attachment issues were further compromised by having lived with six different foster parents during her childhood and adolescent years. It appears that Mary formed a trusting relationship with her first foster parent, but that trust was broken when she was removed from the home and placed in a second foster home. With each subsequent move, her willingness or capacity to form secure attachments, in all probability, diminished. It is hard for Mary to trust. She perceives relationships in terms of disappointment and abandonment. This has resulted in her being very guarded in the group home and unwilling to form relationships with the Transitions staff and her peers.

Mary has been in the foster care system since she was 5 years old. During this time, she has had only one positive parental figure—her first foster mother. Other than during that relationship, Mary most likely received very little parental guidance throughout her journey in foster care. She has been provided with shelter, but not the parental guidance and role modeling that would prepare her for adulthood. As she nears her transition out of foster care and into so-called independent living, she is probably feeling very scared and anxious. Her hostile behavior is her defense from her fears. It is scary to imagine being on one's own at the age of 18 without any family or support system. Mary adopts her hostile and indifferent "I don't care about anything" attitude as a way of protecting herself from her internal fears. Mary's trust issues make it hard for her to share her feelings and be vulnerable with the staff or her peers. She instead lashes out to others and turns inward—isolated, alone, and, more likely than not, very anxious about being on her own and making her way in life as an independent young adult.

CASE PROCESS SUMMARY

Prior to my first meeting with Mary, I discussed her background, her behavior in the group home and program, as well as my field instructor's assessment of what might be influencing Mary's behavior and nonparticipation. Cognitively, I felt that I had a pretty good handle on what to expect in my first meeting with Mary. The case aides also advised me to give her plenty of space and not to force a conversation. They agreed that doing so would just cause a hostile and angry reaction from Mary. During my first week of placement, I had observed Mary being very disrespectful to the staff, argumentative with her peers, and not held accountable for her actions. I did not have any direct interactions with Mary. When Mary was assigned to me in week 2, I was tasked with introducing myself and discussing my role and how we will work together. Needless to say, I was a bit nervous and apprehensive about my ability to engage with my assigned client.

My plan was to initiate a casual conversation with Mary in which I would introduce myself, discuss my role, and offer my help in any way possible. I wanted to keep it casual and informal and hopefully set up a time to meet. I approached Mary in the living room where she was listening to music with her headphones. No one else was in the room. Once I got her attention, I asked whether I could talk with her for a few minutes. She replied with an angry "Who the f*** are you?" I introduced myself and said I was a social work intern. Mary replied, "I am in a bad mood and I hate social workers. Get the f*** out of my face and leave me alone."

Emotionally, I was not prepared for the way Mary treated me. I tried to behave professionally and not respond negatively, but inside I was offended, angry, and judgmental. I tried not to show it, but I am pretty confident my nonverbals revealed how I felt and the effect her behavior had on me. I grew up in a religious home where my parents emphasized respecting others and appropriate behavior when interacting with adults. As a parent myself, I, along with my husband, have tried to instill these values in our children. I found Mary's behavior extremely offensive. I also felt that it was wrong that Mary was allowed to behave this way in the group home with no consequences or accountability. I was also very discouraged that the initial meeting had been a complete failure.

I processed the interaction and my self-reflections in supervision with my field instructor. We discussed how my personal values were influencing my feelings about Mary and our working together. We discussed human behavior and the social environment, person-in-environment, and attachment theory to better understand Mary's behavior. We also discussed ways I might manage my personal feelings and how to become more empathic about Mary's challenges and the reasons behind her hostile and defensive behavior. We used qualitative assessment of the interaction to identify ways to improve my practice effectiveness with Mary.

Janet, MSW Intern

DISCUSSION QUESTIONS

- Based on the preceding case summary, describe how you would manage the conflict between Janet's personal values and Mary's behavior. Discuss how you would cognitively, behaviorally, and emotionally manage your feelings of being disrespected and of being personally offended by Mary's behavior.

- Describe a client interaction you have had that is similar to what Janet experienced in her first meeting with Mary. Describe the interaction, your internal processing, and what you did to engage your client and improve your practice effectiveness.

- In the case summary, identify two mezzo-level organizational issues that Janet could possibly address during her field placement. Describe at least one organizational intervention that she could pursue to improve service effectiveness and staff morale. Briefly describe how you would conduct a qualitative evaluation of the effectiveness of your proposed intervention.

- In the case summary, identify two macro-level issues that have impacted Mary's life and her current situation as an unprepared teenager aging out of foster care. Identify three change goals, and describe how Janet might go about developing a macro-level intervention to address the identified goals.

ELECTRONIC COMPETENCY RESOURCES

WEBSITE LINKS

Council on Social Work Education—Educational Policy and Accreditation Standards (EPAS 2015)
www.cswe.org/Accreditation/Standards-and-Policies/2015-EPAS

VIDEO LINKS

Developing Learning Contracts—UBSSW Field Department
www.youtube.com/watch?v=XbHQ8JpyOak

Developing Goals and Objectives—APIAHF
www.youtube.com/watch?v=MAhs-m6cNzY

Evaluating your Social Work Practice—Michael Vimont
www.youtube.com/watch?v=ZYt4SWD_-uM

Critical Thinking—Macat
www.youtube.com/watch?v=HnJ1bqXUnIM

Reflective Practice—Elevate Training and Development
www.youtube.com/watch?v=1W8pqWU35BQ

REFERENCES

Bogo, M. (2016). Evaluation of student learning. In C. A. Hunter, J. K. Moen, & M. S. Raskin (Eds.), *Social work field directors: Foundations for excellence* (rev. ed., pp. 154–178). New York, NY: Oxford University Press.

Bogo, M., Rawlings, M., Katz, E., & Logie, C. (2014). *Using simulation in assessment and teaching*. Alexandria, VA: Council on Social Work Education.

Collins, E., & Daly, E. (2011). *Decision-making and social work in Scotland: The role of evidence and practice wisdom*. Glasgow, Scotland: Institute for Research and Innovation in Social Services. Retrieved from https://www.iriss.org.uk/resources/reports/decision-making-and-social-work-scotland

Council on Social Work Education. (2015). *Educational policy and accreditation standards*. Alexandria, VA: Author.

Heron, G. (2006). Critical thinking in social care and social work: Searching student assignments for the evidence. *Journal of Social Work Education, 25*, 209–224. doi:10.1080/02615470600564965

Kanno, H., & Koeske, G. (2010). MSW students' satisfaction with their field placements: The role of preparedness and supervision quality. *Journal of Social Work Education, 46*, 23–38. doi:10.5175/JSWE.2010.200800066

McKnight, S. E. (2013). Mental health learning needs assessment: Competency-based instrument for best practice. *Issues in Mental Health Nursing, 34*, 459–471. doi:10.3109/01612840.2012.758205

Poulin, J. (2010). *Strengths-based generalist practice: A collaborative approach* (3rd ed.). Belmont, CA: Cengage.

Poulin, J., & Matis, S. (2015). Social work competencies and multidimensional assessment. *Journal of Baccalaureate Social Work, 20*, 117–135. doi:10.18084/1084-7219.20.1.117

Rubaltelli, E., & Slovic, P. (2008). Affective reactions and context-dependent processing of negations. *Judgment and Decision Making, 3*, 607–618. Retrieved from http://journal.sjdm.org/71204/jdm71204.pdf

CHAPTER 3

Using Supervision to Guide Professional Development and Behavior

CASE VIGNETTE

Elaine is a BSW student placed at a community crisis center. The agency provides 24-hour mobile crisis response to the community, a walk-in clinic for individuals experiencing a crisis, and a referral case management support team to link individuals to resources available in their community. Elaine is very excited to be at this placement because she has also been interested in mental health and thinks she is going to learn a lot during her time at this agency. She feels like she is learning so much every single day at her placement.

Every Thursday afternoon, Elaine meets with her field supervisor, Erin, who is an MSW at the agency. Elaine and Erin spend their time in supervision discussing the events of the week thus far. They talk about how many clients Elaine was able to help at the walk-in clinic or how many calls she went out on with the mobile crisis team. Elaine and Erin also talk about how Elaine helped the clients she encountered that week. Erin will often ask Elaine to share her rationale for why she did what she did with the client. Sometimes, Elaine is not sure of the answer, so she tells Erin that she "doesn't know." Erin understands that as a social work student, Elaine is not going to have all of the answers and part of her role as the field supervisor is to assist Elaine in making connections between what she has learned from her social work courses and what she is currently doing in her field placement.

Elaine values her time in supervision because she knows that Erin has been a social worker for many years and has a lot of experience helping clients. Elaine feels that she is learning how to be a better social worker by talking with Erin about how to approach a client situation. Oftentimes, Erin will share how she would address a situation. By discussing her thought process, Elaine finds a new way to think about a situation with her own clients. Through supervision, Elaine is able to enhance her professional identity and confidence in her ability to be a self-regulating, independent social work professional soon.

Why do you think that Elaine appreciates supervision so much?
How might Elaine's perspective on her field experience change if Erin did not make time for Elaine to process her experiences?
How do you think the role of your field supervisor influences your field placement experience?

© Springer Publishing Company DOI: 10.1891/9780826175533.0003

LEARNING OBJECTIVES

In this chapter, we explore the importance of social work supervision. Supervision is an activity that occurs in a variety of professions, but within social work, especially in field, supervision is a dynamic process. Participating in routine social work supervision is related to Competency 1: Demonstrate Ethical and Professional Behavior. The Council on Social Work Education (CSWE, 2015) asserts that social workers "use supervision and consultation to guide professional judgment and behavior" (p. 2). Social work supervision partners you as the learning social worker with an experienced social work professional to assist you in applying your social work knowledge and skills in the field setting. It also serves as a tool to improve professional problem solving while developing your professional self. By the end of this chapter, you will be able to:

- Describe ethical standards social workers must abide by related to research and evaluation.
- Describe the supportive dimensions of social work supervision.
- Describe the administrative dimensions of social work supervision.
- Describe the educational dimensions of social work supervision.
- Identify and describe your preferred learning style.
- Identify ways that you can increase trust in the supervision relationship.
- Evaluate your current supervisory relationship.
- Distinguish between mentoring supervision and employment supervision.

SOCIAL WORK SUPERVISION

We have discussed how field is the signature pedagogy of the social work profession. At the heart of field is supervision. Social work supervision can be traced back to the early days of the profession in the early 20th century, when it was used with early charity workers in New York (Kadushin & Harkness, 2014). Supervision within social work has long been a means to pass along practice wisdom from the trained professional social worker to the learner. It is through social work supervision that you, the student, can practice and improve your social work skills in a real-world setting. Social work supervision is a collaborative process in which both you and your supervisor work together to enhance your practice skills and develop your professional self (National Association of Social Workers [NASW] & Association of Social Work Boards [ASWB], 2013). Through social work supervision, your professional social work identity can mature (Field, Jasper, & Littler, 2016). Social work supervision serves to ensure that you are developing the appropriate skills necessary to be an ethical and competent social work practice professional (Caras, 2013). Through your field placement, you will have the opportunity to critically engage in practice settings to enhance your social work skills; your social work supervision is a central component to this critical engagement (Zuchowski, 2016).

To supervise is to direct, watch over, or keep an eye on the work of another. Thus, in supervision, the supervisor oversees and monitors the actions of the supervisee. Social work supervision goes beyond this basic definition, however, to include a dynamic engagement between the supervisor and the supervisee. Good-quality supervision provides a foundation for the developing social worker. As a field student, we encourage you to make the most of your weekly supervisions to lay a strong foundation for your future as a professional social worker.

Developing a supervision agreement can be helpful during your field placement (Field et al., 2016). A supervision agreement serves to ensure that both parties are clear on what to expect from each other throughout the supervision relationship. Caras and Sandu (2014) suggest that "supervision requires a learning alliance, which empowers the person to acquire relevant skills and knowledge for his profession. This alliance aims to develop interpersonal skills in supervision relationship" (p. 76). Social work supervision is multidimensional and can have multiple functions or purposes, so it is important that both partners are clear on what they expect from supervision. Often, field supervisors have had students earlier and are familiar with the social work supervision requirements in field. If they are new to supervising social work students, your field faculty liaison can assist them in better understanding the role of supervision in field education.

It is very important that you are participating in regular supervision every week with your field supervisor. If, for whatever reason, you are not participating in supervision at your field placement, you should let your faculty liaison know right away.

Social work supervision in field can serve many purposes:

- Assessing your growth related to the nine social work competencies established by the CSWE

- Developing your professional self and increasing your sense of professional autonomy

- Encouraging personal development by helping you explore how your personal values and beliefs align and merge with those of the profession

- Promoting professional values within all elements of practice

- Enabling you to reflect upon ethical and legal considerations related to social work practice

Social work supervision can be thought of in terms of three primary domains: support, administration, and education (Figure 3.1; Kadushin &

Field Reflection Questions
Consider your field supervision sessions. To what extent do you cover each of the three domains of supervision?

Is there a domain that could be increased during your weekly supervision?

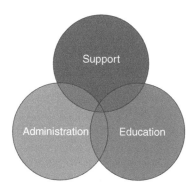

FIGURE 3.1 **Three domains of field education.**

EXHIBIT
3.1

Domains of Supervision

Support	Administration	Education
• Address stress and other hazards of helping (burnout, vicarious trauma, and compassion fatigue)	• Agency policies and procedures • Job tasks • Job functioning	• Incorporation of theory, models, and frameworks • Professional development and training

Harkness, 2014; NASW & ASWB, 2013). Exhibit 3.1 provides an overview of each domain of social work supervision. The three dimensions of support, administration, and education are all necessary during your social work supervision during your field placement.

Social work supervision serves as a means to provide support to you, the learning social worker. As a social work student, receiving support in supervision is vital for your success in the field experience. In fact, support is very important within the entire profession of social work. At times, practicing social work can be quite demanding and stressful. It is important to learn ways to diminish and manage stress whenever possible. Through supportive supervision, you, as the developing social worker, can address situations, experiences, or processes that are difficult for you. Together with the support of your field supervisor, you can brainstorm and problem-solve potential solutions to ameliorate such conditions. There may be simple changes that you are able to make that your supervisor can help you see. In the event that it is something beyond your control, your field supervisor may be able to provide suggestions on ways to cope with or better manage the stressor.

Social work supervision also covers administrative processes. Through supervision, you can review agency policies and procedures. You can review macro-level policies that relate to your practice as well. Likewise, reviewing professional ethical values and standards is part of administrative supervision. Administrative supervision is often a central component of employment supervision, which we discuss later in this chapter. Within administrative supervision, work tasks and assignments are often explored to ensure that the agency's mission, goals, and objectives are being met and clients are being served appropriately, both effectively and efficiently.

Finally, social work supervision can serve as an educational process. Educational supervision seeks to increase your knowledge, skills, and training and help push you toward mastery of the social work competencies. Educational supervision is a pivot aspect of field supervision, as you are a student, and still learning how to be a professional social worker. As a developing social worker in field, you are able to take all of the theoretical concepts that you learned in your social work courses and implement them while engaging in the helping process. It is necessary to understand not only *what* to do in a situation with a client, but also *why* you are doing it. The *why* is often connected to theories, perspectives, models, or evidence-based practices that have been found to be well suited for the situation you are experiencing as a social worker. Good social work practice is grounded in research and derived from the wealth of practice knowledge available to us.

LEARNING STYLES AND LEARNING STYLE ASSESSMENT

As social workers, we appreciate that every person is a unique individual and, as a result, we respect differences. Differences can present in a variety of ways. For example, students learn in a variety of ways. Maybe you have noticed that you do better in a class when the instructor shows videos, or maybe you need to read something for it to sink in, or maybe you need to actually try it out on your own to really understand what is being taught. Those differences refer to individual learning styles. Exhibit 3.2 outlines some common learning styles.

Field Reflection Questions

How do you learn best? Which type of learning style represents your preferred style?

How can your learning style help you in field? Are there any struggles or barriers that you will need to address related to your preferred learning style and the setup of your field placement?

It is important to understand which learning style (or styles) seems to fit you most. Understanding how you learn best requires some self-reflection. Note that your preferred learning style may vary depending on the content that you are learning. For example, in a subject that you really enjoy, you may have a good fit within one learning style; in contrast, in a subject that is more difficult or challenging for you, a different learning style may be more beneficial. Knowing how you learn best can help you during your field placement. You should communicate with your field instructor what your preferred learning style is so that you can discuss ways to help you get the most out of your field placement. Also, because there may be times you will need to take in information in a nonpreferred way, your field instructor can help you to problem-solve ideas to get the most out of those

EXHIBIT 3.2

Learning Styles

Learning Style	Definition	Preferences
Visual	These learners prefer to use images to help them with organization information	Charts, graphs, maps, logic models, visual organizers, pictures, videos
Auditory	These learners prefer to receive new information by listening and speaking	Verbal commands, presentation lectures, discussions
Kinesthetic	These learners prefer to use hands-on learning activities to understand information	Tactile experiences, hands-on learning, learning by doing and then reflecting
Solitary	These learners prefer taking in new information on their own at first	Self-study
Social	These learners prefer working interactively to gain new information	Group projects

experiences as well. Remember that your field placement is part of your social work *education*. You are still a student. You are still learning. Embrace that reality during your field placement, and recognize that you are going to not have all of the answers and will be learning every day how to become a better, more competent social worker. While you are still learning, it is important to make the most of your time as a student and learn as much as you can during this process.

TYPES OF SUPERVISION

The various models of supervision can range from a collaborative engagement to a more authoritarian process. Different styles of supervision provide different opportunities. Collaborative supervision encourages both the supervisor and the supervisee to engage in a dyadic process together, cocreating the supervision relations on an ongoing basis. In this type of supervision, the supervisee is often asked to prepare materials to share and discuss in the supervision session. In contrast, in the authoritarian supervision process, the supervision is more hierarchical. Going beyond styles of supervision, there are other distinctions regarding types of supervision that we discuss in the following text.

MENTORING SUPERVISION

The supervision we have been discussing thus far in this chapter relates to mentoring supervision. Mentoring supervision is supervision using a process to enhance the skills of the supervisee. This type of supervision is required weekly during your field education. Mentoring supervision is also the type of supervision required if you plan to pursue professional clinical licensure later in your career.

EMPLOYMENT SUPERVISION

Employment supervision, though similar, differs from mentoring supervision. It varies from organization to organization. The primary purpose of this type of supervision is to review agency-specific policies, procedures, and other organizational matters. There is often an element of case consultation or sharing of issues, concerns, or progress for clients among team members. Often, this type of supervision lacks an emphasis on professional growth and enhancement.

As a profession, social work values ongoing supervision. Throughout your future career, you can seek out supervision from a licensed social work professional to assist you in deepening your professional skillset. The NASW maintains an active list of members who provide supervision services to social workers on its website.

GROUP SUPERVISION

Most often, social work supervision is provided in an individual context, with just the supervisor and the supervisee being present. Sometimes, however, supervision occurs in a group format. The goals of supervision remain the same whether supervision is provided on a one-on-one basis or in a group. The distinction comes from the number of supervisees participating. Benefits of group supervision include having multiple learners who can share experiences and provide support to one another. A potential drawback of group supervision is that a learner may feel reluctant to be completely open and share some experiences in a group setting. If you are involved in group supervision, it is important that you feel comfortable with your group so that you can get the most benefits from your time in supervision. Often times, supervisors who facilitate group supervision will create ground rules for group supervision that help everyone feel safer when sharing experiences, thoughts, and feelings in this setting. Sometimes, these ground rules include such things as respecting one another, treating what is said in supervision as confidential, promoting open communication with the use of "I-statements," and emphasizing the principle that there are no stupid questions.

> **Field Reflection Questions**
>
> Compare and contrast group and individual supervision. What do you think would be the benefits of each for you at your current field placement?
>
> What, if any, would be the drawbacks to each for you?

STUDENT/SUPERVISOR MATCH

Your relationship with your field supervisor is a very important aspect of your time in field. It is with your field supervisor that you will meet weekly to conduct your social work supervision. The quality of the relationship between you and your field instructor is based on many factors. One factor is how well you and your supervisor are matched. As with any type of relationship, certain qualities and characteristics can enhance a relationship. Regarding your professional supervisory relationship, there can be similarities that bring you and your field instructor closer. Sometimes there may be no obvious similarities other than the fact that both of you love social work, but that is often enough to make a terrific match. A great deal of research has demonstrated that the quality of the relationship between the field student and the field supervisor is associated with student learning and satisfaction from the field placement (Cleak, Roulston, & Vreugdenhil, 2016; Cleak & Smith, 2012; Tangen & Borders, 2016).

As social workers, we appreciate that relationships are very significant. The NASW's *Code of Ethics* (2017) states that we "understand that relationships between and among people are an important vehicle for change" (p. 6). The relationship with your field supervisor is no different. Having a secure, stable relationship with your field supervisor is critically important and related to your overall success in field (Bennet, Mohr, Deal, & Hwang, 2012; Bogo, 2015). As with any relationship, there are ways that you can strengthen your relationship with your field supervisor. Qualities at the heart of the social work supervision relationship are trust, sharing, and vulnerability.

Although we certainly encourage you to have a strong, open relationship with your field supervisor, it is also important to maintain a professional attitude. Your relationship with your field supervisor should remain strictly professional throughout your field experience. Just as we as social workers should avoid dual relationships with clients, while completing your field experience, you should avoid dual relationships with your field instructor. The NASW's *Code of Ethics* sets forth ethical standards regarding supervision and consultation that outline the nature of the professional supervisory relationship (see Exhibit 3.3).

NASW's *Code of Ethics* Standard for Supervision and Consultation

3.01 SUPERVISION AND CONSULTATION

(a) Social workers who provide supervision or consultation (whether in-person or remotely) should have the necessary knowledge and skill to supervise or consult appropriately and should do so only within their areas of knowledge and competence.

(b) Social workers who provide supervision or consultation are responsible for setting clear, appropriate, and culturally sensitive boundaries.

(c) Social workers should not engage in any dual or multiple relationships with supervisees in which there is a risk of exploitation of or potential harm to the supervisee, including dual relationships that may arise while using social networking sites or other electronic media.

(d) Social workers who provide supervision should evaluate supervisees' performance in a manner that is fair and respectful. (NASW, 2017, p. 21)

■ TRUST, SHARING, AND VULNERABILITY

For social work supervision to be most beneficial, it is important that there is trust between the supervisor and the supervisee. Trust involves many factors, but is tied especially closely to the social work value of integrity. Related to the value of integrity, we can increase trust by being honest and truthful. We can follow through with what we say we are going to do and be dependable and reliable.

Field Reflection Questions

What is the level of trust in your supervision relationship?

How can you increase the level of trust?

Open, honest sharing is important in social work supervision. It is important to use your time in supervision not as a time to try to impress your supervisor by saying what you think the "right thing" is, but rather as a time to sort through your thoughts and feelings in an effort to become a competent social work professional. At times, you may need to explore your own personal thoughts, feelings, and beliefs in supervision regarding how they are impacting your practice as a social worker. You may also need to discuss situations or experiences with clients or systems that you work with during your placement that are personal triggers for you. Although social work supervision often involves discussing personal issues, it is not to be confused with personal therapy. Unguru and Sandu (2017) make the following distinction between counseling and supervision:

> While counseling involves the direct relationship between the social worker and the beneficiary, with the reflection on the problem being the responsibility of the beneficiary guided by the counselor, within the supervision the social worker is the one who reflects upon his own practice, with the beneficiaries, identifying the

best professional solutions he approached/is about to approach in working with his customers. (p. 18)

Social work supervision requires self-reflection not only on elements of social work practice, but also on the practitioner's thoughts, feelings, and behaviors. Effective social work professionals must engage in continuous self-reflection. We must be mindful of how our thoughts, feelings, and behaviors influence our practice. We discuss self-reflection in more depth in Chapter 4.

> **Field Reflection Question**
> How can you distinguish between supervision and personal therapy?

Brown (2017) has suggested the mnemonic "BRAVING" as a means to better understand trust. In this acronym, the "B" stands for maintaining boundaries. As social workers, we know that boundaries are very important. We talk about having healthy boundaries with our clients quite often. Regarding social work supervision, it is also important to have boundaries. One way to have clear boundaries in your field supervision is to maintain a professional relationship and be clear on each other's roles and responsibilities during the field process. The "R" in the mnemonic stands for reliability. As you may recall from a research course you have taken, being reliable refers to consistency; thus, we can develop trust by being consistent. As we have discussed, one way we can do this is to demonstrate the social work value of integrity: We can do what we say we are going to do. By following through on our words with actions, we demonstrate integrity, and show that we are reliable. The "A" in the mnemonic stands for accountability. Being accountable requires that you are responsible for what you have done (or maybe did not do). The "V" represents the concept of a vault. By definition, a vault is a storage compartment. In Brown's analogy, the vault refers to holding information as secret or in confidence. To have a relationship of trust, we should not share things that are meant to be kept confidential. The "I" represents integrity. As social workers, through the NASW's (2017) *Code of Ethics*, we understand integrity to mean being "continually aware of the profession's mission, values, ethical principles, and ethical standards and practice in a manner consistent with them" while being honest and responsible (p. 6). The "N" stands for nonjudgment. Trust requires that we integrate a nonjudgmental stance and attitude into our professional persona. Finally, the "G" stands for generosity. Brown suggests that generosity means we give the benefit of the doubt to the person we are in relationship with. By being generous, we assume goodwill toward the person and try not to take offense or become defensive.

> **Field Reflection Questions**
> Using the BRAVING mnemonic for the elements of trust, in which areas is your supervision strong?
>
> In which areas can your supervision relationship be improved? Provide examples.

Once you have a foundation of trust in your supervisory relationship, you can proceed with sharing and vulnerability. Sharing is a necessary aspect of supervision. Sometimes, it can be difficult to determine what to share. Sometimes, we may not want to share certain things because they make us feel vulnerable. Vulnerability refers to a state of being open or exposed to possible attack. It can be scary. Despite that, vulnerability is necessary for many things in life, including true connection and feeling emotions such as joy. Brown (2012) defines vulnerability as "uncertainty, risk, and emotional exposure" (p. 34). Vulnerability is connected to having the courage to speak our truth (Brown, 2012). As a field student, you may at times feel vulnerable

> **Field Reflection Questions**
>
> Has there been a time in your field placement thus far when you had to share something that made you feel vulnerable?
>
> What was that experience like for you? What did you learn from that experience?

during your field placement. For example, if you are presented with a task to complete at the agency and you do not know how to do it, you may feel vulnerable about saying you do not know and asking for help. We encourage you to remember that during your field placement (and throughout your social work career), it is okay to be vulnerable. It is okay not to have all of the answers. It is okay to ask for help. In fact, the NASW's *Code of Ethics* lists competence as one of our values—it is our duty to ask for help when it is needed to ensure we are meeting the expectation of competence in our work.

SUPERVISORY RELATIONSHIP INVENTORY

There are many measures available that you can use to assess your supervisory relationship with your field supervisor (Tangen & Borders, 2016). We have provided an inventory that you can take to rate your current supervisory relationship with your field supervisor (see Exhibit 3.4).

If you score 20 or higher in all three categories in Exhibit 3.4, then it is safe to assume that field supervision is working well. If you score less than 20 in any category, you should evaluate the scores and decide whether the low score is problematic. For example, getting a low score on the administrative component might not indicate a problem given the amount of time in the placement. Maybe you do not need a lot of supervision

> **Field Reflection Questions**
>
> After completing the Supervisory Relationship Inventory, what did you learn about your current supervisory relationship?
>
> Where can your relationship be improved? How can you facilitate these improvements?

related to agency policies and procedures. If your assessment identifies areas that you would like to strengthen, we strongly recommend you share the results with your field instructor so you can discuss ways to address the concern. The purpose of the inventory is to increase your awareness of the three components of field supervision and, if needed, begin a conversation with your field instructor on ways to strengthen any area that is not being addressed to meet your learning needs.

PROBLEM SOLVING

Social work supervision can be an amazing opportunity to engage in problem solving with your field supervisor. Furthermore, through good supervision, you can increase your social work problem-solving skills. In fact, the International Federation of Social Workers (IFSW) has defined social work as a profession that seeks social change, problem solving, and empowerment (IFSW, 2012).

In supervision, it is important to share situations with your supervisor before they become full-blown problems whenever possible. By addressing a situation before it becomes a problem, you can brainstorm potential solutions. Open communication before difficult

EXHIBIT
3.4

Supervisory Relationship Inventory

The following questions are about what you and your supervisor do in your sessions together. Answer each question by circling the response that best describes your interactions with your field instructor using the following rating scale.

1 Not at all	2 A little	3 Some	4 A lot	5 A great deal

Administration: To what extent:

A1. Have you and your supervisor discussed his or her expectations for your field placement?

1	2	3	4	5

A2. Do your supervisory sessions focus on documentation and required paperwork?

1	2	3	4	5

A3. Do your supervisory sessions focus on administrative issues and agency policies?

1	2	3	4	5

A4. Do your supervisory sessions focus on tasks you need to accomplish?

1	2	3	4	5

A5. Have you and your supervisor discussed how your progress is going to be assessed?

1	2	3	4	5

Education: To what extent:

E1. Have you and your supervisor reviewed your progress on the learning goal(s) identified in your learning contract?

1	2	3	4	5

E2. Do your supervisory sessions focus on clinical/case issues?

1	2	3	4	5

E3. Have you and your supervisor discussed your work and progress on the nine social work competencies?

1	2	3	4	5

E4. Does your supervisor help you reflect upon your feelings, reactions, and use of self in working with your clients?

1	2	3	4	5

(continued)

Supervisory Relationship Inventory (*continued*)

E5. Does your supervisor help you think more clearly about your clients/cases?

1	2	3	4	5

Support: To what extent:

S1. Do you feel your supervisor cares about you?

1	2	3	4	5

S2. Does talking with your supervisor have a calming, soothing effect on you?

1	2	3	4	5

S3. Do you feel that your supervisor provides you with emotional support?

1	2	3	4	5

S4. Does talking with your supervisor give you confidence in your abilities?

1	2	3	4	5

S5. Are you willing to take risks and talk about your mistakes and struggles with your supervisor?

1	2	3	4	5

Scoring	Score
Administration: sum of items A1–A5	
Education: sum of items E1–E5	
Support: sum of items S1–S5	
Total: sum of A, E, and S items	

situations arise is the most preferable way to problem-solve (Edmondson, 2014). Oftentimes, your field supervisor can share his or her practice wisdom and previous experiences with you to indicate what he or she has learned on the job. By engaging in supervision and discussing such issues with your supervisor, you can benefit from his or her experiences and insights.

We understand though, that on occasion, things may happen and, as a result, you will be facing a problem. In the event that you find yourself in a predicament during your field placement, it is important that you reach out to your field supervisor as soon as possible to problem-solve together. Even if the problem arose from something that you did (or failed to do), trust us: It is best to address the situation with integrity and directly address it with your field supervisor quickly.

In addition to problems that arise with clients, during your social work supervision, you and your field supervisor can problem solve to identify and address other possible problems that may arise while you are a field student. Being a field student is a time of excitement and anticipation; you are one step closer to becoming a professional social worker. However, we fully understand that students today face many challenges and are often balancing a variety of commitments, trying to make it through the semester. It is common for field students to often be juggling or attempting to balance multiple demands between field, coursework, family, employment, and so forth (Hemy, Boddy, Chee, & Sauvage, 2016). Remember, your social work supervision can provide support as you face these challenges. Coupling support and problem solving, together with input from your supervisor, you may be able to find ways to better balance the demands you are facing and incorporate ways to take care of yourself while undergoing this process.

SUMMARY

Social work supervision is a cornerstone in the field education experience. It focuses on multiple domains—support, administration, and education. Through these three dimensions of supervision, a supervisor can pass along practice wisdom and skills to the learner social worker. To get the most out of field supervision, it is important that the relationship between the supervisor and the supervisee is one imbued with trust, where both parties are able to freely share with each other. It is necessary to be vulnerable at times in supervision, especially as a developing social worker. In supervision, it is appropriate to identify personal limitations and to process these in this setting. Problem solving can occur in supervision, and supervision can also facilitate the development of better problem-solving skills in the supervisee.

CRITICAL THINKING QUESTIONS

In this chapter, we discussed Competency 1: Demonstrate Ethical and Professional Behavior in terms of the use of social work supervision to develop your professional social work self. The following discussion questions focus on how social work supervision relates to Competency 1:

1. Describe the supervision you participate in at your field placement. How does your supervision help your growth as a social worker?

2. How would you rate your supervisory relationship with your field supervisor? How does your relationship with your field supervisor influence your field placement experience?

3. In what ways can you improve your professional supervisory relationship by using trust, sharing, and vulnerability?

4. How do you balance appropriate self-disclosure and being open during your social work field supervisions?

5. How can you use what you now know about your preferred learning style to assist you in getting the most out of your field supervision? What is one way that you can incorporate your preferred learning style into each dimension of supervision?

6. If you were having problems with your supervisory relationship during your field placement, what would you do? How would you try to address the situation? With whom would you talk about this issue?

COMPETENCY 1: DEMONSTRATE ETHICAL AND PROFESSIONAL BEHAVIOR

Social workers understand the value base of the profession and its ethical standards, as well as relevant laws and regulations that may impact practice at the micro, mezzo, and macro levels. They understand frameworks of ethical decision making and how to apply principles of critical thinking to those frameworks in the practice, research, and policy arenas. Social workers recognize personal values and the distinction between personal and professional values. They also understand how their personal experiences and affective reactions influence their professional judgment and behavior. Social workers understand the profession's history, its mission, and the roles and responsibilities of the profession. They also understand the role of other professions when engaged in interprofessional teams. Social workers recognize the importance of lifelong learning and are committed to continually updating their skills to ensure they are relevant and effective. They also understand emerging forms of technology and the ethical use of technology in social work practice. Social workers:

- Make ethical decisions by applying the standards of the NASW's *Code of Ethics*, relevant laws and regulations, models for ethical decision making, models of ethical conduct of research, and additional codes of ethics as appropriate to context.

- Use refection and self-regulation to manage personal values and maintain professionalism in practice situations.

- Demonstrate professional demeanor in behavior; appearance; and oral, written, and electronic communications.

- Use technology ethically and appropriately to facilitate practice outcomes.

- Use supervision and consultation to guide professional judgment and behavior.

CASE SUMMARY—"IT IS OKAY TO NOT KNOW"

PRACTICE SETTING DESCRIPTION

Hope is a BSW student who is completing her field placement at Redstone Hospital. Redstone Hospital is a 300-bed community hospital in a rural area of Ohio. This hospital is the only hospital in a three-county radius. The hospital has a social work staff of five full-time and three part-time social workers. Hope's field supervisor, Christa, is a full-time social worker with over a decade of experience working at Redstone Hospital. Christa's primary responsibility is covering the emergency department.

IDENTIFYING DATA

While covering the emergency department, the social worker must be prepared to deal with a variety of situations. The medical staff will often call upon the social worker for a consult if there is a suspicion of abuse or neglect. The social worker will also be called if there is a concern that the patient is experiencing a mental health crisis or has a substance abuse problem. Sometimes, the social worker is called to a patient's room to assist with locating resources for the patient or arranging transportation for the patient to return home if he or she is not being admitted to the hospital. As you can see, the social workers who cover the emergency department could be called in for a consult on a variety of issues at any time. When Hope's placement first started, she and Christa went on all consults together. As Hope and Christa became more comfortable, Hope would start going on consults on her own and then report back to Christa regarding the patient.

PRESENTING PROBLEM

One evening Hope was working with Christa covering the emergency department. The night had been a very busy one so far. It seemed as if the social workers were being requested for everyone in the emergency department. While Christa was in the social work office looking to find a bed in a rehab facility for a patient who came in high and was willing to get treatment, a request for another consult came in from the medical staff, requesting a social worker right away for a patient who needed transportation home. Christa asked Hope whether she wanted to work on finding a bed at a rehab or whether she felt comfortable going to see the resource consult. Hope had never had to find and secure a bed at a rehab facility before. She thought it would be easier to go and talk to the patient who needed transportation because she had done that before.

When Hope arrived at the patient's room for the consult, she was startled by the patient, who was standing on her bed. The patient was talking so fast that it was hard for Hope to understand what she was saying. The patient kept talking with an urgency that alarmed Hope. When she had said she would take this consult, she thought that she was going to find out where the patient lived and get some bus tickets to take care of the problem. Hope was not sure what was going on with this patient, but she knew that she needed more than just bus tickets. Hope hesitated for a moment because she did not know what she was going to do. She thought for a second and then paged Christa to come and meet her in the patient's room.

Christa arrived right away. As soon as Christa got to the room, Hope apologized for not knowing what to do and calling her to come down. Christa patted Hope on the shoulder and said, "You knew exactly what to do. You knew your limits and you asked for help when you needed it. I am proud of you."

ASSESSMENT

The next day, during their regular group supervision, Christa brought up the incident from the night before. At first, Hope thought that maybe Christa changed her mind and was upset with her for not knowing what to do. Christa asked Hope to talk about how she came to the decision to call for her to come and help out on that case. Hope thought for a second and then realized that, even though she felt like she should have known what to do and did not want to admit she did not know what to do to help this patient, Christa had never made Hope feel bad for asking for help or not knowing what to do. Hope explained that she felt safe asking Christa for help because she knew that Christa would be supportive and nonjudgmental.

CASE PROCESS SUMMARY

After supervision, Hope thought about the past 2 days and how much she had been learning at Redstone Hospital with Christa. She realized that she was learning so much because she was asking for help when she was not sure what to do. Christa would always help her in the moment and then spend time talking about the situation during their next supervision session. Hope knew that it was safe to share and be vulnerable with Christa because she had a strong foundation of trust with Christa. Hope felt lucky to have Christa as her field supervisor because she knew she was learning a lot.

DISCUSSION QUESTIONS

- Hope felt comfortable asking Christa for help because they had a strong supervisory relationship. How do you think this scenario would have been different if Hope felt her supervisory relationship with Christa was poor?
- Sometimes, it can be difficult to ask for help. Has there been a time in your field placement when, like Hope, you were in over your head and were not sure what to do? How did you respond?
- The day after Hope asked Christa for help, they discussed the situation again in supervision. Why do you think it is important to process specific client situations in supervision? Is there a benefit to talking about such situations soon after they happen? If so, what are those benefits?

ELECTRONIC COMPETENCY RESOURCES

WEBSITE LINKS

Guidelines for social work practice supervision and consultation by NASW-Colorado
www.naswco.org/page/43/Guidelines-for-Social-Work-Practice-Supervision
-and-Consultation

Social Work podcast titled "Supervision for Social Workers" (2008)
socialworkpodcast.blogspot.com/2008/01/supervision-for-social-workers.html

Article: "Supervisor, Beware: Ethical Dangers in Supervision" by Claudia J. Dewane (2007)
www.socialworktoday.com/archive/julyaug2007p34.shtml

Article: "Ethics Alive! Ethical Concerns in Social Work Field Supervision" by Allan Barsky (2013)
www.socialworker.com/feature-articles/ethics-articles/ethics-alive-ethics-in
-social-work-field-supervision

Article: "Your First Supervisor—Finding Your Alice" by Nancy White-Gibson (2015)
www.socialworker.com/feature-articles/practice/your-first-supervisor-finding
-your-alice

VIDEO LINKS

NASW presentation on supervision (2011)
www.youtube.com/watch?v=HQmRpV0xXgc

Brené Brown, social work researcher, discusses "The Power of Vulnerability"
www.ted.com/talks/brene_brown_on_vulnerability

Tips on preparing for clinical supervision
www.youtube.com/watch?v=UJa2CDiQYT8

Ted Talk on how good leaders make you feel safe (discusses the importance of trust)
www.ted.com/talks/simon_sinek_why_good_leaders_make_you_feel_safe?
share=18bcab0a22

REFERENCES

Bennet, S., Mohr, J., Deal, K. H., & Hwang, J. (2012). Supervisor attachment, supervisory working alliance, and affect in social work field instruction. *Research on Social Work Practice, 23*(2), 199–209. doi:10.1177/1049731512468492

Bogo, M. (2015). Field education for clinical social work practice: Best practices and contemporary challenges. *Clinical Social Work Journal, 43*(3), 317–324. doi:10.1007/s10615-015-0526-5

Brown, B. (2012). *Daring greatly.* New York, NY: Gotham Books.

Brown, B. (2017). *Braving the wilderness: The quest for true belonging and the courage to stand alone.* New York, NY: Random House.

Caras, A. (2013). Ethics and supervision process: Fundaments of social work practice. *Procedia—Social and Behavioral Sciences, 92*(10), 133–141. doi:10.1016/j.sbspro.2013.08.649

Caras, A., & Sandu, A. (2014). The role of supervision in professional development of social work specialists. *Journal of Social Work Practice, 28*(1), 75–94. doi:10.1080/02650533.2012.763024

Cleak, H., Roulston, A., & Vreugdenhil, A. (2016). The inside story: A survey of social work students' supervision and learning opportunities on placement. *British Journal of Social Work, 46*(7), 2033–2050. doi:10.1093/bjsw/bcv117

Cleak, H., & Smith, D. (2012). Student satisfaction with models of field placement supervision. *Australian Social Work, 65*(2), 243–258. doi:10.1080/0312407X.2011.572981

Council on Social Work Education. (2015). Educational policy and accreditation standards for baccalaureate and master's social work programs. Retrieved from https://www.cswe.org/getattachment/Accreditation/Accreditation-Process/2015-EPAS/2015EPAS_Web_FINAL.pdf.aspx

Edmondson, D. (2014). *Social work practice learning.* London, UK: Sage.

Field, P., Jasper, C., & Littler, L. (2016). *Practice education in social work: Achieving professional standards* (2nd ed.). St. Albans, UK: Critical Publishing.

Hemy, M., Boddy, J., Chee, P., & Sauvage, D. (2016). Social work students "juggling" field placement. *Social Work Education, 35*(2), 215–228. doi:10.1080/02615479.2015.1125878

International Federation of Social Workers. (2012). Statement of ethical principles. Retrieved from ifsw.org/policies/statement-of-ethical-principles

Kadushin, A., & Harkness, D. (2014). *Supervision in social work.* New York, NY: Columbia University Press.

National Association of Social Workers. (2017). *Code of ethics.* Silver Spring, MD: Author. Retrieved from https://www.socialworkers.org/About/Ethics/Code-of-Ethics/Code-of-Ethics-English

National Association of Social Workers & Association of Social Work Boards. (2013). Best practice standards in social work supervision https://www.socialworkers.org/LinkClick.aspx?fileticket=GBrLbl4BuwI%3D&portalid=0

Tangen, J. L., & Borders, D. (2016). The supervisory relationship: A conceptual and psychometric review of measures. *Counselor Education and Supervision, 55*(3), 159–181. doi:10.1002/ceas.12043

Unguru, E., & Sandu, A. (2017). Supervision: From administrative control to continuous education and training of specialists in social work. *Romanian Journal for Multidimensional Education, 9*(1), 17–35. doi:10.18662/rrem/2017.0901.02

Zuchowski, I. (2016). Getting to know the context: The complexities of providing off-site supervision in social work practice learning. *British Journal of Social Work, 46*(2), 409–426. doi:10.1093/bjsw/bcu133

CHAPTER 4

Using Reflection and Self-Regulation to Promote Well-Being Through Self-Care

CASE VIGNETTE

Mary has been at her social work placement field site, a local crime victims center, for about a month. She was initially really excited about her placement because in addition to social work, she was always intrigued by the criminal justice system. Mary thought that working at the crime victims center would be a great way to merge her two interests. She would be supporting clients who have been victims of crimes.

Mary has a small, but growing, caseload and sits in on the rape survivor support group that meets twice a week. During the support group, the survivors process their experiences and share sometimes graphic details of what they have experienced.

Mary is starting to get headaches more often than ever before and she feels very tired. Her sister recently told her that she seems so "on edge" lately. Mary chalks all of this up to being a busy student who has a lot on her plate. She has needed to ask for time off from her part-time job and field placement because she has been so exhausted and not feeling like herself.

Mary has been staying in a lot more than usual. She used to be quite social and enjoy going out on the weekends with her friends. One night, after some coaxing from her friends, Mary went out with a couple of her girlfriends. While out, someone came over and started talking to one of her friends; Mary yelled at this person and told the person to get away right now. Her friends do not understand what is wrong with Mary and why she overreacted in such a way. Mary is not sure why she responded that way, either.

What do you think is going on with Mary?

How do you think her field placement is influencing these changes in her?

What should Mary do?

© Springer Publishing Company DOI: 10.1891/9780826175533.0004

LEARNING OBJECTIVES

In this chapter, we explore using reflection and self-regulation to promote well-being through self-care, which is closely related to Competency 1: Demonstrate Ethical and Professional Behavior. This competency puts forth that social workers should "understand how their personal experiences and affective reactions influence their professional judgment and behavior" by using "refection and self-regulation to manage personal values and maintain professionalism in practice situations" (CSWE, 2015, pp. 1–2). By the end of this chapter, you will be able to:

- Describe reflection, self-regulation, and self-awareness as it relates to being a professional social worker.
- Describe various potential hazards (vicarious trauma, burnout, and compassion fatigue) as they relate to social work practice.
- Describe self-care.
- Identify self-care strategies that you can implement.
- Identify personal supports.
- Develop a personal self-care plan.

PROMOTING PERSONAL WELL-BEING

As social workers, we often encourage our clients to advocate for themselves. We encourage our clients to be empowered to speak up regarding what they need. We suggest to our clients that they take care of themselves so that they will be able to take care of other responsibilities in their lives—family, work, and so forth. On the basis of this, we, as a profession, understand the importance of self-care for our clients. However, at times, we lose sight of the importance of self-care for ourselves. In this chapter, we explore the concept of self-care and how it is necessary to promote well-being and to avoid such things as burnout, vicarious trauma, and compassion fatigue.

The importance of self-care for social work professionals cannot be understated. It is as vital as ongoing training. To truly be competent professionals, we need to engage in regular self-care. To be effective in helping others, social workers must be able to help themselves first. There is the old adage that you cannot pour from an empty cup, meaning that you must replenish yourself before you can serve others. This expression is quite true for social workers. Despite the value of self-care, many helping professionals often find themselves caring for others and neglecting their own self-care (Kanter, 2007). It is impossible to give to others when you as a person have nothing left to give. Restoring yourself cannot be perceived as self-indulgent. but rather should be viewed as a component of competent practice, which is required by the National Association of Social Workers (NASW's) *Code of Ethics*.

Throughout this chapter, as with all of your social work education, we encourage you to have an open mind. Curiously explore your current state of well-being and your relationship with self-care. Explore ways that you could be more compassionate to yourself, creating a personal self that is better able to serve your clients. In addition to having an open mind, self-awareness is a really important component of self-care.

KNOW THYSELF

To be an effective professional social worker, you will need to engage in reflection and self-regulation. When we are thinking deeply or carefully about something, we are engaging in reflection. Self-regulation refers to our ability to maintain or control ourselves regarding our thoughts, feelings, and behaviors. Successful reflection and self-regulation require self-awareness. It is impossible to engage in reflection and self-regulation if you are unaware of your thoughts, feelings, and behaviors. Effective social workers are self-aware and continually examine their own selves so that they can be more effective helping professionals.

SELF-AWARENESS

Self-awareness is a term used to describe the recognition of personal thoughts, feelings, and behaviors. When your stomach growls and you feel the sensation of hunger, that is self-awareness. When you are texting with someone you are interested in and you feel butterflies in your stomach, that is self-awareness. Anytime that you can recognize your thoughts, feelings, and behaviors, you are being aware of your *self*. Some people naturally seem to do a better job at self-awareness than others, but do not worry: Self-awareness is something that you can practice and improve. Being present in the moment and practicing mindfulness (which we talk about later in this chapter) are ways that you can improve your self-awareness.

Field Reflection Questions

Practice some self-awareness right now. What are you thinking about? Which feelings are you experiencing?

Do you notice any bodily sensations or strong emotions?

Self-awareness is critical and necessary in social work practice. Social workers often use their *self* in helping clients. Just as accountants would use a calculator to do their job, social workers use their self to do their job. A big piece of social work is being present with the client. We must be present with ourselves to be fully present with the client.

How do we get to know our *self* better? Ideally, your education, especially your social work courses, will have served as a catalyst for self-exploration and critical thinking. Throughout your social work education, you have learned about the use of self in your practice classes. In addition to what you learn in the classroom, you may have gained insights into yourself from a variety of other sources. Maybe you have received feedback from people you are close to or maybe you have sought your own avenues to get to know yourself better through books, groups, or activities designed with such a purpose. Self-awareness, or personal knowledge about the social worker's self and needs, can be achieved in a variety of ways (Bogo, 2010). Throughout your field experience, you can explore your self-awareness and use of self in the following ways: field supervision, process recordings, feedback from others (including field supervisors, faculty members, colleagues, peers, and clients), and personal reflection.

Focusing on self-awareness as a component of field education is critical. To provide sound, ethical social work services, social workers need to be aware of their biases, beliefs, and values and how those are connected to their personal experiences, feelings, and reactions. Throughout your social work education, you have learned to pay attention to your verbal and nonverbal behaviors (e.g., making eye contact, nodding) to demonstrate to the client that you are concerned and listening. In a similar way, now that you are in the field, you must turn your attention inward and pay attention to your thoughts and feelings while working with others. Although it is important that you are aware of what is going on with you, you cannot allow that to be the focus of the session. It is a delicate balance, and requires some practice, to be able to be reflective while still focusing on the clients in front of you. During your time in field, you will be able to practice this skill to become a more effective social work professional.

Everyone has a bad day every now and then; however, as social workers, we are mandated by the NASW's *Code of Ethics* to hold our commitment to the clients we serve in the highest priority. It is inappropriate, and unethical, to allow your personal issues to interfere with your client's treatment. So what are social workers to do? Self-awareness is a strategy that can be one potential solution (see Case Example 4.1). By being self-aware, you can identify concerns before they become an issue in treatment. Through self-awareness, you can be alert to and care for your own needs to ward off the hazards of helping in the form of burnout, compassion fatigue, and vicarious trauma. One way you can care for your own needs is by engaging in consistent self-care.

CASE EXAMPLE 4.1: SELF-AWARENESS

When Sara was a young girl, her father was diagnosed with cancer. He battled cancer for much of her adolescence. On the basis of her experiences in the hospital setting, Sara knew that when she grew up, she wanted to work in a hospital to help others who were going through the same thing. While in college working on her BSW degree, Sara was assigned a field placement at a local hospital to support patients and families in the oncology unit. One day, while completing rounds, Sara walked into the room of a new patient who looked very much like her father. Immediately Sara was flooded with a wave of emotions and felt her stomach getting tight. Sara took a deep breath and did a quick scan of herself. She recognized that this man looked very much like her father, and that her mind and body had just transported her back to her adolescence when she watched her dad battle the same disease.

What Should Sara Do?

This situation, much like many other situations in social work, does not have a clear black-and-white solution. There are a lot of other variables that impact what Sara should do next in this situation. Sara was aware of her response and she obviously has good insight because she was able to recognize what triggered this reaction. If Sara is able to contain her personal feelings and not let them interfere with her work with the client, she can proceed. If she does not feel that she can support the client, for whatever reason, then she should reach out to another social worker for support. Either way, using supervision to process this experience is strongly recommended. Supervision is an amazing tool in the toolkit for social workers (refer Chapter 3 for more on supervision).

■ HAZARDS OF HELPING

Hazards are dangers or risks that can be potentially harmful. Sometimes we encounter hazards through our work environments or working conditions. Nearly all professions have some potential hazards. Firefighters, for example, experience the hazard of running into burning buildings to fight fires, which obviously can be quite dangerous and potentially life-threatening. However, they do not just run into the hazards. First, before ever rolling up to a fire, they spend countless hours training, learning, and preparing for what to do when they encounter the hazard. Then, when they are presented with the hazard, they put on their gear to protect and buffer against the dangers that they are about to be exposed to in the line of duty. We expect firefighters to put on their heavy jackets, helmets, and breathing devices so that they can do their job effectively and safely. In social work, we clearly do not need the same gear as firefighters, but to protect ourselves from the potential hazards of our profession, we should put on our own proverbial gear. The potential hazards of helping professions (see Exhibit 4.1), such as social work, that we must safeguard against are burnout, vicarious trauma, and compassion fatigue. These phenomena are found within helping professions and are at times referred to as "the cost of caring." In addition to our training, the gear that we can put on to protect us from these hazards is self-care. Self-care serves to buffer us against these hazards and serves as a defense. Self-care cannot prevent these hazards, much like an umbrella cannot prevent the rain, but it can help negate the impact of these hazards nonetheless.

It is important to note that these factors are potentially hazardous—not all helping professionals will be impacted by these phenomena during their careers. There are a multitude of factors that influence whether an individual will be negatively impacted by any one of these hazards (we talk about some of these factors later in this chapter). It must be stated that not all stress is bad. Some stress is actually a good thing; it can keep us motivated and performing optimally. Some researchers have found that optimal levels of stress can not only increase motivation but also improve energy levels, alertness, and perceptions (Craig & Sprang, 2010). Where we must be careful is when stress goes beyond the optimal range and becomes detrimental and counterproductive. Excessive stress can lead to decreased motivation, feelings of hopelessness, lack of productivity, and fatigue.

The noted humanitarian and Nobel Peace Prize recipient, Mother Teresa, devoted her life to working with the poor and sick in the poorest sections of India. She and her fellow sisters served individuals who were viewed as outcasts by society—a very vulnerable population, to say the least. In their service, they witnessed poverty, disease, famine, and neglect on a daily basis. Mother Teresa once said, "The miracle is not that we do this work, but that we are happy to do it." It is a paradox of sorts. Mother Teresa and the other sisters of her order bore witness to sadness and suffering, but somehow found a joy in what they did. They had high levels of compassion satisfaction with the work they were doing. Compassion satisfaction refers to the positive sense that one derives from enjoying one's work and feeling that one is making a positive impact in the lives of others.

Social work can present demanding workloads and a great deal of responsibility; however, it is important to keep in mind that there can be great reward from doing this difficult work. Some roles for social workers require them to bear witness to sadness and suffering more often than others. During your field placement, you may be supporting individuals who have experienced significant difficulties, and sometimes you may have limited resources available to support your work. Some students experience feelings of frustration, helplessness, or even failure at what they perceive to be their inability to promote effective change. During your field placement, and throughout your social work career, it is important to be aware of any such feelings that may arise and to reflect upon them and seek support through appropriate supervision to address your feelings.

It is important to be aware and understand that at times, being a social worker requires that you sit in the uncomfortable darkness (e.g., sadness, fear, anger, trauma) with those with whom you are working. Sometimes, after spending time in the proverbial darkness, we can be affected. There can be an emotional impact as a result of witnessing tragedy and injustice. This effect can take on several different forms. Ethically, social workers must be mindful of any such issue that could cause impairment in their practice. The NASW's (2017) *Code of Ethics* has an ethical standard (2.08) related to professional impairment, which states:

> Social workers who have direct knowledge of a social work colleague's impairment that is due to personal problems, psychosocial distress, substance abuse, or mental health difficulties and that interferes with practice effectiveness should consult with that colleague when feasible and assist the colleague in taking remedial action. (para. 91)

The *Code of Ethics* is clear that as professional social workers, we must acknowledge impairments when they could interfere with the services being provided to clients. As reflective, self-regulated professionals, we should be aware of our own functioning and not allow personal impairments to impact our work by seeking out treatment, remediation, or support for such impairments. Being the best version of ourselves to serve our clients is consistent with the ethical principle of integrity as well. It is necessary that all social workers also practice responsibility; ensuring that we are well is part of being a responsible professional.

Impairments could come from a variety of sources. The impairments that we focus on in this chapter relate to the potential hazards of helping we noted earlier. It is important to note that no matter the source of the impairment or etiology, it is essential that social workers take any possible impairment seriously and seek action to ameliorate it.

BURNOUT

Burnout is often described as a state of exhaustion affecting the person mentally, physically, and spiritually as a result of ongoing exposure or involvement in the helping profession (Newell & Nelson-Gardell, 2013). Craig and Sprang (2010) indicate that burnout is often associated with "feelings of hopelessness and difficulties in dealing with work or in doing one's job effectively and that the feelings usually have a gradual onset and reflect the feeling that one's efforts make no difference" (p. 322). Burnout is a gradual process that intensifies over time, causing mental, physical, and spiritual exhaustion (Fahy, 2007). The symptoms of burnout are outlined in Exhibit 4.1.

CASE EXAMPLE 4.2: BURNOUT

Kevin is completing his foundation MSW social work field placement in a community mental health center. The center is located in an area with high levels of poverty and crime. The majority of clients who seek treatment at the center have experienced multiple traumas. Kevin has his own caseload and sees about five or six clients a day for individual therapy. At the end of the day, Kevin feels exhausted, mentally and physically, but he often has unfinished paperwork that he brings home with him. When he goes home, he does not want to talk to his partner. Rather, he wants to just "zone out" on the couch, eat his dinner, and stream TV reruns before he has to start on the paperwork from the day. One night, when Kevin is utterly overwhelmed by his work, he decides he cannot keep this up. He does not enjoy his placement or seeing his clients anymore. Some days he feels so exhausted that he does not know how he will make it through the day, much less his field placement.

What Should Kevin Do?

In this scenario, we see the way that burnout can impact a social worker. Using supervision to discuss and process what is going on with Kevin might be helpful. Kevin and his supervisor can explore some of the factors that are probably adding to his level of burnout, such as the size of his caseload and his need to take paperwork home. The supervisor may be able to provide Kevin with strategies to address his paperwork issue so that he can get his work done at the office; then he can have a break from work at home in the evenings. One thing is for sure, Kevin needs support to be able to support his clients.

VICARIOUS TRAUMA

Vicarious trauma, sometimes called secondary traumatic stress (STS), describes when the worker is traumatized because of being exposed to the traumatic experiences of clients. The manifestation of vicarious trauma in the worker can mirror the symptoms of posttraumatic stress disorder (PTSD) within the victimized client. If the worker has been vicariously traumatized, he or she may experience symptoms of PTSD including re-experiencing the trauma in the form of nightmares and intrusive thoughts, avoiding reminders of the trauma, problems sleeping, hypervigilance and increased arousal or startle responses, altered cognitive functioning, or regression.

Vicarious trauma is not a diagnosis in the *Diagnostic and Statistical Manual of Mental Diseases* (5th ed.; *DSM-5*). However, under the diagnosis of PTSD in the *DSM-5* (American Psychiatric Association, 2013), exposure to the traumatic event can take several forms, including direct exposure, witnessing the traumatic event in person, learning of the traumatic event from someone with whom you are close, or firsthand repeated exposure to details of a traumatic event. Vicarious trauma overlaps with the firsthand repeated exposure to details of a traumatic event.

Symptoms of vicarious trauma can be categorized into the following areas: cognitive behavioral, affective, somatic, and spiritual. Cognitive behavioral symptoms include such things as feeling irritable or preoccupied, withdrawing from others, poor concentration and memory, and experiencing changes in sleep or appetite. Affective symptoms encompass a variety of emotional reactions that can range from being numb and shutdown to feeling angry and hostile. At times, the affective symptoms could even present like a roller coaster of emotions and mood swings for the individual. Somatic symptoms include physical, bodily reactions such as aches and pains—these can lead to physical exhaustion, which in turn leads to compromised immune system functioning. The last category of symptoms, spiritual, relates to the meaning and purpose an individual assigns to experiences. Spiritual symptoms related to vicarious trauma may include the individual questioning his or her worldview and feeling hopeless or lost.

It has been suggested that vicarious trauma can alter a worker's worldview (Cox & Steiner, 2013). For example, a social worker who works primarily with victims of violent crimes may begin to have beliefs that the world is unsafe—Case Example 4.3 illustrates such a scenario. As a social work placement field student, it is imperative that if you notice any of the symptoms noted in this chapter or start to feel traumatized by the work that you are doing, you immediately speak with your supervisor and your faculty liaison about your experiences. You will not be judged for your experience; rather, you can be supported and given the tools and supports that you need to address it head-on. There is no shame in reaching out for help when you need it. Please remember that field education is just that—*education.* You are not expected to have all of the answers and know everything from the very beginning; if you did, you would not need the education. Take advantage of your time in field and learn all that you can, including learning about yourself!

CASE EXAMPLE 4.3: VICARIOUS TRAUMA

Jessica is a social work intern completing her foundation MSW field placement at a sexual assault support center. Her daily responsibilities include conducting intake assessments with all new clients who come to the center. Each day, Jessica usually meets with three to four victims of sexual assault who share their experiences with her. Jessica begins to have nightmares and intrusive thoughts that resemble the stories that the clients have told her. She also notices that she feels more on edge when she goes out in the community. Jessica is afraid to tell her supervisor about these feelings because she is worried that they reflect poorly on her performance and potential to become an effective professional social worker.

If you were Jessica's coworker and she shared her feelings with you, how would you handle this situation?

What would you encourage Jessica to do?

COMPASSION FATIGUE

The final occupational hazard we discuss in this chapter is compassion fatigue. In comparison to burnout and vicarious trauma, compassion fatigue is a broader term used to describe the overall experience of mental fatigue within the worker as a result of ongoing treatment and the chronic display of empathy with individuals who are, in some way, suffering (Newell & Nelson-Gardell, 2014). To understand this better, it may be helpful to explore compassion on a deeper level.

Compassion can be defined as an awareness or understanding of what another person is going through that is accompanied with a strong desire to help that person in order to reduce or eliminate their suffering. At the core, compassion means to suffer with or be concerned regarding the suffering of another person and is often coupled with a desire to help (Johnson, 2008). Buchanan-Barker and Barker (2004) suggest that compassion is a form of fellow feeling in that "we (helping professionals) participate in the process of suffering by caring with the suffering person" (p. 18). It is no secret that there is suffering in the world. Frankly, many of you have chosen the field of social work to ameliorate such suffering. Many within the profession of social work feel "called" to make a difference (Newell & Nelson-Gardell, 2014). Although it is a noble pursuit to make a difference, we must realize that the negative effects of chronic exposure to traumatic, violent, and stressful experiences or stories can take a toll on the worker. When this chronic exposure begins to overwhelm the individual, compassion fatigue can develop.

Craig and Sprang (2010) define compassion fatigue as "cognitive-emotional-behavioral changes that caregivers experience from indirect exposure" within helping professions such as social workers (p. 320). Slocum-Gori, Hemsworth, Chan, Carson, and Kazanjian (2011) suggest that compassion fatigue is a "stress response that emerges suddenly and without warning and includes a sense of helplessness, isolation, and confusion" (p. 173). Onset of compassion fatigue can occur rapidly and is often initially undetected (Lester, 2010; Potter et al., 2010). Compassion fatigue can lead to other serious mental health concerns and illnesses, including depression, anxiety, irritability, and PTSD (Craig & Sprang, 2010; Finke, 2006; Lester, 2010; Melvin, 2012). In addition to the toll compassion fatigue takes on the individual worker, it impacts the workplace in terms of more sick days used, high turnover rates of employees, and lower productivity (Potter et al., 2010).

**EXHIBIT
4.1**

Hazards of Helping

	Burnout	Vicarious Trauma	Compassion Fatigue
Onset	Gradual	Rapid	Rapid
Symptoms	• Exhaustion, tired, lack of energy • Unable to cope, overwhelmed • Easily frustrated, cynical related to job (coworkers, clients) • Difficulty concentrating, lack of creativity	• Intrusive memories, flashbacks • Distressing dreams • Hypervigilance, exaggerated startle response • Avoidance • Memory distortions, difficulty concentrating • Negative worldview (thoughts that the world is unsafe)	• Mental fatigue • Decreased empathy • Depleted levels of compassion for clients • Can lead to mental health concerns if untreated

RISK AND PROTECTIVE FACTORS

The hazards that we have just discussed—burnout, vicarious trauma, and compassion fatigue—are real conditions that exist within all helping professions, including social work. Although these are real occupational hazards, as we have said, not all workers will experience them. There are a variety of factors to consider when exploring why some workers are affected by these hazards and others are able to avoid them. In doing so, it is important to consider personal risk and protective factors.

A risk factor is some sort of characteristic or attribute that makes an individual more susceptible, or vulnerable, to developing or being influenced by something. Risk factors that indicate individuals may be at a higher likelihood of developing these hazardous conditions include the following:

- *The nature of the work*: The population with which you work can be considered a risk factor. If you are working in a setting where you are exposed to high volume of difficult or traumatic cases, you may be more vulnerable. This also includes working within a setting where you are exposed to high-risk experiences and meet with resistance from the client systems. An example would be working within an agency when, at times, families are not cooperative and view the helper's role in a negative light.

- *Organizational factors*: Characteristics of the organization where you work may increase the likelihood of developing an occupational hazard. Having high caseloads and a lack of supervision can result in feeling chronically overwhelmed and may even trigger feelings of helplessness. Poor morale within an agency can foster isolation and lack of unity and support. Insufficient training and support can be extremely detrimental to the workers as they are unprepared to appropriately handle what may come their way through the course of their employment.

- *Unrealistic expectations*: It is a noble pursuit to wish to change the world, but we must be realistic in our endeavors. It is unreasonable to think that within 1 week on the job, you will be able to eradicate all of the world's social problems. It is important to maintain perspective, be realistic in your goals, and celebrate small victories. Just as you work to establish achievable goals with your clients, you should also strive to set such goals for yourself and your work.

- *Poor boundaries*: A boundary is an invisible line that marks limits. Within social work, we are called upon by our code of ethics to maintain appropriate professional boundaries at all times with clients. It is the responsibility of the worker at all times to be alert to, and when possible avoid, dual relationships. Understanding boundaries is a cornerstone of the social work profession. Regarding burnout, vicarious trauma, and compassion fatigue, boundaries are important both with clients and with the job itself. With clients, the social worker must establish and maintain healthy boundaries for their mutual benefit. With the job itself, the social worker must be mindful to not take the work home and establish a separation between his or her personal and professional lives.

- *Personal issues*: Unresolved emotional issues can derail your social work practice. It is important to be aware of your personal experiences and seek out support to address concerns so they do not interfere with your professional work. Unaddressed personal issues can lead to barriers in treatment that will halt work with those whom you should be serving. Furthermore, it is necessary that you are aware of any countertransference responses that arise while you are working as a social worker. Countertransference refers to a situation in which your personal feelings are projected onto the client or become entangled in the work you are doing with your clients.

Field Reflection Questions

Which risk factors are present for you at this time in your placement? Is there anything you can do to lessen these?

Which protective factors are present for you? Are there any protective factors you can add?

Protective factors can serve as a buffer warding against the development of occupational hazards. They are characteristics or attributes that serve to strengthen the resistance to developing negative conditions. These factors, which can mediate against potential hazards, include such things as routine self-care practices, thoughtful self-awareness (reflection and self-regulation), appropriate training, and healthy, clear boundaries.

Support is a protective factor that is quite important. As a field student, you may draw upon support from others in many ways. Personal support may come from your family and friends. Sometimes it is difficult trying to manage your time with friends and family while completing your schoolwork and field hours, but we encourage you to stay connected with your personal supports, as they represent a protective factor that will actually help you to be a better social worker. Peer support is another form of support available to you as a field student. In your field class, you have a group of other social work students who are going through the same process as you are right now. It can be very helpful to have a peer who is having the same experience to provide support and encouragement. The shared experience is something that can quickly bond you and allow you to be there to help each other throughout your time in field. As we discussed at length in the previous chapter, supervision is another source of support while you are in your field placement. Using your field supervisor and any other organizational supports available to you is an excellent way to increase your personal protective factors.

Personal resilience is a protective factor that can support you throughout your social work career. Resilience is a general term used to describe your ability to bounce back or overcome adversity. It is something that can be fostered and nurtured within an individual. Resilient individuals are resourceful and adaptive, maintain a sense of hopefulness and a positive outlook despite circumstances, can draw upon appropriate coping strategies, and use supports.

SELF-CARE

Prior to take-off on any airline, flight attendants go through a list of instructions for the passengers in the event of an emergency situation. One of the directions given is that, in the event of an emergency, once the oxygen mask comes down from the ceiling, you are to put the oxygen mask on yourself before you attempt to help anyone else. In an airline emergency, if you do not put your oxygen mask on first, you will quickly be unable to help anyone else. This advice from 30,000 feet in the sky is also really good advice for helping professionals such as social workers.

We have talked about the necessity of being self-aware, but it is equally necessary to take care of yourself so that you can be effective in taking care of others. As social workers, we must take care of ourselves to be effective in our professional practice. Once you are aware of what is going on within you, the compassionate next step is to care for yourself. Returning to an earlier example of self-awareness, when you recognize that you are hungry, the simplest way to take care of that need is to eat something. With that being said, it is not uncommon for social workers to get busy at work helping others and to skip lunch, dismissing their own feelings and needs. Self-awareness allows us to acknowledge our needs, and self-care requires us to take care of these acknowledged needs.

Self-care is important for all social workers regardless of the area of level of practice (Lee & Miller, 2013). Whether you practice at the micro, mezzo, or macro level, you are still using your *self* as a tool for change and, as a result, you must take care of yourself. Your car will not make it far without gasoline. You. too. need fuel; your fuel takes the form of self-care.

DEFINING SELF-CARE

Self-care is a term used to describe the habits, routines, and activities that an individual engages in to promote well-being, support health, and maintain balance in his or her personal and professional lives (Lee & Miller, 2013). It refers to a continuum of activities that seek to reduce stress and promote optimal well-being. Self-care is intentional. It is "an empowering tool that allows practitioners to take ownership of their health and wellbeing holistically and with consideration to both their personal and professional lives" (Lee & Miller, 2013, p. 96). Self-care is especially important for helping professionals like social workers.

Self-care strategies can serve as a buffer against hazards of burnout, vicarious trauma, and compassion fatigue, which we discussed earlier in this chapter. Adopting this perspective serves to empower social workers to enhance their own well-being and address their own needs. It is important that we as social workers honor our well-being and take steps to ensure that we are functioning as best as we can so that we can fully support the clients we serve.

SELF-CARE ACTIVITIES

Self-care is best viewed as a holistic, multidimensional construct encompassing the following areas: physical, psychological and emotional, social, spiritual, and leisure (Lee & Miller, 2013). Self-care practices, which are sometimes called "rituals," can take on many forms. Most often, self-care focuses on three dimensions of individual well-being: the mind, body, and spirit (Figure 4.1).

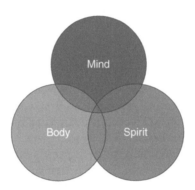

FIGURE 4.1 Dimensions of self-care.

Self-care rituals (Figure 4.2) are quite subjective and individualistic, reflecting personal preferences and interests. For example, one person may find running to be extremely enjoyable, whereas another person may despise running but find a similar joy in drawing. With that in mind, the following are some examples of self-care strategies for the mind (emotional or psychological self-care), body (physical self-care), and spirit (spiritual self-care) that you may wish to consider for yourself. A great place to start when considering which self-care rituals are appropriate for you would be to take a self-care inventory. There are a variety of inventories available that you can use to rate yourself and determine which areas of self-care are current strengths and which areas of self-care you could improve. Exhibit 4.2 is a simple self-care inventory for you to use to explore your current levels of self-care. It is important to be honest with yourself when completing the self-care inventory, as this gives you a baseline to start when assessing your current self-care behaviors.

Self-Care Rituals

Mind	Body	Spirit
• Keep a journal • Be curious • Say "no" when necessary • Love yourself • Play	• Eat healthy • Excercise (running, yoga, weight-training) • Quality sleep • Take care of yourself medically • Go for a walk	• Time for reflection • Be open to inspiration • Spend time in nature • Meditate • Engage in service activities

FIGURE 4.2 Examples of self-care.

EXHIBIT
4.2

Self-Care Inventory

Use this inventory to determine your current levels of self-care for each dimension. Please note that this is not an exhaustive list of self-care activities, but rather a sample of potential self-care activities. At the end of each section, you will see lines marked "other." If you have a self-care strategy that you engage in that is not on the list, please add it in the spaces provided. For each activity, please use the following scale:
3: I do this really well (frequently).
2: I occasionally do this.
1: I rarely do this.
0: I never thought to do this (never).

Physical Self-Care	0	1	2	3
Eat three meals a day				
Chose nutritious foods				
Drink water				
Rest				
Get enough sleep				
Go to the doctor when sick				
Go to the doctor for routine preventive/wellness visits				
Exercise				
Walk				
Stretch				
Other: _____				
Other: _____				
Emotional/Psychological Self-Care	0	1	2	3
Express thoughts and feelings				
Ask for help				
Maintain healthy boundaries				
Take personal responsibility				
Obtain personal therapy or coaching				
Engage in self-awareness				

(continued)

**EXHIBIT
4.2**

Self-Care Inventory (*continued*)

Emotional/Psychological Self-Care	0	1	2	3
Journal				
Color, draw, create				
Read				
Practice self-compassion				
Other: _____				
Other: _____				
Spiritual Self-Care	0	1	2	3
Pray				
Spend time in nature				
Participate in a community				
Reflect				
Engage in service				
Set intentions				
Practice mindfulness				
Meditate				
Other: _____				
Other: _____				

Self-Care for the Mind

Rituals that promote psychological and emotional well-being are part of this category of self-care. Lee and Miller (2013) assert that the target of this dimension of self-care is to "maintain a positive and compassionate view of the self and negotiate the demands that arise from the intersection of the individual and environment" (p. 99). As social workers, the core of our work involves providing compassion for others. Despite this compassion we can hold for others, often it is more difficult to display

Field Reflection Questions

What did you learn about yourself and your current self-care strengths and areas for improvement after completing the self-care inventory?

How will you strengthen the areas that need improvement?

the same compassion toward ourselves. We are often our own toughest critics. One simple self-care strategy for the mind would be to demonstrate more compassion toward yourself.

Social work researcher Brené Brown has conducted a great deal of research on topics of worthiness, vulnerability, shame, and courage. According to Brown (2010), to be able to help others fully, we ourselves must be willing to ask for help. As a field student, you will need to ask for help during your placement; you do not need to know all of the answers all of the time. Use this time in field to practice getting comfortable asking for help and assistance when you need it.

Other self-care strategies for the mind include things such as recognizing personal strengths, problem solving, journaling thoughts and feelings, and seeking individual treatment to address personal issues when appropriate. These strategies closely tie back into the concepts of reflection and self-regulation that we discussed earlier in this chapter. By promoting self-care of the mind, it can serve to promote self-awareness, which we know is critically important for effective professional social work practice.

Self-Care for the Body

Our bodies are fascinating and complex machines. Let us consider another machine—a car. You routinely put gas in your car and from time to time take your car to the garage to get a tune-up so it can continue to take you where you want to go. Our bodies also require fuel and from time to time tune-ups and routine maintenance to keep us functioning at our best.

Goals for physical self-care target optimizing physical function and personal safety (Lee & Miller, 2013). Examples include such things as eating well-balanced meals throughout the day, getting enough quality sleep at night, exercising your body, and addressing medical illnesses and injuries by seeking medical attention when appropriate.

Self-Care for the Spirit

Caring for the spirit encompasses all activities that ignite an inner passion or resonate deep within yourself. For some, spiritual self-care practices are tied to their religious practices. However, it is noteworthy that in this context, the concept of spirit does not have to be viewed within the context of religious beliefs.

Mindfulness is one strategy of spiritual self-care that has grown in popularity in recent years. For social workers, some posit that mindfulness training can allow the worker to more closely attend to clients and encourages a sense of acceptance and openness that enhances the helping relationship (Gockel, Burton, James, & Bryer, 2012). Studies have shown that workers who participate in mindfulness training report lower levels of stress and anxiety and higher levels of positive emotions and compassion (Shapiro, Brown, & Biegel, 2007).

So what is mindfulness? For some, the first picture in their mind may have been of a monk sitting cross-legged on the floor engaging in chanting and breath work. Yes, this is one type of mediation, but it is just that—one type. There are a variety of mindfulness exercises that involve all of the senses for individuals across the life span. There has been much attention focused on mindfulness practices that can be used in everyday life for the average individual. All mindfulness activities revolve around the focus of being present in the current moment. Mindfulness encourages us to experience the world through all of our senses—what we are seeing, tasting, hearing, smelling, and feeling. Mindfulness is about self-acceptance as well. It is recommended that mindfulness is practiced regularly to fully reap its many benefits. Some links to resources on mindfulness are given at the end of this chapter (Electronic Competency Resources) for you to try out. Remember, just like self-care rituals, mindfulness is not a "one size fits all" proposition. Try a few different types of mindfulness strategies to see what works best for you.

SUPPORTIVE RELATIONSHIPS

The value of support should not be understated. After all, we are *social* workers, not *solitary* workers; the word "social" is in our title for a reason. We as a profession understand the value and importance of human relationships. The NASW's *Code of Ethics* (2017) cites the importance of human relationships as one of the professions' guiding principles:

> Social workers understand that relationships between and among people are an important vehicle for change. Social workers engage people as partners in the helping process. Social workers seek to strengthen relationships among people in a purposeful effort to promote, restore, maintain, and enhance the wellbeing of individuals, families, social groups, organizations, and communities. (para. 5)

As social workers, we must not neglect our own relationships and must continually seek to strengthen our supports. Our relationships may change over time and include a variety of formal and informal supports. We may have a network of family and friends from whom we can draw upon for support. Maybe we belong to a community or organization where we can feel refreshed by engaging with others who share a common bond with us. Although you are still a social work student and in field, there are several people whom you may wish to consider as a part of your social support system.

Field Reflection Questions

Which supportive networks do you have in your life that you can rely on for support? Be sure to include both personal and professional support systems.

Make a list of your supports. How are these people helping you? How could they be more supportive of you?

Throughout your field placement, you have several relationships that can support you throughout this process; the first and foremost is your relationship with your field supervisor. The role of the field supervisor is one defined by support. Field supervisors are not only tasked with providing you with an orientation to the organization and overseeing your daily tasks. but also charged with creating a meaningful learning environment in which you can engage your social work skills while being supported by trained practitioners. In addition, your weekly supervision with your supervisor is designed to be the time when you can not only review routine questions related to the job, but also seek support as you grow throughout the field process.

Another supportive relationship you have while you are in field is with your faculty liaison. This staff member has been assigned to assist you during your field journey. The role of the faculty liaison includes being available to support both you, as the student, and the field supervisor. Your faculty liaison is a great resource of support if you have something you want to discuss related to the field.

Field can, at times, be difficult. Who better to understand what you are going through than those who are going through it with you right now? Your social work peers are a great source of support during the field process. The shared experience of field can serve as a bond for your connection.

DEVELOPING A SELF-CARE PLAN

As you have read, self-care is necessary to serve as a buffer against the helping profession hazards we have discussed. We started this chapter by asking you to approach self-care with curiosity; now we ask you to approach self-care with creativity as we discuss developing a self-care plan.

What is a self-care plan? Well, it is simply a written plan of which self-care rituals you are going to incorporate into your life. You can reflect back on the self-care inventory that you completed earlier in this chapter to give you a good place to start in developing your self-care plan. There are a variety of formats available for self-care plans, which range from quite simple to more reflective and engaging. A quick online search for "self-care plans" will result in a myriad of options. No matter the template, a basic self-care plan should address the dimensions of self-care (mind, body, spirit) and allow you space to identify which rituals you plan to complete.

Much like a treatment plan that we work with clients to develop, self-care plans are ways that we can clearly outline our goals (for ourselves) and hold ourselves accountable (Did I do what I said I was going to do for myself?). You can even use your social work skills and create specific, measurable, attainable, relevant, time-bound (SMART) objectives for yourself in your self-care plan. We have included a sample of a simple self-care plan for you (Exhibit 4.3) as well as a template for you to create your own self-care plan (Exhibit 4.4). Take some time to engage in reflection and consider which self-care rituals you can incorporate into your life. Remember that self-care is intentional and proactive—so it is helpful to plan ahead.

EXHIBIT 4.3

Sample Self-Care Plan

Tara's Self-Care Plan
In the space below each dimension of self-care, list two to three rituals that would promote care of your *self*.

Mind	Body	Spirit
• Color a mandala once a week • Keep a gratitude journal every night	• Eat three meals a day • Go for a walk at least three times a week • Drink eight glasses of water each day	• Read an inspirational story or passage every morning • Meditate twice a week

**EXHIBIT
4.4**

Self-Care Plan

_____'s Self-Care Plan
In the space below each dimension of self-care, list two to three rituals that would promote care of your *self*.

Mind	Body	Spirit
•	•	•
•	•	•
•	•	•

After completing your plan, it is important to set yourself up for success. Consider which barriers are present that may hinder your ability to stick with your plan. Once you have identified these barriers, develop strategies to address them so that you can stick with your plan. For example, you may identify time as a barrier to engaging in self-care, because you are a busy student who is trying to manage the demands of coursework and field with other demands from your personal life. One possible strategy to address this time barrier is to schedule time in your day to take some time to engage in self-care. You may schedule just 5 minutes a day to sit and meditate or 30 minutes early in the morning to go for a jog. Self-care is effective only when it is being practiced: It does no good to have an amazing self-care plan if you cannot implement it.

One strategy that may be helpful is to find a self-care partner. Having someone to support you in your self-care endeavors and to help hold you accountable for taking care of yourself can be a great motivator. Just as you are probably more likely to go to the gym or exercise class if you have a workout partner, you will be more likely to engage in self-care if you have a self-care partner. Identify your self-care partner and have a conversation with him or her about where you are and where you would like to be with your self-care. Ideally, if your self-care partner is engaging in his or her own self-care, you can be mutually supportive of each other. Talk with each other about what type of support motivates and encourages you most, and decide how you will check in with each other to hold each other accountable. Something as simple as a text message to touch base can serve this purpose.

Think of your self-care plan as a compassionate contract with yourself. It has been said that you cannot give what you do not have, so for us, as social workers, to give compassion to our clients, it is important for us to show compassion to ourselves. Consider your self-care plan an ever-evolving document that demonstrates your commitment to try and take care of your *self*. Because it is something that will change over time, it is important to revisit this plan periodically to see what you need to adjust. Take another self-care inventory and then revisit your plan every couple of months.

CASE EXAMPLE 4.4: SELF-CARE

Nicole is in the middle of her MSW field placement at a residential treatment facility with individuals with intellectual disabilities. To defray the costs of her education, she also works full-time at a psychiatric hospital. She is scheduled to work 40 hours a week but because of call-offs from other staff members, she is often asked to pick up other shifts at her job. Between her field placement, full-time job, and classes, Nicole is constantly on the go. Sometimes she has to work an overnight shift at her job and then go straight to her field placement, going sometimes 24 hours without sleep. Nicole has no time for a life outside of work and school, because when she is not at work, she spends her time catching up on sleep and trying to keep up with her laundry and other household tasks that need.

Is Nicole taking care of herself?

How do you think this will influence Nicole in the short term and the long term?

What should Nicole do?

How can support systems help in this scenario?

SUMMARY

In this chapter, we discussed the importance and necessity of multidimensional self-care. Through reflection, self-regulation, and self-awareness, social workers can be better able to use their *self* as a tool in the helping relationship and change process. Occupational hazards such as burnout, vicarious trauma, and compassion fatigue were identified and symptomology for each was reviewed. We discussed risk and protective factors to ward against the development of such hazards. Remember that risk and protective factors are things that you can work to promote or diminish as you progress throughout your lifetime. The importance of social supports should not be underestimated. Connections should be strengthened during your field placement and throughout your social work careers. Developing a self-care plan is one strategy to address personal needs and identify personal rituals that will increase self-care.

The profession you have chosen to pursue can, at times, be difficult and challenging; however, do not lose sight of the great rewards that come from a fulfilling career as a social worker who is making a real difference in the lives of many!

CRITICAL THINKING QUESTIONS

In this chapter, we discussed Competency 1: Demonstrate Ethical and Professional Behavior in regard to using reflection and self-regulation to promote well-being through self-care. As a social worker, you are expected to be able to recognize how your personal experiences, thoughts, feelings, and behaviors can influence your professional judgment and behavior. Reflection, self-regulation, and self-awareness are strategies for you to use to manage your personal self to remain a consummate social work professional. The following discussion questions focus on how reflection and self-regulation relate to Competency 1:

1. In your field placement, how can you use reflection and self-regulation to maintain professional social work behavior? On days that are exceptionally difficult, which strategies can you use to promote well-being in a professional environment?

2. What would you do if you began to recognize signs of vicarious trauma in a fellow student at your field placement? Which steps would you take and why?

3. How can you use reflection and self-regulation to promote well-being through self-care for yourself? How would you describe self-care to someone who is unfamiliar with it? How could you encourage it for others? How do your personal experiences influence your professional judgment and behavior as a social work field student?

4. How do you use refection and self-regulation to manage personal values and maintain professionalism in the field?

5. How can you improve your self-awareness as a professional social worker?

6. How can you ensure that you will engage in self-care not only as a field student but also as a practicing social work professional after graduation?

COMPETENCY 1: DEMONSTRATE ETHICAL AND PROFESSIONAL BEHAVIOR

Social workers understand the value base of the profession and its ethical standards, as well as relevant laws and regulations that may impact practice at the micro, mezzo, and macro levels. They understand frameworks of ethical decision making and how to apply principles of critical thinking to those frameworks in practice, research, and policy arenas. Social workers recognize personal values and the distinction between personal and professional values. They also understand how their personal experiences and affective reactions influence their professional judgment and behavior. Social workers understand the profession's history, its mission, and the roles and responsibilities of the profession. They also understand the role of other professions when engaged in interprofessional teams. Social workers recognize the importance of lifelong learning and are committed to continually updating their skills to ensure they are relevant and effective. They also understand emerging forms of technology and the ethical use of technology in social work practice. Social workers:

- Make ethical decisions by applying the standards of the NASW's *Code of Ethics*, relevant laws and regulations, models for ethical decision making, models for ethical conduct of research, and additional codes of ethics as appropriate to context.

- Use refection and self-regulation to manage personal values and maintain professionalism in practice situations.

- Demonstrate professional demeanor in behavior; appearance; and oral, written, and electronic communications.

- Use technology ethically and appropriately to facilitate practice outcomes.

- Use supervision and consultation to guide professional judgment and behavior.

CASE SUMMARY—"I CAN'T CRY NOW ... SOMEONE ELSE IS DYING"

PRACTICE SETTING DESCRIPTION

Prairie Homecare and Hospice Services is a small organization that operates in a rural community in Pennsylvania. The staff consists of several nurses and medical staff, but there are only two full-time social workers to support all of the clients, who currently include more than 150 patients. This is the first time that Prairie Homecare and Hospice is hosting a social work field student. As the field student, I am going to work with both the social workers and eventually have my own small caseload of clients.

IDENTIFYING DATA

Early on in my field placement, my days were spent totally with the two social workers. I would ride with them to and from client visits, and we would cofacilitate sessions with the patients and their families. I did feel really comfortable from the beginning, especially with the elderly female patients. I guess I felt this way because they reminded me of my own grandmother, who had lived with my family for the past 12 years until about 6 months ago, when she passed away after a long bout with cancer. My grandmother and I were always really close. When my parents worked, she would be at home to take care of me and my sisters. Due to my comfort around these older women, my supervisors thought I was ready to have my own caseload. I started off with 10 clients of my very own. Of the 10, nine were older women, eight were on hospice.

Now that I had a caseload of my own, I did not spend as much time with my supervisors. Actually, because our work involved so much traveling, I would really see them only at the start of each day for a few minutes and then on Friday afternoon for our weekly supervision. They kept telling me how great I was doing and that they were hearing great things about the work I was doing with the clients. Because I was doing such a good job, they quickly increased my caseload—in fact, they actually doubled it. Now I have 20 clients whom I am responsible for seeing and documenting. I think I should be grateful to have so much responsibility because it must mean I am doing a good job. The only problem is some days I feel like I am running around in circles driving from one home to the next without any breaks.

PRESENTING PROBLEM

About 2 weeks after being assigned 20 cases, one of the first cases that had been assigned to me, Mrs. Charlotte, started taking a turn for the worse as her health declined. Mrs. Charlotte was one of my favorite patients to visit, probably because she looked so much like my grandmother and she said I was like the granddaughter she never had. Previously, my visits with Mrs. Charlotte were filled with laughter and chatting, but recently she has mostly been sleeping. The lead nurse says, "It won't be long now."

For a couple of weeks, I continue to see all of my clients, but it seems like everyone is getting sicker. I am starting to get angry that my patients are not recovering. I wonder what they are doing wrong or why they will not go back to the hospital to try and get better. I am frustrated that I cannot make them better. I do not know what I am doing wrong!

This week has been the worst. First, on Monday morning I learned about another patient passing away over the weekend. While I was sitting in the staff meeting, my work cell phone rang that I was needed by the family at Mrs. Charlotte's house. I got there as fast as I could, but I was too late. She was gone. Mrs. Charlotte passed away and I was not there for her. As I stood on her porch, talking to the nurse from my office, I could feel tears welling up inside of me. My stomach hurt. I remembered that I was here as a social work intern and I told myself internally that I should not cry. To remain professional, I quickly took a deep breath, said goodbye to the nurse, and got in my car. I thought I would be able to cry in my car once I pulled away. As soon as I got in the car, my phone rang, it was a different office nurse telling me that another one of my clients was close to passing and the family was requesting a social worker. When I hung up the phone with her, I plugged the address into my GPS and started driving to where I was needed. I thought to myself, "I can't cry now; someone else is dying."

That week, three clients on my caseload passed away. I guess I should have expected it because I am working for a hospice after all.

ASSESSMENT

For the past week, I have been feeling irritable and I am just so tired. It does not seem to matter how much sleep I get, I just want to stay in bed and sleep some more. I also noticed that I have been thinking about my grandmother a lot recently. During supervision this week, both the social workers at the agency who I work with met me. They shared that they bet the past week was really hard for me experiencing several losses of patients. I did not want to seem bothered by it, so I quickly downplayed my reaction to it and said, "Oh, it's fine, just part of the job." One social worker nodded and said, "Sometimes our patients do pass away, but a loss is still hard, even if we expect it to happen." There was something about how she said and how she looked at me in such a comforting way that I lost it right there in her office. I started to cry. When she asked me about my tears, I said this past week has reminded me a lot about my grandmother. She handed me a box of tissues and we started unpacking some of my reaction.

CASE PROCESS SUMMARY

Through my supervision, I was able to process with my supervisor that in part my reaction was due to some of my own unresolved feelings surrounding my grandmother's death that I had not yet dealt with. I realized that I should have asked for help earlier, when my caseload started feeling overwhelming. I also saw that maybe I was having some counter-transference reactions with Mrs. Charlotte and that is why I felt so attached to her. I also learned through supervision that it is okay to have feelings as a social worker. Feelings are normal and natural, but it is important to be aware of these feelings and to process them in a place like supervision so that they do not interfere in my practice with my clients. I plan to start journaling about my feelings and taking breaks throughout the day to do things I enjoy, such as going for a walk at lunch or listening to my favorite music while driving in my car.

Alice, MSW intern

DISCUSSION QUESTIONS

- In what ways could Alice have promoted personal well-being better in the scenario?

- On the basis of the scenario, how do you think Alice did in managing her personal experiences and professional behaviors? If you were Alice, what would you have done differently?

- If Alice wanted to talk to her supervisor about what she was feeling (before the supervisor brought it up), how could she have initiated that conversation? What should that conversation look like?

- Are there any personal issues that you need to be mindful of as you progress through your field placement or possible triggers that may elicit a countertransference response from you in field? How can you use reflection and self-regulation to manage these?

- As a social worker, how can you manage personal experiences and professional expectations to remain ethical and demonstrate professional behavior?

ELECTRONIC COMPETENCY RESOURCES

WEBSITE LINKS

Self-Care Starter Kit, from University at Buffalo's School of Social Work
http://socialwork.buffalo.edu/resources/self-care-starter-kit.html

The American Institute of Stress homepage
www.stress.org

The *Mindful* website provides various media exploring mindfulness
www.mindful.org

The Compassion Fatigue Awareness Project provides links to self-assessments (PROQOL, compassion fatigue self-test, life stress self-test) that can be done online or PDF versions
www.compassionfatigue.org/index.html

VIDEO LINKS

Ted Talk featuring Megan McCormick discussing her own self-care journey
www.youtube.com/watch?v=sUKKJapwUXc

NASW; member Lisa Wessan shares her "Top 10 List" of self-care practices for social workers based on her article "Preventing Compassion Fatigue" in NASW's *Focus* newsletter of September, 2013
www.youtube.com/watch?v=vJ5fqsWskkE

Social Work Tech Video 5—Self-care Plan
www.youtube.com/watch?v=GWwwPb6akqA

Article: "Brené Brown on Self-Criticism, Judgment and the Power of Compassion" (with video and OWN eCourse links)
www.huffingtonpost.com/2014/02/25/brene-brown-self-criticism-compassion_n_4848895.html

Health Equity Institute's "Release: Self-Care for Trauma Workers"—Trauma workers discuss burnout, vicarious trauma, and self-care
www.youtube.com/watch?v=CoLupPSmmoU&index=3&list=PLoqWbfSB28TspN27SF9DVdufULmyvj39E

"What is Compassion Fatigue?" Dr. Frank Ochberg discusses both compassion fatigue and burnout
www.youtube.com/watch?v=VubmnvCl9sk

"Social Work and Compassion Fatigue Webinar" by Maretter Monson
www.youtube.com/watch?v=7kBHNpUMo0g

REFERENCES

American Psychiatric Association (APA). (2013). *Diagnostic and statistical manual of mental disorders* (5th ed.). Arlington, VA: American Psychiatric Publishing.

Bogo, M. (2010). *Achieving competence in social work through field education.* Toronto, ON, Canada: University of Toronto Press.

Brown, B. (2010). *The gifts of imperfection: Let go of who you think you're supposed to be and embrace who you are.* Center City, MN: Hazelden Publishing.

Buchanan-Barker, P., & Barker, P. (2004). More than a feeling. *Nursing Standard, 19*(11), 18–19. doi:10.7748/ns.19.11.18.s26

Council on Social Work Education (2015). *Educational policy and accreditation standards for baccalaureate and master's social work programs.* Retrieved from https://www.cswe.org/getattachment/Accreditation/Accreditation-Process/2015-EPAS/2015EPAS_Web_FINAL.pdf.aspx

Cox, K., & Steiner, S. (2013). Preserving commitment to social work service through the prevention of vicarious trauma. *Journal of Social Work Values & Ethics, 10*(1), 52–60.

Craig, C. D., & Sprang, G. (2010). Compassion satisfaction, compassion fatigue, and burnout in a national sample of trauma treatment therapists. *Anxiety, Stress, and Coping, 23*(3), 319–339. doi:10.1080/10615800903085818

Fahy, A. (2007). The unbearable fatigue of compassion: Notes from a substance abuse counselor who dreams of working at Starbucks. *Clinical Social Work Journal, 35,* 199–205. doi:10.1007/s10615-007-0094-4

Finke, L. (2006). The bond and burden of caring. *Journal of Child and Adolescent Psychiatric Nursing, 19*(1), 1–2. doi:10.1111/j.1744-6171.2006.00035.x

Gockel, A., Burton, D., James, S., & Bryer, E. (2012). Introducing mindfulness as a self-care and clinical training strategy for beginning social work students. *Mindfulness, 4,* 343–353. doi:10.1007/s12671-012-0134-1

Johnson, M. (2008). Can compassion be taught? *Nursing Standard, 23*(11), 19–21.

Kanter, J. (2007). Compassion fatigue and secondary traumatization: A second look. *Clinical Social Work Journal, 35,* 289–293. doi:10.1007/s10615-007-0125-1

Lee, J. J., & Miller, S. E. (2013). A self-care framework for social workers: Building a strong foundation for practice. Families in Society. *Journal of Contemporary Social Services, 94*(2), 96–103. doi:10.1606/1044-3894.4289

Lester, N. (2010). Compassion fatigue. *Mental Health Practice, 14*(2), 11. doi:10.7748/mhp.14.2.11.s14

Melvin, C. S. (2012). Professional compassion fatigue: What is the true cost of nurses caring for the dying? *Journal of Palliative Nursing, 18*(12), 606–611. doi:10.12968/ijpn.2012.18.12.606

National Association of Social Workers (NASW). (2017). *Code of ethics.* Silver Spring, MD: Author. Retrieved from https://www.socialworkers.org/About/Ethics/Code-of-Ethics/Code-of-Ethics-English

Newell, J. M., & Nelson-Gardell, D. (2014). A competency-based approach to teaching professional self-care: An ethical consideration for social work educators. *Journal of Social Work Education, 50,* 427–439. doi:10.1080/10437797.2014.917928

Potter, P., Deshields, T., Divanbeigi, J., Berger, J., Cipriano, D., Norris, L., & Olsen, S. (2010). Compassion fatigue and burnout: Prevalence among oncology nurses. *Clinical Journal of Oncology Nursing, 14*(5). E56–E62. doi:10.1188/10.CJON.E56-E62

Shapiro, S. L., Brown, K. W., & Biegel, G. M. (2007). Teaching self-care to caregivers: Effects of mindfulness based stress reduction on mental health of therapists in training. *Training and Education in Professional Psychology, 1,* 105–115. doi:10.1037/1931-3918.1.2.105

Slocum-Gori, S., Hemsworth, D., Chan, W. W., Carson, A., & Kazanjian, A. (2011). Understanding compassion satisfaction, compassion fatigue, and burnout: A survey of the hospice palliative care workforce. *Palliative Medicine, 27*(2), 172–178. doi:10.1177/0269216311431311

Building Relationships and Interprofessional Collaboration

CASE VIGNETTE

Josh is a senior BSW field placement student interning as a client advocate at a county-based resource center for individuals with disabilities. He participated in a care plan meeting to discuss his client, Scott, and review his treatment plans. Scott, 57 years old, had received a variety of services most of his life, as he was diagnosed with autism and learning disabilities at the age of 4. Each of Scott's service providers explained the issues they had encountered in providing him with care. His service providers from the respite program, his adult day-care center, and his in-home care provider shared their concerns. Scott was expressing frustration and confusion about his care plan, stating that he was hearing different things from different people. After attending the meeting, it became clear that everyone on the team was giving Scott the same information, but the differences in how they described the information made it challenging for Scott to understand. Josh met with Scott's social worker and debriefed her. After reviewing the information, the social worker suggested that each of the care providers brainstorm a potential alternative approach for Scott's care and regroup for another interprofessional meeting in 2 weeks' time. The meeting was attended by Scott's social worker, all of his care providers, and Josh. After sharing potential approaches, the interprofessional team decided to use the suggestion that Scott's in-home care provider had: Identify one member of the team as Scott's go-to person for clarification about his treatment plan. All questions that any member of the team received from Scott would be routed to that go-to person, ensuring that Scott would know who to go to with his questions and that he would not get differently worded answers from multiple people essentially saying the same thing. A second meeting was set for 4 weeks into the future to review the effectiveness of the new approach.

What relationship qualities need to be present between all members of Scott's care team for the interprofessional approach to be effective? What are some of the strengths of the work the team did in this case example? What are some of the potential pitfalls? Suppose one of the care team members becomes hostile or resistant to continued meetings. What would be Josh's next steps? What would be the potential downside to not having all of Scott's care providers at the meeting?

© Springer Publishing Company DOI: 10.1891/9780826175533.0005

LEARNING OBJECTIVES

The focus of this chapter is on the importance of engaging with individuals, families, groups, organizations, and communities (Competency 6). The chapter begins with an exploration of the importance of trust building and collaboration to the engagement at all levels within the helping relationship. This is followed by a deeper dive into interprofessional collaboration—building relationships within the professional realm, the roles and responsibilities of inter professional relationships, and challenges and benefits to working interprofessionally. By the end of this chapter, you will be able to

- Describe the role that engagement plays in the helping relationship and the change process.
- Understand the importance of collaboration and trust building across all levels of social work practice.
- Understand the importance of interprofessional collaboration.
- Use skills that will make you more effective in collaboration with clients, colleagues, and interprofessional teammates.
- Identify potential pitfalls that may arise in the interpersonal and interprofessional collaborative relationship.

THE HELPING RELATIONSHIP

When reading about the helping relationships, the term "client" is used to describe individual clients, as well as families, groups, communities, and organizations. The quality of the helping relationship between the social worker and the client is vital to the outcome that the client experiences. Indeed, this phenomenon has been consistently cited within the empirical research (Glicken, 2009; Norcross, 2011; Warren, 2001). Saleebey (2008) discusses the importance of nonjudgment, trust, care, and competence as necessary regardless of the issue that the client is focused on. According to Bisman (1994), the helping relationship requires a leap of faith: In essence, both you, as the social worker, and the client must believe that you have something to offer in regard to assisting on the presenting issue, and you must believe in the client'a capacities to engage in some sort of change behavior. Many scholars and clinicians believe that the actual helping relationship does not commence until all parties have established confidence in the others' competence and care. Glicken (2009) believes that the helping relationship is the trust that all parties put into the belief that their collaboration will lead to a positive outcome.

Authenticity has also been identified as a necessity for the helping relationship. Approaching the client with genuine concern, empathy, and warmth improves the relationship (Glicken, 2009). Empathy is the "act of perceiving, understanding, experiencing, and responding to the emotional state and ideas of another person" (Barker, 2014, p. 149). This means you, as a social worker, have to allow yourself to be genuinely concerned for the client, and respond with warmth to what the clients say. The importance of language is also discussed in Chapter 8. Given that most individuals seeking services have experienced trauma, loss, poverty, discrimination, and injustices, it is our responsibility as social workers to provide them with a helping relationship that has the highest potential for meaningful, positive outcomes. We must lay the foundation for clients to thrive in the helping relationship by using the skills of non-judgmental care, competence, and empathy. The social work practice elaboration and empathy practice skills also contribute significantly to the development of a positive helping relationship.

ELABORATION SKILLS

Elaboration skills are microintervention techniques that encourage clients to tell their stories in detail. These techniques can be used with individual, family, small group, organizational, and community client systems. To understand a client's situation and perspective, we need to have the client's story told in detail. The power of the story lies in the specifics. Most people tend to avoid specifics and begin discussing their situation in very general terms. The social worker's job is to help the client tell a detailed story rich in facts and feelings. There are seven elaboration skills: using open-ended questions, using minimal prompts, seeking concreteness, summarizing, containment, exploring silences, and reframing.

Using Open-Ended Questions

There are basically two types of questions: those with predefined responses and those without predefined responses. The former are usually referred to as closed-ended questions. They do not encourage a detailed and elaborate response, and generally should be avoided. An example of a closed-ended question is, "Do you get along well with the other kids at school?" If the client responds at all, the answer will be yes or no. This is the only answer called for. Not much information is obtained from this type of question.

Alternatively, one can ask open-ended questions that elicit more information from the client. For example, the social worker could ask, "How do you get along with the other kids at school?" This cannot be answered with just a yes or no response. The client has to formulate a more detailed or elaborate response to answer the question. Although the questions are similar, the open-ended one encourages elaboration, whereas the closed-ended one does not.

Limit your use of closed-ended questions. If a question is warranted, ask an open-ended one.

Using Minimal Prompts

As the term implies, minimal prompts are brief nonverbal or verbal indications of encouragement. Nonverbal minimal prompts include "nodding the head, using facial expressions, or employing gestures that convey receptivity, interest, and commitment to understanding" (Hepworth, Rooney, Rooney, & Strom-Gottfried, 2017). These nonverbal prompts can be very effective in encouraging elaboration. They communicate in an attentive and nonintrusive way that you would like the client to tell you more and that you are interested in hearing his or her story.

Verbal minimal prompts are brief utterances such as "Mm-mmm" or "Ah-ha" or other short phrases such as "Tell me more" or "I see." As with the nonverbal prompts, the verbal ones encourage the client to go on without interrupting or asking a series of questions.

Another type of minimal prompt is an **accent response,** in which the worker repeats a client's word or short phrase in the form of a question. The word or phrase selected should be the core component of the client's message. For example, if the client says, "I just hate all the kids at school," the social worker might say, "Hate?" or "The kids?" to prompt the client to give more information about the client's feelings about the kids at school. Accent responses are easy to use, do not interrupt the flow of communication, and are very effective in getting clients to explore their feelings and concerns in depth.

Seeking Concreteness

As noted earlier, clients tend to introduce their concerns and describe their experiences in vague, general terms. Beginning social workers often do not probe for specifics and may allow clients to keep the conversation at a general level. Hepworth et al. (2017) point out that communicating one's feelings and experiences requires specificity. They call the process of helping clients to respond in specific terms "seeking concreteness"; Shulman (2009) refers to it as moving from the general to the specific.

Often clients begin their stories in general terms because they have never put their feelings and experiences into words. They need help in exploring their feelings and experiences. Asking for specifics helps clients articulate their stories. Thus, seeking concreteness not only deepens your understanding of clients' stories, but also helps clients understand and articulate their feelings and experiences.

Seeking concreteness is easy to do. The key is to recognize and respond to vague and overly general comments. For example, a community member might say, "The neighborhood is falling apart. It is just not the same anymore." This is a fairly vague statement. At this point, the social worker really does not know what is causing the frustration. The worker could seek more concrete information by asking an open-ended follow-up question, such as "How has it changed?" or "What do you mean by falling apart?" Both responses invite the client to elaborate on his or her concerns.

Asking for specific information deepens the worker's and client's understanding of the topic. The technique of seeking concreteness has the added benefit of contributing to the natural flow of the conversation. It helps the worker stay on the topic introduced by the client. Seeking clarification helps the worker avoid jumping from topic to topic, a common mistake made by beginning social workers. It also communicates to the client interest in hearing his or her story.

Summarizing

Summarizing is a basic interviewing skill that is often used to highlight key points in a conversation with a client. When used this way, summarizing can help the client and the worker make the transition to a different topic. Summarizing, however, can also be used as an elaboration technique. This entails making connections between relevant aspects of a client's story. Summarizing can help clients explore in depth feelings and experiences that they might not recognize as being connected. This can be a powerful tool in helping them gain insight and understanding.

Summarizing is a more difficult skill to use than the other elaborating skills discussed earlier. It is a filtering and feedback process. It requires the ability to identify the key components of the story, pull them together, and repeat them back to the client in a combination statement–question form. The statement–question form prevents the social worker from taking the position of knowing or presuming to know that the different points are connected for the client. Typically, a summary statement is concluded with a question to see if the worker's perception or summary is consistent with the client's view of the situation.

Using Containment

Shulman (2009) defines containment as the skill of not acting. Many beginning social workers, in their desire to be helpful, rush in with solutions before the client has told his or her story. Containment is the ability to hold back on this impulse. It also is an important skill for those who have a tendency to finish a client's sentences or to focus on identified outcomes very early in the helping process.

Exploring Silences

This skill involves attempting to explore the meaning of the silence. It is hard to understand the meaning of silences. The client might be processing a thought, struggling with powerful emotions, feeling bored, or any number of things. Beginning social workers are often uncomfortable with silence and rush in to fill it up. Doing so ensures that the meaning of the silence will be lost as the worker moves on to something else. The social worker needs to actively explore the silence. A clue to its meaning is the worker's own feelings (Shulman, 2009). Understanding one's own feelings at a particular moment helps one to make an educated guess about the meaning of the client's silence and actively explore the meaning of the silence.

The first strategy for dealing with silence is containment. Give the client some time, and stay with the silence. A simple probing question, such as "You are quiet right now. What's going on?", is often sufficient to get the client to open up. You have acknowledged the silence and encouraged the client to elaborate. If your feelings suggest that the client is feeling (*hurt*), then you could ask an open-ended question, such as "Are you struggling with the (*hurt*) you feel?" The client needs to be encouraged to let the worker know if the guess is wrong. Even if the worker is off base, there is little harm done. The client can correct the misperception. Either way, the silence has been acknowledged and its meaning explored. Rather than feeling uncomfortable during periods of silence, view them as opportunities to better understand your client and his or her story.

Reframing

Reframing is a technique that is used often in family therapy. It is sometimes referred to as relabeling. Reframing is the process of giving a positive interpretation to what the client sees as a negative or concern. It is reframing a negative into a positive. In strengths-based social work, this is an important technique. It provides the worker with a way to highlight positives and help clients view their concerns from a different, more positive perspective. It also helps with the identification of strengths and coping abilities. Reframing is an elaboration skill, in that it invites clients to explore their stories from a different perspective. For example, a mother might say that she is a bad parent because her daughter was suspended from school. A social worker might reframe this negative comment by pointing out how well she had done in raising her other children and noting that her daughter up to this point has done well in school and that they have a strong mother–daughter relationship.

EMPATHY SKILLS

Conveying understanding and empathy are critical to the development of trust and a positive helping relationship. The skilled use of empathy in your interactions with your clients will enable you to help your clients engage in the change process. The key empathy skills are focused listening, reflective empathy, and additive empathy.

Focused Listening

Focused listening (Shulman, 2009) or active listening (Chang, Decker, & Scott, 2018) is the process of concentrating on a specific part of the client's message. The worker tries to identify the primary themes in the client's story and be sensitive to clues the client may give regarding the underlying feeling content of the message. The worker also tries to understand what the message means to the client (Chang et al., 2018). What is the client really saying, and what meaning does it have for the client?

Focused listening requires the social worker to tune into the meaning behind the client's words. This involves attending to the client's words, nonverbal communication, and affect as well as what is not being said. Listening and understanding the client's message is the first component of empathy. The second component is communicating back to the client your understanding.

Reflective Empathy

Conveying empathy and understanding is vital in developing a helping relationship. Clients need to feel understood. Those who do not feel are unlikely to share personal thoughts and feelings. Why risk vulnerability with someone who does not understand you? Disadvantaged and oppressed clients' experiences of discrimination, abuse, or exploitation have left many feeling profoundly misunderstood (Cournoyer, 2017). The ability to respond empathetically is a critical social work practice skill, particularly when one has to overcome mistrust and reluctance.

In its simplest form, empathic responding is "reflecting" back to clients their message. At this level, the empathic response accurately captures the factual content and feelings expressed by the client. The response communicates an equivalent message. Reflective empathy is more effective if you paraphrase the client's words rather than just "parrot back" the same words.

The use of empathetic responding is vital to the development of trust and the building of a strong helping relationship. Respond empathetically whenever your client is dealing with or expressing affective content. If there is an emotional component in the message, either on the surface or below it, an empathic response is needed. The power of the relationship lies in helping clients deal with and manage their feelings. Understanding the facts is important, but understanding the feelings is essential. Doing so will communicate that you are listening, that you care about the client, and that you understand or, at the very least, are trying to understand.

Responding to the affective component is beneficial even if you have incorrectly described the client's feelings or their intensity. An incorrect empathetic response gives clients an opportunity to clarify their feelings.

Additive Empathy

This level of empathetic responding occurs when the social worker accurately identifies implicit underlying feelings. The social worker not only responds to the surface and underlying feelings, but that response also connects the message to other themes of feelings expressed by the client. The use of additive empathy communicates a deeper level of understanding than the more basic reflective empathy. Both require the social worker to "risk" responding to the affective component of the client's message. Many beginning social workers shy away from dealing with clients' feelings directly, because it is easier to stick to the facts and ignore the feelings. If one wants to build trust, however, responding to the feeling content is necessary.

TRUST BUILDING

Trust, as found in the supervisory relationship, is an important aspect of the helping relationship. Establishing trust between the social worker and the client has an impact on the collaborative decision-making process, improves communication, and increases the likelihood that the client will follow through with the plan developed with the social worker (Gamble, 2006). Because of the importance of trust, many theories have been proposed regarding how to develop trust within the working relationship. Although some conceptualize the trust development as an individual predisposition (one's ability to trust others) or an individual characteristic (one is either trustworthy or not), others have identified specific characteristics that exist within the helping relationship.

> **Field Reflection Questions**
>
> Consider your current field placement. How do you begin to lay the foundation for trust with your clients?
>
> Can you think of a time when you used empathetic listening skills? How do you convey that you perceived and understood the client's experience? How did you respond?

As Behnia (2008) points out, life would be literally unbearable if we did not have the ability to trust. We, as humans, would be frozen by fear and uncertainty. For example, we would be unable to drive to work each day if we did not trust that the other drivers on the road would obey traffic laws—stop at red lights, stop at stop signs, and so forth. Without trust, we would lose all relationships because of paranoia and suspicion. We would be unable to obtain services because of our inability to trust the competence of our care providers. The same idea applies to the social work care provider as well.

Although an extensive literature focuses on trust, Behnia (2008) used multiple sources to land on the definition that trust is the ability and will to allow oneself to be vulnerable with others because of one's belief in other individuals' intentions and competence. This means that individuals have confidence that others will behave in a way that is nonharmful or even potentially beneficial (Levin, Whitener, & Cross, 2006).

At the start of the helping relationship, the only trust that exists is on a surface level. The client may trust the approach more than the individual social worker. He or she may be willing to try to work with the social worker because of the worker's training or expertise or reputation (Behnia, 2008). The client enters into the helping relationship with the expectation that the social worker's intentions are positive. However, once the helping relationship is initiated, the client begins to define the social worker's trustworthiness and competence. The client does this by collecting data from the client–social worker interactions. Behnia (2008) believes that this information is categorized into three realms: self-concept, perceived self, and definition of the professional.

The client's self-concept refers to his or her own feelings and beliefs about his or her own attributes. This matters, because the client's own beliefs about his or her sense of self will impact how he or she perceives interactions with others. The perceived self is how the client thinks others perceive, or think of, him or her. It is vital that the client develops a positive perceived self with the social worker. If the client thinks that the social worker views him or her negatively, the client will be unwilling to be vulnerable and move forward in the helping relationship. A client's imagined perception could conjure feelings of pride, shame, anger, or a whole host of other reactions (Rosenberg, 1979). This also plays a role in stereotypes for nondominant groups. If a client is a member of a nondominant group that has experienced discrimination, he or she may be hesitant to disclose some thoughts, feelings, and actions, out of concern that this may potentially reinforce the stereotypical perceptions that exist about the group to which the client belongs. This phenomenon is referred to as stereotype threat (Steele & Aronson, 1995).

Clients use a host of tactics to obtain information to arrive at their definition of the social worker. Especially at the beginning of the helping relationship, the client is gathering information about the social worker's competence (Behnia, 2008). Questions going through the client's head can include the following: Does the social worker know what he or she is doing? Does he or she know enough about my specific issue? Does he or she actually care? What does he or she think of me? As a social worker, you must recognize that the client is intensely attuned to your verbal and nonverbal cues in an effort to answer all of the questions listed earlier, and more. An example would be a social worker breaking eye contact or attempting to change the subject when a client attempts to share a trauma experience. With these cues, the client may come to the conclusion that the social worker is unable to handle the topic emotionally, or lacks the expertise to help him or her work through his or her trauma (Behnia, 2008).

Clients may ask direct questions about your training and/or intentions; they may make assumptions on the basis of your office presentation; they may test your knowledge about a multitude of topics, including a specific diagnosis to your understanding of oppression and racism; and they may ask you personal questions to see if you may have had personal experience with the topic they want to discuss. Clients may also try to gather information to inform their perception of you as a worthwhile individual. Behnia (2008) shares that this is often done by disclosing potentially jarring information to be able to observe the social worker's reaction. If you react negatively, showing signs of disgust, disapproval, or discomfort, the client may perceive you as judgmental and unsafe.

Reading about these client tactics may have you feeling anxious, but there are strategies you can use to help build trust within the helping relationship. First, you must realize that the client is engaging in this fact-finding mission for his or her own protection: It is not an insult to you as a human being or a professional. Understand where the client is coming from—voluntary or mandated; no matter which applies, the client must go through the steps he or she needs to establish an understanding of your intentions and abilities to move forward to a collaborative working relationship. As discussed in further detail in Chapter 8, the helping relationship occurs in a social context that is shaped by factors such as social locations, social stratification, setting, and identities of all parties involved. Race, ethnicity, sexual orientation, class, age, disability status, religion, and more massively impact the lived experiences of individuals, and their access to resources. Previous experiences of discrimination at the hands of agencies and service providers may make clients much more suspicious of the helping professional. Because agencies have exploited their power to assist in the domination of members of certain groups, this suspicion is not unwarranted (Falvo, 2004).

Now that you know some of strategies that clients use, you may be able to identify them when they occur, and can provide answers that contribute to their search for definition of you as a helping professional. Behnia (2008) notes that other ways to convey care and competence include the following:

- Sit beside the client instead of behind a desk.

- Do not rush the session or meeting. Take the time necessary.

- Use a soft tone; speak respectfully.

- Remember information the client provides you (e.g., names, events). Take notes and review them prior to meeting.

- Express an interest in what is going on.

- Be helpful when appropriate.

- Be explicit about your motivations in engaging in the work with the client.

- Use personal disclosure to an appropriate extent.

Using personal disclosure can be powerful, but must be done appropriately. An example provided by Basescu (as cited in Behnia, 2008, p. 1437) was that when a client disclosed her anxiety about how long she had been in therapy, the professional disclosed that he himself was in therapy for 8 years. In doing so, the professional alleviated the client's concerns that the helping professional might be judging her while not disclosing information that redirected attention to his own personal experiences. Self-disclosure is best left for after the helping relationship is established, so clients are not concerned that you are rushing them to disclose before they are ready to do so. In addition, you must be mindful of cultural beliefs around self-disclosure, as using self-disclosure with a client who is not culturally accustomed to it may cause concern for the client. Always ensure that you are using self-disclosure for the benefit of the clients, and not to elicit sympathy or rush the clients into a deeper level of intimacy than they are ready for (Behnia, 2008).

Remember that relationships are built over time. A key factor in developing a strong helping relationship is having shared experiences. In a professional relationship, this occurs by undertaking the activities or tasks of the helping process, such as identifying a client's strengths and concerns and developing goals and a plan of action. Engaging in these purposeful activities helps build trust. Trust, in turn, helps strengthen the interpersonal connection or worker–client bond, which then strengthens the client's motivation to engage in the structural activities.

A key to developing a strong positive collaborative relationship is establishing some level of trust. The client must be able to trust the social worker. Relationships cannot be built in the absence of trust. A certain degree of trust must be established between the client and the social worker for the client to engage in a collaborative helping process.

Trust is essential for relationships to develop and grow between social workers and their clients. To build a strong collaborative relationship, the social worker must reduce the client's fear, suspicion, and mistrust at the same time as the worker promotes feelings of acceptance, support, and affirmation.

Building trust with reluctant clients is an interactional process. Trust cannot be built in the absence of interpersonal interactions between the client and the social worker. Instead, it is built upon a sequence of trusting and trustworthy interactions. Your client must act in a trusting manner by taking some level of risk, and you as the social worker must respond with trustworthy actions. Building a positive helping relationship is a process. Trust is earned by your behavior and trustworthy responses; it is not given freely, especially if your clients have experienced oppression, discrimination, poverty, abuse, and/or trauma in their lives.

COLLABORATION

Collaboration must occur at all levels of social work practice. At a micro level, the client and the social worker enter into a collaborative working relationship once trust has been established to work toward goals the client has established with the assistance of the social worker. At the mezzo level, social workers may collaborate to address a myriad of potential issues: program effectiveness, uncoordinated social services programming, duplicative services, referral barriers, lack of sufficient opportunity to empower clients, expansion of service delivery, service and program advertising, service delivery development, and barriers to shared decision making (Graham & Barter, 1999). At the macro level, collaboration is at the heart of community organizing, coalition building, advocacy, citizen participation, and resource mobilization.

Collaboration is crucial within all levels of intervention in the field of social work, as collective problem solving, pooling resources, and developing efficient and cost-effective service delivery become necessary as funding streams shrink and funders begin to require evidence of collaborative relationships (Schaefer, 2014). As Graham and Barter (1999) explain, this provides opportunities to improve based on the collective experience—to promote a better understanding of clients' needs, improve service delivery, reduce professional burnout, share resources, and empower clients and stakeholders.

"The collaborative social worker is less protective of territorial expertise," and views himself or herself as a consultant, with an emphasis on respecting clients' and team members' rights to fully participate in decisions that impact them (Graham & Barter, 1999, p. 8). Although the collaborative process has the goal of joint decision making for positive change, parties involved will be coming to the collaborative relationship with varying degrees of power. This lack of a shared footing impacts the collaborative relationship—within collaboration there will inevitability be conflict (e.g., opposing viewpoints, conflicting motivations). Compromise and a continued focus on the desired outcomes are essential to an effective collaboration.

INTERPROFESSIONAL COLLABORATION

As touched upon earlier, interprofessional collaboration should be varied and diverse (Kvarnström, 2008). Collaborative care requires providers from different disciplines to work together to provide services to clients in an effective and caring way (Craven & Bland, 2013). Ambrose-Miller and Ashcroft (2016) discuss the factors that facilitate and enhance interprofessional collaborative practice:

- Adopting values and ethics for interprofessional practice
- Understanding interprofessional roles and responsibilities
- Enhancing interprofessional communication
- Facilitating teams and teamwork
- Understanding organizational structure
- Understanding professional identity
- Knowing scope of practice
- Understanding and addressing problematic power differentials

As social workers, it may be easiest to conceptualize interprofessional collaboration through systems theory (Crawford, 2011). Imagine if you were asked to make a list of all the people you interact with in your daily life. It would be extensive, and you could potentially categorize all of the individuals on the list into different groups. You may even be able to map the groups, as a way to visualize the connections and interrelationships between them all. That is essentially how systems theory helps us to describe interprofessional collaboration.

How different systems operate and how open they are to information, resources, and energy crossing into other systems depend on a multitude of conditions: legal obligations, funding obligations, the system's attitude toward collaboration, and the system's own self-interest (Crawford, 2011). The key benefit of open systems is that they can be flexible and easily adapt to needs; however, open systems can also impede collaboration if they do not have an understanding of their own boundaries and the boundaries of their partners (Crawford, 2011).

Whittington's (2003) two-stage model of collaboration explains interrelationships between collaborative systems. In the first stage, you identify the main systems that are participating in the collaborative process. In the second stage, you describe the relationship and interchanges between all the systems in the process. This nonhierarchical model helps to clearly define the boundaries of each system in the collaborative process.

Field Reflection Questions

Consider your current field placement. How might Whittington's (2003) two-stage model be applied to your own experience? What examples from field can you identify?

Using the example given earlier, who were the key participants? What were the interactions that took place?

BUILDING PROFESSIONAL RELATIONSHIPS

Understanding your own professional identity is vital to your effective collaboration with other professionals (Ambrose-Miller & Ashcroft, 2016). To have this understanding, you must first understand what it means to be a professional in the field of social work. Is it being recognized as part of the field, perhaps by the licensure that is bestowed on you through your state board? Is it adherence to the National Association of Social Workers' (NASW's) *Code of Ethics*? Is it something else entirely? Once you have identified what the key elements of professional social work are, you can then apply those standards to your own practice as a social worker (Crawford, 2011). You will develop your professional identity through the interactions you have within your field placement, your educational experiences, and your other environments. Crawford (2011) points out that professional identity can also be tied to professional contributions, achieved status, uniqueness, power and authority, and self-interest.

Your professional identity comes into play in interprofessional collaboration because many of the aspects of professionalism are required to be an effective member of an interprofessional collaborative team. This can include a commitment to service recipients, explicit values, agreed-upon standards, and the *Code of Ethics*; recognition of the specific disciplinary contribution; and more (Crawford, 2011). One could also argue that it is more challenging to resist protectiveness of territorial expertise if social workers are not confident in their professional identity. This lack of confidence would lead to social workers trying to "prove themselves" to other members of the collaborative process.

Also, the need for all interprofessional collaborators to recognize the benefits of collaborating is vital. Crawford (2011) highlights the following benefits of collaboration: knowledge of professional roles; trust and mutual respect; skillful communication; ability to recognize which member of the team is best suited to meet the needs of the client; and, most importantly, having a shared set of values that includes beliefs, ideas, and assumptions about the service recipients, the goals, and the approach. Clearly, this can be a challenge given that different professions adhere to different professional values.

Field Reflection Questions

Reflect on yourself in your field placement.

What does it mean to you to be a professional? Do you consider yourself to be a professional? Why or why not?

Can you give examples from your field placement that explain your answer? How might this inform your professional identity?

Even though this is the case, Hammick, Freeth, Copperman, and Goodsman (2009) have identified some core values for interprofessional collaboration. These include the following:

● Respect for every member of the collaborative team

● Confidence in what you know and what you do not know, and in what others know

● A willingness to engage with others, rather than taking a detached view of proceedings

● A caring disposition toward your colleagues

● An approachable attitude

● A willingness to share what you know as a means to the best possible outcome for the user of your service (p. 23)

Crawford (2011) also identified the following skills as necessary for interprofessional collaboration: interpersonal skills such as negotiating, listening, articulating, dealing with conflict, and empathy; person-centered practice skills; the ability to demonstrate trust and respect; and personal skills that include self-awareness, reflexivity, confidence in practice, emotional awareness, problem-solving skills, critical thinking skills, and a sense of responsibility.

ROLES AND RESPONSIBILITIES

Having an awareness of one's own role, and the role of others, within the interprofessional collaboration has been noted as being important to the effectiveness of the process. Social workers should be able to clearly and accurately describe their own role and the roles of others in the collaborative process. You should be able to recognize and respect that there are a myriad of roles, responsibilities, and competencies across disciplines. You must consider the impact that performing your role may have on other professionals within the interprofessional group, and recognize that other professions may view the world differently. Although this task might seem easy, understanding one's own and other professionals' roles and responsibilities can be complicated—boundaries between professional roles and responsibilities can become blurred, leading to potential confusion about which professional is responsible for what and when.

Seabury, Seabury, and Garvin (2011) identified three steps that social workers often use to clarify roles within practice, and they can be applied to interprofessional collaboration as well: explicating various expectations, comparing and identifying discrepancies in expectations, and negotiating agreements on expectations. The first step requires collaborators to identify what they expect from each member of the interprofessional team, including their own responsibilities. In the second step, collaborators compare and examine the different expectations. Conflict and ambiguity that exist are identified. Finally, collaborators come to an agreement on the conflicting perspectives and reinforce areas of agreement. As stated earlier, conflict is to be expected in collaboration, and, as such, differences should be viewed as constructive and informative. Done early in the process, role clarification saves time, resources, and potential emotional stress.

As a social worker, you will have multiple accountabilities and responsibilities. You are accountable to the clients you work with, to your licensure board, to the NASW's *Code of Ethics*, to your employer, to your colleagues, and to the other professionals with whom you work with. Responsibility and accountability are inextricably linked to trust, discussed earlier in the chapter, and they also require integrity, self-awareness, and a clear sense of responsibility. Interprofessional collaboration can make the lines of accountability difficult to distinguish, and it is your responsibility to make clear your multiple accountability levels to those team members with whom you are collaborating.

Field Reflection Questions

What can you achieve in your field placement by working across systems? Which systems can you identify as interconnecting with your field agency?

From your experience in field, how does the system you are in and the systems you work across impact service delivery to clients?

WORKING ON A TEAM

Ambrose-Miller and Ashcroft (2016) discuss social workers' perspectives on interprofessional collaboration, including what you can expect while working in a team environment. Some of the perspectives reported include the following:

- Get confortable in a leadership capacity.

- Attract team members who are seeking out collaboration.

- Be prepared to nurture the collaborative process.

- Advocate for an organizational culture that favors collaboration over time saving.

- Be prepared to advocate for social work's contribution to the team.

- Embrace the flexibility of your role as a social worker as a strength.

- Know that your role as client advocate can create tension within the collaborative team.

Social workers have identified leadership qualities as important, because those qualities help the social worker to collaborate and speak up within the team environment. They also help to reinforce collaborative ideas. In addition, it has been suggested that individuals who gravitate toward collaboration and egalitarian work environments thrive in the interprofessional process. As such, identifying potential team members who have the skills and mindset for that process and encouraging them to join in is useful. Those interviewed by Ambrose-Miller and Ashcroft (2016) explained that the collaborative process requires nurturance in the form of intentional planning and carving out time for the process. This is easier to do when the overall organization also supports and values interprofessional collaboration. The attitudes of both leadership and employees about interprofessional collaboration seem to greatly influence the nurturance, of lack thereof, of a collaborative culture. Because so many organizations are overly concerned about efficiencies, you may need to advocate for an intentional push toward collaborative models.

In some settings, your contribution as a social worker will be clear to all members of the collaborative team. In other settings, such as a health care setting, the social worker must use his or her expertise to ensure that a humanizing, broad perspective is being taken by the interprofessional team. This takes confidence, and its speaks to the necessity to have confidence in your role and competence, as discussed earlier in the chapter. Also identified as a strength is social workers' ability to be flexible in their role and fill a variety of service gaps when necessary. Finally, recognize that the social worker is, at times, the interprofessional team member who is filling the role as client advocate. This role can create tension between team members, as when all other members have a different, often more expedient, plan in mind.

Field Reflection Questions

How does professional supervision allow you to evaluate your own practice?

How does this process prepare you for interprofessional social work practice?

COLLABORATION CHALLENGES

Although there are many benefits to interprofessional collaboration, as discussed in detail in the "Beneifts" section, there are also potential challenges. Ambrose-Miller and Ashcroft (2016) reported that in-place decision-making procedures at times create a barrier to a more collaborative decision-making process within the interprofessional team. Typically, interprofessional team members call for a collaborative decision-making process; however, differences may arise across professions regarding the most appropriate decision-making process, especially for team members who often have the final call on decisions in their everyday work life.

In addition, because of ethical and legal mandates regarding confidentiality, fears around information sharing can be another potential barrier to interprofessional collaboration. Radford (2010) points out that the efficient sharing of information is vital to intervention and risk reduction, so a clear delineation of what information is truly confidential and what is appropriate to be shared with the interprofessional team is necessary if the team is to operate in the most beneficial way. O'Sullivan (2011) highlights the dire need for effective information-sharing strategies, describing how lack of communication between social services agencies has resulted in cases with tragic consequences for children and vulnerable adults. Clear protocols shared with the interprofessional team early in the process will allow for fewer delays as team members try to establish the confidentiality of specific, vital information.

Power imbalances within the interprofessional team can also create barriers (Crawford, 2011). Lymbery (2006, as cited in Crawford, 2011) identified three types of interprofessional rivalries that can be a result of power imbalances: professional identity and territory; relative status and power of professions; and different patterns of discretion and accountability between professions. This underlines the importance of a shared purpose, as well as an atmosphere of teamwork. Sharing differing opinions with the same goal looks very different than personal feuds or infighting. A constant focus on the goal of the interprofessional team—the outcome for the client—helps interprofessional collaborators refocus their energies within disagreements.

BENEFITS

Interprofessional collaboration allows professionals from different fields to come together, develop proficiency as a group, share information and knowledge, and see circumstances from a variety of perspectives. Research on the topic of interprofessional collaboration has found multiple benefits from this practice (Darlington & Feeney, 2008), including lower anxiety levels of team members, faster access to services for clients, and fewer instances of separation in child welfare cases.

In the health care area, research has shown that interprofessional collaboration results in improved client experiences, improved health outcomes, and reduction of costs (Vega & Bernard, 2016). This is because of a reduction in the number of potential errors that may occur when clients are switched to a different provider. The interprofessional collaboration approach supports the sharing of essential information with all team members, thereby reducing the risk of errors associated with transitions. In addition, interprofessional collaboration requires a client-centered approach, as discussed earlier. This requires a shift of all team members, including those in the health care setting, away from the physician-centered system, which has also been found to improve outcomes (Vega & Bernard, 2016). Finally, research indicates that clients and patients who receive interprofessional care are more satisfied and have better health outcomes, including a 30% reduction in emergency room visits. Healthcare professionals also report being more satisfied with interprofessional collaboration than traditional approaches—with more than 95% of professionals in one study stating that it was an improvement (Vega & Bernard, 2016).

Although interprofessional collaboration has been found to be an effective practice model in multiple settings (Darlington & Feeney, 2008; Vega & Bernard, 2016), it is also becoming an expectation for social services and medical providers—an expectation codified in policy or organization mandates in some cases. A shift toward interprofessional collaboration has been documented in the United States, the United Kingdom, other parts of Europe, and Australia (Darlington & Feeney, 2008). Perhaps this mandate is justified, as O'Sullivan (2011) points out that information sharing between agencies may provide social workers with the information they need to intervene and potentially avoid tragic outcomes for vulnerable individuals.

SUMMARY

This chapter explored the importance of collaboration and trust building across all levels of social work. The quality of the helping relationship between the social worker and the client is vital to the outcome that the client experiences. Nonjudgment, authenticity, trust, care, and competence are vital for the helping relationship to grow. In addition, belief that a positive outcome is possible through the collaborative effort is required for the helping relationship to have a chance of success. The process of trust building, including its necessity and skills that can be used to build trust, was also explored in this chapter.

Collaboration was explored at all levels of social work practice. It results in collective problem solving, pooling resources, developing efficient and cost-effective service delivery, promoting a better understanding of clients' needs, improving service delivery, reducing professional burnout, sharing resources, and empowering clients and stakeholders. The skills necessary for building interprofessional collaborative practice strategies were also discussed.

After a thorough review of the skill set that lends itself to effective interprofessional practice, benefits and challenges to collaboration across disciplines were examined.

CRITICAL THINKING QUESTIONS

Competency 6 focuses on the importance of engagement within social work practice. As a social worker, you are expected to understand that engagement is not a one-size-fits-all approach. You are also expected to understand that your own experiences and biases will impact your ability to engage with various groups. It is your responsibility to use supervision to appropriately address those biases that impede your ability to collaborate with individual clients, group clients, or members of other professions. In addition, you must remember that collaboration takes a balance of competence and confidence, with the understanding that all partners have something important to contribute to the collaborative working relationship. The following questions focus on engaging diversity in practice:

1. Earlier in the chapter, we discussed the trust-building process. How might the trust-building process for a mandated client differ from that for a voluntary client?

2. In thinking about interprofessional collaboration, how do the necessary skills discussed in this chapter also apply to the competency of demonstrating ethical and professional behavior?

3. Similar to engaging diversity and difference in practice, interprofessional collaboration, as well as collaboration with groups and organizations, involves humility, curiosity, and ongoing self-reflection. Can you identify a time when you found yourself making an assumption about a professional in another field (e.g., a doctor, a teacher)? In reflecting upon your experience working interprofessionally, how might these assumptions impact your ability to be a fully engaged member of an interprofessional team?

4. Earlier in the chapter, the trust-building process was described as a two-way street. The client must trust your intentions and competence as the helping professional, but you must also trust that the client has the capacity to make positive changes. Reflect on your experience in your field placement. Have you ever worked with a client for whom you were unsure of his or her capacity or desire to make positive changes? Or perhaps you were convinced otherwise? Identify how this may have impacted your practice with that client. Do you agree that, to be effective, both parties must trust that a positive outcome is possible?

COMPETENCY 6: ENGAGE WITH INDIVIDUALS, FAMILIES, GROUPS, ORGANIZATIONS, AND COMMUNITIES

Social workers understand that engagement is an ongoing component of the dynamic and interactive process of social work practice with, and on behalf or, diverse individuals, families, groups, organizations, and communities. They value the importance of human relationships. Social workers understand the theories of human behaviors and the social environment, and critically evaluate and apply this knowledge to facilitate engagement with clients and constituencies, including individuals, families, groups, organizations, and communities. They understand strategies to engage diverse clients and constituencies to advance practice effectiveness. Social workers understand how their personal experiences and affective reactions may impact their ability to effectively engage with diverse clients and constituencies. They value principles of relationship building and interprofessional collaboration to facilitate engagement with clients, constituencies, and other professionals as appropriate. Social workers:

- Apply knowledge of human behavior and the social environment, person-in-environment, and other multidisciplinary theoretical frameworks to engage clients and constituencies.

- Use empathy, reflection, and interpersonal skills to effectively engage diverse clients and constituencies.

CASE SUMMARY—"NOT SURE WE WILL EVER CLICK"

PRACTICE SETTING DESCRIPTION

My name is Brianna and I am a first-year MSW student completing an internship at a family services agency in a medium-sized city on the East Coast. The agency provides individual and family counseling services on a sliding fee scale. The agency also accepts mandated clients referred to fulfill counseling requirements, often tied to sentencing related to nonviolent felonies. I was assigned to work with R., who was sentenced to counseling after being charged with possession of illegal prescription medications.

IDENTIFYING DATA

R. is 16 years old and has been in legal trouble once before, related to marijuana possession. R. lives with his mother and two younger siblings. R. attends an alternative high school and was working part-time, but lost his employment because of missing from work after his arrest. The judge in R.'s case decided that R. might benefit from counseling because of his defiant attitude over the course of the proceedings. The judge believes that R. may have some anger issues and required counseling as a part of a deal to avoid jail time.

PRESENTING PROBLEM

R. is resistant to counseling and has shown little interest in forming a helping relationship. He has indicated that he does not think he needs to be there and will not benefit from the counseling. He has come in for three sessions and has spoken only about four sentences.

ASSESSMENT

Although R. has not shared much information, I do know a little about him from the records we received upon accepting him as a client. I know that R.'s mother is a single parent who is employed in two part-time jobs, he has two younger siblings age 8 and 6, and R. used a public defender for his trial. R.'s mother was supportive of R. receiving counseling.

Although R. is obviously extremely reluctant to actually share anything with me during his sessions, I have identified some obvious strengths. First, R.'s mother is supportive of R.'s receipt of counseling. Second, R. has mentioned wanting to fulfill the obligations of his probation, including continuing with the counseling, so he can "move on with his life." When pressed, he shared he wants to complete high school and obtain training to become an auto mechanic because it pays well, and he believes he would be able to help out his family with that decent income.

CASE PROCESS SUMMARY

I will admit that I am feeling frustrated with the lack of progress that we have made so far. Although three sessions over 3 weeks is not a significant amount of time, I am much more used to working with voluntary clients. So, this slow speed is challenging. My typical conversation starters result in one-word answers from R. I know that R. is resistant to the idea of counseling in general, but I also have to wonder whether the fact that I am a fairly young White woman and he is a teenage Latino male may be impacting his ability to see me as someone capable of helping him in any way. I wonder whether I should transfer R. to one of the two male social workers who work in the agency, even though there would be a bit of a wait. I am just not sure if we will ever "click."

Brianna, MSW student intern

DISCUSSION QUESTIONS

- If you were Brianna's supervisor, what questions might you ask Brianna to gauge how she is attempting to build trust with R.?
- If R. was your client, how would you attempt to engage him beyond simply asking him questions? What are some of the potential pitfalls of your suggested approaches?
- Thinking back to what you read in this chapter, why might Brianna believe that referral to another social worker makes the most sense in this case? Do you believe it is solely because of the pair's inability to "click," or might there be some other potential barrier for Brianna?
- Imagine that Brianna needed to build an interprofessional team to ensure R.'s successful completion of his sentence. Who should Brianna consult to be a part of that interprofessional team? How might this team be able to help R. be successful?

ELECTRONIC COMPETENCY RESOURCES

WEBSITE LINKS

Interprofessional Collaboration: A Social Work Ethic—Shelley Cohen Konrad
www.slideshare.net/CEIPE/social-work-leadership-in-ethics

Communication Skills in the Client–Social Worker Relationship—Rebecca Davis
www.youtube.com/watch?v=mJoZG7jfolk

VIDEO LINK

Social Work and Models of Interprofessional Education—Center for Health Administration Studies, University of Chicago
www.youtube.com/watch?v=HDvd9_sgdOg

REFERENCES

Ambrose-Miller, W., & Ashcroft, R. (2016). Challenges faced by social workers as members of interprofessional collaborative health care teams. *Health and Social Work, 41*(2), 101–109. doi:10.1093/hsw/hlw006

Barker, R. L. (2014). *The social work dictionary* (6th ed.). Washington, DC: NASW Press.

Behnia, B. (2008). Trust development: A discussion of three approaches and a proposed alternative. *British Journal of Social Work, 38,* 1425–1441. doi:10.1093/bjsw/bcm053

Bisman, C. D. (1994). *Social work practices: Cases and principles.* Pacific Grove, CA: Brooks/Cole.

Chang, V. N., Decker, C. L., & Scott, S. T. (2018). *Developing helping skills: A step-by-step approach to competency* (3rd ed.). Belmont, CA: Cengage.

Cournoyer, B. R. (2017). *The social work skills workbook* (8th ed.). Belmont, CA: Cengage.

Craven, M. A., & Bland, R. (2013). Depression in primary care: Current and future challenges. *Canadian Journal of Psychiatry, 58,* 442–448. doi:10.1177/070674371305800802

Crawford, K. (2012). *Interprofessional collaboration in social work practice.* Thousand Oaks, CA: Sage.

Darlington, Y., & Feeney, J. A. (2008). Collaboration between mental health and child protection services: Professionals' perceptions of best practice. *Children and Youth Services Review, 30,* 187–198. doi:10.1016/j.childyouth.2007.09.005

Falvo, D. R. (2004). *Effective patient education: A guide to increased compliance* (3rd ed.), Boston, MA: Jones & Bartlett Publishing.

Gamble, V. N. (2006). Trust, medical care, and racial and ethnic minorities. In D. Satcher & J. Rubens (Eds.), *Multicultural medicine and health disparities* (pp. 437-448). New York, NY: McGraw-Hill.

Glicken, M. D. (2009). *Evidence-based practice with emotionally troubled children and adolescents.* San Diego, CA: Academies Press.

Graham, J., & Barter, K. (1999). Collaboration: A social work practice method. *Families in Society: Journal of Contemporary Human Services, 80,* 6–13. doi:10.1606/1044-3894.634

Hammick, M., Freeth, D. S., Copperman, J., & Goodsman, D. (2009). *Being interprofessional.* Cambridge, UK: Polity Press.

Hepworth, D. H., Rooney, R. H., Rooney, G. D., & Strom-Gottfried, K. (2017). *Direct social work practice: Theory and skills* (10th ed.). Boston, MA: Cengage.

Kvarnström, S. (2008). Difficulties in collaboration: A critical incident study of interprofessional healthcare teamwork. *Journal of Interprofessional Care, 222,* 191–203. doi:10.1080/13561820701760600

Levin, D. Z., Whitener, E. M., & Cross, R. (2006). Received trustworthiness of knowledge sources: The moderating impact of relationship length. *Journal of Applied Psychology, 91*(5), 1163–1171. doi:10.1037/0021-9010.91.5.1163

Lymbery, M. (2006). United we stand? Partnership working in health and social care and the role of social work in services for older people. *British Journal of Social Work, 36*(7), 1119-1134.

Norcross, J. C. (Ed.). (2011). *Psychotherapy relationships that work: Evidence based responsiveness* (2nd ed.). New York, NY: Oxford University Press.

O'Sullivan, T. (2011). *Decision making in social work* (2nd ed.). Basingstoke, UK: Palgrave Macmillan.

Radford, J. (2010). Serious case review under chapter VIII. Working together to safeguard children in respect of the death of a child: Case number 14. Retrieved from https://cscb-new.co.uk/downloads/Serious%20Case%20Reviews%20-%20exec.%20summaries/SCR_Archive/Birmingham%20SCR%20-%20BSCB200892%20(2010).pdf

Rosenberg, M. (1979). *Conceiving the self.* New York, NY: Basic Books Publishing.

Saleebey, D. (2008). The strengths perspective: Putting possibility and hope to work in our practice. In K. M. Sowers & C. N. Dulmus (Eds.), *Comprehensive handbook of social work and social welfare* (pp. 123–142). Hoboken, NJ: John Wiley & Sons.

Schaefer, C. (2014). Human services groups collaborate to survive. *The Non-profit Times.* Retrieved from http://www.thenonprofittimes.com/news-articles/human-services-groups-collaborate-to-survive/

Seabury, B. A., Seabury, B. H., & Garvin, C. D. (2011). *Foundations of interpersonal practice in social work: Promoting competence in generalist practice* (3rd ed.). Los Angeles, CA: Sage.

Shulman, L. (2009). *The skills of helping individuals, families, groups and organizations* (6th ed.). Belmont, CA: Cengage.

Steele, C. M., & Aronson, J. (1995). Stereotype threat and the intellectual test performance of African Americans. *Journal of Personality and Social Psychology, 69*(5), 797–811. doi:10.1037/0022-3514.69.5.797

Vega, C. P., & Bernard, A. (2016). Interprofessional collaboration to improve health care: An introduction. *Medscape Education Clinical Briefs.* Retrieved from https://www.medscape.org/viewarticle/857823

Warren, C. S. (2001). Book review: Negotiating the therapeutic alliance: A relational treatment guide. *Psychotherapy Research, 11*(3), 357–359. doi:10.1093/ptr/11.3.357

Whittington, C. (2003). Collaboration and partnership in context. In J. Weinstein, C. Whittington, & T. Leiba (Eds.), *Collaboration in social work practice* (pp. 13–38). London, UK: Jessica Kingsley Publishing.

Demonstrating Professional Behavior in Oral, Written, and Electronic Communications

CASE VIGNETTE

Jocelyn is completing her BSW field experience as a case manager with a large human services organization. She meets with clients to establish goals and then works with the clients to achieve these goals. Oftentimes, she is helping her clients with housing, health care, and social and vocational goals. Much of Jocelyn's time is spent communicating with other professionals over the phone, in person, or electronically. She often collaborates with other professionals and participates in interdisciplinary team meetings for many of her clients. Jocelyn needs to follow up with other professionals who are also working with her clients to monitor progress toward goals. She often has to request information and documentation from other providers to include in her records.

People have always told Jocelyn that she is a very social and outgoing person. Jocelyn is excited about all of the communication she will have with other service providers because she loves to talk to people. She thinks that this is going to be easy because she is so social. As Jocelyn meets new service providers with whom she needs to collaborate, she adds them to her Facebook account so that they can chat with each other over Messenger. Within a couple of weeks, Jocelyn has added more than 20 service providers on her personal Facebook page. Despite now using her personal Facebook to connect with other professionals, Jocelyn continues to post about her personal social life, including nights out with friends, stories about how stressed she is with school, and how she feels about her coworkers at her field site.

Is Jocelyn communicating like a professional?

What, if any, ethical concerns arise from Jocelyn's current communications?

LEARNING OBJECTIVES

In this chapter, we examine what professional social work behavior in communication looks like as it relates to Competency 1: Demonstrate Ethical and Professional Behavior. This competency requires that social workers "demonstrate professional demeanor in behavior; appearance; and oral, written, and electronic communication" (Council on Social Work Education [CSWE], 2015, p. 2). Regarding professional electronic communication, we also explore "emerging forms of technology and the ethical use of technology in social work practice" (CSWE, 2015, p. 1).

By the end of this chapter, you will be able to

- Describe professional oral, written, and electronic communications.
- Distinguish between professional and casual (informal) communications.
- Describe elements of an effective case note.
- Complete a process recording.
- Describe the components of a biopsychosocial–spiritual assessment.
- Compose professional email correspondence.
- Describe the ethical use of technology regarding social work practice.
- Develop a personal social media policy.
- Identify the National Association of Social Workers' (NASW's) ethical standards related to technology.

ORAL COMMUNICATION

Most of us have heard the phrase, "it is not what you said, but how you said it," at some point in our lives. Words are powerful, and how they are used is something we must be considerate of in all contexts. As social workers, we must constantly behave professionally. As professionals, our communication—whether it be oral, written, or electronic—should demonstrate our professionalism. To achieve this, we must have a clear understanding of what it means to be a professional. Professionalism is possessing competence or expertise expected in one's field. For social workers, the CSWE outlines the competencies that you must possess to be a professional social worker and that are discussed throughout this text.

PROFESSIONAL SPEAKING

To be an effective professional social worker, you must be aware of the spoken language you are using. In this role, it is important to distinguish between casual and formal speech. Casual speech has its place, but as professional social workers, we should use formal speech in most circumstances to present our best professional selves. Formal speech for professional social workers is usually the adoption of the speech of the dominant culture. In the dominant U.S. culture, this means use of proper elocution (clear speech, proper pronunciation), appropriate speed and tone (inflection), and proper syntax. When engaging in formal speech, you should avoid words that are informal (e.g., *hey, yeah, kinda, nah, gonna, ain't*). Slang terms should be avoided, as they may be misunderstood. When speaking professionally, you should remember your manners as well. Use terms such as *please, thank you,* and *you are welcome.* If you are not accustomed to speaking formally, you should practice. As with anything, practice can improve your performance and help you in getting more comfortable with professional speaking.

JARGON AND ACRONYMS

CBT, BHRS, RTF, ADHD, OCD, LTSR, EBP, IOP, DBT—sometimes social work can feel like a bowl of alphabet soup! All of these letters mean something, but they lose their meaning if you do not know what they stand for (see Case Example 6.1). First and foremost, if during your field placement you come across an acronym that you do not understand, *ask.* It may also be helpful to keep a list of commonly used acronyms for your placement, especially while you are settling in and getting familiar with the jargon that professionals are using. These acronyms and other forms of professional jargon all have their place, but we need to be cautious when using this type of language in our communication. We need to be sure not to just throw out a list of jargon and acronyms to our clients or others who are not familiar with our professional terminology.

> **Field Reflection Question**
> What are some common acronyms or jargon used at your field placement?

CASE EXAMPLE 6.1: OVERWHELMED BY ACRONYMS AND JARGON

Jim has an MSW field placement as a mobile family therapist. His MSW supervisor handed him a stack of charts for the clients he will be shadowing this week. As Jim started to look at the first chart, he read, "The IP has been dx with OCD by Dr. Rudd. F/U in 2 weeks for med mgmt." He stopped and read that sentence again (and again), but it did not make sense to him. He was afraid to ask his supervisor about it because he felt self-conscious thinking it was something that he should have already known. By the time Jim made it through the fourth chart, he was pretty discouraged because he did not feel as if he was able to understand what was going on with any of the clients he was supposed to be seeing this week.

What Should Jim Do?

As we have said earlier (and will say again), your field placement is a time for learning and growing as a social worker. You are not expected to have all of the answers. It is okay to ask for help, support, or, in this case, clarification when you are presented with something you do not understand. Your field supervisor is there to help you with issues just like this.

(And in case you were wondering, the sentence given earlier can be translated to "The identified patient [client] was diagnosed with obsessive-compulsive disorder by Dr. Rudd. Follow-up in two weeks for medication management.")

WRITTEN COMMUNICATION

Written communication is all around us; we read articles, books, and emails all the time. As a college student, you most certainly have had your share of written assignments, many of which assessed your ability to effectively communicate your thoughts and ideas through written words. For social workers, good writing skills are crucial to demonstrate professionalism. Rai and Lillis (2013) assert that "writing plays a central role in social work practice" (p. 1), and we could not agree more. In this section, we discuss several ways in which social workers will need to express themselves through written communication, including case notes, process recordings, and biopsychosocial assessments. Later we talk about electronic communication that involves written communication as well.

Field Reflection Questions

How would you assess your current communication skills? Are you stronger at oral or written communication? Why?

How can you improve your communication skills?

CASE NOTES

In social work, it is often said, "If it is not documented, it did not happen." Clear, accurate, and timely documentation is necessary for effective social work practice. Documentation not only is critical to ensure continuity of care and measure change over time, but is often necessary for reimbursement from third-party payers such as insurance companies and other funding sources.

As social workers, our written words are quite powerful, so we must recognize the latent power and also be considerate of this when documenting information. McDonald, Boddy, O'Callaghan, and Chester (2015) suggest that social workers must constantly be mindful that "*how* and *why* we write as well as *what* we write reflects our commitment to the values and ethics of professional practice" (p. 360). Your documentation of client interactions becomes a lasting record that can follow clients long after your helping relationship with them has been terminated. Your written documentation of your interactions with clients can serve to enhance or diminish the lives of your clients—this is a big responsibility (Alter & Adkins, 2006). As a result, as social workers we must be sure that we are using our best written communication skills to document in a way that is ethical and professional.

Each social services agency will have its own documentation requirements for case notes, and it is important that you familiarize yourself with these forms and requirements early on during your field placement. If you are unsure what the requirements are at your field placement, ask your field supervisor right away. Although specifics for case note requirements will vary from agency to agency, there are several things that we, as professional social workers, should always consider.

Professional social workers provide clear documentation. Clarity in our writing refers to it being easy to understand or interpret. Our documentation is direct. We should avoid ambiguous writing that could lead to misinterpretations. Also, clear documentation is complete, without any missing gaps or interactions that are unaccounted for within the chart. For example, if a social worker documents that during the visit she witnessed a "touching event between siblings," this could have multiple meanings. Did the social worker witness an event that was heartfelt and kind, or did the social worker witness a sexual or physical interaction between siblings that involved inappropriate personal contact? This example, which McDonald et al. (2015) cite in their work, illustrates the necessity for clarity in written communication. Had the social worker been referring to a heartfelt interaction and another worker read the documentation and mistook it for inappropriate physical touching, that misunderstanding could lead to significant difficulties for the family involved. We should try to avoid language such as this that can have different meanings and can easily be misinterpreted.

Professional social workers provide accurate documentation. At the heart of ethical written communication is the truth. Lying, misleading, or fabricating information is forbidden. Our documentation should reflect the whole truth, even when it may not be pleasant. Sometimes, social work students fear that if they document that a client is having negative experiences or not progressing in treatment, it will negatively reflect upon them, so they do not accurately document what the client is experiencing. First, client progress, or lack thereof, does not necessarily reflect your ability to be an effective social worker. A variety of factors influence client progress throughout treatment. By not accurately documenting the client and his or her situation, you are breaking the core social work value of integrity and doing a disservice to your client (and yourself as the helper). Professional social workers must always practice with integrity, which includes being honest in our written communication.

To meet the previous two standards of documentation—clear and accurate—our documentation must also be timely. Timely documentation serves multiple purposes. First, the sooner we can document our interactions with clients, the more likely our documentation is to be clear, accurate, and complete. It is natural to lose details of interactions as time passes. As professional social workers, we must make every effort possible to capture the details that are important for our clients' records so that we can effectively document those details in our case notes. Whenever possible, you should complete your documentation immediately following a client interaction. Should you not have the time or ability to document immediately, we recommend that you jot down some notes of the details you feel should be included in the case note so that you can reflect back on your notes later when you sit to write them. If you are finding it difficult to complete your field documentation in a timely manner, this is an important conversation to have with your field supervisor. Together you can review your schedule and documentation requirements and then brainstorm solutions.

In addition to being sure that your documentation is clear, accurate, and timely, one common record-keeping practice is writing a SOAP note. In a SOAP note, S is for subjective observations, O is for objective data, A is for assessment, and P is for plan (Hepworth, Rooney, Rooney, & Strom-Gottfried, 2017). Subjective observations refer to how the client views his or her situation or experience. You can document this by writing, "client reports that …" or "parents voiced concerns about …" within your case notes. In contrast, objective data refer to facts and descriptions— the things you see, hear, smell, count, or measure in some other way. The assessment section of the case note should include your clinical judgments, impressions, and diagnosis information. The

Field Reflection Questions

In your current field placement, what documentation requirements do you have regarding your interactions with clients and other professionals?

How can you ensure that your documentation is clear, accurate, and timely?

last section of the case note should include your plan or next steps in working with this client, including any expectations for the worker or the client.

PROCESS RECORDING

A process recording is a tool used in social work education and supervision to assist the learning social worker in exploring client–worker dynamics and examining the use of self in the helping process. Process recordings are often very detailed written works, but can at times include audio or visual recordings as well. They have long been used in social work education as a means to examine what was said and done in the helping process while exploring the motives, thoughts, and behaviors associated with the interaction. Although process recordings are most often used with microinteractions, they can also be used at the mezzo and macro levels of practice (Medina, 2010). Formats for process recordings can vary, but most include the following elements:

- Background Information
  - Description of the setting (place, date, time) in which the interaction took place
  - First names of parties involved

- Purpose

- Content
  - Description of the interaction (verbal and nonverbal; see Exhibit 6.1 for a sample of how to display the content of a process recording)

- Impressions and assessment
  - Social worker's comments and feelings about what happened and why

- Plans
  - Future plans with this client

- Issues, questions, and problems
  - Any questions the social worker has regarding the interaction or content

We have included a sample process recording in Exhibit 6.2.

Tips for Success

For process recordings to be most beneficial, we recommend that you complete them as soon as possible after the interaction, while your recollections and reactions are as fresh as possible. As we discussed earlier, timely documentation is highly desirable because of its ability to capture the most accurate details of the interaction. We also recommend that you take full advantage of the educational benefits of process recordings by being as honest as possible when reconstructing the interaction and your reactions. Do not try to include what you think is the "right thing" to write down. Rather, use the process recording for its intended purpose, as a tool to help you reflect on your practice skills and become a more effective and efficient social work professional. Most social work programs that require students to complete process recordings also require that the process recording be reviewed by the field instructor and discussed in supervision. Process recordings are helpful learning tools only if you are honest and open to feedback.

EXHIBIT 6.1

Sample SOAP Note

Client Name: Carolyn D.   Date/Time: 3-1-2018 11:15 AM to 12:00 PM

Met with client to continue cognitive behavioral therapy (CBT) intervention to address symptoms of depression. Client arrived on time and reported feeling "a little bit down" today. Client appeared to be unkempt and dressed much more casually than had ever previously presented. Eye contact was minimal and at times, client appeared tearful during session. Client stated she has "no energy" to take care of herself in regard to showering and washing her hair. Social worker readministered a depression inventory previously taken by the client. On this date, the client's score indicates a rise in depressive symptoms from 2 weeks ago. Social worker plans to collaborate with client's psychiatrist regarding the recent medication adjustment made and share client's current presentation to ensure continuity of care. Social worker and client will continue to use CBT interventions to address depressive thoughts but will meet more frequently (weekly instead of every other week).

EXHIBIT 6.2

Sample Process Recording

Jenna, an MSW field student who is placed at a local hospital, completed the following process recording. In the example, the social work student, Jenna, and her field supervisor, Janet, received a page from the emergency department (ED) requesting a consult. After reviewing the patient's information in the electronic medical record, the social workers determined the purpose of this session. The social workers planned to meet with Nick (a 10-year-old Caucasian male) and his biological mother in the ED to discuss an incident of assault between siblings to assess the situation and gather pertinent information.

Interview Content (May Also Include Client Behavior—That Is, Nonverbal Communication)	Client's Feelings/ Affect	Student's Gut-Level Feelings	Analysis of Your Intervention and Identification of Any Themes or Issues in This Section
Jenna: We were called in by the doctors to talk with you a little bit. Can you tell us what brought you to the hospital tonight?	Mother is upset.	Nick does not seem to be in much pain; mother is very emotional.	Gather information to be able to best assist the family.

(continued)

EXHIBIT
6.2

Sample Process Recording (*continued*)

Interview Content (May Also Include Client Behavior—That Is, Nonverbal Communication)	Client's Feelings/ Affect	Student's Gut-Level Feelings	Analysis of Your Intervention and Identification of Any Themes or Issues in This Section
Mom: My children were fighting; Nick got kneed in the head.	Mother is tearful.	Mother seems very upset for such a minor injury. There are probably more family dynamics the team needs to uncover.	
Janet: So, Nick, can you tell us a little about your siblings? Brothers? Sisters?	Nick is looking down, avoiding eye contact with social workers.	Nick appears to be shy.	Prior to going into the room, team knew there were other siblings in the home and that Nick had been in a fight with his younger sister. However, this question was appropriate to attempt to engage Nick in conversation. Also, it was a way for the team to check the information received in the initial consultation referral, which can sometimes be inaccurate.
Nick: I have one brother and one sister.	Nick is soft-spoken.	It may be challenging to get Nick to open up.	
Jenna: What are their names?			
Nick: Holly and Noah.		Nick is not interested in talking.	Try to engage Nick in other ways: Use age-appropriate language, and try to build a rapport.
Jenna: Are you the oldest?			
Nick: Yes.			
Janet: So, buddy, who were you fighting with tonight?			Using "buddy" to simulate relationship/ rapport.

(continued)

**EXHIBIT
6.2**

Sample Process Recording (*continued*)

Interview Content (May Also Include Client Behavior—That Is, Nonverbal Communication)	Client's Feelings/ Affect	Student's Gut-Level Feelings	Analysis of Your Intervention and Identification of Any Themes or Issues in This Section
Nick: My sister.			
Jenna: How old is your sister?			
Mom: Holly is 7. Holly and Nick fight all of the time. I cannot take it anymore. Both of them have problems. Nick has an attention deficit hyperactivity disorder diagnosis. Holly was diagnosed with bipolar but that has been ruled out. I have wrap-around coming into the home for a year, but it is not getting any better.	Mother is crying. Nick is not interested in the conversation. He is playing with his ice pack and other hospital equipment in the room.	Mother is overwhelmed by her children's mental health and their behaviors.	
Janet: So, what caused the fight tonight?			
Mom: Nothing ever causes the fight; they just do not care. I have no life because of them. I do not even have silverware or real dishes in my house because they fight so much.	Mother is crying and appears anxious as well as overwhelmed.	I wonder what role mother plays in all of this. I wonder what her parenting style is like and what she has attempted to reduce these negative behaviors in her home.	
Jenna: Which services do you currently have for your family?			
Mom: We only have wrap-around for Holly. Nick sees a psychiatrist at school once a month. He sees a therapist sometimes, too.			

(continued)

**EXHIBIT
6.2**

Sample Process Recording (*continued*)

Interview Content (May Also Include Client Behavior—That Is, Nonverbal Communication)	Client's Feelings/ Affect	Student's Gut-Level Feelings	Analysis of Your Intervention and Identification of Any Themes or Issues in This Section
Janet: Are services helping at all?		On the basis of the mother's testimony to behaviors in the home, it does not seem as if services are working.	
Mom: No, things are just as bad. Every 3 months they have a review. There is never any progress.		Services should be looking to refer to a more appropri-ate service if they have not had any progress in 1 year.	
Medical student and attending doctor enter the room to examine Nick. Conversation between social workers and family ceased.	Nick did not appear to be in much pain while the doctors were examining him. Nick seemed disinter-ested in the doctors. He remained very restless. Mother continued to appear overwhelmed.	Nick is definitely displaying signs of ADHD such as hyperactivity and impulsivity. Mother seems so overwhelmed, as if she is drown-ing; she needs help (additional resources, services, etc.).	
After the medical staff left, the social workers resumed their conversation with mother.	Nick is spin-ning around in a doctor's chair.		
Janet: So, tell us a little more about who is at home with you.			

(continued)

EXHIBIT 6.2

Sample Process Recording (*continued*)

Interview Content (May Also Include Client Behavior—That Is, Nonverbal Communication)	Client's Feelings/ Affect	Student's Gut-Level Feelings	Analysis of Your Intervention and Identification of Any Themes or Issues in This Section
Mom: My three children and my husband. But my husband is not their father.			
Mom: Nick, stop spinning.	Nick does not acknowledge mother.	I doubt he is going to listen to his mother. Nick seems to be in control in the family.	There are hierarchical family issues. The family could benefit from structural family therapy.

BIOPSYCHOSOCIAL ASSESSMENTS

At the heart of what we do as social workers are comprehensive assessments. As social workers, we are trained to view the whole person as well as his or her environment when we conduct an assessment. One of the most common social work assessments is a biopsychosocial–spiritual assessment. In this one assessment, we look at the whole person, his or her environment, and his or her functioning to determine individual strengths and areas for growth (see Table 6.1). You will need to call upon your human behavior in the social environment coursework as a foundation for this assessment. NASW (2016) states that:

> A biopsychosocial–spiritual perspective recognizes the importance of whole person care and takes into account a client's physical or medical condition; emotional or psychological state; socioeconomic, sociocultural, and sociopolitical status; and spiritual needs and concerns. (p. 10)

TABLE 6.1 CONSIDERATIONS FOR A HOLISTIC ASSESSMENT OF A PERSON				
Biological	Psychological	Social	Spiritual	Environmental
• Physical illnesses and disease • Exercise • Use of pharmaceuticals • Nutrition	• Mental health (e.g., depression, anxiety, mood disorders) • Developmental stage • Intellectual functioning	• Friends • Family • Formal supports • Group membership • Culture	• Connection to a higher power • Participation with a faith community • Sense of meaning • Hope	• Macro influences

When completing a biopsychosocial assessment (see Exhibit 6.3), several areas should be included to ensure that it is comprehensive:

- Identifying information
- Presenting problem
- Mental status
- Biological determinants
- Psychological determinants
- Social determinants
- Spiritual determinants
- Environmental determinants
- Impressions: summarizing conclusions on the basis of previous sections and asserting recommendations for treatment

EXHIBIT 6.3

Sample Biopsychosocial Assessment

Identifying Information. Chad is a young Caucasian male with dark features who is 12 years old. Today Chad's father and stepmother are seeking help in dealing with his persistent mental health condition. Chad resides with his biological father, Pete; his stepmother, Josie; and his four siblings. He has some contact with his biological mother, Beth, but it is intermittent. He last saw his mother approximately 3 months ago. Through therapy, Chad has been able to identify that he was deeply hurt by his parents separating and subsequent divorce. He has also stated on several occasions that he is scared that Josie will leave like Beth did.

Presenting Problem. For approximately 1 year, Chad has been outwardly manifesting symptoms in the form of "rage," including verbal and physical aggression. At first, his outbursts would be months apart; recently, they are occurring much more frequently. The parents report that they have needed to use the county crisis line at least a couple times a month. They also report an increase in the duration of his episodes. They state that earlier the acting-out would last only an hour, but now Chad can be in an altered state for hours or even days. His episodes of rage occur only within the family setting. There are no negative behavior reports at school.

When defining Chad's behaviors, all present agree that Chad is a great kid who can be extremely helpful. However, when he becomes overwhelmed, he will act out. Past outbursts include verbally accosting his parents and siblings, making threats of bodily harm, and stating "odd" things. When asked to further define what "odd" things are, his stepmother reported that last summer Chad would ask his siblings to use a knife

(continued)

EXHIBIT
6.3

Sample Biopsychosocial Assessment (*continued*)

to cut the bad out of him. Stepmother reports several instances where Chad would talk about his "evilness." In the home, Chad has acted out physically by biting his step-mother in the stomach, which broke the skin. He also stabbed his stepmother in the foot with a piece of a broken broom, which partially paralyzed her foot. When Chad reaches this level, his father states that he attempts to restrain him but, despite being so small, Chad is very strong when he is upset.

Mental Status. Chad is alert and oriented to time, person, place, and situation. He demonstrates consistent eye contact with the interviewer and appears to have a bright affect. He is slim and short for his age. Chad appears to look younger than his chronological age. He smiles frequently while he sits slouched in his chair, close to his stepmother, Josie. Chad is more affectionate with his stepmother than would typically be expected for a boy his age. His rate of speech is normal, and his tone is appropriately varied throughout the interview. He denies auditory or visual hallucinations, as well as suicidal or homicidal ideation.

Biological Determinants. All present agree that Chad is a generally healthy child. He has no history of chronic or acute physical health conditions. He has no known allergies. Currently, Chad takes 5 milligrams of an antianxiety medication twice daily that was initially prescribed to him while he was hospitalized approximately 2 months ago.

Psychological Determinants. Chad has a current diagnosis of intermittent explosive disorder, major depressive disorder, and anxiety not otherwise specified that was given to him by a psychiatrist while Chad was hospitalized approximately 2 months ago. Chad's intellectual functioning is average for his age. In school, he earns mostly A or B grades.

Social Determinants. Regarding his siblings, Chad gets along well with his sisters and there is usually little, if any, conflict between them. However, he frequently acts out on his brother Jack. The parents report that during the past summer vacation months, Chad "terrorized" Jack. Chad would constantly make demeaning comments to Jack. He would physically fight with his brother and one time hit Jack in the face with a metal object that caused a deep laceration. To ease the conflict, parents imple-mented a safety plan in which both boys were not in the home at the same time. The parents used family members and other natural supports throughout this time.

The parents report that Chad's behaviors put a big strain on the whole family. His stepmother describes life in the house with Chad as "living on eggshells." The parents report that they enjoy doing things together as a family. Family game nights and movie nights are consistent activities within their home. The family also enjoys spending time outdoors in the nearby mountain region.

(continued)

Sample Biopsychosocial Assessment (*continued*)

Spiritual Determinants. The family does not engage in any formal religious services; however, they describe their faith as something that is very important to them. The family engages in collective prayer before meals and bedtime.

Environmental Determinants. The family is unhappy with their current housing and is actively searching for a new residence. The parents have been looking for a new home for months but report little success finding a location that can meet the needs of such a large family within their budget. The stepmother has a close friend who resides about 35 minutes away and is interested in moving to that area of the county.

Currently, the family is not involved in any community activities and does not report having any ties to the community. The children do not participate in any extracurricular activities; however, they did attend a summer school program at their school this past summer.

Impressions. Chad is a pleasant young male who resides within a newly blended stepfamily. He has had ongoing mental health concerns that have increased in severity, frequency, and duration over the past year. Chad admits to having concerns regarding separating from his stepmother, fearing she will leave the family as his biological mother, Beth, did when he was younger.

Josie and Pete claim they strive to promote a warm and loving environment in which to raise their children. Josie is extremely active in seeking out and maintaining mental health treatment for the children. Overall the children are able to work together and can get along. All of the children have identified strengths.

At present, the parents (Josie and Pete) feel that Chad's outbursts are of great concern for the family because of the impact on the family's ability to interact. The parents state that they feel if they could get Chad's outbursts under control, then they would be better able to function as a family system.

Chad's outbursts are in part a by-product of his mental health and attachment issues. However, there is also a distinct similarity between Chad's behaviors and Pete's negative behaviors. There is a predictive tendency for paternal symptoms and behaviors and externalizing behaviors of children in the home.

Intense structural family therapy would be beneficial at this time with Chad as the IP. With a family therapy team in the home three times a week, they would be able to teach Chad coping skills he would be able to use. This in-home, 32-week service could also work with the parents to improve coparenting skills. Treatment should be devised so that during the three sessions a week, time can be spent individually with Chad, privately with the parents, and in group sibling and/or family sessions.

IP, identified patient.

ELECTRONIC COMMUNICATION

We are living in a technologically advanced era. Many of us have technology with us at all times. Our ability to be electronically connected is greater than ever before. As with most things in life, technology comes with both advantages and potential disadvantages. As professional social workers, we must be able to successfully navigate the use of technology in electronic communication in its various forms.

Our professional code of ethics addresses the use of technology in social work practice. Technology can be used in a myriad of services, including, but not limited to, counseling, therapy, advocacy, education, supervision, research and evaluation, as well as program administration. All principles and standards set forth by the *Code of Ethics* should be followed whether the interactions, relationships, or communications occur in person or electronically (NASW, 2017). According to the NASW's *Code of Ethics* (2017):

> With growth in the use of communication technology in various aspects of social work practice, social workers need to be aware of the unique challenges that may arise in relation to the maintenance of confidentiality, informed consent, professional boundaries, professional competence, record keeping, and other ethical considerations … For the purposes of this Code, technology-assisted social work services include any social work services that involve the use of computers, mobile or landline telephones, tablets, video technology, or other electronic or digital technologies; this includes the use of various electronic or digital platforms, such as the Internet, online social media, chat rooms, text messaging, e-mail, and emerging digital applications. Social workers should keep apprised of emerging technological developments that may be used in social work practice and how various ethical standards apply to them. (p. 4)

Field Reflection Questions

How are you connected online? What does your online identity look like today?

Does your current online identity align with that of a professional social worker? If so, how? If not, how can you improve your online identity to be more professional?

SOCIAL MEDIA

Twitter, Facebook, Instagram, Snapchat, LinkedIn, and other similar apps and sites are great ways to stay connected with family and friends. They are commonplace in today's society for most people; however, we, as social workers, need to be aware of our social media presence. Social media serve as more than just a means to connect with others; Westwood (2014) suggests that social media have an "awareness angle which brings important social issues and the impact of social inequalities" to light (p. 3). It is estimated that social workers use social media at high rates to share professional information in the form of blogs, podcasts, and articles (Hitchcock & Battista, 2013).

Before your next tweet, post, link, or snap, consider your digital footprint, including whether it is demonstrating the professionalism of a social worker. In this age of technology, we must be mindful of our digital footprint. The term *digital footprint* refers to the online record trail we leave on the World Wide Web. We suggest that you take a moment to Google yourself and see what comes up; you may be surprised. Knowing what is online is the first step in being able to manage your online identity.

Privacy settings are something else that are important to consider. With technology being so easily accessible, it is easy for others to search for you online. The NASW's *Code of Ethics* (2017) states that:

> Social workers should be aware that personal affiliations may increase the likelihood that clients may discover the social worker's presence on Web sites, social media, and other forms of technology. Social workers should be aware that involvement in electronic communication with groups based on race, ethnicity, language, sexual orientation, gender identity or expression, mental or physical ability, religion, immigration status, and other personal affiliations may affect their ability to work effectively with particular clients. (p. 11)

Regardless of privacy settings, we urge you to post with caution. Bottom line: If you would not want the picture or post to be put on a billboard on the side of the highway, we strongly suggest that you reconsider posting it online. Once it is out there, it is very difficult, if not impossible, to totally erase.

EMAIL

With email so readily accessible on mobile devices, it is sometimes easy to forget that this form of communication also requires professionalism from social workers. When composing or responding to an email, although it may be convenient to respond quickly, we urge you to take a moment and consider your message.

How can you increase professionalism in an email? First, thoughtfully consider your subject line; do not leave it blank. The subject line does not have to be (and should not be) a novel, but it should identify the purpose of the email. Then, start your email off with a salutation or greeting. Something as simple as "Good morning" or "Dear (name)" is a great way to start off your email. This starts your message off right.

When typing your email, be sure to use appropriate grammar and punctuation. Capitalize the appropriate words and use professional language (avoid the pitfalls we have been discussing in this chapter so far). At the end of your email, include a closing such as "Sincerely" or "Thank you" and do not forget to include your name. With email, it is often taken for granted that the person knows who the email is coming from; the recipient probably does, but that does not negate your responsibility to send a professional message.

Remember, how you email in your personal life is one thing; how you email as a professional social worker is a completely different matter. Always proofread your emails before sending them to catch typos or autocorrect errors that may be hiding in your message. Exhibit 6.4 illustrates a simple professional email message for your review.

As a student in field, you most likely have access to your campus-issued email that you can use for correspondence. It is important to consider what email address you will be using when you begin applying for social work jobs and networking. Be mindful that your email address should be professional. Shy away from using email addresses such as 2cute4u@mymail.com or superherogamer2003@yourmail.com. Although these might be fine for your personal correspondence, something more professional might be a better choice for your career. A professional email choice may be as simple as your first and last name or first initial and last name.

When communicating electronically, it is important to be mindful that at times our message can be lost in translation. When communicating electronically, we do not

Professional Email Example

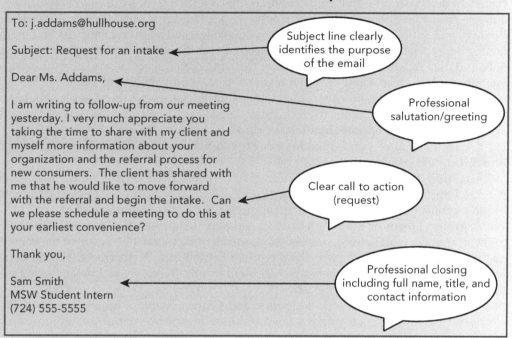

To: j.addams@hullhouse.org

Subject: Request for an intake ◄—— Subject line clearly identifies the purpose of the email

Dear Ms. Addams, ◄—— Professional salutation/greeting

I am writing to follow-up from our meeting yesterday. I very much appreciate you taking the time to share with my client and myself more information about your organization and the referral process for new consumers. The client has shared with me that he would like to move forward with the referral and begin the intake. ◄—— Clear call to action (request) Can we please schedule a meeting to do this at your earliest convenience?

Thank you,

Sam Smith ◄—— Professional closing including full name, title, and contact information
MSW Student Intern
(724) 555-5555

EXHIBIT 6.5

General Netiquette Guidelines

Consider your audience.
Assume that your written message is permanent.
Avoid sarcasm or harsh rhetoric.
Be clear if you are asserting opinion or fact.
Use appropriate formality.
Avoid typing in all capitals, excessive punctuation, or the use of emojis.

have access to tone of voice, inflection, or other nonverbal cues to help us interpret the messages we receive. To be sure that our electronic communication is professional, we should try to follow general "netiquette" rules. Netiquette refers to appropriate and clear electronic communication (see Exhibit 6.5). It is a "broad concept that captures the sense of morality and ethical values that are applied to the online world" (Park, Na, & Kim, 2014, p. 75). Following netiquette guidelines demonstrates a level of online etiquette or politeness (Khani & Darabi, 2014).

PROFESSIONAL AND ETHICAL USE OF TECHNOLOGY

It is important that as professional social workers, we are caring and genuine with our clients. In demonstrating that connection, we may be friendly toward our clients, but we must be clear that although we are friendly, we are not our clients' friends. Throughout this text, and your social work education, you have learned about establishing and maintaining appropriate boundaries. The responsibility for the development and maintenance of boundaries falls totally upon the social worker. So as the social worker, you need to establish and be clear about these professional boundaries with your clients. It is inappropriate to be friends with clients on social media. Social work professionals should not accept requests and invitations from clients on social media platforms "to prevent boundary confusion, inappropriate dual relationships, or harm to clients" (NASW, 2017, p. 11). Furthermore, social workers should not engage in personal communication with clients through any electronic forum.

According to Loue (2016), "social workers are increasingly relying on the internet to provide information to clients/patients, to seek advice about patients, to provide mental health treatment, and as part of an ongoing supervisory or consultant relationship" (p. 1). With a growing focus on telehealth services and a rise in app-based video conferencing as a way to connect with helping professionals, social workers must be aware of the benefits and potential limitations of such advances (see Exhibit 6.6). Furthermore, several social work professional organizations came together recently to release technology standards for social workers. The National Association of Social Workers, Association of Social Work Boards, Council on Social Work Education, and Clinical Social Work Association (2017) clearly set forth that social workers must continue to practice within the guides of the NASW's *Code of Ethics.* In addition:

> [w]hen using technology to provide services, practitioner competence and the well-being of the client remain primary. Social workers who use technology to provide services should evaluate their ability to assess the relative benefits and risks of providing social work services using technology … reasonably ensure

EXHIBIT 6.6

Professional Use of Technology

Benefits	Limitations
• Offers services to those who may be unable to access in-person services (because of transportation issues, for example) • Can be more convenient (related to client scheduling) • Services are often less expensive for clients • Increased access to professionals (no longer limited to those in the geographic area) • Real-time monitoring • The ability to respond rapidly • Ease of communication	• Potential breaches in confidentiality because of hacking and lack of encryption • Lack of connectivity or access to technology in some areas (particularly rural regions) as well as the possibility for technology failures • Lack of in-person interaction/connection • Cost of technology (devices, Internet access)

that electronic social work services can be kept confidential … reasonably ensure that they maintain clear professional boundaries … confirm the identity of the client to whom services are provided electronically at the onset of each contact with the client … assess individuals' familiarity and comfort with technology, access to the Internet, language translation software, and the use of technology to meet the needs of diverse populations, such as people with differing physical abilities. (pp. 11–12)

PROFESSIONAL ONLINE IDENTITY

Developing a professional online identity is another important step to consider. For some social workers, developing this professional online identity is necessary (especially if they deliver services electronically). Curington and Hitchcock (2017) suggest that professional social workers who use social media for professional purposes should create a professional online identity, post for professional reasons, and create a social media policy. Your professional online identity is different than your personal online identity, which we discussed earlier in this chapter. Your professional online identity may use social media platforms, blogs, business websites, or other online forums. Through these forums, you are clearly identifying yourself as a professional social worker. Because this is a professional presentation, your postings should be aligned with social work values and principles while following guidelines set forth by professional organizations. As this is a professional presentation, you should develop a social media policy regarding how you use technology and your response to various situations (see Exhibit 6.7 for tips on developing a professional social media policy).

EXHIBIT 6.7

Tips for Developing a Professional Social Media Policy

Your social media policy serves to "to inform clients, constituents, colleagues and others about when, how and why you use social media in a professional capacity" (Curington & Hitchcock, 2017, p. 10). Your social media policy is a personal policy in which you will include standards that are applicable to your professional situation; however, it is recommended that you include risks and benefits of the use of technology in professional practice (refer back to Exhibit 6.5).

Your social media policy should include (at least) the following:

The goals of your technology presence

Your policies related to friending, following, and contacting clients

Identification of the professional standards from which your policy is derived

Ethical concerns created by the use of technology

How you hope to use technology in your professional practice

CONFIDENTIALITY AND PRIVACY

As professionals, we must always consider the intended and unintended consequences of behaviors. When using electronic communication and the assistance of technology, we must be aware of our limitations to safeguard information. In this day and age, it is common to hear about hackings and data breaches, but we must never get too accustomed to these terms to forget what that means for us as social workers and for the clients we serve. When serving vulnerable populations and dealing with sensitive and confidential information, we must take all steps possible to protect the information of our clients. We should follow all state and federal guidelines related to privacy and compliance. There are many considerations in ensuring confidentiality while using technology-driven social work practices (Groshong & Phillips, 2015).

For example, we should ensure that we are HIPAA compliant when using technology, which often involves adhering to levels of encryption and agreements with servers. HIPAA— that is, the Health Insurance Portability and Accountability Act—was passed into law in 1996 in the United States and serves to safeguard protected health information (PHI). HIPAA also has provisions to ensure that any PHI that is transmitted electronically (ePHI) is safeguarded to ensure confidentiality and privacy.

Field Reflection Question

If, as a social worker, you were providing services electronically, how would you describe the risks to confidentiality to the client?

SUMMARY

In this chapter, we explored ways to demonstrate professional behavior in various forms of communication with others. As a social worker, you will have the opportunity to interact with many people in a variety of venues, and it is necessary that you act as the professional that you are at all times. Considering oral communication, social workers need to distinguish between causal and informal speech and select which is more appropriate on the basis of the audience and the goal of the communication. Professional jargon and acronyms should be used cautiously. Related to written communication, we reviewed common forms of social work documentation that professional social workers may encounter. We explored process recordings, which can be beneficial tools during your field education and during supervision sessions. Formats for case notes and biopsychosocial assessments were also discussed. Electronic communication was reviewed and the importance of cordial communication using netiquette skills was underscored. With an increase in technology-related platforms and social media, social workers must be aware of not only their personal identities, but also their professional online identities. Ethical standards for professional communication and professional use of technology were reviewed.

CRITICAL THINKING QUESTIONS

In this chapter, we focused on Competency 1: Demonstrate Ethical and Professional Behavior, in regard to demonstrating professional behavior in oral, written, and electronic communications. As a social worker, you are expected to demonstrate professionalism at all times no matter the platform of communication. The following discussion questions focus on professional communication as it relates to Competency 1:

1. How would you define professionalism and being a professional? How is being a professional social worker different than being simply a professional?

2. In your field placement, how can you ensure that your communication is always professional? Are there differences in how you would professionally communicate with a client as opposed to with another professional? If so, what are they?

3. How can you ensure that you are using technology in an ethical way as a social work professional?

4. What would you do if a client sent you a friend request on a social media site? What would you say to the client during your next session about this request?

5. How can you improve your online identity as a professional social worker?

6. What are two ways you can improve your oral communication so as to be more professional? What are two ways you can improve your written communication so as to be more professional? What are two ways you can improve your electronic communication so as to be more professional?

■ COMPETENCY 1: DEMONSTRATE ETHICAL AND PROFESSIONAL BEHAVIOR

Social workers understand the value base of the profession and its ethical standards, as well as relevant laws and regulations that may impact practice at the micro, mezzo, and macro levels. They understand frameworks of ethical decision making and how to apply principles of critical thinking to those frameworks in practice, research, and policy arenas. Social workers recognize personal values and the distinction between personal and professional values. They also understand how their personal experiences and affective reactions influence their professional judgment and behavior. Social workers understand the profession's history, its mission, and the roles and responsibilities of the profession. They also understand the role of other professions when engaged in interprofessional teams. Social workers recognize the importance of lifelong learning and are committed to continually updating their skills to ensure they are relevant and effective. They also understand emerging forms of technology and the ethical use of technology in social work practice. Social workers:

- Make ethical decisions by applying the standards of the NASW's *Code of Ethics*, relevant laws and regulations, models for ethical decision making, models for ethical conduct of research, and additional codes of ethics as appropriate to context.

- Use refection and self-regulation to manage personal values and maintain professionalism in practice situations.

- Demonstrate professional demeanor in behavior; appearance; and oral, written, and electronic communications.

- Use technology ethically and appropriately to facilitate practice outcomes.
- Use supervision and consultation to guide professional judgment and behavior.

CASE SUMMARY—"SOCIAL MEDIA BLUNDER"

PRACTICE SETTING DESCRIPTION

Newport Community Ministries is a small not-for-profit organization that strives to meet the needs of community members by providing resources such as food, clothing, and financial assistance to community members who are afflicted by poverty. In addition to supporting individuals and families directly, the organization works to engage members of the local business community. By engaging businesses, Newport Community Ministries strives to create opportunities such as jobs as well as educational and training opportunities that will assist individuals in becoming more employable in the future. Newport Community Ministries also connects with local politicians to advocate for poverty reform initiatives.

This semester, I have been placed at Newport Community Ministries as a BSW intern. There is only one social worker employed with this agency, Todd, and he serves as my field supervisor. Todd is excited to be working with me this semester because sometimes it gets overwhelming keeping up with everything he needs to do.

IDENTIFYING DATA

One of my learning objectives this semester is to create an online social media presence for Newport Community Ministries. Todd assigned me this task because it has been on his "to-do list" for a while. Since I am a lot younger than him, he thought that I would have the skills to develop these electronic resources. Because I do have a lot of experience on social media (not to brag, but I have more than a thousand followers on Instagram), I was excited to have this opportunity; I believe that I will really be able to use my creativity. Todd said that he wants to have a platform for Newport Community Ministries to be able to share their achievements (e.g., relationships with business partners, policy successes) and reach out for help (ask for donations from the community, request volunteers, and so on) online.

PRESENTING PROBLEM

A few weeks after I launched the Newport Community Ministries social media accounts (I created Twitter, Snapchat, and Facebook accpints), I started having some problems. First, to boost the followers on these platforms, I decided to share them on my social media sites, asking my followers to follow the Newport Community Ministries pages. That worked and got a lot of followers on the new page. The only problem is that because I connected my personal page with the Newport Community Ministries page, people now can access my personal accounts. I noticed that I was starting to get "likes" and "follows" from community business partners, current volunteers, and even a couple of individuals who have come to Newport Community Ministries for services.

At first, I did not think it was that big of a deal. Then one day this week, I posted a meme on my personal social media page that had a funny saying about having a tough day at work because of people who are clueless. A friend had posted it and the meme had my favorite actor in it, so I shared it on my page. Actually, I did not even have a bad day at work, so the content of the meme did not apply to me; I just thought that it was funny and liked the actor. I guess I shared it without thinking.

Within a couple of hours, I noticed that I had a ton of notifications. One client who I had worked with at Newport Community Ministries that day commented on my post, asking if it was him who ruined my day. He posted again saying that he hopes I do not quit working at Newport Community Ministries because I am really friendly and always help him when he comes in. He also sent me a few private direct messages about my post, asking about how I was feeling and saying that he was concerned about me. He said he was there if I needed someone to talk to about it. I did not respond to the messages from the client; I did not know what to say.

ASSESSMENT

The next day when I went in to Newport Community Ministries, I knew I should talk to Todd about it—but to be honest, I was embarrassed and thought it would just go away on its own. I mean, I did not message the client back; that was the right thing to do, I think. Well, I was wrong.

That afternoon, the client who had messaged me on my personal social media came in to Newport Community Ministries and demanded to see me. He was really agitated and visibly upset. When I went out to see him, he started yelling at me and he called me a "liar." He said that he thought we were friends and he could not believe that I ignored his messages online. I felt bad because I could see how upset he was; at the same time I was a little scared because I was being yelled at by this client.

Thankfully, Todd was in his office near where the client and I were standing. When the client started getting loud, Todd quickly came out of his office to intervene. Todd asked the client if he would talk with him for a little bit, to which the client agreed. Todd and the client went into his office and talked for almost an hour!

After the client left, Todd came to my office and shut the door. I was really nervous. Thankfully, Todd just wanted to talk to me about what happened. I came clean and shared what happened. I told Todd how I thought I was doing the right thing by ignoring the client online, but now I realized that ignoring the client made the situation worse. The client took my post personally and felt dismissed by me. Even if it was not my intention to offend anyone with what I posted, as a professional social worker, it is my responsibility to consider such things before I make such a post.

Todd and I were able to process the entire situation and explore how we were using social media professionally for Newport Community Ministries and how I was using it personally as well. Todd and I looked online and found copies of ethical standards set forth by NASW and other professional social work organizations.

CASE PROCESS SUMMARY

Through my supervision with Todd, I was able to see that I was not in compliance with social media standards set forth by NASW and as a result I risked the well-being of my clients. Now that I have a clearer understanding of what is required ethically by social workers when using technology, I am better able to manage my personal social media and distinguish between my personal and professional online identities. On the basis of my conversation with Todd, we both agreed that it would be a good idea to develop a social media policy for Newport Community Ministries to post on the social media pages. By posting our social media policy, it can serve to inform clients of how and why we have our online pages and what they can expect from us as professionals.

Holly, MSW student

DISCUSSION QUESTIONS

- On the basis of this scenario, what steps could Holly have taken to avoid this problem in the first place? Once the problem occurred, what should Holly have done to address the situation?

- How did Holly's personal social media interfere with her ability to be a professional social worker? How could she avoid such issues in the future?

- How could developing a social media policy at the launch of the Newport Community Ministries social media pages have helped in this scenario?

- As a social worker, working at an organization like the one described in this scenario, create a social media policy that could be included on the agency's social media site.

ELECTRONIC COMPETENCY RESOURCES

WEBSITE LINKS

Essay: "What Makes a Professional" by Daniel Lombard (2011)
www.communitycare.co.uk/2011/01/28/what-makes-a-professional

Article: "5 Ways to Ace Your Social Work Job Interview" by Valerie Arendt (n.d.)
www.socialworker.com/feature-articles/career-jobs/5-ways-to-ace-your-social-work
-job-interview

Article: "What Does it Mean to Be a Professional at Work?" by Alison Green (2013)
https://money.usnews.com/money/blogs/outside-voices-careers/2013/07/22/
what-does-it-mean-to-be-professional-at-work

Article: "Professionalism in the Workplace: How to Conduct Yourself on the Job" by
Dawn Rosenberg McKay (2017)
www.thebalance.com/professionalism-526248

NASW, ASWB, CSWE, and CSWA Standards for Technology in Social Work Practice (2017)
www.socialworkers.org/includes/newIncludes/homepage/PRA-BRO-33617.
TechStandards_FINAL_POSTING.pdf

This Social Work podcast discusses biopsychosocial–spiritual assessments
http://socialworkpodcast.blogspot.com/2007/02/bio-psychosocial-spiritual-bpss.html

Article: "Must I Un-Friend Facebook? Exploring the Ethics of Social Media" by
Lisa Kays (n.d.)
http://www.socialworker.com/feature-articles/ethics-articles/Must_I_Un-Friend_
Facebook%3F_Exploring_the_Ethics_of_Social_Media%E2%80%94

Infographic by University at Buffalo School of Social Work (n.d.)—Social worker's guide
to social media
https://socialwork.buffalo.edu/resources/social-media-guide.html

Common social work terms (vocabulary list)
www.carthage.edu/social-work/student-resources/vocabulary

U.S. Department of Health and Human Services list of acronyms and abbreviations
www.state.nj.us/humanservices/resources/acronyms.html

VIDEO LINKS

Ted Talk by Dale Atkins, "Being a Professional" (2013)
www.youtube.com/watch?v=sLv7sdGJWPI

Stanford Graduate School of Business presentation, "Think Fast, Talk Smart: Communication Techniques" (2014). This presentation provides tips and techniques to improve oral communication in spontaneous conversations.
www.youtube.com/watch?v=HAnw168huqA

A short video by *Forbes* on composing professional emails
www.youtube.com/watch?v=sErI3d2E4P4

REFERENCES

Alter, C., & Adkins, C. (2006). Assessing student writing proficiency in graduate schools of social work. *Journal of Social Work Education, 42*(2), 337–354. doi:10.5175/JSWE.2006.200404109

Council on Social Work Education. (2015). Educational policy and accreditation standards for baccalaureate and master's social work programs. Retrieved from https://www.cswe.org/getattachment/Accreditation/Accreditation-Process/2015-EPAS/2015EPAS_Web_FINAL.pdf.aspx

Curington, A. M., & Hitchcock, L. I. (2017). The Social Media Toolkit for Social Work Field Educators. Retrieved from http://www.laureliversonhitchcock.org/2017/07/28/social-media-toolkit-for-social-work-field-educators-get-your-free-copy/

Groshong, L., & Phillips, D. (2015). The impact of electronic communication on confidentiality in clinical social work practice. *Clinical Social Work Journal, 43*, 142–150. doi:10.1007/s10615-015-0527-4

Hepworth, D. H., Rooney, R. H., Rooney, G. D., & Strom-Gottfried, J. (2017). *Direct social work practice: Theory and skills* (10th ed.). Belmont, CA: Cengage.

Hitchcock, L. I., & Battista, A. (2013). Social media for professional practice: Integrating Twitter with social work pedagogy. *Journal of Baccalaureate Social Work, 18*, 33–45.

Khani, R., & Darabi, R. (2014). Flouting the netiquette rules in the academic correspondence in Iran. *Procedia: Social and Behavioral Sciences, 98*(6), 898–907. doi:10.1016/j.sbspro.2014.03.498

Loue, S. (2016). Ethical use of electronic media in social work practice. *Romanian Journal for Multidimensional Education, 8*(2), 21–30. doi:10.18662/rrem/2016.0802.02

McDonald, D., Boddy, J., O'Callaghan, K., & Chester, P. (2015). Ethical professional writing in social work and human services. *Ethics and Social Welfare, 9*(4), 359–374. doi:10.1080/17496535.2015.1009481

Medina, C. K. (2010). The need and use of process recording in policy practice: A learning and assessment tool for macro practice. *Journal of Teaching in Social Work, 30*(1), 29–45. doi:10.1080/08841230903479474

National Association of Social Workers. (2016). NASW standards for social work practice in health care settings. Retrieved from https://www.socialworkers.org/LinkClick.aspx?fileticket=fFnsRHX-4HE%3D&portalid=0

National Association of Social Workers. (2017). *Code of ethics*. Silver Spring, MD: Author. Retrieved from https://www.socialworkers.org/About/Ethics/Code-of-Ethics/Code-of-Ethics-English

National Association of Social Workers, Association of Social Work Boards, Council on Social Work Education, & Clinical Social Work Association. (2017). NASW, ASWB, CSWE, & CSWA standards for technology in social work practice. Retrieved from https://www.socialworkers.org/includes/newIncludes/homepage/PRA-BRO-33617.TechStandards_FINAL_POSTING.pdf

Park, S., Na, E. Y., & Kim, E. (2014). The relationship between online activities, netiquette, and cyberbullying. *Children and Youth Services Review, 42*, 74–81. doi:10.1016/j.childyouth.2014.04.002

Rai, L., & Lillis, T. (2013). 'Getting it write' in social work: Exploring the value of writing in academia to writing for professional practice. *Teaching in Higher Education, 18*(4), 352–364. doi:10.1080/13562517.2012.719157

Westwood, J. (2014). *Social media in social work education*. Northwich, UK: Critical Publishing.

CHAPTER 7

Engaging Diversity and Difference in Practice

CASE VIGNETTE

Chanté was a first-year MSW student doing her placement at a community-based counseling center that provided free and reduced-cost counseling services. A few months into her placement, Chanté was starting to feel more confident in her abilities providing services to members of different populations. Chanté recently began working with a client who is gender nonconforming. Although Chanté had learned some about the lesbian, gay, bisexual, transgender (LGBT) population in her Diversity class, working with someone who is gender nonconforming was a new experience for her. In her personal life, she had not much interaction with gender-nonconforming individuals.

In her work with this client, Chanté has noticed that she feels uncomfortable and is unsure where these feelings are coming from. Chanté does recall getting the message from her parents that gender-nonconforming individuals were abnormal, and perhaps confused. Thinking back to her Diversity class, Chanté consulted the National Association of Social Workers' (NASW's) Code of Ethics in hopes that it would provide her some clarity.

Unfortunately, Chanté's reading of the Code of Ethics left her feeling even more confused. Is she able to competently provide counseling services to her client when having these conflicting feelings? Is it more appropriate to refer her client to another counseling intern? What is in her client's best interest?

LEARNING OBJECTIVES

This chapter focuses on Competency 2: Engaging in Diversity and Difference in Practice. It begins with a brief introduction of the ways in which social work values and ethics uniquely support diversity in practice. This is followed by a review of the conceptual framework for diversity and bias in social work practice. The chapter then reviews standards for cultural competence, the importance of empathy and humility, and the various ways that individuals and groups are oppressed by the majority culture. By the end of this chapter, you will be able to

- Recognize the role of oppression in your clients' lived experiences.
- Recognize the importance of self-awareness and personal biases in working with diverse clients.

(continued)

LEARNING OBJECTIVES *(continued)*

- Engage in practices that are anti-oppressive by recognizing the myriad of factors that affect clients and client systems.
- Use ongoing supervision to do continual work on cultural awareness.

■ SOCIAL WORK VALUES AND ETHICS

Our personal identity is our cultural identity—it impacts how we see ourselves in the world and how we move through the world. Culture is the most influential determinant of identity (McGoldrick, Giordano, & Garcia-Preto, 2005). When social workers do not address implications of culture in their work with their clients, they may, unintentionally, be further oppressing their clients instead of helping them. The field of social work is developing different ways of conceptualizing models of practice for students in social work programs regarding cultural competence (Hall & Lindsey, 2014). In particular, the field is moving away from focusing solely on knowledge about specific cultures as the means of reaching a level of cultural competence in practice (Locke, 1992; Rodgers & Potocky, 1998). There is now an acknowledgment that the competency level of social workers is narrowed when they do not, in conjunction, learn the skills necessary to recognize how their own identity greatly impacts the work that is done with diverse individuals, groups, and communities.

The foundation of social work is based on practices that advocate for social, environmental, and economic justice in a culturally sensitive way. The NASW's (2017) *Code of Ethics* explains to social workers that their responsibility is to "obtain education about and seek to understand the nature of social diversity and oppression" [Standard 1.05(c), para. 3]. The NASW (2015) "promotes and supports the implementation of cultural and linguistic competence at three intersecting levels: the individual, institutional, and societal. Cultural competence requires social workers to examine their own cultural backgrounds and identities while seeking out the necessary knowledge, skills, and values that can enhance the delivery of services to people with varying cultural experiences associated with their race, ethnicity, gender, class, sexual orientation, religion, age, or disability [or other cultural factors]" (p. 65).

As future social workers join the field, the importance of identity in practice will continue to further nurture a "more comprehensive view of cultural competence" (Garran & Rozas, 2013, p. 99). This emphasis will also promote concepts of effectiveness and well-being within the profession. Focusing on continual growth in the skills related to cultural sensitivity will greatly help the incoming generation of social workers to be mindful of the ways in which their identity can benefit or hinder the work they do with the clients. In contrast, ignoring issues related to race, ethnicity, sexuality, religion, and other factors will result in poor service delivery to the client (Seipel & Way, 2006).

Field Reflection Questions

In your current field placement, which skill sets do you need to strengthen in regard to your cultural competence and humility?

In what ways can you, as a new social worker, integrate ongoing learning around cultural competence and cultural humility as a part of your continued growth?

■ CONCEPTUAL FRAMEWORKS FOR DIVERSITY, BIAS, AND CULTURAL COMPETENCE

This section of the chapter is devoted to defining important concepts that play a role in engaging diversity in practice in culturally competent and culturally humble ways. Diversity, intersectionality, bias, culture, competence, and culturally competent practice are explored.

DIVERSITY AND BIAS

Diversity is considered to reference difference, and, more specifically, human difference, and refers to every individual, given that all individuals are unique (Lum, 2000). Ridlen and Dane (1992) point out that discussions around diversity often originate when individuals or groups in power have defined certain behaviors as problematic. Often, those in power determine the values, negative or positive, assigned to behaviors in a way that creates preferences for those with fewer differences. This predisposition to favor those with the fewer differences is considered a bias that can impede an individual's or group's ability to be impartial (Bias, 2017). This preference may be extended to justify the exploitation of others for the benefit of those in power. As Van Dijk (1997) explains, this process, coined "othering," stifles the development of people who do not conform to the norms and expectations of the majority group, which has been White Anglo-Saxon Protestants with Eurocentric worldviews throughout the entire history of the United States.

The field of social work has had a difficult time defining the depth of human experience on the basis of dual concern for both "person and environment." Intersectionality examines how multiple social constructions of oppression or privilege can intersect to shape an individual's lived experiences (Battle-Walters, 2004). Intersectionality acknowledges that identities are not separate from one another, and that discrimination and oppression of marginalized individuals and groups have interactive effects. For example, Kornblum and Julian (2007) point out that African American women older than 70 years are among the poorest population subgroups, which highlights the ways in which race, gender, and age can intersect to layer oppression.

CULTURE

The worldview of social workers and the clients they serve is based in large part on their culture. Because culture is such a vital component of worldview, it also greatly impacts the ways in which social workers deliver services. Pinderhughes (1989) states that social workers who acquire positive self-identities show more ability to respect their clients' identities. Social work has defined culture differently over time. In the past, scholars limited which components of individuals' identity and experience were considered to constitute their culture. Early definitions used by social workers did not always acknowledge the impact of race, religion, gender, and other cultural components on the lived experiences of individuals (Mitchell, 1999). In reality, culture is a multidimensional concept that includes life experiences, behavioral patterns, and intergenerational messages (Lum, 2000).

COMPETENCE

Aponte (1995) aptly defines competence as encompassing ways of moving through the world that are acquired by individuals as a way to survive, and as including the skills and abilities they acquire to complete necessary functions in a successful manner. Competence suggests that one is capable of completing a task and has the sufficient skill set that can result in an adequate outcome (Lum, 2000). When thinking about competence in terms of social workers, competence refers to the acquisition of skills needed to provide services that are therapeutic, not oppressive, to all clients.

CULTURAL COMPETENCE

The Council on Social Work Education (2008) defines cultural competence as the ability of professionals to effectively interact with individuals of all cultures on the basis of curiosity and respect about differences related, but not limited, to race, ethnicity, culture, class, gender, sexual orientation, religion, physical or mental ability, age, and national origin. Unlike the linear acquisition of skills, cultural competence is an ongoing process that involves attentiveness to one's own biases and is built on a framework of respect and validation of difference. The ongoing work of cultural competence often begins with self-reflection to fully understand how our own cultural beliefs and practices result in different truths than others may have. It also includes the humility to understand that our way may not be the only "right" way.

STANDARDS FOR CULTURAL COMPETENCE

In 2015, the NASW revised the Standards for Cultural Competence in Social Work Practice. That revision highlights the importance of an intersectional approach to social work practice, the acknowledgment of social work professionals' own position of power in their work, and the fact that cultural competence is an ongoing process. This section provides a brief overview of the standards, including some examples taken from the NASW's Standards of Cultural Competence in Social Work. Social workers are encouraged to review the document in its entirety; it can be found on the NASW's website.

STANDARD 1: ETHICS AND VALUES

Social workers are required to practice in full accordance with the NASW's *Code of Ethics* (2015). In regard to cultural competence, social workers must understand the significant role that culture holds in effective practice, while also acknowledging that all cultures have strengths. It is the responsibility of the social worker to seek out knowledge about his or her clients' cultures and to infuse that knowledge into his or her service delivery with clients. Social workers also need to acknowledge and engage in continued education about the nature of oppression and discrimination.

STANDARD 2: SELF-AWARENESS

All social workers must continually assess their assumptions and biases, and identify how those beliefs impact their attitudes, worldview, and behaviors, which directly impact their service delivery. Simply identifying information about one's cultural heritage is not sufficient. Social workers must also take the time to learn about and celebrate other cultural heritages, and identify how their own cultural heritage may encourage damaging beliefs. Armed with this self-awareness, social workers must work in the community with others to identify strategies to change detrimental beliefs and acknowledge and correct those beliefs when they are impacting service delivery. Self-reflection is the basis for professional development in social work, and that process is never completed.

STANDARD 3: CROSS-CULTURAL KNOWLEDGE

It is the responsibility of social workers to obtain a grounded sense of their own identity, and then move on to learning about and valuing other identities. Cultural competence is an ongoing activity that requires continual learning, unlearning, and relearning of a multitude of different topics related to diversity. Examples include religious traditions, historical experiences, communication styles, help-seeking behaviors, and other cultural traditions. To be effective in our service delivery, we must expand our knowledge and understanding of these topics to better accommodate the needs of clients with whom we are working. In addition, understanding the applicability of practice models to specific client populations is vital to ensure effective service delivery.

STANDARD 4: CROSS-CULTURAL SKILLS

This standard applies specifically to the attainment of skills to work with individuals and groups of different cultures, as well as the broad range of skills necessary to advocate for clients at the micro, macro, and mezzo levels. It includes sharpening one's ability to convey authenticity and warmth, assessing policies for cultural inclusiveness, selecting and developing appropriate service interventions that take into account clients' cultural experiences, and effectively identifying resources in each client's life—including those with which you may be unfamiliar (e.g., healers, spiritual guides, families of choice).

Field Reflection Questions

After reviewing the cultural competency standards, which standard do you feel you have the most difficulty applying in your field placement work?

Which standard is the easiest for you to apply? What makes one standard harder to incorporate into your practice than the others?

STANDARD 5: SERVICE DELIVERY

Social workers are responsible for making culturally appropriate referrals, identifying service gaps that impact specific groups, evaluating service delivery models for cultural sensitivity and inclusiveness, assessing the cultural competence of other social work agencies, and including clients in the development of service delivery plans. Agencies should actively recruit and work to retain multicultural staff, and should include cultural competence skills as requirements in social work positions.

STANDARD 6: EMPOWERMENT AND ADVOCACY

Social policies, programs, and systems greatly impact client populations, especially those clients who are vulnerable and oppressed. Social workers should advocate on behalf of their clients and participate in the development and implementation of policies that empower marginalized and oppressed populations. They should be socially aware and confront stereotyping, discrimination, and other oppression of their clients and their clients' communities. This includes advocacy and action that works toward the empowerment of communities.

STANDARD 7: DIVERSE WORKFORCE

Social workers should encourage recruitment, admissions, hiring, and retention efforts that ensure diversity in social work programs and organizations. Recruiting and retaining multicultural students and staff naturally increase cultural competence through the expertise of those social workers. Statistics show that although social work aspires to be a diverse and inclusive field, U.S. social workers are predominantly White females, who account for 86% of all social workers (NASW & Center for Workforce Studies, 2006). Given that social work client populations are significantly more diverse than the profession, an intentional push toward aligning these demographics would help the field of social work bridge cultural differences. This intentional push should be evident within all levels in social work organizations. Moreover, social workers who possess unique knowledge or a specific skill set, such as bilingual speaking abilities, should be compensated appropriately.

STANDARD 8: PROFESSIONAL EDUCATION

As mentioned earlier in the chapter, it is imperative that social workers embrace a culture of lifelong learning around topics related to cultural competence. Just as social workers continue to improve their skills through the use of continuing education credits to learn cutting-edge therapeutic techniques, they must also use those and other avenues to participate in education and training that provide a continued focus on the current and changing needs of diverse client populations.

STANDARD 9: LANGUAGE AND COMMUNICATION

As the NASW's Standards (2015, pp. 43–44) point out, "[l]anguage is a source and extension of personal identity and culture and, therefore, is one way that individuals interact with others in their families and communities and across different cultural groups." Given that language is a part of an individual's identity, it is a part of our clients that we must accept without judgment or agenda. Clients have a right to use the language they are most comfortable using; in turn, it is the social worker's responsibility to ensure access to services in each client's preferred language. Social work professionals should promote diversity in language and confront discrimination on the basis of linguistic abilities. They should also seek out opportunities to be trained in how to work effectively with interpreters and translators.

STANDARD 10: LEADERSHIP TO ADVANCE CULTURAL COMPETENCE

The field of social work is committed to advancing cultural competence within and beyond the profession, and has a responsibility to confront oppressive systems and promote diverse and inclusive environments in the communities that social work professional serve. Part of leadership in social work is having a skill set that includes the ability to facilitate challenging conversations that promote growth and understanding in areas related to diversity and cultural competence. Social workers should recognize their formal and informal positions of power and privilege, and use them to advance cultural competence and challenge problematic practices.

EMPATHY AND HUMILITY

Engaging diversity in practice requires cultural humility. According to Tervalon and Murray-García (1998):

> Cultural humility incorporates a lifelong commitment to self-evaluation and self-critique, to redressing the power imbalances in the patient–physician dynamic, and to developing mutually beneficial and nonpaternalistic clinical and advocacy partnerships with communities on behalf of individuals and defined populations. (p. 117)

Incorporating a lifelong commitment to self-critique in practice requires both empathy and humility in practice. Reflecting the work of Carl Rogers, the person-centered approach of working with clients with unconditional positive regard, congruence, and empathy has been recognized as the foundation of clinical social work practice (Holosko, Skinner, & Robinson, 2007; Rogers, 1951; Rothery & Tutty, 2001).

EMPATHY

According to Sinclair and Monk (2005), empathy is the most productive therapeutic condition, even across varying treatment modalities. Empathetic therapeutic relationships have been identified as an agent of change in multiple outcome evaluations (King, 2011). Vanaerschot (2007) explains the use of empathy in the therapeutic relationship as the helping professional seeking to understand the unique experience of the client, and the personal meaning that he or she ascribes to it. This approach is incomplete without acknowledgment of the client's cultural identities and experiences.

One way that empathy plays a role in the helping relationship is through the social worker's desire to understand the meanings a client has attributed to the events in his or her life. This requires the social worker to encourage the client to explore different explanations, and to be open to different explanations himself or herself. For example, often an individual who experienced childhood abuse will attribute that experience to something he or she as the victim did to provoke the abuser's violent outburst, as opposed to attributing that experience to deficiencies in the abuser's coping mechanisms. When a social worker uses the therapeutic relationship to direct the client toward healing through an alternative attribution of that experience, the professional becomes what Vanaerschot (2007, p. 317) calls a "surrogate experiencer."

Gerdes and Segal (2011) have identified three different components of empathy that contribute to the surrogate experiencer concept. The first is affective sharing with the other—a mainly automatic process of the brain. Neuroscience research suggests that when human beings hear another individual express his or her feelings or see his or her non-verbal communication (e.g., gestures, facial expressions), the neural pathways in the brain simulate a "shared representation" and generate mirrored feelings. Although important, affective sharing can be detrimental without the second component, self–other awareness. This allows human beings to separate their own feelings from the feelings of others. For example, such awareness enables the social worker to make inferences about the information being provided. This "brake" allows social workers to avoid emotional overloading from the experiences shared by clients. The third component described by Gerdes and Segal (2011) is mental flexibility. An important skill for social workers, it allows humans to receive the perspective of the client, yet also turn it off, as necessary to move forward with accomplishing the goals of the working relationship.

Specific to empathy and cultural competence in the social work is the critique of the absence of an emphasis on cultural context. Buckman, Reese, and Kinney (2001) aptly point out that much of the empathy literature fails to recognize that self-actualization is not available to all clients because of the power of cultural forces such as racism, sexism, and economic disparities, among others. Ignoring cultural context emphasizes damaging dominant discourses and can contribute to further harm of the client (King, 2011; Sinclair & Monk, 2005). The lived experiences of clients exist in direct relation to the biased experiences forced upon them by the dominant groups, which results in severe consequences for vulnerable and oppressed populations, including lower placement in the hierarchy of social structure (Buckman et al., 2001; Sinclair & Monk, 2005).

Humility and empathy are vital within service to clients, as they allow the privileged social worker to acknowledge how the harmful societal systems function to oppress clients and cause—or at the very least contribute to—the problems they are facing within the work they hope to do. The social worker must use the surrogate experience to assist the clients in moving past attributions that may be paralyzing them through feelings of fault, and assist them in viewing their struggle in light of oppressive cultural contexts (Sinclair & Monk, 2005).

HUMILITY

Tervalon and Murray-García (1998) coined the term *cultural humility* to recognize the fact that culture is central to all human interactions, and to emphasize that competence is never truly achieved because the needs of groups and the dynamics of oppressive social systems continually shift. The need for humility is vital in the context of cultural competence, because engaging diversity in practice requires the social worker to learn with and from the client. This requires the vulnerability to admit to self and others that you do not have all of the answers, and the readiness to acknowledge that education, licensing, and other credentials do not solely qualify you to fully address the many ways that inequality pervades society. We are not just limited through lack of knowledge. but also because of our unconscious biases and use of stereotyping to explain client behaviors (Ortega & Faller, 2011).

Although at first this focus on humility and vulnerability may feel intimidating to the new social worker, it actually liberates the social worker from the pressure of being the expert on everything the clients have experienced and will experience. The social worker is a collaborator with the client in the helping relationship. Collaboration allows the client to teach the social worker about the uniqueness of his or her intersectionality. This allows for a mutually beneficial relationship and helps to reduce the harmful effects of power dynamics within the helping relationship.

Considering cultural humility in mezzo and macro terms, it is easy to recognize how agencies and organizations can easily go astray. Decisions about programming are often made in a vacuum—with respect to funding requirements or guidelines, but also without input from the true experts, the individuals who will be using the services. Cultural humility charges social workers to advocate for client and community voice in decision making.

> **Field Reflection Questions**
>
> What do empathy and cultural humility look like to you in direct practice? What about in mezzo and macro practices?
>
> With which aspect of cultural humility do you feel most comfortable? With which aspect are you least comfortable?

FORMS OF OPPRESSION

As discussed earlier in the chapter, oppression is the result of inequities in power that allow groups in power to act out their biases, prejudices, and stereotypes in ways that deprive those not in power of full access to resources, self-actualization, and autonomy (Thomas & Schwarzbaum, 2017).

There are many ways in which oppression, discrimination, and prejudice are seen in everyday life: prejudicial talk, avoidance of certain groups or individuals, segregation or exclusion in social systems (e.g., employment, education), violence to person or property, exploitation, marginalization (exclusion from social life), cultural imperialism (repressing the nondominant group's norms and values), and organized extermination of a group of people on the basis of their membership (Allport, as cited in Thomas & Schwarzbaum, 2017; Young, 1990). Social workers will be able to identify the ways that these oppressive actions take place on micro, mezzo, and macro levels. Daily microaggressions (common, regularly occurring humiliations—intentional or not—on the basis of stereotypes and prejudices; Sue et al., 2007), imbalances of power within interpersonal relationships, and systemic institutional and cultural discrimination and exclusions deny individuals the ability to be seen, and see themselves, as spiritually, mentally, and emotionally whole.

The damaging effects of oppression reach their height when individuals begin to internalize the negative stereotypes about the group in which they have membership (Sue & Sue, 2012). Internalization of oppression can manifest itself in a variety of ways, including self-hatred, engaging in self-harming behaviors, and acting in ways that are in accordance with the stereotypical messages received, among others. Kagan and Burton (2005) argue that the helplessness that many oppressed individuals feel is also a form of internalized oppression: They have internalized the dominance of those in power, and are rendered incapable, helpless, and powerless. Although some are able to prevent this internalization through the coping skills they have developed, others are overwhelmed by the ongoing assault on

Field Reflection Questions

What are some instances of microaggressions or interpersonal acts of oppression you have heard from clients, or witnessed yourself in your field placement?

What other ways, beyond the examples listed, can internalized oppression impact individuals?

their sense of self. Because of this, social workers must remember to use an ever-present lens of culture and oppression when working with clients. The following subsections define the ways in which individuals are often targets for oppression—but note this list is not exhaustive.

RACISM

Racism is pervasive, rooted in assumptions of superiority on the basis of race, and deeply infused in the history of the United States, and it requires the critical attention of all social workers (Rodgers, 2015). As overt racism (e.g., legalized segregation, lynching) became less acceptable during the civil rights era, the acting out of racist ideologies evolved into a more concealed form of racism that is persistent in the institutions of society. The resulting policies create unequal outcomes for people of color, including higher rates of incarceration; unequal access to financial, employment, and educational resources; inequity in representation; disparities in health outcomes; and more (Rodgers, 2015). A very important and often confusing concept is color-blind racism (Bonilla-Silva, 2003). Perhaps some of you reading this passage were even coached as children to "see people, not color." Although usually well intentioned, claiming to not see people with regard to their race is actually an exceptionally damaging approach—not acknowledging and celebrating the differences in culture imposes the dominant (White) culture on everyone, robs people of color of their cultural uniqueness and pride, and assumes that everyone has the privilege of moving through the world in the same way, with a total disregard for the impact of discrimination, oppression, and ongoing microaggression (Bonilla-Silva, 2003). Very recently, the United States has been experiencing a significant increase in the expression of overt forms of racism, including the use of brazenly racist slogans, aligned with belief systems of the Ku Klux Klan and Nazism, with the intention of inciting violence and discrimination toward people of color (Siddique & Laughland, 2017).

XENOPHOBIA AND ETHNOCENTRISM

Often fueled by racism, xenophobia is the fear or hatred of other countries and individuals from other countries. It is often seen in conjunction with ethnocentrism—the belief that one group (ethnic, religious, or specific culture) is superior to others—and leads to prejudice and oppression on the basis of ethnicity, religion, or country of origin (Sue & Sue, 2012). This greatly impacts beliefs and policies around immigration and globalization. Targeting immigrants as the cause of society's ills has long been a practice in the history of the United States. Which groups of immigrants are targeted and what those forms of discrimination look like fluctuate significantly on the basis of political and economic factors (Thomas & Schwarzbaum, 2017). However, racism often plays a role in who is most often targeted, with people of color at a greater risk of discrimination because of racial profiling. An example is the ongoing targeting, since the terrorist attacks of September 11, 2001, of Arab individuals, Muslim individuals, and South Asian individuals for questioning related to immigration violations (American Civil Liberties Union, 2017).

CLASSISM

Classism is the differential treatment on the basis of (actual or perceived) social class. Lott and Bullock (2007) point out that classism occurs both individually and institutionally. Individual classism refers to the stereotypes and prejudices that are believed about individuals living in poverty as well as working-class individuals. Institutional classism refers to the social institutions that enact policies and procedures that negatively impact, marginalize, and harm individuals living in poverty. This can be seen in the education system, legal system, political system, and beyond. In addition, denying the fact that class difference has systemic roots and blaming the poor for their poverty are additional forms of classism (Thomas & Schwarzbaum, 2017).

RELIGIOUS OPPRESSION

The pervasive oppression on the basis of minority religious status is the product of the intersection of the historical tradition of Christian hegemony in the United States, the unequal power relationships of minority religious groups with the Christian majority, and the often-held belief of "one true religion." Christian beliefs and norms are hegemonic in that they are assumed status and are interwoven into society. Some examples are the addition of "In God We Trust" and the observance of Christian holidays by governmental agencies. Religious persecution on the basis of these beliefs has resulted in violence and religious cleansing (systematic extermination of groups on the basis of religious belief).

SEXISM

Sexism is discrimination on the basis of gender, most commonly occurring by men toward women. This form of discrimination is often rooted in a belief that women should be subservient to men, and that men are superior to women intellectually (Thomas & Schwarzbaum, 2017). Traditional notions of gender link behavioral, cultural, and social characteristics to an individual's gender. Sexism and gender-based discrimination and inequality include violence; restricted access to education, economic, and governmental opportunities; resource restriction that results in health disparities; and other practices (Littlefield, McLane-Davison, & Vakalahi, 2015). Moral, religious, and cultural practices often reinforce traditional gender roles and attitudes. These beliefs are so strongly held that violence is perpetrated against those who violate them. Challenging traditional beliefs of gender and advocating for policies that decrease gender discrimination and sexual harassment are some of the ways that discrimination on the basis of gender can be confronted (Littlefield et al., 2015).

HOMOPHOBIA, BIPHOBIA, AND HETEROSEXISM

Homophobia is the intense fear, hatred, or dread of homosexuals and homosexuality (Moses & Hawkins, 1982). Biphobia is an aversion to bisexuals and bisexuality. It is important to remember that individuals of any sexual orientation can hold homophobic and biphobic beliefs. Similar to other forms of oppression, homophobia and biphobia can manifest themselves in a variety of ways, including violence and discrimination in education, employment, and housing. State-sponsored homophobia includes practices and policies that criminalize homosexuality; governmental figures engaging in hate speech toward gay, lesbian, and bisexual individuals; and withholding certain rights and privileges (e.g., marriage, health care decision-making capacity) from same-sex couples.

Often, many homophobic and biphobic beliefs are rooted in heterosexism (sometimes referred to as heterocentrism)—the systematic preferencing of opposite-sex sexuality and relationships (Jung & Smith, 1993). Heterosexism is pervasive in societal customs and institutions, and serves to keep homosexuality and bisexuality invisible. Some examples include denial that bisexuality and homosexuality exist, the assumption that sexual orientation can and should be changed, hostility toward same-sex relationships (with same-sex marriage only recently becoming legally recognized nationally), the existence of sodomy laws in one-third of all U.S. states, and resistance to the addition of sexual orientation to nondiscrimination statutes, resulting in a lack of legal protection from discrimination on the basis of sexual orientation. In addition, social workers often unintentionally use heterosexist language in service delivery to clients, such as asking a female client if she has a boyfriend or husband. Evaluating service delivery for inclusion and making changes, such as moving away from exclusive language, require intentionality and practice by social workers.

TRANSGENDER OPPRESSION

Transgender oppression refers to the devaluing, discrimination, stereotyping, and violence that individuals face when their appearance or identity does not conform to conventional beliefs about gender—namely, that only two genders exist, and that they are fixed at birth and are determined solely by the chromosomal and anatomic sex of an individual. Common beliefs tied to transgender oppression include that transgender individuals do not actually exist, individuals presenting as gender nonconforming are doing so for an ulterior motive (e.g., attention, political motivation), and transgender individuals are defying nature or acting against the will of God. These beliefs are tied to transphobia—disgust, fear, hatred, or disbelief of the existence of transgender and gender-nonconforming individuals (Chakraborti & Garland, 2009). Transgender oppression includes bullying, physical violence, harassment, false arrest, and sexual assault. Transgender and gender-nonconforming individuals are often discriminated against in employment, education, and health care settings, and they often lack legal protection from discrimination owing to the absence of gender identity in many nondiscrimination statutes. Data collected by the Federal Bureau of Investigation (FBI) show that lesbian, gay, bisexual, and transgender individuals are more likely to be targets of hate crimes than any other minority group—with transgender women of color being the most frequent targets of violence (Park & Mykhyalyshyn, 2016). Transgender oppression is further reinforced throughout the social systems in the United States, most notably through transgender and gender-nonconforming invisibility. One obvious example is that most federal, state, institutional, organization, and agency forms provide only two options for gender or sex: male or female.

ABLEISM

Ableism is discrimination in favor of able-bodied people, the negative judgment about the capabilities of individuals with disabilities, the expression of hate for people with disabilities, and the denial of accessibility and resources (Smith, Foley, & Chaney, 2008; Thomas

& Schwarzbaum, 2017). Smith et al. (2008) aptly point out that discrimination against individuals with disabilities is often characterized by the belief that they are abnormal, have some sort of deficit, need to be fixed, and cannot fully function in society. This framing of disability as deficient as opposed to difference has resulted in the ignoring of it as a dimension of cultural competence (Smith et al., 2008). Discrimination on the basis of ableism manifests as discrimination in employment (most specifically the rejection of disabled applicants for housing and jobs); failing to provide accessibility at all, or anything beyond wheelchair ramps; using ableist language; individuals without disabilities using resources allocated for those with disabilities (e.g., parking spaces, restrooms); making assumptions about an individual's disability status on the basis of the visibility (or invisibility) of his or her disability; and policies and systems that, intentionally or not, keep people with disabilities in poverty.

Field Reflection Questions

What are some ways you may have unintentionally participated in discriminatory or exclusive ways?

What are some ways you can change your practice to become more inclusive of nondominant groups?

SUMMARY

This chapter focused on different concepts related to engaging diversity in practice. Understanding that culture plays a huge role in our thoughts, feeling, behaviors, privileges, and experiences of oppression is vital to competent service delivery to clients. Without such acknowledgment, social workers can unintentionally harm clients through a variety of unintentional practices.

In this chapter, diversity, bias, cultural competence, and humility were operationally defined and discussed in regard to the field of social work. Recognition of society's predisposition to favor the values and norms of the dominant group is important to recognizing how we may be imposing those dominant expectations on the clients and communities we work with. Also explored were the ways in which cultural identities intersect to layer oppressive experiences and marginalized individuals who belong to multiple oppressed communities. Intersectionality helps social workers conceptualize how these identities exist in conjunction with one another, rather than separately—all of the uniqueness to be celebrated, and all of the oppression to be recognized.

A deeper dive into the Standards for Cultural Competence in Social Work Practice as defined by the NASW was also part of this chapter. Just a snapshot was presented here; the full document is available online (the link is available in the "Electronic Competency Resources" section). These standards are a useful contribution to social work education, as many of the concepts can be difficult to understand in regard to practice. This chapter, and more so the full document, provide examples of how these standards are put into practice for social workers at the micro, mezzo, and macro levels.

The necessary acceptance of empathy and humility as key components of culturally competent practice were discussed in the chapter as well. Research has regularly examined the usefulness of empathy in the helping relationship, and newer neuroscience research has started to hone in on where empathic skills come from. Humility—and, more specifically, cultural humility—recognizes both the importance of culture to all interactions and the fact that competence is never truly achieved; it is an experience of ongoing self-assessment and learning practices. All social workers can benefit from putting these frameworks into practice, as they recognize the inherent power imbalances between social worker and client, and seek to place client and social worker in the roles of collaborators. As a social worker, you do not know everything, and you cannot know everything—so allow the client to teach you about his or her unique identity.

The final section of the chapter focused on forms of oppression, including how oppression is acted out within society and within social work practice, and what the damaging impacts of oppression are. It reviewed some, though not all, of the groups that are targeted for oppression. Forms of oppression may be applied to individuals and groups on the basis of (actual or perceived) race, ethnicity, country of origin, socioeconomic class, religion, gender, sexual orientation, gender identity, and disability status. The chapter provided a brief overview of these forms of oppression and discussed what they look like in practice, ranging from ignoring the existence of the identity to engaging in murder and systematic extermination.

CRITICAL THINKING QUESTIONS

Competency 2 focuses on the interrelationship of diversity and difference and the development of individual identity. As a social worker, you are expected to understand that oppression and discrimination are a direct result of exploitation by the dominant group, on the basis of difference and perceived superiority. Their effects may manifest as poverty, violence, alienation, lack of access to resources, and more. You are expected to evaluate your work in the context of the client's or community's culture, assume the role of collaborator, continually reflect on the ways in which your biases can and do impact your work, and seek out opportunities to develop your skill set around cultural competence and humility through ongoing education regarding the most recent concepts and approaches. Above all, you must remember that culture always matters, and that competence is never achieved with no further work to be done. The following questions focus on engaging diversity in practice:

1. Ella, a White, straight woman, has had three sessions with her client, who is Black and bisexual. Ella has been using active listening and empathetic reflection as she learns more about her client and the experiences that brought her in to receive services. Sometimes, after she reflects back what she has heard, her client will respond with, "Yeah, but I'm sure you have no idea what I'm talking about." Although Ella agrees with her client that she cannot truly understand what those experiences have been like, she knows that she should appropriately respond with a statement or question that allows her and the client to explore cultural differences that exist between them. She is not completely sure how she could bring this up. Identify the potential for missteps on Ella's behalf. Describe how you would avoid or minimize these risks. Discuss how you would approach this scenario. Reflect on and describe your affective reaction to this scenario.

2. Think back to earlier chapters—identify which engagement and assessment skills you would use during this conversation with Ella. Which skills are you less confident about using in this scenario? Identify how you may be able to strengthen those skills so that you are able to more effectively approach this conversation with the client.

3. You must be able to engage your clients in a helping relationship beyond difference. In reflecting upon your work with clients in your field placement, describe a situation

in which you were unable to fully grasp an experience that your client attempted to share with you. On reflection, was this because of a cultural or linguistic difference? How did you deal with this situation? Reflect on and describe how you would approach a similar situation in the future.

4. Engaging diversity and difference in practice involves humility, curiosity, and ongoing self-reflection on your automatic stereotypical and biased assumptions about your clients. Everyone holds implicit biases. After reflecting upon your work with clients in your field placement, describe an experience in which you recognized yourself having a stereotypical or biased assumption about a client you were working with. Reflect on and describe your affective reaction to this experience. Describe how you handled this experience. Reflect on and describe how you could improve your reaction when it happens in the future.

COMPETENCY 2: ENGAGE DIVERSITY AND DIFFERENCE IN PRACTICE

Social workers understand how diversity and difference characterize and shape the human experience and are critical to the formation of identity. The dimensions of diversity are understood as the intersectionality of multiple factors including, but not limited to, age, class, color, culture, disability and ability, ethnicity, gender, gender identity and expression, immigration status, marital status, political ideology, race, religion/spirituality, sex, sexual orientation, and tribal sovereign status. Social workers understand that, as a consequence of difference, a person's life experiences may include oppression, poverty, marginalization, and alienation or, alternatively, privilege, power, and acclaim. They also understand the forms and mechanisms of oppression and discrimination and recognize the extent to which a culture's structures and values, including social, economic, political, and cultural exclusions, may oppress, marginalize, alienate, or create privilege and power. Social workers:

- Apply and communicate understanding of the importance of diversity and difference in shaping life experiences in practice at the micro, mezzo, and macro levels.

- Present themselves as learners and engage clients and constituencies as experts of their own life experiences.

- Apply self-awareness and self-regulation to manage the influence of personal biases and values in working with diverse clients and constituencies.

CASE SUMMARY—"HOW DO I HELP?"

PRACTICE SETTING DESCRIPTION

My name is Makayla and I am a first-year MSW student completing an internship at a family service agency in a medium-sized city in the Midwest. The agency provides individual and family counseling services on a sliding fee scale. The agency also runs a number of educational and treatment groups. I was assigned to work with T., who is seeking assistance in finding resources for herself and her two children, and to manage stress.

IDENTIFYING DATA

T. has two children, Maria and Luisa. T. fled to the area to escape her abusive husband. T. is 30 years old, and her children are age 8 and 6. T. and her daughters are undocumented. T. works as a house cleaner while her children are at school. T. and her children have temporary shelter.

PRESENTING PROBLEM

T. and her children are facing multiple obstacles. They need to find permanent, affordable housing. They also need to find ways to supplement T.'s income, because she is currently not making enough to pay rent, cover the bills, and feed her children.

In addition, T. is experiencing an immense amount of stress and anxiety. She has described an instance where she could not calm down her breathing, and she felt lightheaded. She is concerned about meeting her children's needs and finding a permanent housing situation, and she is always concerned that either her ex-husband or the government will locate her.

ASSESSMENT

Although T. and her family are facing many stressors, the most immediate and pressing need is to find permanent housing for them. T. was reluctant to even come into the agency for counseling services out of fear of service refusal and fear of being turned in due to her undocumented status. The majority of the housing services in the area require applicants to be citizens or permanent residents.

In addition, T.'s anxiety is causing her potential panic attack symptomology. Although T. reports that this has occurred only one time, her increased levels of stress are certainly impacting her physical well-being. She reports difficulty sleeping at night, as well as exhaustion during the day.

T. is extremely reluctant to sign up for any federally funded services, even those that she and her children are entitled to receive. Upon hearing the suggestion that we connect the family with Supplemental Nutrition Assistance Program (SNAP) services, T. became nervous and refused. She has heard that participation in SNAP services, and others like them, may draw the attention of Immigration and Customs Enforcement, and she had heard stories on the news of individuals being deported after signing up for such programs.

T. and her daughters have many strengths. They are all happier after relocating away from their abusive family member. While they moved away from family and friends, they moved to this specific location because of a small support system that already lived here. It is this support system that is providing them with food and shelter until T. can establish permanent arrangements. In addition, T. is already employed, and her working hours are increasing. All of the family members fluently speak and read English.

Another obvious strength is T.'s determination and resilience, which she has already amploy demonstrated. The family's support network is growing further in part because of their new church community. In addition, T. is highly motivated to find her own accommodation and support her children.

CASE PROCESS SUMMARY

I feel I have built significant rapport with T. She is very open with me, which took quite a bit of time. In discussion with my field supervisor, I shared that T.'s unwillingness to sign up for certain services that she and her daughters are allowed to use, even with their undocumented status, was a big challenge, and I was unsure why T. was being so resistant to most of the options I shared. Because resources are so limited here, we do not really have the option of turning down what is available. In many ways, I find myself wondering, "How do I help?" Upon reflection, my field instructor shared that she sensed my frustration with the situation, and she wondered if perhaps T. could sense my frustration as well.

Makayla, MSW student intern

DISCUSSION QUESTIONS

- On the basis of the information provided, how would you, as Makayla's field supervisor, encourage her to work through this apparent frustration? Would you encourage her to bring this topic up with T.? Why or why not?

- Evaluate and critique Makayla's assessment of T. through the lens of engaging diversity and difference in practice. What are the strengths of the assessment? Which areas need to be strengthened?

- Consider the case example in terms of intersectionality. From the information provided, what are the different identities that T. may inhabit? How does that change her situation when compared with others? What additional information do you wish you had?

- Thinking about cultural competence and cultural humility, what is something you would want to focus on with T. if you were working with her?

ELECTRONIC COMPETENCY RESOURCES

WEBSITE LINKS

Standard and Indicators for Cultural Competence in Social Work Practice—National Association of Social Workers
www.socialworkers.org/LinkClick.aspx?fileticket=PonPTDEBrn4%3D&portalid=0

Cultural Humility, Part I—What Is "Cultural Humility"?—The Social Work Practitioner
https://thesocialworkpractitioner.com/2013/08/19/cultural-humility-part-i-what-is
-cultural-humility

Intersection Theory—Dustin Kidd
www.slideshare.net/dustinkidd1/intersectional-theory

VIDEO LINKS

Race and Racism—Camera Jones
www.youtube.com/watch?v=GNhcY6fTyBM

Power of Vulnerability—Brené Brown
www.ted.com/talks/brene_brown_on_vulnerability

Unconscious Bias—J. Renee Navarro
https://diversity.ucsf.edu/resources/unconscious-bias

Social Inequalities in Health—Ann Morning
www.youtube.com/watch?v=roAQHn5rEoQ

It Gets Better Promo—It Gets Better Project
www.youtube.com/watch?v=3IYv1__mSpE

The Urgency of Intersectionality—Kimberlé Crenshaw
www.ted.com/talks/kimberle_crenshaw_the_urgency_of_intersectionality

REFERENCES

American Civil Liberties Union. (2017). Racial profiling: Definition. Retrieved from https://www.aclu.org/other/racial-profiling-definition

Aponte, H. J. (1995). *Bread & spirit: Therapy with the new poor.* New York, NY: W. W. Norton.

Battle-Walters, K. (2004). *Sheila's shop: Working-class African American women talk about life, love, race, and hair.* Lanham, MD: Rowman & Littlefield.

Bias. (2017). *American Heritage Dictionary.* Retrieved from https://ahdictionary.com/word/search.html?q=bias

Bonilla-Silva, E. (2003). "New Racism," color-blind racism, and the future of whiteness in America. In A. W. Doane & E. Bonilla-Silva (Eds.), *White out: The continuing significance of racism* (pp. 271–284). New York, NY: Routledge Taylor & Francis.

Buckman, R., Reese, A., & Kinney, D. (2001). Narrative therapies. In P. Lehmann & N. Coady (Eds.), *Theoretical perspectives for direct social work practice: A generalist-eclectic approach* (pp. 279–302). New York, NY: Springer Publishing.

Chakraborti, N., & Garland, J. (2009). *Hate crime: Impact, causes and responses.* London, UK: Sage.

Council on Social Work Education. (2008). *Council on Social Work Education curriculum policy statements.* Alexandria, VA: Author.

Garran, A. M., & Rozas, L. W. (2013). Cultural competence revisited. *Journal of Ethnic & Cultural Diversity in Social Work, 22*(2), 97–111. doi:10.1080/15313204.2013.785337

Gerdes, K. E., & Segal, E. (2011). Importance of empathy for social work practice: Integrating new science. *Social Work, 56*(2), 141–148. doi:10.1093/sw/56.2.141

Hall, E., & Lindsey, S. (2014). Teaching cultural competence: A closer look at racial and ethnic identity formation. *The New Social Worker.* Retrieved from http://www.socialworker.com/feature-articles/ethics-articles/teaching-cultural-competence

Holosko, M. J., Skinner, J., & Robinson, R. S. (2007). Person-centered theory. In B. A. Thyer (Ed.), *Comprehensive handbook of social work and social welfare: Human behavior in the social environment* (pp. 297–326). Hoboken, NJ: John Wiley & Sons.

Jung, P. B., & Smith, R. F. (1993). *Heterosexism: An ethical challenge.* Albany: State University of New York Press.

Kagan, C., & Burton, M. (2005). Marginalisation. In G. Nelson & I. Prilleltensky (Eds.), *Community psychology: In pursuit of liberation and well-being* (pp. 292–308). New York, NY: Palgrave Macmillan.

King, S. H. (2011). The structure of empathy in social work practice. *Journal of Human Behavior in the Social Environment, 21*(6), 679–695. doi:10.1080/10911359.2011.583516

Kornblum, W., & Julian, J. (2007). *Social problems* (10th ed.). Englewood Cliffs, NJ: Prentice Hall.

Littlefield, M. B., McLane-Davison, D., & Vakalahi, H. F. (2015). Global gender inequality. *Encyclopedia of Social Work.* doi:10.1093/acrefore/9780199975839.013.932

Locke, D. C. (1992). *Increasing multicultural understanding: A comprehensive model.* Newbury Park, CA: Sage.

Lott, B., & Bullock, H. E. (2007). *Psychology and economic injustice: Personal, professional, and political intersections.* Washington, DC: American Psychological Association.

Lum, D. (2000). *Social work practice and people of color: A process stage approach.* Belmont, CA: Wadsworth.

McGoldrick, M., Giordano, J., & Garcia-Preto, N. (2005). *Ethnicity and family therapy.* New York, NY: Guilford.

Mitchell, E. R. (1999). Assessment and development of cultural competence. *Dissertation Abstracts International, 61*(03B), 1699.

Moses, A. E., & Hawkins, R. O. (1982). *Counseling lesbian women and gay men: A life issues approach.* St. Louis, MO: C.V. Mosby.

National Association of Social Workers. (2015). *Standards and indicators for cultural competence in social work practice.* Washington, DC: Author. Retrieved from https://www.socialworkers.org/LinkClick.aspx?fileticket=7dVckZAYUmk%3d&portalid=0

National Association of Social Workers. (2017). *Code of ethics.* Washington, DC: Author. Retrieved from https://www.socialworkers.org/About/Ethics/Code-of-Ethics/Code-of-Ethics-English

National Association of Social Workers & Center for Workforce Studies. (2006). *2004 national study of licensed social workers: Demographic factsheet—Female social workers.* Washington, DC: Author.

Ortega, R. M., & Faller, K. C. (2011). Training child welfare workers from an intersectional cultural humility perspective: A paradigm shift. *Child Welfare, 90*(5), 27–49.

Park, H., & Mykhyalyshyn, I. (2016). L.G.B.T. people are more likely to be targets of hate crimes than any other minority group. *The New York Times.* Retrieved from https://www.nytimes.com/interactive/2016/06/16/us/hate-crimes-against-lgbt.html

Pinderhughes, E. (1989). *Understanding race, ethnicity, and power: The key to efficacy on clinical practice.* New York, NY: Free Press.

Ridlen, S., & Dane, E. (1992). Individual and social implications of human differences. *Journal of Multicultural Social Work, 2*(2), 25–42. doi:10.1300/J285v02n02_03

Rodgers, A. Y., & Potocky, M. (1998). Preparing students to work with culturally diverse clients. *Social Work Education, 17*(1), 95–100. doi:10.1080/02615479811220081

Rodgers, S. T. (2015). Racism. *Encyclopedia of Social Work.* doi:10.1093/acrefore/9780199975839.013.1009

Rogers, C. R. (1951). *Client-centered therapy.* Boston, MA: Houghton-Mifflin.

Rothery, M., & Tutty, L. (2001). Client-centered theory. In P. Lehmann & N. Coady (Eds.), *Theoretical perspectives for direct social work practice: A generalist-eclectic approach* (pp. 223–239). New York, NY: Springer Publishing.

Seipel, A., & Way, I. (2006). Culturally competent social work: Practice with Latino clients. *New Social Worker, 13*(4), 4–7.

Siddique, H., & Laughland, O. (2017, August 23). Charlottesville: United Nations warns US over "alarming" racism. *The Guardian.* Retrieved from https://www.theguardian.com/world/2017/aug/23/charlottesville-un-committee-warns-us-over-rise-of-racism

Sinclair, S. L., & Monk, G. (2005). Discursive empathy: A new foundation for therapeutic practice. *British Journal of Guidance & Counselling, 33*(3), 333–349. doi:10.1080/03069880500179517

Smith, L., Foley, P. F., & Chaney, M. P. (2008). Addressing classism, ableism, and heterosexism in counselor education. *Journal of Counseling & Development, 86*, 303–309. doi:10.1002/j.1556-6678.2008.tb00513.x

Sue, D. W., Capodilupo, C. M., Torino, G. C., Bucceri, J. M., Holder, A. M., Nadal, K. L., & Esquilin, M. (2007). Racial microaggressions in everyday life: Implications for clinical practice. *American Psychologist, 62*, 271–286. doi:10.1037/0003-066X.62.4.271

Sue, D. W., & Sue, D. (2012). *Counseling the culturally diverse: Theory and practice.* Hoboken, NJ: John Wiley & Sons.

Tervalon, M., & Murray-García, J. (1998). Cultural humility versus cultural competence: A critical distinction in defining physician training outcomes in multicultural education. *Journal of Health Care for the Poor and Underserved, 9*(2), 117–125. doi:10.1353/hpu.2010.0233

Thomas, A. J., & Schwarzbaum, S. (2017). *Culture and identity: Life stories for counselors and therapists.* Thousand Oaks, CA: Sage.

Vanaerschot, G. (2007). Empathic resonance and differential experiential processing: An experiential process-directive approach. *American Journal of Psychotherapy, 61*(3), 313–331. doi:10.1176/appi.psychotherapy.2007.61.3.313

Van Dijk, T. A. (1997). Political discourse and racism: Describing others in Western parliaments. In S. H. Riggins (Ed.), *The language and politics of exclusion: Others in discourse* (pp. 31–64). Thousand Oaks, CA: Sage.

Young, I. M. (1990). *Justice and the politics of difference.* Princeton, NJ: Princeton University Press.

CHAPTER 8

Advancing Human Rights and Social Justice in Your Field Placement

CASE VIGNETTE

Kendall was a second-year MSW student doing her placement at an agency on an Indian reservation in the midwestern United States. A few months into her placement, Kendall began to hear complaints from her clients about health issues that were cropping up within families and the community. Concerned about this trend emerging in her placement, Kendall decided to do a little research to gather recent health data from the community and found few resources available that could provide any information.

Kendall began to ask service recipients at the agency about their experiences, and documented that information. It was not long before she heard about community groups that had formed to identify the cause of the issues that her clients were reporting to her—with a main hypothesis that a local oil refinery was causing both air and water pollution. They struggled to find any definitive data, but similar symptoms among residents began popping up near another oil refinery a few states away. Kendall began to attend the community group meetings in an effort to assist in data collection and brainstorming potential action efforts.

However, Kendall has noticed that some in the community have cooled off to her, and others have started to get openly hostile to all of her work in the community—not just her efforts to stop the pre sumed pollution and poor health issues. Jobs are hard to come by on the reservation and in the nearby areas, and any position at the refinery—from janitor to engineer—is extremely coveted. Plus, the wages of the refinery workers support local businesses. New restaurants have opened, and a new grocery store is planned to open soon. For the first time that many can recall, the flood of people away from the community has slowed, and anecdotal accounts suggest alcohol and drug abuse is also slowly declining.

What should Kendall do if her own values around environmental justice conflict with community leaders' steadfast support of the refinery and the economic benefits it has provided?

How should Kendall approach her work in the community if the large majority of community members, including many of her own clients, want her to stop volunteering with the community agency that they see as racial?

(continued)

© Springer Publishing Company DOI: 10.1891/9780826175533.0008

CASE VIGNETTE *(continued)*

How does Kendall reconcile her desire to adhere to the National Association of Social Workers'
(NASW's) Code of Ethics, which include advocating for environmental justice, economic justice,
and upholding her clients' rights to self-determination?

LEARNING OBJECTIVES

This chapter focuses on Competency 3: Advance Human Rights and Social, Economic, and
Environmental Justice within your field placement and beyond. It begins with a brief overview of
the conceptual theories and frameworks for social justice. This is followed by an exploration of the
types and sources of power, social locations, social constructions, social processes, social identities, conflicts, and the ways these concepts interact in relation to the field experience. The chapter
then reviews visions and strategies for change. By the end of this chapter, you will be able to

- Recognize the importance of advancing social, economic, and environmental justice.
- Understand the conceptual theories and frameworks for social justice work.
- Understand the facets of power and social aspects that contribute to injustices in these areas.
- Use change strategies to implement social justice strategies in your field placement and beyond.

CONCEPTUAL THEORIES AND FRAMEWORKS FOR SOCIAL JUSTICE

Social justice is a broad concept that encompasses fair and unbiased treatment of all individuals, eradication of discriminatory practices and institutionalized oppression, and
establishment of equality for members of historically marginalized and oppressed groups—
achieved through the establishment of truly equal opportunity and access to resources
(Barsky, 2010; Reisch, 2002; Young, 2001). The Council on Social Work Education (CSWE)
addresses the social justice mandate by stating that "social work's purpose is actualized
through its quest for social justice, the prevention of conditions that limit human rights,
the elimination of poverty, and the enhancement of the quality of life for all persons"
(2015, p. 5). It specifically calls upon all social workers to "understand the global interconnections of oppression and human rights violations; advocate for human rights [...]; and
engage in practices that advance social, economic, and environmental justice" (2015, p. 8).

The meanings of social justice have wide implications, yet can be ambiguous, and moving from interpretation to practice is challenging. It is important to remember that the concept
of social justice is bound by context and history. Attempts to define the correct relationship
between individuals, communities, states, and countries have been explored for centuries by
philosophers, political theorists, and social workers (Finn & Jacobson, 2017).

The notion of social justice within the field of social work is generally based on Western
ideologies and the Judeo-Christian religious tradition (Finn & Jacobson, 2017). Beliefs
around social justice are generally abstract and are in line with what is moral and/or
right—with a specific focus on the notion that all citizens are equal and have the right to

meet their basic needs, the desire to share opportunities as equitably as possible, and the obligation to work toward eliminating unjustified inequalities. Caputo (2002) points out that although many notions of social justice within social work actually maintain the status quo, social justice remains an important goal of social work.

Some scholars examine social justice through the always-present tension that exists between individual liberty and the common good. These scholars would argue that social justice is endorsed to the degree that we can promote collective good without violating basic individual freedoms (Finn & Jacobson, 2017). Others contend that social justice incorporates fairness within fundamental rights and duties, economic opportunities, and social conditions (Miller, 1976).

A perspective often used by social work is that of a distributive approach to social justice—advocating for an organization of societal institutions that assures human rights and access to meaningful social participation, as well as equitable distribution of resources. Distributive justice focuses on what society owes an individual. Other frameworks focus on what people owe society—legal justice—and what individuals owe one another—commutative justice (Reichert, 2003; Van Soest, 1992).

Social work generally addresses the conflicting philosophical frameworks used to explain choices in the realm of social justice using three dominant theories: utilitarian, libertarian, and egalitarian (Finn & Jacobson, 2017). Utilitarian theories consider decisions that result in greater good and less harm for the most people to be the appropriate course of action. The right of the individual is deemed less important than the needs of the community or society at large; as such, those rights may be infringed on if a particular decision results in assisting the greater good (McCormick, 2003). Libertarian perspectives focus on individual freedom from external control or influence. This framework rejects the concept of equitable resource distribution, instead arguing that individuals have the right to any resources they acquire as long as no law is broken (Nozick, 1974). Clearly, this is in direct contrast to the utilitarian perspective as the obligation to society lies in the protection of individual freedoms. Finally, egalitarian theoretical frameworks argue that everyone should be guaranteed the same rights, opportunities, and access to goods and resources (Rawls, 1971). This approach advocates for the redistribution of resources to the vulnerable, oppressed, or disadvantaged in society to guarantee that unmet needs are rectified (Rawls, 1971).

> **Field Reflection Questions**
>
> In your current field placement, which human rights and social justice theoretical perspective(s) do you see in action?
>
> In what ways do those perspectives manifest? (For example, who is allowed to receive services? What theoretical framework would that decision likely be classified as?)
>
> How are the theoretical perspectives similar to your own? How are they different?

Political philosopher Rawls (2001) examines what would need to be present in a society that meets basic human needs, reduces excessive stress, encourages individuals' abilities, and reduces threats to well-being. Rawls advocates for an equal distribution of resources and burdens from tangible resources (good and services) and intangible resources (power and opportunity). Social justice comes down to two principles (Rawls, 2001, pp. 42–43):

- Each person has the same indefeasible claim to a fully adequate scheme of equal basic liberties, the scheme which is compatible with the same scheme of liberties for all.

● Social and economic inequalities are to satisfy two conditions: (a) They are to be attached to offices and positions open to all under conditions of fair equality of opportunity, and (b) they are to be to the greatest benefit of the least advantaged members of society (the difference principle).

Distributive justice, as defined by Rawls, helps the field of social work to integrate social justice into both micro and macro practice settings (Wakefield, 1988). This theoretical framework focuses counteracting inequalities by advocating for unequal distribution of resources only if it is done to advance the least advantaged groups in society (Reisch, 1998).

TYPES AND SOURCES OF POWER

In Chapter 7, we discussed forms of oppression that exist because of inequities in power that allow groups in power to act out their biases, prejudices, and stereotypes in ways that deprive those not in power of full access to resources, self-actualization, and autonomy (Thomas & Schwarzbaum, 2017). This section does a deeper dive into the types of power that exist, as well as the social dimensions that contribute to these power differences.

Although power is a complex term with multiple meanings depending on the context, the type of power we focus on in regard to social justice refers to power within social structure and systems. Legitimately or otherwise, certain individuals and groups have power, and with that power they use force (of varying types) to exploit others for their own gain. The purpose of focusing on power within social relationships and societal structures is to better understand how we, as social workers, can better understand that social justice advocacy can attempt to address the connections between privilege and exploitation.

Three types of power exist (Dobratz, Waldner, & Buzzell, 2012):

1. Coercive and dominant power: Likely the most obvious use of power, coercive power uses the command of resources to dominate others and force them into submission. For example, coercive power in the form of physical force could include military strength, brute force, and violence.

2. Authority and legitimate power: Society creates order by acknowledging power on the basis of tradition, norms, and laws. Authority and legitimate power is the form of power that arises from this acknowledgment. Members of society accept that specific individuals or groups have power on the basis of a sense of legitimacy and obedience or duty. This type of power is able to be obtained because individuals believe that placing power in states offers protection to members of society and preserves community interests.

3. Privileged and interdependent power: This type of power tends to be more subtle, but still has dramatic implications for social interactions and distribution of power in a society. It power focuses specifically on the power relationship between two actors. Often, the actors do not realize exactly how much influence they have in a given situation. Piven and Cloward (2005) point out that people have potential power when others depend on them for the contributions they make to the interdependent relationships that make up society. Johnson (2006) also points out that privilege links to the ways society deems certain differences to be important or

significant. These include
unearned advantages (one
specific group rewarded) and
conferred dominance (when
one group pressures another
group, or groups, into con-
forming to that privilege) as
ways that privilege is created
in society.

Field Reflection Questions

In your current field placement, which of these types of power do you currently see play out?

Can you think of an example of each of these types of power in your field placement? If so, what are they? If not, can you imagine an example that could poten-tially exist?

Framing societal power within the field placement experience, it is important to rec-ognize that power is the ability of individuals, groups, and/or structures to attain a plan through authority, influence, or even force (Dobratz et al., 2012). This is important because it recognizes that power exists on the micro level as well as on the macro level. When we are thinking about social justice and human rights, we are particularly concerned with the ways that dominant power, individually or collectively, is exploited by privileged indi-viduals or groups. Often within the guise of preserving societal interests, certain groups end up marginalized, scapegoated, and exploited for the benefit of more powerful groups.

SOCIAL IDENTITIES

According to Kirk and Okazawa-Rey (2010), identity is how we define ourselves at any specific instance in time and is a process of growth, change, and renewal. Identity may seem fixed, but over the course of the life span, it is more fluid. An interplay of individual choices, particular life events, community recognition and expectations, societal categorization, classifications, and socialization all come into play in identity formation. Most definitions of identity point to the connections among us as individuals, how we are perceived by other people, and how we are classified by social institutions. You can conceptualize social identities through the lens of social work practice. The micro level is usually the level at which individuals are most comfortable with themselves and their social identities. At the mezzo level, individual identi-ties and needs meet group standards, expectations, obligations, responsibilities, and demands. Comparisons are made, and individuals either have their identities affirmed or discover incon-gruities in who they believe they are and how they are viewed by others. "Classifying and labeling human beings, often according to real or assumed physical, biological, or genetic dif-ferences, is a way to distinguish who is included and who is excluded from a group, to ascribe particular characteristics," and to prescribe social locations (Kirk & Okazawa-Rey, 2010, p. 52).

SOCIAL LOCATIONS

Social location is a way of expressing the core of a person's existence in the social and political world. Social locations are the groups people are a part of because of their place or position in history and society. Individuals all have a social location that is based on the intersection of all of their identities and group memberships. These identities include race, gender, ability, religion, sexual orientation, social class, age, actual geographic location, and more. As discussed in Chapter 7, our identity, how we see the world, and how we are able to move through the world are greatly influenced by our group memberships. Specific roles, rules, power, and the existence or lack of privilege are a result of these memberships as well.

SOCIAL CONSTRUCTIONS

Social constructions are difficult to define because social construction scholars are generally averse to the limitations of definitions. When thinking about social constructions in regard to field placement, it is the understanding that the world we live in and the world our clients live in are not simply there, but are actually continually constructed in elements of everyday life (Holstein & Gubrium, 2008). Instead of viewing the world as something that exists and can be discovered, social constructions are the variety of social interchanges that make up the reality of the world. In essence, the clients you work with participate in the creation of their own world, just as you participate in the creation of your own world.

In addition, social constructionists recognize that there is no reality, only descriptions—an understanding that lends an immense amount of importance to language. Everything about the world is mediated by language, and because of this, you as the social worker benefit from focused attention on how language functions for your clients, within your agency, and within society as a whole.

Important aspects of social construction, as described by Witkin (2011), include the understanding that knowledge is dependent on historical and cultural aspects; a recognition that language has the power to establish and give organized existence to something; a critical lens concerning any knowledge that is taken for granted (regularly seen in our dichotomous, categorical society); an understanding that knowledge is social action; and a belief that knowledge is sustained by social processes. The belief that human beings, in relation to one another, construct the world is often difficult for individuals to accept because it is antithetical to Western cultures' emphasis on individualism.

SOCIAL PROCESSES

Originating from sociology theories, social processes refer to the various patterns of social interactions in which individuals and groups interact and establish social relationships. Examples of different forms of social interaction include competition, cooperation, conflict, assimilation, exploitation, accommodation, and others (Ginsberg, 1956). Although there are a large number of social processes (e.g., education, political, religious, economic), Ruhela (2005) argues that the vast array of social processes all fall under two large categories:

Field Reflection Questions

Which social identities and social locations can you identify when thinking about the clients with whom you work within your field placement?

Can you think of an example from your field placement in which social constructions would be a useful lens to use in your work? In what ways are realities socially constructed in your current work?

1. Integrative, conjunctive, or associative processes: These social processes bring individuals and groups together to produce unity among members of a group or

society. These processes take the interests of all members in to account. Examples are cooperation and accommodation.

2. Disintegrative, disjunctive, or dissociative processes: These social processes AudioVolumeMute produce hatred, tension, and bring disagreement among the members of a group or society. Competition, rivalry, and conflict are the main disintegrative processes.

Oppression and discrimination are embedded in the complexity of ever-changing and constant social processes.

CONFLICT

Conflict is an important social process that is a huge part of society as a whole. It is a codified form of struggle that is deliberate in its attempt to oppose or resist the will of others. Conflict is universal, ever present, and personal. Although there are a multitude of theories on the origin of conflict, we do know that social change can be a direct cause of conflict, and conflict can result in social change. Conflict may seem overwhelmingly negative, because of the fact that it resists cooperation and can cause chaos; however, conflict can perform positive functions as well. It can result in a redefinition of circumstances by the individuals or groups in conflict. Generally, the groups in conflict have to give up outdated value systems and accept new value systems at the end of the conflict—this may result in new efforts of cooperation and accommodation.

There is perhaps no better known example of using conflict in the pursuit of social justice than that documented in a passage from Martin Luther King, Jr.'s "Letter From Birmingham Jail" (1963, p. 5), in which King states:

> You express a great deal of anxiety over our willingness to break laws. This is certainly a legitimate concern. Since we so diligently urge people to obey the Supreme Court's decision of 1954 outlawing segregation in the public schools, it is rather strange and paradoxical to find us consciously breaking laws. One may well ask, "How can you advocate breaking some laws and obeying others?" The answer is found in the fact that there are two types of laws: there are just laws, and there are unjust laws. I would agree with St. Augustine that "An unjust law is no law at all."

IMPLICATIONS FOR FIELD AND STRATEGIES FOR CHANGE

The previous section invited you to reflect on what is, potentially, a new way of thinking about the world, and your experience in your field placement. All too often, social justice is considered something that a social worker simply carves time out for (e.g., on something like an advocacy day), as opposed to being a framework for practice. It can be challenging to envision a practice philosophy that infuses these theories in an effort to have a human rights and social justice focus in daily work in your field placement. For example, traditional assessments in clinical practice often focus on problems that a social construction framework will remind you are culturally and relationally bound. This opens up the possibility of seemingly endless interpretations with no one interpretation as the truth.

However, the social worker can use collaborative approaches to seek to understand the client's theory of problem, which helps the social worker toward collaboration solutions.

Within practice, these lenses provide the social context necessary to recognize the impacts of oppression and economic disadvantages experienced by clients. As mentioned in Chapter 7, social justice requires practitioner transparency, collaboration, and respectful curiosity and humility in work with clients. Major (2011) emphasizes how social constructions are well suited for practice with families in the child welfare system because of their emphasis on contextual meanings—so often low-income families are judged according to the same standards as those with significantly more opportunities and resources.

Harrison, VanDeusen, and Way (2016) identify three strategies for implementing a social justice–infused practice framework even in micro-level social work practice. The first of these is, as discussed in Chapter 7, increased self-awareness. Bonnycastle (2011) provides a helpful continuum for examining this critical theme of the self-awareness needed for effective justice-focused micro practice. This includes moving from a simple recognition that discrimination is bad to a full confrontation of the privilege the social worker holds, and the impact of the social worker's practice in relation to the social locations of the clients served. This process involves overcoming the social worker's denial and struggle to change.

Field Reflection Questions

In what ways do you infuse a justice-informed lens in your current field placement practice? In what ways could you be more intentional about the infusion of the justice focus?

Which therapeutic approaches lend themselves to justice-informed micro practice? Which of these could you apply in your current field placement?

The second strategy discussed by Harrison et al. (2016) is justice-informed engagement, assessment, and intervention. Because of their person-in-environment perspective, social workers are better prepared to infuse justice through their micro practice skills. This includes a focus on enhancing individuals' economic, psychological, and social conditions through collaborative approaches. The quest for social justice within micro practice can be infused into many theoretical approaches and intervention models. Examples include client-centered and collaborative approaches; strengths-based and empowerment approaches; biopsychosocial assessment that includes the historical and political bases for social constructions; and a focus on the ways in which oppression, discrimination, and historical trauma can contribute in the development of individual difficulties.

The final strategy discussed by Harrison et al. (2016) is justice-informed policy and systems advocacy. As discussed in greater detail in Chapter 10, social workers must infuse social justice in their micro work by addressing social and organizational policies that perpetuate inequities. Similarly, social workers work in concert with their clients toward social and economic justice, as they may strive to address inequities in their own lives as their awareness of such inequities arises in their therapeutic experience (Moradi, 2012).

Reisch and Garvin (2016) stress the importance of using social justice–infused approaches, especially as they relate to processes and outcomes. Although you are unable to deeply scrutinize every action you take, every facial expression, every word decision, and so on, it benefits you to critically self-reflect on the implications of these social interactions with clients. You need to consider the social justice implications of such processes, including how each part of the process reveals information about power differentials; how the actions reflect considerations of the empowerment of clients and oppressive social conditions; how you have informed your work through critical self-reflection on sources of injustice; which roles you are fulfilling in your social interactions with clients and whether those are reflective of the needs and rights of others; and, finally, what a critical self-reflection on the potential of abuse of power reveals.

In thinking about social justice implications in mezzo and macro levels of practice, it is important to relate the personal and the political. The concerns that clients bring into their work with you do not arise solely because of individual shortcomings, but also because of unjust policies and practices that occur within agencies and the larger society. The driving force for social justice–infused social work practice is the skill of challenging inequalities, which creates opportunities for change. You must understand that not every mezzo and macro challenge you attempt will be successful, and the process of challenging oppressive practices and policies can be uncomfortable and tedious for you as you undertake the challenge. The most effective and appropriate challenges need to be person-centered; use an egalitarian value approach; use empowerment approaches to assist individuals in reducing unjust policies; and, like micro work, focus on process and outcome.

As an example of challenging a potential abuse of power, consider this experience. In your placement with Child Protection Services, one of your clients, a 17-year-old foster youth, was denied a request to begin attending an after-school church youth group. The agency made this decision on the basis of some bullying the client had experienced. On reflection, you recognize that the agency you are working within may have misused its power under the guise of "protecting" the client from harm. You decide to challenge this decision by approaching your supervisor and explaining that you appreciate the agency's concern for the client's safety; however, you are concerned about the organization taking away the client's right to self-determination. You share with your supervisor the importance of this client, who is approaching the age of 18, having the opportunity to make his own decisions, and not being denied the opportunity to attend an activity that may benefit him greatly. Using the NASW's *Code of Ethics* as your guide, how could you challenge this decision in a constructive way, and assert the client's right to self-determination and his right to nonoppressive service delivery from the agency?

CASE EXAMPLE 8.1: IT'S A SHAME, REALLY

Bianca is a senior BSW student completing her field placement at Prairie View Middle School, located in a low-income area in a mid-Atlantic state. She was pulled aside by Mrs. Iverson, a science teacher at the school. Mrs. Iverson has concerns about a student named Andrea, a seventh-grader who is having a difficult time turning in her homework, even though she is one of the top-performing students on tests and in-class activities. Mrs. Iverson has tried to reach out to Andrea's parents by phone and email, but has never gotten a response. She tells Bianca that she is pretty sure that Andrea's parents are unengaged and are not supporting her in her education. Mrs. Iverson says, "It's a shame really. We see it time and again. Really bright kids with parents who just don't care about education."

Bianca decides to reach out to other teachers who have Andrea in their classes—they report a similar pattern. She decides to reach out to the teachers of Andrea's younger siblings and finds out that they do not have the same issue with turning in their homework. In fact, neither of them had any missing assignments.

Perplexed, Bianca sets up an appointment to chat with Andrea. Andrea insists that she has simply "dropped the ball" and "will do better on her upcoming assignments." Bianca is unconvinced and discusses the issue with her supervisor. Her supervisor suggests a home visit. Bianca attempts to contact the parents but does not have any luck. She receives permission to drop by the home over the weekend along with her supervisor.

Bianca and her supervisor learn that both Andrea's father and mother work multiple part-time jobs to support their family, and neither of them gets home until after the children are asleep. Andrea has taken on the role of caretaker for her two younger siblings, which includes assisting them on their studies and getting them dinner. She simply does not have time to complete nightly homework on top of her other responsibilities.

Bianca knows that a justice-infused approach to this situation is one that advocates for equitable approaches that consider the impact of the economic conditions for the student. She sets up a meeting with Mrs. Iverson, Andrea's other teachers, and her supervisors to brainstorm alternative approaches for Andrea's learning. However, she does not stop there—Bianca recognizes that this situation is likely happening to other students. Bianca wants to know, on an institutional level:

What biases might be stopping teachers from trying to improve the situation for other students? How can these biases be addressed?

What opportunities exist to create more equitable policies?

Who needs to be at the table when brainstorming these solutions?

SUMMARY

Many of the issues facing the people you work with are rooted in far-reaching social, political, economic, and environmental conditions. Simultaneously, much of the assistance we as social workers are able to provide is done at an individual level. We must resist the urge to assume that the majority of problems are personal, rather than reflecting wider societal and structural problems. This chapter focused on different concepts related to injustices at multiple levels. First, conceptual and theoretical concepts around social justice were explored. This section focused on how social justice calls for the fair and unbiased treatment of all individuals, eradication of discriminatory practices and institutionalized oppression, and establishment of equality for members of historically marginalized and oppressed groups.

Although the previous chapter discussed various types of oppression and discrimination that your clients may face, this chapter explored the sources of power that allow dominant groups to exploit and marginalize others, including coercive and dominant power, authority and legitimate power, and privileged and interdependent power. Power can exist on all levels—micro, mezzo, and macro. Social identities and social locations were defined in this chapter, and how those relate to power and privilege was discussed.

Social constructions were also explored, as was their relation to the field placement experience. Grasping the fact that what "reality" is or is not is greatly influenced by our own experiences and social interchanges, which is also the case for your clients, is important when we are confronted with what some deem to be truth or fact. Language is highly important because it is the only way that we can collaborate with the clients to truly understand their lived reality. Because of this, attention to language is vital to the justice-informed helping relationship. Social processes were defined in the chapter, and examples of them were given. Conflicts, which have a unique and often contradictory relationship to the field of social work, were discussed.

The final section of this chapter explored strategies infusing a justice lens into your practice in the field. Increased self-awareness; justice-informed engagement, assessment, and intervention; and justice-informed policy and systems advocacy were explained. All of these strategies require intentional, critical self-reflection on the choices you make, the language you use, and the ways you, and others, are potentially abusing your power. Multiple theoretical frameworks and intervention models lend themselves to justice-informed practice, if you are intentional about applying them in such a way.

CRITICAL THINKING QUESTIONS

Competency 3 focuses on advancing human rights and social, economic, and environmental justice. As a social worker, you are trained to maintain a person-in-environment perspective as you engage with your clients. This uniquely positions you to maintain a justice-informed framework in your work. You must move beyond the understanding that discrimination is bad, and move toward a full confrontation of your own power and privilege, and how it impacts the clients you wish to serve. You are also expected to recognize the impacts of oppression and economic disadvantages experienced by clients. Social justice requires practitioner transparency, collaboration, and respectful curiosity and humility in work with clients. An understanding that social constructions are well suited for justice-informed practice because of their emphasis on contextual meanings is vital. It helps you to identify ways in which individuals, families, and groups are judged on unbalanced standards. Advancing human rights and social justice is an ongoing, intentional process that is actively infused in every aspect of practice, not simply something that the social worker does on the side with his or her free time (although engaging in additional forms of advocacy above and beyond the workplace is fantastic as well). The following questions focus on advancing human rights and social, economic, and environmental justice:

1. Charlotte is a BSW intern placed with a housing agency. Many of the clients in low-income housing face housing discrimination. Charlotte knows it is her duty to advocate for her clients both inside her agency and outside. Identify potential injustice-infused micro-level practice steps that Charlotte can take. Identify mezzo-level justice-infused practice steps Charlotte can take. Identify macro-level justice-infused practice steps Charlotte can take. Discuss how you would approach this scenario.

2. Consider some of the conflicts that Charlotte may encounter as she engages in the multilevel justice-infused practice you identified. How might she work through those conflicts? Is it Charlotte's role to bring justice-informed perspectives to her colleagues?

3. Concepts of social constructions encourage us to be critically self-reflective of our language usage with clients. Can you identify problematic language you have heard used with clients? Reflect on and describe what was problematic about it, and how the situation could have been approached in a justice-informed way.

4. Advancing social justice requires practitioner transparency, collaboration, and respectful curiosity and humility in work with clients. It also requires that you consider the social justice implications of your interactions with clients. In reflecting upon your work with clients in your field placement, describe an experience in which you identified a potential abuse of power, by yourself, someone else, or the agency as a whole. Reflect on and describe your affective reaction to this experience. Describe how this situation could be approached if it were to happen in the future.

■ COMPETENCY 3: ADVANCE HUMAN RIGHTS AND SOCIAL, ECONOMIC, AND ENVIRONMENTAL JUSTICE

Social workers understand that every person, regardless of position in society, has fundamental human rights such as freedom, safety, privacy, an adequate standard of living, health care, and education. They understand the global interconnections of oppression and human rights violations, and are knowledgeable about theories of human need and social justice and strategies to promote social and economic justice and human rights. Social workers understand that strategies designed to eliminate oppressive environmental, economic, social, and cultural human rights are protected. Social workers:

- Apply their understanding of social, economic, and environmental justice to advocate for human rights at the individual and system levels.

- Engage in practices that advance social, economic, and environmental justice.

CASE SUMMARY—"PUTTING ON A SHOW"

PRACTICE SETTING DESCRIPTION

My name is Sara and I am a senior BSW student completing an internship at a local family services agency in a small city on the West Coast. The agency provides individual and family counseling services on a sliding fee scale. The agency also works with Child Protection Services on reunification causes. I was assigned to work with J. for 6 months in an effort to reunify her with her three children.

IDENTIFYING DATA

J., a 28-year-old Latina female, has three children: Brenda, Tasha, and Darren. J.'s children were removed due to substantiated charges of neglect. The children are ages 12, 6 and 3. The children stayed with J.'s sister after they were removed from J.'s care. J. has been battling a drug addiction and she was unable to care for her children—their home was found to be squalid. After the removal of the children, J. began her third attempt at completing a drug treatment program. She was successful and 2 months ago was reunified with the children.

PRESENTING PROBLEM

J. comes to weekly sessions, and reports that she is doing well maintaining her sobriety. We spend a significant amount of time in our work discussing coping strategies for her stressors. She reports that the majority of her stresses include the demands of parenting three children with little support and financial stressors.

In field seminar, one of my peers, who is placed at a local middle school, shared a situation from her field placement that she was conflicted about. My peer shared that a student named

"Jane" was expressing concerns about the fact that her mother had begun using marijuana at home. The personal use of marijuana is legal in our state, but it is not allowed under the conditions of the reunification agreement. This concerned Jane because she and her younger siblings just barely moved back in with their mom. Jane also shared that her mother recently got a new boyfriend and he has been spending more and more time in the home. Her mom told Jane not to say anything about the marijuana because they could be split up again. Jane is very stressed that someone is going to find out and she and her siblings will be forced to move back in with her aunt. This is causing Jane a lot of stress and anxiety.

I recognized the similarities in the story, and I know that Brenda attends the same school that my peer is at for her field placement. It is clear that the young woman being described is my client's daughter.

ASSESSMENT

When assessing the situation only from my interactions with J., she appears to manage this transition fairly well. The most important aspect of our work together is the focus on coping strategies for her to use so she does not relapse. In addition, J. is focused on finding a new job, because her current job stocking shelves at a local grocery chain is providing her with only 20 hours of work per week. J. has reported that although she is stressed and anxious, she has not had the urge to use drugs or alcohol to cope with the stress.

J. has many strengths. She is highly motivated to maintain custody of her children. She mentioned that the thought of losing custody of the children was what motivated her to finally complete a treatment program. While in treatment, she became aware of the myriad of services that her family qualified for, but she is not receiving Supplemental Nutrition Assistance Program (SNAP) benefits, and her children are not covered by Medicaid.

My interactions with J.'s children indicate that they are much happier now that they are back with their mother. In talking with Brenda specifically, she noted that her aunt's house was "fine," but it was not the same as being with her mother. They were relieved that they were able to stay with their aunt, and not a "stranger," while J. worked on her sobriety.

J. has shown great resilience in achievement and maintenance of abstinence from drugs, and in her quest to be reunified with her children. She has identified ways that she can support her family, and took the initiative to access services they needed. She is also actively looking for a full-time job or a second part-time job.

CASE PROCESS SUMMARY

I was very surprised when I made the connection between my peer's story and my client. J. and I have worked together for 6 months and I believe that we have worked very well together. It seemed as though she was being very open with me, and now I am questioning if perhaps J. felt the need to put on a show with an overly happy face in our work together. Although she has been honest with me about the ongoing stressors in her life, she has remained positive and open to collaborating on solutions and strategies for facing these stressors. During supervision I shared that I felt a simultaneous sense of betrayal and hurt, given that J. has possibly been lying about her sobriety to me. I began to self-reflect on how my actions may have encouraged J.'s actions.

Sara, BSW student intern

DISCUSSION QUESTIONS

- On the basis of the information provided, what issues related to human rights and social, economic, and environmental justice can you identify within this case?
- Consider the case example in terms of social location. From the information provided, what are the different social identities that J. may inhabit? How might these locations be influencing J.'s construction of reality?
- Similarly, think about Sara's social identities and social locations. How might they impact Sara's construction of reality?
- What are some of the areas that Sara should focus her self-reflection on using a justice-infused lens? Identify which of the strategies discussed in the chapter that Sara may be able to use in her work with J.

ELECTRONIC COMPETENCY RESOURCES

WEBSITE LINKS

Defining Economic Justice and Social Justice—Center for Economic and Social Justice
www.cesj.org/learn/definitions/defining-economic-justice-and-social-justice

Community Voices Heard: Engaging Constituents for Social, Economic, and Racial Justice—Emerging Practitioners in Philanthropy
www.slideshare.net/EPIPNational/community-voices-heard-engaging
-constituents-for-social-economic-and-racial-justice?qid=c6ee9dc7-4ff1-44f2-a
19e-b38286c6d6e3&v=&b=&from_search=31

Environmental Social Work: A Call to Action—Claudia Dewane
www.socialworkhelper.com/2017/10/09/environmental-social-work-call-action

VIDEO LINKS

Who Am I? Think Again—Hetain Patel and Yuyu Rau
www.ted.com/talks/hetain_patel_who_am_i_think_again?language=en

Developing a Human Rights Approach to Strengthen Practice—Jane McPherson
www.youtube.com/watch?v=2PHTaqYeB1M

Social Work Education: Environmental Justice—Sondra Fogel
www.youtube.com/watch?v=TB_9fVGQNdI

Social Constructionism—Sydney Brown
www.youtube.com/watch?v=gVCkJ7jLnz0

REFERENCES

Barsky, A. E. (2010). *Ethics and values in social work: An integrated approach for a comprehensive curriculum.* New York, NY: Oxford University Press.

Bonnycastle, C. R. (2011). Social justice along a continuum: A relational illustrative model. *Social Service Review, 85,* 267–295. doi:10.1086/660703

Caputo, R. K. (2002). Social justice, the ethics of care, and market economies. *Families in Society, 83,* 355–364. doi:10.1606/1044-3894.10

Council on Social Work Education (2015). *Educational policy and accreditation standards for baccalaureate and master's social work programs.* Retrieved from https://www.cswe.org/getattachment/Accreditation/Accreditation-Process/2015-EPAS/2015EPAS_Web_FINAL.pdf.aspx

Dobratz, B., Waldner, L., & Buzzell, T. L. (2012). *Power, politics, and society: An introduction to political sociology.* Boston, MA: Pearson.

Finn, J. L., & Jacobson, M. (2017). *What is social justice?* Oxford University Press. Retrieved from https://blog.oup.com/2017/03/what-is-social-justice

Ginsberg, M. (1956). *On the diversity of morals.* London, UK: William Heinemann.

Harrison, J., VanDeusen, K., & Way, I. (2016). Embedding social justice within micro social work curricula. *Smith College Studies in Social Work, 86*(3), 258–273. doi:10.1080/00377317.2016.1191802

Holstein, J. A., & Gubrium, J. F. (Eds.). (2008). *Handbook of constructionist research.* New York, NY: Guilford.

Johnson, A. G. (2006). *Privilege, power, and difference.* New York, NY: McGraw-Hill.

King, M. L., Jr. (1963). Letter from Birmingham jail. *The Atlantic.* Retrieved from https://www.theatlantic.com/politics/archive/1963/08/martin-luther-kings-letter-from-birmingham-jail/274668

Kirk, G., & Okazawa-Rey, M. (2010). Living in a globalizing world. In G. Kirk & M. Okazawa-Rey (Eds.), *Women's lives: Multicultural perspectives* (pp. 371–392). New York, NY: McGraw-Hill.

Major, D. R. (2011). Mostly we played whatever she chose. In S. L. Witkin (Ed.), *Social construction and social work practice: Interpretations and innovations* (pp. 154–187). New York, NY: Columbia University Press.

McCormick, P. T. (2003). Whose justice? An examination of nine models of justice. *Social Thought, 22*(2-3), 7–25. doi:10.1080/15426432.2003.9960338

Miller, D. (1976). *Social justice.* Oxford, UK: Clarendon Press.

Moradi, B. (2012). Feminist social justice orientation: An indicator of optimal functioning? *Counseling Psychologist, 40*(8), 1133–1148. doi:10.1177/0011000012439612

Nozick, R. (1974). *Anarchy, state, and Utopia.* New York, NY: Basic Books.

Piven, F. F., & Cloward, R. (2005). Rulemaking, rulebreaking, and power. In T. Janoski, R. R. Alford, A. Hicks, & M. A. Schwartz (Eds.), *Handbook of political sociology* (pp. 33–53). New York, NY: Cambridge University Press.

Rawls, J. (1971). *A theory of justice* (1st ed.). Cambridge, MA: Harvard University Press.

Rawls, J. (2001). *Justice as fairness: A restatement.* Cambridge, MA: Belknap Press of Harvard University Press.

Reichert, E. (2003). *Social work and human rights: A foundation for policy and practice.* New York, NY: Columbia University Press.

Reisch, M. (1998). *Economic globalization and the future of the welfare state: Welfare reform and social justice visiting scholars program.* Ann Arbor, MI: University of Michigan School of Social Work.

Reisch, M. (2002). Defining social justice in a socially unjust world. *Families in Society: The Journal of Contemporary Social Services, 83,* 343–354. doi:10.1606/1044-3894.17

Reisch, M., & Garvin, C. D. (2016). *Social work and social justice: Concepts, challenges, and strategies.* New York, NY: Oxford University Press.

Ruhela, S. P. (2005). *Introduction to sociology.* Gurgaon, India: Shubhi Publications.

Thomas, A. J., & Schwarzbaum, S. E. (2017). *Culture and identity: Life stories for counselors and therapists.* Thousand Oaks, CA: Sage.

Van Soest, D. (1992). *Incorporating peace and social justice into the social work curriculum.* Washington, DC: National Association of Social Workers.

Wakefield, J. C. (1988). Psychotherapy, distributive justice, and social work. Part 2: Psychotherapy and the pursuit of justice. *Social Service Review, 62,* 353–382. doi:10.1086/644555

Witkin, S. L. (2011). *Social construction and social work practice: Interpretations and innovations.* New York, NY: Columbia University Press.

Young, I. M. (2001). Equality of whom? Social groups and judgments of injustice. *Journal of Political Philosophy, 9*(1), 1–18. doi:10.1111/1467-9760.00115

Engaging in Research to Inform and Improve Practice, Policy, and Service Delivery in Your Field Placement

Irene is completing her MSW field placement at an elementary school with a school social worker. She is really enjoying her work and all of the things she is exposed to at this placement. She spends nmvost of her time working with students, either individually or in a group setting. She works with the children on a variety of concerns, including behavioral issues, upsetting or strong feelings, and social skills issues. Recently, Irene thought that it might be beneficial if the students who were coming to see her for social skills issues would come at the same time and play an interactive game together during part of the session.

During her weekly supervision, Irene shared with her field supervisor that she had an idea to help students with social skills issues. The supervisor listened to what Irene wanted to do related to introducing a game in the group so that the children could practice their social skills in a play activity. The supervisor was intrigued by Irene's enthusiasm. The field supervisor asked Irene to research her idea—that is, her belief that having the students play interactive games helps build social skills.

At the next supervision, Irene came prepared with copies of the scholarly research articles she found that supported the use of a variety of play therapy techniques, including interactive games, to promote social skills with children in a group setting. Irene felt confident in her ability to find research articles because she had a research methods course last semester.

After the field supervisor and Irene reviewed the research together, they started planning a social skills group session to meet twice a week. After a couple of weeks of running the group, the field supervisor asked Irene to bring some data on her social skills groups to their next supervision to discuss how the group was working out.

Irene reviewed the student records to get actual data, looking at length of stay in treatment with the school social worker as well as severity of symptoms (using a checklist that was completing routinely while the kids were seeing the social worker) to compare students who had been participating in Irene's group with students who were coming only to meet with Irene individually. After reviewing the data, Irene found that the students who participated in the group showed

CASE VIGNETTE *(continued)*

much more progress than the children with social skills deficits who were coming to the social work office individually. Irene was proud of her ability to use research to inform her decision to add games to her social skills groups and to evaluate the effectiveness of her group sessions.

How is Irene using research to inform her professional practice as a social worker?

How could Irene use her practice to inform research?

LEARNING OBJECTIVES

In this chapter, we discuss practice-informed research and research-informed practice as it relates to Competency 4. We explore how different types of research, quantitative and qualitative, serve to advance the profession and evaluate professional practice. The Council on Social Work Education (CSWE, 2015) states that competent, professional "social workers understand that evidence that informs practice derives from multi-disciplinary sources and multiple ways of knowing" (p. 3). In this chapter, we explore the process "for translating research findings into effective practice" (CSWE, 2015, p. 4). By the end of this chapter, you will be able to

- Describe ethical standards that social workers must abide by related to research and evaluation.
- Distinguish between research and evaluation.
- Identify the common elements of a logic model.
- Create a logic model.
- Conduct a search for relevant literature.
- Critically evaluate sources of research.

RESEARCH AND EVALUATION

Social work is an amazing profession that integrates art and science. It requires the use of intuition and common sense while being a "legitimate scientific endeavor, with a specified knowledge base" (Samson, 2015, p. 119). Although for many students, the scientific inquiry is the lesser of the two sides of the profession, being capable in both is essential for effective professional social work practice at all levels. Throughout your career, you will need to make many important decisions; it is critical that you integrate both the art and the science of social work in the process of making those decisions. It is important that you have a thorough social work knowledge base to make these decisions. It is simply not enough to just speculate or take information for granted; you must be an active seeker of the truth and a careful consumer of research.

Historically, social work researchers and social work practice professionals were siloed into different arenas, and there were few interconnections between the two groups. On the one hand, the practice professionals viewed

Field Reflection Questions

At your placement, how are social work interventions evaluated?

How do you know what you are doing is effective?

the researchers as out of touch with the hands-on, day-to-day practice of social work. On the other hand, the researchers viewed the practice professionals as lacking in regard to understanding and valuing research findings. In the 1970s, the CSWE and the National Association of Social Workers (NASW) sought to bring together these two factions of social workers (Yegidis, Weinbach, & Myers, 2018). According to Cabassa (2016), "bridging the gap between research and practice is a critical frontier for the future of social work" (p. 539). This merging, or closing of the gap, between practice professionals and researchers serves to create the idea of a clinical scientist. A clinical scientist is a social worker who, if focused on research, still connects with practice, or, if focused on practice, still connects with research.

Research is a systematic, or ordered, process that attempts to explore, examine, or explain information. Gibbs and Stirling (2013) suggest that "research at its simplest level is about asking questions and finding something out" (p. 317). In social work research, there is often an orientation toward change, an emphasis on an equal relationship between the researcher and participants, accountability, as well as a holistic perspective on the different aspects of the person and problems (Dominelli, 2005). Furthermore, research in social work often approaches the "subject matter with a particular orientation, that is based on a commitment to understanding—and improving—what happens in the practice setting. This in turn leads to what we see as a unique and valuable perspective on the design and implementation of empirical inquiry" (Worsley, Smith, & Hardwick, 2016, p. 11).

Research allows us, as social workers, the means to challenge perceptions and explore relationships between the people we serve and the experiences they are going through (Engel & Schutt, 2010). It provides us with a foundation to challenge stereotypes, untruths, and false propaganda that oftentimes target vulnerable populations. As social workers striving for social justice and advocating for all people, research serves as a strong resource for us to rely on to gain credibility and strength in our positions.

It is necessary for social workers to be well informed and understand research to have "the practical foundation and theoretical orientation" to be successful in their careers (Szuchman & Thomlison, 2011, p. 4). When you get a new client, how will you know which intervention works best? Granted, there are no absolute, one-size-fits-all interventions; however, there are well-researched and scientifically grounded practice interventions that have been shown to be effective with individuals. We call these well-researched interventions evidence-based practices. Social workers who use evidence-based practices are "using research findings to guide their practice decisions" (Rubin & Bellamy, 2012, p. 4). Social workers should strive to use evidence-based practices as long as they fall within the social workers' scope of competence and training.

Research and evaluation are often discussed as if they were synonymous. We should point out that there is a distinction between the two. When we consider evaluative research, we are concerned with the effectiveness of a program or practice (Royse, Thyer, & Padgett, 2016). Evaluation is critically important for social workers, as we need to determine whether what we are doing is effective, efficient, or even necessary.

■ CONNECTION TO NASW'S *CODE OF ETHICS*

Social workers need to understand and be able to apply research to their practice. The professional *Code of Ethics* provided by the NASW sets forth ethical standards regarding research and evaluation for social workers that have 17 points (see Exhibit 9.1). It is imperative that social workers use research to make clinical decisions and select best practices when working with clients. Our clients deserve the best services available.

Excerpt From the NASW's *Code of Ethics*

5.02 EVALUATION AND RESEARCH

(a) Social workers should monitor and evaluate policies, the implementation of programs, and practice interventions.

(b) Social workers should promote and facilitate evaluation and research to contribute to the development of knowledge.

(c) Social workers should critically examine and keep current with emerging knowledge relevant to social work and fully use evaluation and research evidence in their professional practice.

(d) Social workers engaged in evaluation or research should carefully consider possible consequences and should follow guidelines developed for the protection of evaluation and research participants. Appropriate institutional review boards should be consulted.

(e) Social workers engaged in evaluation or research should obtain voluntary and written informed consent from participants, when appropriate, without any implied or actual deprivation or penalty for refusal to participate; without undue inducement to participate; and with due regard for participants' well-being, privacy, and dignity. Informed consent should include information about the nature, extent, and duration of the participation requested and disclosure of the risks and benefits of participation in the research.

(f) When using electronic technology to facilitate evaluation or research, social workers should ensure that participants provide informed consent for the use of such technology. Social workers should assess whether participants are able to use the technology and, when appropriate, offer reasonable alternatives to participate in the evaluation or research.

(g) When evaluation or research participants are incapable of giving informed consent, social workers should provide an appropriate explanation to the participants, obtain the participants' assent to the extent they are able, and obtain written consent from an appropriate proxy.

(h) Social workers should never design or conduct evaluation or research that does not use consent procedures, such as certain forms of naturalistic observation and archival research, unless rigorous and responsible review of the research has found it to be justified because of its prospective scientific, educational, or applied value and unless equally effective alternative procedures that do not involve waiver of consent are not feasible.

(i) Social workers should inform participants of their right to withdraw from evaluation and research at any time without penalty.

(j) Social workers should take appropriate steps to ensure that participants in evaluation and research have access to appropriate supportive services.

(k) Social workers engaged in evaluation or research should protect participants from unwarranted physical or mental distress, harm, danger, or deprivation.

(l) Social workers engaged in the evaluation of services should discuss collected information only for professional purposes and only with people professionally concerned with this information.

(continued)

Excerpt From the NASW's *Code of Ethics (continued)*

(m) Social workers engaged in evaluation or research should ensure the anonymity or confidentiality of participants and of the data obtained from them. Social workers should inform participants of any limits of confidentiality, the measures that will be taken to ensure confidentiality, and when any records containing research data will be destroyed.

(n) Social workers who report evaluation and research results should protect participants' confidentiality by omitting identifying information unless proper consent has been obtained authorizing disclosure.

(o) Social workers should report evaluation and research findings accurately. They should not fabricate or falsify results and should take steps to correct any errors later found in published data using standard publication methods.

(p) Social workers engaged in evaluation or research should be alert to and avoid conflicts of interest and dual relationships with participants, should inform participants when a real or potential conflict of interest arises, and should take steps to resolve the issue in a manner that makes participants' interests primary.

(q) Social workers should educate themselves, their students, and their colleagues about responsible research practices.

Going beyond the ethical standards outlined in the *Code of Ethics*, the core value of competence also relates to engagement in research. The value of competence sets forth that "social workers continually strive to increase their professional knowledge and skills and to apply them in practice. Social workers should aspire to contribute to the knowledge base of the profession" (NASW, 2017, p. 6). To be competent, social workers must continue learning beyond earning their degrees. They must seek out knowledge and skills and apply them to their practice. Furthermore, professional social workers are called upon by this ethical principle to contribute to the knowledge base of the profession as well. Contributing to the knowledge base of the profession can take a variety of forms. It can be done formally by publishing findings and presenting at conferences. Contributions can also be done more informally. Sharing your findings with other social workers or individuals interested in researching such things can be seen as a contribution as well.

MICRO EVALUATIONS

MEASUREMENT TOOLS

There are a number of measurement methods that involve clients, are easy to construct and implement, and are appropriate for generalist social work practice. The more frequently used methods are the following:

- Client logs
- Behavioral observations

- Rating scales
- Goal attainment scales
- Standardized measures

Client Logs

Having clients prepare narrative accounts of their activities, thoughts, and feelings is an effective method of monitoring progress. Client logs or journals help clarify the nature of client problems and the circumstances that contribute to the problem situation. Clients often find that keeping a log helps them increase their understanding and awareness of the factors that contribute to the identified problem situation. It enables them to "track the antecedents and consequences, or the feelings and thoughts, surrounding the occurrence of a specific event" (Berlin & Marsh, 1993, p. 99). Client logs allow a client to systematically take notes on the occurrence of a target problem and the events surrounding each occurrence. Doing so prevents distortions and misperceptions caused by faulty memory (Bloom, Fischer, & Orme, 2009).

Client logs also are an excellent source of baseline data on the frequency of the target problem. Baseline data obtained from logs serve as clinical measurements of the client's thoughts, feelings, and behaviors. These recordings help the client gain insight and help the practitioner monitor clinical progress during treatment (Jordan & Franklin, 2015).

Client logs are easy to construct. Most are divided into columns, with the types of information the client should record listed at the top of each column. The columns should record the incident or behavior, when it occurred, and how the client responded to it (Bloom et al., 2009). Information about circumstances just prior to and just after the problem event may also be included in client logs.

Two decisions need to be made regarding the completion of logs. The first is when to record the information, and the second is what to record. Clients can record at preset time periods or immediately following the occurrence of the target event. Recording at preset time periods works if you have narrowed down the occurrence of a target event to a specific period—that is, if you know in advance approximately when the target problem is likely to occur. For example, a family might complain about sibling fights after school and during dinner. The client log then might cover the time period of 3:00 to 7:00 p.m. in the evening. The client keeping the log would record all the sibling fights that occurred during this time period.

The second option is to use open time categories. This method is sometimes referred to as critical incident recording (Bloom et al., 2009). With this type of log, the client decides whether to record an event. The client decides whether the event is related to the problem or target and then records it as soon as possible after it occurs. This method works best when you need information about events that are likely to be spread out over the entire day.

In addition to specifying when the recording will take place, you need to clarify in advance what will be recorded. By design, client logs give the client control over the content. Clients choose which of the many thoughts, feelings, and behaviors they experience daily to include and exclude. They use a great deal of subjective judgment in completing logs. Information recorded on the log should be limited to what the client believes is important (Bloom et al., 2009). Thus, you and the client need to be clear about what constitutes a critical incident. Discuss with the client the types of events that would be appropriate for inclusion in the log. In the beginning, encourage clients to be inclusive rather than exclusive in their recordings. Review the first logs together, with an eye toward the appropriateness of the entries as well as events that the client did not record but should have.

(**Note:** A **Client Log Form** can be found in the Student Toolbox available on the Springer Publishing Company's website at www.springerpub.com/fieldwrk.)

Behavioral Observations

Behavioral observations are direct client behavior (Jordan & Franklin, 2015). The frequency and duration of specific client behaviors can be observed and recorded (Bloom et al., 2009). Behavioral observation can provide detailed information on the occurrence of client behaviors and the context of those behaviors. It represents one of the most reliable and valid methods of measuring client change.

> **Field Reflection Questions**
> How could you use behavioral observation with a client in your field placement?
> Which behaviors would you want to have observed?
> How would you use the data in your work with your client?

Typically, the first step in using behavioral observation is to operationally define the target behavior. An example would be specifying the types of disruptive behavior a child displays in the classroom, such as getting out of his or her seat or talking with classmates while the teacher is talking. The target problem must be clearly defined in behavioral terms and must be observable. Observation cannot be used to measure target problems that focus on feelings or thoughts. It is limited to measuring the frequency, duration, and context of behaviors.

The second step is to select the observer or observers. Often, the observers are significant others, family members, or other professionals who have access to the client's person-in-environment interactions. For example, a young child having a problem controlling his or her temper can be observed at home by a parent and at school by a teacher or teacher's aide.

The third step is to train the observers. Observers must know in advance exactly what behavior to look for and how to recognize the behavior when it occurs (Jordan & Franklin, 2015). In addition, they have to be trained to conduct the observations. "Deciding how to sample the behaviors is the fundamental question in conducting a structured observation" (Berlin & Marsh, 1993, p. 107). You must decide whether to record all instances of the behavior or just a sample. Continuous recording involves recording every occurrence of a target behavior every time it occurs (Bloom et al., 2009). A simple form can be created that includes, at a minimum, the date, time, location, and brief description of the behavior. The continuous recording approach requires the observer to be willing and available, and it works best when the target behavior does not occur with great frequency. Often, these conditions cannot be satisfied, so a sampling strategy is used instead.

Time sampling is appropriate when events occur continuously or frequently. "Time sampling requires the selection of specific units of time, either intervals or discrete points, during which the occurrence or nonoccurrence of a specific behavior is recorded" (Berlin & Marsh, 1993, p. 107). The assumption is that the sample behavior would be the same if all occurrences of it were recorded (Haynes, 1978). There are two types of time sampling: interval and discrete.

Interval sampling involves selecting a time period and dividing it into equal blocks of time. The observer records the occurrence or nonoccurrence of the behavior during each interval. The behavior is recorded once for each interval regardless of how many times it occurs (Bloom et al., 2009).

Discrete time sampling involves selecting specific time periods and recording all instances of the target behavior that occur during the selected periods. The key issue in this type of recording is to select periods that are representative in terms of the target behavior. If the behaviors occur often and regularly, you would need fewer periods to obtain a representative sample of them (Bloom et al., 2009). If the behaviors occur during certain time periods—for example, during meals—then the selected periods must correspond to the behavioral patterns of the client.

Overall, direct observation is an excellent method for assessing client outcomes. It is one of the most effective tools we have for measuring behavior. When it is used with two or more observers, it can provide reliable and valid outcome data. It also has the potential to provide valuable clinical information on the context within which target problems occur. Direct observation should be seriously considered when a target problem is behavioral in nature, the situation allows for direct observation, and implementing direct observation is feasible.

(**Note:** A **Behavioral Observation Form** in the Student Toolbox available on Springer Publishing Company's website www.springerpub.com/fieldwrk.)

Rating Scales

Individualized rating scales are measures of client problems that are created by the client and the social worker together (Bloom et al., 2009). These types of measures are also referred to as self-anchored rating scales (Jordan & Franklin, 2015). The major advantage of an individualized rating scale is that it measures the specific problem or concern that you and your client have identified as the focus of intervention. Thus, a rating scale is directly linked to the feeling, thought, or event that is being addressed in the helping process.

Another advantage of individualized rating scales is that they are based on the client's unique experiences and perceptions. The anchor points of the scale are defined by the client. The low, middle, and high points of the scale are labeled with short, succinct terms. The labels (anchors) describe what the numbers represent (e.g., behaviors, thoughts, and feelings that the client would experience at various points along the scale). Having the client define the anchor points gives the measure great relevance for the client. It becomes a unique measure of the client's feelings, thoughts, or behaviors; it represents his or her perceptions and experiences.

Individualized rating scales usually have 5 to 10 points. Scales that have more than 10 points are difficult for clients to score and, therefore, are not recommended (Bloom et al., 2009). For example, if a self-esteem scale had 1 to 100 points, it would be very difficult to determine the difference between ratings of 70 and 75. Scales with 7 points are considered ideal (Jordan & Franklin, 2015). An example of an individualized rating scale is shown in Exhibit 9.2.

Individualized rating scales are easy to construct. Identify with the client the behavior, thought, or feeling that is targeted for change. A wide range of characteristics of the target can be rated (Bloom et al., 2009). It is important for the target to be clearly articulated and for each rating scale to measure only one aspect or dimension of the target (Gingerich, 1979). Bloom, Fischer, and Orme (2009) warn against using different dimensions at each

EXHIBIT
9.2

Individualized Rating Scales

Comfort in social situations						
1	2	3	4	5	6	7
Terrified, overwhelmed, completely unable to engage in conversation with strangers			Somewhat anxious, yet able to respond when spoken to		Relaxed, confident, able to initiate conversations with strangers	

end of the scale, such as happy at one end and sad at the other. People often experience contradictory feelings and can feel happy and sad at the same time. It is preferable to develop two measures, a sadness scale and a happiness scale, rather than one scale on which both dimensions are rated. Bloom et al. (2009) also recommend that the target and its measurement be worded positively, as something the client wants to achieve, not just something eliminating a negative. For example, if the problem is feelings of sadness, the goal might be to increase feelings of happiness, and the rating scale would measure the level of happiness.

The next step is to decide on the number of scale points and develop anchor descriptions for the two end points and possibly the middle point. Scales with seven or nine points are popular because they have a clear midpoint. The numbers on the scale represent gradations for the target problem from low to high. The higher the score, the more frequent, serious, important, or problematic the target problem is. The end points of the scale are defined by the client, as are the descriptions or examples of the low, middle, and high numbers. These anchor descriptions define the meaning of the numbers on the rating scale. Begin by asking the client to describe what it would be like at one end of the scale for the given target problem. Repeat the process for the other end of the scale and for the midpoint. Anchors should describe the behaviors, thoughts, or feelings the client would experience along the continuum of the scale (Bloom et al., 2009).

After you and your client construct the scale, make sure that the anchors fit the client's perception of the situation and that both of you are clear about what constitutes a low or high score. This is best accomplished by practicing using the scale and asking the client to retrospectively complete a rating for different points in his or her life. This will increase the client's comfort in using the scale and provide an opportunity to determine whether the anchor points provide adequate differentiation of the target problem.

An important point to keep in mind in constructing individualized rating scales is that they must be truly *individualized*. The anchors reflect images and pictures of what the situation is like for the client. Your job is to help the client put those images into words. Make sure the words are the client's, not yours or someone else's. The strength of individualized rating scales is that they are client defined and derived directly from the identified target problem.

An alternative to individually constructed anchors is general anchor descriptions. Rating scales with general anchors can be used for different client situations. For example, a general rating scale measuring feelings of connectedness could be used to measure a client's relationships with each member of his or her family. The disadvantage of general anchors is that they are more ambiguous and less precise than individually tailored anchors (Coulton & Solomon, 1977). Exhibit 9.3 shows general rating scales.

Individualized and general rating scales are excellent tools for measuring client progress and change on identified target problems. They have a high level of face validity because they are derived directly from client problems or concerns. There is some evidence that the validity of single-item rating scales is comparable to that of standardized measures (Nugent, 1992). However, the validity and reliability of individualized rating scales cannot be readily established, because they are designed for use with individual clients (Berlin & Marsh, 1993). Rating scales do, however, have a high level of clinical applicability and are excellent tools for measuring client target problems and assessing progress.

Goal Attainment Scales

Goal attainment scaling (GAS) was developed in the field of mental health during the 1960s (Royse et al., 2016). It has been used in a large number of settings and with a wide range of client populations. GAS is similar to individualized rating scales in that the client develops and defines the scale anchors or descriptors. The two methods differ, however, in that goal attainment scales are based directly on the client's goals rather than on behaviors, thoughts, or feelings. A strength of GAS is that it can be used to monitor the client's perception of progress toward the identified treatment goals (Jordan & Franklin, 2015). Thus, GAS has been effective in assessing client change related to the identified goals (Corcoran, 1992).

To use GAS, you and your client need to have specified change goals. A question that arises is which goals or how many should be measured (Seaburg & Gillespie, 1977). In general, the number of goals measured should correspond to the number of goals being addressed in the helping relationship. The number of goals being addressed at any given time should be limited. As discussed earlier in this chapter, the goals selected should be those that are most significant to the client and that intervention is most likely to change (Royse et al., 2016).

In conjunction with the client, list each goal on a five-point scale ranging from 0 to 4. The scale categories are the following:

(4) Optimal progress

(3) Major progress

EXHIBIT 9.3

General Rating Scales

Amount of anxiety

1	2	3	4	5	6	7
Little or no anxiety			Moderate anxiety		Extreme anxiety	

Frequency of feeling lonely

1	2	3	4	5	6	7
Never			Sometimes		All the time	

(2) Moderate progress

(1) Some progress

(0) No progress

Work with the client to develop anchors for each scale point. The anchors should represent potential outcomes related to each category and should be as specific as possible. Avoid vague, general outcome statements. Exhibit 9.4 shows a sample goal attainment scale that was developed with an 80-year-old woman who was caring for her 55-year-old mentally retarded son. The social worker was helping the woman address her anxiety and concern about her son's future.

GAS is a client-focused method of measuring progress. It is a direct extension of the goal-oriented approach to practice and is easily incorporated into generalist social work practice with a diverse range of client populations. GAS also empowers clients by placing responsibility for defining and monitoring progress with them. The client is viewed as the expert on what constitutes progress and on determining the extent to which progress is being made. In these respects, GAS is useful as a clinical measurement tool for engaging clients in the helping process.

EXHIBIT 9.4

Goal Attainment Scale

Level	Goal 1: Increase Ability to Deal With Panic Attacks	Goal 2: Make Plans for Son's Future
No progress (0)	Unable to calm myself down, unable to catch breath, heart racing, extreme anxiety	Unable to discuss with son his future needs and plans
Some progress (1)	Limited ability to calm myself down, some difficulty breathing, pacing the floor, moderate anxiety	Discussed son's future with other members of the family
Moderate progress (2)	Able to calm down using breathing/relaxation techniques, maintain composure, low anxiety	Discussed with son his future needs
Major progress (3)	Able to verbalize feelings, remain calm in stressful situations, almost no anxiety	Discussed with son his future needs and involved family and outside agencies in assessing son's needs
Optimal progress (4)	Able to deal with stressful situations without experiencing panic attacks, very low anxiety, calm and relaxed	Working with son, family, and outside agencies and services to prepare son to care for himself in the future

Standardized Measures

Standardized measures are instruments developed following empirical scale construction techniques with uniform administration and scoring procedures (Jordan & Franklin, 2015). Their reliability is known, and their validity has usually been empirically tested.

Standardized measures are available for a wide range of client behaviors, including marital satisfaction, self-esteem, anxiety, and family relations. Some standardized measures assess global behaviors, such as generalized contentment, whereas others assess specific behaviors and problems, such as fear, depression, or sexual satisfaction. Standardized measures are available in rapid assessment formats with up to 25 scale items, as well as in lengthy, comprehensive formats with hundreds of scale items. Rapid assessment instruments are easy to use and to incorporate into generalist social work practice.

"Standardized measures represent the most useful quantitative clinical measurement tools that are available to practitioners" (Jordan & Franklin, 2015, p. 53). There are numerous sources of standardized measures. *Measures for Clinical Practice* by Corcoran and Fischer (2013) is an excellent two-volume collection of rapid assessment instruments. Volume 1 contains measures for use with couples, families, and children, and Volume 2 contains instruments for individual adults. The two-volume set contains more than 300 different brief assessment instruments, with supporting information on each instrument's purpose, scoring, reliability, and validity. Another great source of rapid assessment instruments is *Measures of Personality and Social Psychological Attitudes* (1991) by Robinson, Shaver, and Wrightsman. In this book, measures are organized by clinical topic (e.g., self-esteem, depression, anxiety).

A useful list of commercially available measures can be found in *Clinical Assessment for Social Workers* by Jordan and Franklin (2015). The WALMYR Publishing Company is also an excellent source for commercially available measurement instruments designed specifically for use in social work practice. WALMYR sells a number of individual and family adjustment scales as well as comprehensive multidimensional assessment instruments.

Standardized measures, especially the rapid assessment variety, are well suited for use in generalist social work practice. If you can locate one that closely corresponds to identified client problems or concerns, standardized measures offer several advantages. They have known psychometric properties—that is, their reliability and validity have been established. They are also efficient, do not require extensive training, and are easy to administer and score (Corcoran & Fischer, 2013).

DESIGNING THE EVALUATION

At the micro level of practice, social workers can engage in evaluation to determine whether the intervention they are using is effective. The most common method of evaluation at the micro level is a very practical research design—single-subject design. In the simplest terms, single-subject designs compare baseline phases (referred to as the A phase) with treatment phases (referred to as the B phase). Several types of single-subject designs may be used (see Exhibit 9.5). For the sake of clarification, note that in single-subject design, the single subject refers to a single case that can be an individual person, a family unit, a group, an organization, or a community. For our purposes, we discuss single-subject design as a micro intervention with a single client.

The process of single-subject design involves collecting and recording data, analyzing data, and then making treatment decisions on the basis of the findings. When completing a single-subject design, it is necessary to clearly identify the target problem

EXHIBIT
9.5

Common Types of Single-Subject Designs

Design Type	Description of Design
B	Measurement occurs during the intervention phase. There is no baseline data collection phase. Example: A client enters an inpatient drug and alcohol rehabilitation program. On entry into the program, he immediately begins receiving medication to treat his physical symptoms of withdrawal and begins individual cognitive behavioral therapy with a social worker. Because the social worker did not have a baseline period prior to starting her therapeutic work with this client, all of the data collected while providing the therapy would be considered the treatment phase (B).
AB	There is a period of baseline data collection where no intervention is given. Following the baseline phase, the intervention is administered, and data are collected. Example: A new student has recently transferred into an autism support classroom. The first week that the student is in the classroom, she is observed and evaluated to determine her current levels of functioning and behavioral needs. Data collected during this initial week would be considered baseline (A). Starting in her second week in the classroom, an applied behavior analysis intervention is implemented. Data collected during the intervention of applied behavior analysis would be considered the treatment phase (B).
ABA	There is a period of baseline data collection where no intervention is given. Following the baseline phase, the intervention is administered, and data are then collected. After a period of time, the intervention is withdrawn, and another period of baseline data collection occurs. Note that treatment carryover effects can interfere with the second baseline in this type of design. Example: A child with behavioral outbursts begins BHRS. During the intake process, the treatment team collects data in the forms of observations, interviews, and scales to determine current needs and establish goals. This is the baseline phase (A). After collecting the baseline data, the team implements a behavior modification plan that includes reinforcements and punishments in an attempt to increase positive behaviors and eliminate undesired behaviors. While the behavior modification plan is being implemented, data are collected (B). Once the child has met his treatment goals, before discharging him from services, the treatment team stops implementing the behavior modification plan and tracks rates of behaviors. The period in which data are being collected after the intervention has been removed is the second baseline phase (A).

(continued)

EXHIBIT
9.5

Common Types of Single-Subject Designs (*continued*)

Design Type	Description of Design
BAB	Measurement occurs during the intervention phase. The intervention is then withdrawn so as to collect baseline data. Following collection of baseline data, the intervention is reintroduced. Example: A woman with anxiety comes to a community mental health clinic for support. During her first session, the treatment begins, with the social worker teaching her techniques to calm down, focus on her breath, and engage in mindfulness. The therapist asks the client to continue this intervention. Because there was no baseline period before the intervention was introduced, this case starts with the treatment phase (B). After several successful weeks using the intervention, the social worker stops the intervention and continues to collect data. Because there is no intervention being delivered, this is a baseline phase (A). The social worker eventually reintroduces the intervention and data are collected during the second treatment phase (B).

BHRS, behavioral health rehabilitation services.

and to operationally define that problem. An operational definition is a very specific definition that serves to clearly illustrate the behavior. For example, a vague target problem would be "aggression." An operational definition for this target behavior could be "throwing items at peers, pinching, poking, slapping, or hitting." Whenever possible, we should always try to define our targets in positive terms, rather than as the absence of something. When creating our operational definitions, we should also consider terminology related to measurement, including frequency, duration, interval, and intensity.

Once you have collected your single-subject design data, you can graph your data using a line graph. Simple line graphs are quite easy to make in a variety of computer programs. Exhibit 9.6 has a sample single-subject design graph. Notice that both the horizontal (y) axis and the vertical (x) axis are labeled. When creating a graph, it is very important that you label the axes. You should also give your chart a title so that the reader understands what he or she is looking at in the graph. When graphing single-subject design data, it is customary to point out the break in data between the baseline and treatment phases. In Exhibit 9.5, the break between the baseline and treatment phases is indicated in three ways. First, the line graph is not continuous, which shows the change in phases. Second, a vertical line in the graph marks the change in phases. Finally, we labeled each section as baseline or treatment.

Field Reflection Questions

At your current field placement, how might single-subject design be a useful evaluation strategy?

Which type of single-subject design would you be able to incorporate into your social work practice?

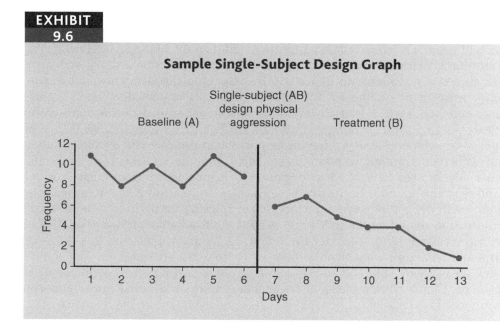

EXHIBIT 9.6

Sample Single-Subject Design Graph

MACRO EVALUATIONS

Evaluations at the macro level are commonly referred to as program evaluations. Program evaluation is a subset of research activities that are practical activities (Royse et al., 2016). These evaluations can take place prior to the inception of a program or within an established program. They include needs assessment, process evaluation, and outcome evaluation. Ideally, a needs assessment is done first to determine the nature or scope of a particular problem or need and determines which type of program would best address that problem. Both process and outcome evaluations assess programs. A process evaluation explores how services are delivered, whereas an outcome evaluation looks at whether the program is meeting its stated objectives. We explore each of these evaluations in more detail next.

NEEDS ASSESSMENTS

Social workers are trained to identify needs. A needs assessment is a systematic method of exploring the extent of social problems while determining the target population who need to be served considering the nature of their service needs (Rossi, Lipsey, & Freeman, 2003). As stated earlier, ideally needs assessments are conducted when new programs are being launched, but they can actually be completed at any time. A needs assessment should be considered, even if completed earlier, if there have been changes in the community, the understanding of the social problem, interventions, funding, or mandates.

There are several steps to conduct a needs assessment. First, the evaluator must identify which problem is occurring and determine how to collect information on the need related to this problem. In addition to recognizing the problem, it is often quite helpful to have an understanding of possible solutions available to ameliorate the problem.

Data will need to be collected and analyzed, and then the findings, or conclusions, should be shared with others. Data analysis does not need to be a scary endeavor. Many resources are available to assist you in managing the data collected during such an assessment or evaluation. It is also a good idea to consider your personal preference and work style. If you are unsure of how to use spreadsheet or data analysis software packages, we encourage you to ask for help from your faculty, field supports, peers, or even online. A variety of helpful video tutorials are available online that can walk you through computer-based data analysis step by step. Once the data are analyzed, you will need to decide how to present your findings, conclusions, and recommendations to the interested parties. Determining how to share your information will depend on several factors. A key question in deciding how to share your information should be the following: Who is your audience? It is a good idea to start with the end in mind. Consider the following: Who am I sharing this information with, and what do I want them to take away from my presentation? You should be considerate of where your audience is coming from regarding their potential beliefs and positions. Chapter 12 on mezzo assessments contains additional information on community needs assessments.

ORGANIZATIONAL EVALUATIONS

Social workers need to evaluate whether organizations and programs are meeting their goals and objectives and operating effectively and efficiently (see Chapter 12 for additional information on assessing organizations). For our purposes, we are considering a program to be an organized set of activities that are designed to reach specific objectives and have an influence on a predetermined set of participants (Royse et al., 2016). Programs can vary in size, funding, and organizational structure. Because of the natural variation among programs (even programs within the same agency), it is very important for you to familiarize yourself with the program you are working. It is a good idea to gather background information about such things as the following:

> **Field Reflection Questions**
>
> How much do you know about the background of the program where you are placed for field?
>
> Where did you get this information? How can you learn more about the background of your field placement program?

- History of the program: When was the program founded? Why was the program created?

- Operations: What does the administrative structure look like for this program?

- Target population: Who is this program designed to support? What are the characteristics of the typical program participant?

- Purpose: What is the mission statement of the program? Does it have a vision statement? What are the goals of the program? What are the objectives of the program?

- Funding: How are services provided from this program financed?

- Diversity: How are issues related to diversity addressed within this program?

Process Evaluations

The process program evaluation is sometimes called a formative evaluation. Grinnell, Gabor, and Unrau (2010) suggest that this type of evaluation serves to examine "how a program's services are delivered to clients and what administrative mechanisms exist within the program to support these services" (p. 129). In addition, process evaluations look at routine aspects of daily operations. Within a process evaluation, activities and administration systems are explored regarding how they are organized and function. A process evaluation can be conducted at any time within an organization, but often occurs early in program development. When used early in programs, process evaluations can be extremely helpful in identifying issues or glitches with the programs' functioning that can be addressed and rectified. A process evaluation seeks to determine whether there is program fidelity, which means that the program is operating as intended. If outcomes are not being met, it may also be quite helpful to conduct a process evaluation to determine whether an issue in program implementation is causing the unmet outcomes. As you can see, process evaluations can be quite useful for a variety of reasons as they not only serve to improve a program's operation, but can also provide great insights into program practices and structure.

Once you decide to undertake a process evaluation, you should start by deciding what information you are hoping to gather. Once you know what information or data you would like to collect, you can then create your questions. As important as deciding what questions to ask, you need to decide who you are going to ask. When conducting organizational evaluations, you need to be aware of the various stakeholders involved who may have vital information. *Stakeholder* is a term used to refer to those people who have an interest in your program. Stakeholders can be staff, administration, board of directors, funding sources, clients, community members, and other business or community partners.

Field Reflection Question

Who are the stakeholders for your current field placement?

It is important to consider from whom you are going to collect information, because your approach may need to be varied for each group. When collecting data for any purpose, it is important that your data collection methods are clear and straightforward. It is also a good idea to be considerate of the participants' time. Although you may want to collect as much data as possible, it would be impossible for most people to complete surveys or interviews that ask hundreds of questions. When conducting an organizational evaluation, such as a process evaluation, you are often collecting data from staff. Be mindful that staff already have a lot on their plates so, whenever possible, try to incorporate your data collection process into the existing flow of current program operations. It can be helpful to ask the staff what they think would be a good way to collect such data. User input can provide valuable insights when you are conducting a process evaluation.

You will then need to collect your information and create a system to manage the incoming data. Once you have gathered your data, you will need to analyze the findings. After analyzing the results, you should share your findings with others: After doing all of the work associated with a process evaluation, it is important to disseminate your results to others. As we have mentioned, you should tailor the delivery of your findings to meet the needs of the stakeholder groups again. For example, you may wish to present a written report or slide show presentation to the board of directors of the program, but clients or community members may prefer something less formal, like a conversation and handouts.

Outcome Evaluations

An outcome evaluation is a type of program evaluation that is sometimes called a summative evaluation. The primary purpose of an outcome evaluation is to determine to what extent the program is meeting its intended target by achieving its objectives. Through outcome evaluations, feedback related to program results can be given to program stakeholders, which increases the overall accountability of the program. It is beneficial to have a mechanism of providing feedback on a program so as to make program decisions, and an outcome evaluation can do just that.

The first step in conducting an outcome evaluation is to examine the program objectives. Ideally, the program will have clearly outlined SMART objectives. SMART is an acronym used to describe objectives that are specific, measurable, attainable, relevant, and time-bound. It is important to understand where program objectives come from. Figure 9.1 illustrates the flow of purpose statements in most organizations. Typically, a program begins with a mission statement. A mission statement is a written conceptual foundation that anchors the program on the basis of what it is about and what it intends to do. From the mission statement, a vision statement can be derived. A vision statement is similar to a mission statement but focuses more on the future direction of the program. From these statements, goals are developed. Goals are broad statements that reflect the program's desired results. Then, from the goals, the objectives are created.

> **Field Reflection Questions**
>
> What are the objectives at your current field placement?
>
> Are the objectives SMART? If not, how can you make them into SMART objectives?

After exploring the program objectives, the next step in an outcome evaluation is to operationalize the variables you will be analyzing in your evaluation. You can then design your data collection and analysis process and procedures. Then, similar to a process evaluation, you will want to share your findings with program stakeholders.

LOGIC MODELS

A logic model is a graphic that visually represents the interrelations and connections between various parts of a program (Grinnell et al., 2010). There are numerous advantages of using logic models, including that their construction requires a focus on what is necessary for a program to meet its intended outcomes. Logic models are powerful tools to share what is happening within a program by illustrating the key steps, actions, and requirements to meet the long-term goals of the program. Sometimes, logic models are referred to by other names—for example, result maps, program logic models, outcomes models, theories of change, and strategy maps. If created in the right way, they can be useful for a variety of purposes. A well-constructed logic model can serve as a foundation for setting priorities within a program, evaluating and monitoring a program, and developing a strategic plan.

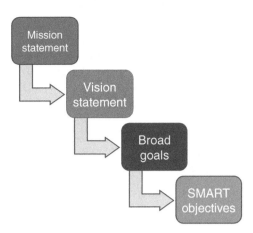

FIGURE 9.1 Flow of purpose statements in an organization.

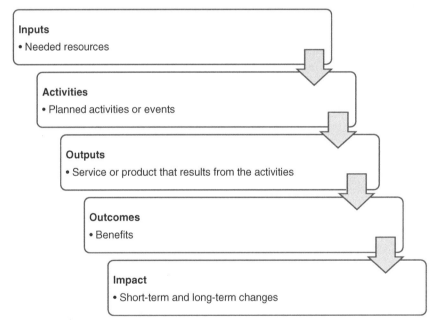

FIGURE 9.2 Elements of a logic model.

A variety of templates are available for creating a logic model. The basic components of a logic model are included in Figure 9.2. In Exhibit 9.7, we have provided you with a sample logic model that has been created for Case Example 9.1.

CASE EXAMPLE 9.1: SMART OBJECTIVES

Ellie was completing her MSW field placement at a large community mental health organization. As a part of her field placement, she was working with her field supervisor to evaluate the newly developed Trauma Services Program being offered by the large organization.

Ellie already had background information on the organization from a field activity she did early on to learn about the agency where she was placed. She had knowledge about the agency's history, services offered, and organizational structure. She was also familiar with the agency's mission statement and goals. Although there were several goals, there were no objectives. Ellie discussed this with her field supervisor, and together they worked to establish SMART objectives for the Trauma Services Program. The objectives they came up with were the following:

- *Within 1 month of intake, a trauma screening assessment will be completed in conjunction with the consumer, family, and treatment team.*

- *Within 1 month of intake, a treatment plan will be developed that incorporates the consumer's trauma history.*

- *During each session, consumers (and/or family) will participate in the session as evidenced by talking and participating in therapeutic activities.*

- *Throughout treatment, the clinician will provide psychoeducation to consumers orally or in writing related to the consumer's trauma experience and symptomology.*

- *Consumers will identify 10 coping strategies to be used when upset.*

- *Consumers will demonstrate a reduction of trauma-related symptoms as evidenced by consumer self-reporting during monthly treatment plan reviews.*

- *Consumer functioning will increase as evidenced by the ability to engage socially with the environment two times per week.*

- *Consumers will increase positive relationships as evidenced by the engagement in at least one safe relationship.*

- *Consumers will increase their safety awareness within the natural environment four out of five opportunities for 4 consecutive weeks.*

- *Clinicians will use their trauma training as evidenced by maintaining an active caseload with trauma consumers.*

- *Clinicians will continue to attend trauma trainings in two out of four opportunities per year.*

- *Clinicians will attend individual supervision once a month to gain additional support and review cases.*

After creating operational definitions, Ellie and her field supervisor discussed what type of evaluation would be best to complete. They decided to complete an outcome evaluation on the last three objectives (related to clinical staff). Ellie determined how she was going to collect her data and designed data collection tools. To avoid placing an additional burden on the staff, Ellie planned to review existing documentation that she had access to, so as to determine whether these objectives were being met.

After retrieving the data, Ellie entered the data into a computer data analysis program to create spreadsheets of her findings. She was able to create graphs to illustrate her data as well. After completing the data analysis, Ellie shared her findings with her field supervisor, and then both of them decided to share the information with the agency's board of directors, the director of outpatient services, and the clinical staff at the next regularly scheduled trauma meeting.

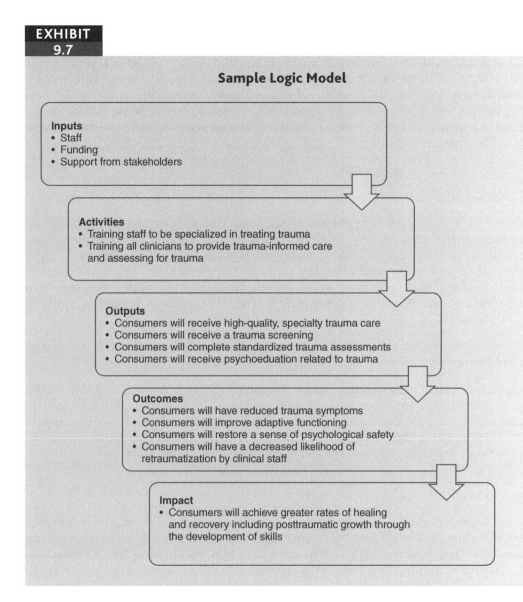

EXHIBIT
9.7

Sample Logic Model

Inputs
- Staff
- Funding
- Support from stakeholders

Activities
- Training staff to be specialized in treating trauma
- Training all clinicians to provide trauma-informed care and assessing for trauma

Outputs
- Consumers will receive high-quality, specialty trauma care
- Consumers will receive a trauma screening
- Consumers will complete standardized trauma assessments
- Consumers will receive psychoeduation related to trauma

Outcomes
- Consumers will have reduced trauma symptoms
- Consumers will improve adaptive functioning
- Consumers will restore a sense of psychological safety
- Consumers will have a decreased likelihood of retraumatization by clinical staff

Impact
- Consumers will achieve greater rates of healing and recovery including posttraumatic growth through the development of skills

USING RESEARCH TO INFORM PRACTICE DECISIONS

In field, how do you make decisions regarding what to do with the people you are working with? Ideally, you are calling upon your foundation of knowledge from your social work courses regarding building relationships, interviewing and assessing, and intervening. In field, you also have the advantage of having a field supervisor to help guide you through your learning process in addition to your faculty liaison. It is important that you are aware of what you are doing and why you are doing it. In field education, supervisors will often pass along their practice wisdom to you, which can be a very valuable thing. However, professional social workers cannot rely solely on the practice wisdom of others. Good, competent, professional social workers must actively seek out information that is relevant, trustworthy, and sound to make practice decisions. McLaughlin (2012) suggests that social workers should "be in a continuous reflective relationship with their practice seeking to find evidence and answers that help them to identify whether their intervention is effective or more interference" (p. 1). It is important that you engage with research to improve your practice skills. Also, as discussed earlier in this chapter, as a competent social worker, you must continually be learning, knowing, and growing to provide the best services possible to your clients. To be able to engage with research, you must first be able to find (good) research.

LITERATURE SEARCHES

Research is available from a variety of sources. Yes, you can go to a library for information, but often more resources are available online. As a student, you most likely have access to online search tools such as EBSCO, but there are a variety of other sources, including the popular Google Scholar and other publicly hosted database sites. For example, the Child Welfare Information Gateway is a great public resource where you can find a wealth of research related to children and families.

Online Searching

Computers are amazing machines that have the ability to provide us with access to a lot of great information. However, we have to know how to access the quality information, because sometimes there is not-so-great information online as well. As the old phrase suggests, "Garbage in, garbage out." This cliché is very true regarding online searching. To improve your search results, we urge you to consider how you are searching.

Boolean Logic

Boolean logic is a simple yet powerful tool that allows you to refine your search results using three simple words: "and," "or," and "not." By using these three words, you can expand or narrow your search on the basis of what you need. The term "and" will narrow your search by requiring that both of the concepts you joined by this word be present in your results. The term "not" will also narrow your results by eliminating specific concepts. Finally, your search can be expanded by using the term "or," which allows for another concept to be included in your results.

EVALUATING YOUR SEARCH RESULTS

Now that you have found the research, you must evaluate it. In a perfect world, all of the information available for public consumption would be sound, empirically based research that has high levels of validity and reliability, is collected with good sampling procedures, and is obtained through an ethically sound design. Sadly, that is not always the case. As a result, we must be cautious and careful consumers of research. An old adage says, "Numbers never lie." In evaluating your search results, you need to understand that numbers can, in fact, lie. People have the ability to manipulate numbers to tell the narrative they desire. This is unethical, but it does occur.

The Internet has a wealth of information ready for you to explore, but not all of that information is created equal. A quick and easy way to evaluate the quality and integrity of a website and its information is to consider the following questions:

- Does it list an author?
- Is there a reference list?
- Is there a date of publication?
- What is the website URL? Generally, websites that end in .edu, .org, or .gov are more likely to contain scholarly material than .com sites.

Positive responses to these questions suggest that the website and the information are probably legitimate and okay for your use. If you are unsure, however, we strongly urge you to take a closer look and conduct a more comprehensive assessment. A number of guidelines for evaluating websites are available from universities and government organizations on the World Wide Web. In fact, your university or college library probably has guidelines for your use. Most of the guidelines list five criteria: accuracy, authority, objectivity, currency, and coverage. Examining the five criteria will give you a reliable assessment of the quality and integrity of the website. Guidelines from Western Connecticut State University, found at http://people.wcsu.edu/reitzj/res/evalweb.html, describe the five categories and provide helpful tips on how to apply the criteria in evaluating websites.

SUMMARY

In this chapter, we explored how professional social workers must be engaged in research and evaluation to provide the best-quality services to their clients. Social workers are ethically obligated to engage with research and evaluation throughout the course of their practice. As a practicing social worker, you can engage in evaluation at various levels of practice. At the micro level, social workers can conduct single-subject designs to determine the effectiveness of interventions. At the macro level, social workers can conduct program evaluations. Needs assessments are important tools to assist in identifying needs or participants in regard to specific social problems. On a program level, process and outcome evaluations can be used to determine whether programs are operating effectively and efficiently and meeting their objectives. We explored logic models as powerful tools to visually outline the steps, actions, and resources required to produce the desired outcomes. Finally, we explored how to search for information and how to evaluate websites to determine whether they are credible.

CRITICAL THINKING QUESTIONS

This chapter focused on Competency 4: Engage in Practice Informed Research and Research Informed Practicee. As a social worker, you must continually refer to research to inform your practice. You must also evaluate your own practice to determine whether what you are doing is effective and beneficial.

1. Why is it important for social workers to remain aware of research related to their area of practice? What does it mean to you to be a competent social worker?

2. In your field placement, how do you use research to inform your practice decisions? How do you gather the research you need to be an effective social work professional in field?

3. How are research and evaluation similar? In what ways do they differ from each other?

4. How can you ensure that you are following the standards set forth by the NASW's *Code of Ethics* related to research and evaluation at your field placement? Provide three specific examples.

5. Conduct an online search for scholarly research related to your field placement. What strategies did you implement to find the research? What criteria did you use to determine whether it was trustworthy?

6. Create a logic model for your field placement. What are the resources necessary for your program to run? What activities are required within your program? What are the outputs of your program? Identify the outcomes and impact of your program as well.

COMPETENCY 4: ENGAGE IN PRACTICE-INFORMED RESEARCH AND RESEARCH-INFORMED PRACTICE

Social workers understand quantitative and qualitative research methods and their respective roles in advancing the science of social work and in evaluating their practice. They know the principles of logic, scientific inquiry, and culturally informed and ethical approaches to building knowledge. Social workers understand that the evidence that informs practice derives from multidisciplinary sources and multiple ways of knowing. They also understand the processes for translating research findings into effective practice. Social workers:

- Use practice experience and theory to inform scientific inquiry and research.
- Apply critical thinking to engage in analysis of quantitative and qualitative research methods and research findings.
- Use and translate research evidence to inform and improve practice, policy, and service delivery.

CASE SUMMARY—"STOPPING MEDICATION"

PRACTICE SETTING DESCRIPTION

My name is Brantley and I am an MSW field student. This semester, I have been placed at a long-term structured residence (LTSR). An LTSR is a therapeutic mental health treatment facility for adults. On the continuum of care, an LTSR is less restrictive than an inpatient hospitalization, but more intense than outpatient treatment. While participating in LTSR services, clients live at the facility and receive mental health treatment from a team of professionals including social workers, therapists, and medical staff. The staff work together to support the residents. We meet weekly to have interdisciplinary team meetings to discuss resident progress, concerns, and other treatment information. My primary responsibilities at the LTSR are to facilitate therapy, both group and individual, with the residents.

IDENTIFYING DATA

The first resident assigned to me was Joel, a 26-year-old male. Joel has been a resident at the LTSR for a little over 1 month. He has an extensive history of psychiatric hospitalizations that began when he was approximately 20. Joel has been diagnosed with schizophrenia. He experiences auditory hallucinations and delusions. Joel engages in ritualistic behavior and can at times be compulsive as well. Joel does not like to socialize with the other residents and has a hard time opening up to peers or staff as a result of a general distrust related to some of his delusions that are paranoid.

PRESENTING PROBLEM

Joel was admitted directly to the LTSR from his most recent inpatient psychiatric hospitalization. At the time of discharge, Joel's psychotropic medications had been adjusted to a level where he reported no positive symptoms related to his schizophrenia (hallucinations and delusions). Despite the reprieve from these symptoms, Joel does not like taking his medication because of the side effects he has been experiencing. Some of those side effects include weight gain, dizziness, muscle spasms, and nausea. Joel has shared with the doctor that he wants to try a different course of treatment because he reports being so miserable on the medication.

During an interdisciplinary team meeting, Joel's request to stop his psychotropic medications was discussed. My field supervisor, a licensed social worker, advocated for Joel's right to self-determination. She told the others on the team that Joel is coherent and capable of making his own treatment decisions, and that we should respect his wishes to try another course of treatment. A nurse at the meeting disagreed with my field supervisor. She shared that she felt strongly that because Joel's hallucinations and delusions have been virtually eliminated on the medication, stopping the medication should not be up for discussion. She added that research suggests medication and therapy together are the standard of treatment for individuals with this diagnosis. The group talked about the ethics related to this situation and in the end agreed that Joel was indeed competent to make the decision to attempt another course of treatment at this time. The psychiatrist plans to wean Joel off his current medications and try another family of medications that are known to have less harsh effects. Everyone agreed that it would be very important for Joel to continue to participate in therapy to continue to address his mental health needs. Everyone also agreed that Joel needed to be monitored quite closely during this transition of medications to evaluate whether the new course of treatment is beneficial for him.

After the meeting, I met with my field supervisor about the meeting and decision to allow Joel to try an alternative course of treatment. My supervisor asked me how I planned to evaluate Joel during this transition. At first, I was not sure what to do. I told my field instructor that I really was not sure. Together, we brainstormed ways to collect data. We also talked about the benefits of collecting data from various sources. After my conversation with my field instructor, I designed a data collection tool that I could use with Joel during my individual sessions. I also designed a self-reporting data tool for Joel to use as well so that he could share his experiences. I also created a general data collection tool that I put in Joel's chart where any staff member who needed to record an incident at the LTSR regarding Joel could make a notation of the event.

ASSESSMENT

Two weeks after the initial interdisciplinary team meeting where it was agreed to transition Joel to new medication, we came together to discuss Joel's case again. At the meeting the nurse who was initially resistant to the change of medication said that she thought Joel was decompensating since changing medications. Another therapist said that he thought Joel was doing better. Luckily, I had been collecting data for 2 weeks, from a variety of sources. I shared the data I had collected and analyzed; it illustrated that Joel was actually doing quite well with his new course of treatment. On the basis of my observations, client self-reports, and reports from other staff, it appeared that Joel was engaging with peers and staff more, still not experiencing any positive symptoms, and not experiencing any of the previously concerning side effects. My data were able to demonstrate that Joel's treatment is successful for him at this time.

CASE PROCESS SUMMARY

I have been learning so much at field placement, and with Joel's case especially, I feel like I am really learning how to be an effective social worker. With the help of my field supervisor, I was able to design data collection tools that allowed me to gather the data necessary to be able to share treatment progress. Because I had actual data, I was able to advocate for Joel's current treatment in the interdisciplinary team meeting. Without the data, I am not sure if Joel's current course of treatment would have been continued. With this experience, I learned that as a social worker I can use evaluation to improve the lives of my clients and at the end of the day that is why I want to be a social worker!

DISCUSSION QUESTIONS

- Why do you think the field supervisor encouraged Brantley to collect actual data?
- Why do you think Brantley decided to collect data from multiple sources (himself, Joel's self-reports, and notes from other staff)? What are the benefits from having multiple sources of data when conducting an evaluation?
- If you were the social work student and needed to collect data on this case, how would you set up your data collection tool? What questions would be on your tool? How would your tools differ depending on who was using it (e.g., how would your data tool be different from the one for the resident and from the one for the other staff)?
- In your field placement, if you needed to collect data on a client, how would you go about gathering those data? What sources would you use? What data would be important to collect?

ELECTRONIC COMPETENCY RESOURCES

WEBSITE LINKS

Public website with the mission of "connecting child welfare and related professionals to comprehensive resources to help protect children and strengthen families"
www.childwelfare.gov

Article: "The Evolution of a Social Worker" by Melissa B. South and Carolyn Bartick Ericson (n.d.)
www.socialworker.com/feature-articles/practice/The_Evolution_of_a_Social_Work_ Researcher

Website with a variety of information on creating a logic model (video included)
https://cyfar.org/what-logic-model

VIDEO LINKS

Video on how to find social work research—Diana Shull, University of Wisconsin-Whitewater
www.youtube.com/watch?v=yoJH75DCxEc

"How To Review a Research Paper"—Patricia Morton
www.youtube.com/watch?v=7lf3Q5BlNWo

"Evaluating Journal Articles With the CAARP Test"—Melissa Mallon, Wichata State University
www.youtube.com/watch?v=Q5Se7lxSANM

Short video about the importance of needs assessments by Penn State Hershey Medical Center
www.youtube.com/watch?v=iH_8EWbHpAU

Short video on using Google Scholar—CCPS Training
www.youtube.com/watch?v=uF5CXAgBPGM

REFERENCES

Berlin, S., & Marsh, J. (1993). *Informing practice decisions*. New York, NY: Macmillan.

Bloom, M., Fischer, J., & Orme, J. G. (2009). *Evaluating practice: Guidelines for the accountable professional* (6th ed.). New York, NY: Pearson.

Cabassa, L. J. (2016). Implementation science: Why it matters for the future of social work. *Journal of Social Work Education*, *52*(suppl 1), 538–550. doi:10.1080/10437797.2016.1174648

Corcoran, K. (1992). Practice evaluation: Setting goals, measuring and assessing change. In K. Corcoran (Ed.), *Structuring change: Effective practice for common client problems* (pp. 28–47). Chicago, IL: Lyceum.

Corcoran, K., & Fischer, J. (Eds.). (2013). *Measures for clinical practice: A sourcebook* (Vols 1–2., 5th ed.). London, UK: Oxford University Press.

Coulton, C. J., & Solomon, P. L. (1977). Measuring outcomes of intervention. *Social Work Research and Abstracts*, *13*, 3–9. doi:10.1093/swra/13.4.3

Council on Social Work Education. (2015). Educational policy and accreditation standards for baccalaureate and master's social work programs. Retrieved from https://www.cswe.org/getattachment/Accreditation/Accreditation -Process/2015-EPAS/2015EPAS_Web_FINAL.pdf.aspx

Dominelli, L. (2005). Social work research: Contested knowledge for practice. In R. Adams, L. Dominelli, & M. Payne (Eds.), *Social work futures: Crossing boundaries, transforming practice* (pp. 223–236). Basingstoke, UK: Palgrave McMillian.

Engel, R. J., & Schutt, R. K. (2010). *Fundamentals of social work research*. Thousand Oaks, CA: Sage.

Gibbs, A., & Stirling, B. (2013). "It's about people and their environment": Student social workers' definitions of social work research. *Social Work Education*, *32*(3), 317–330. doi:10.1080/02615479.2012.658365

Gingerich, W. J. (1979). Procedure for evaluating clinical practice. *Health and Social Work*, *4*, 105–130. doi:10.1093/hsw/4.2.104

Grinnell, R. M., Gabor, P. A., & Unrau, Y. A. (2010). *Program evaluation for social workers: Foundations of evidence based programs* (5th ed.). New York, NY: Oxford University Press.

Haynes, S. N. (1978). *Principles of behavioral assessment*. New York, NY: Gardner.

Jordan, C., & Franklin, C. (2015). *Clinical assessment for social workers: Quantitative and qualitative methods* (4th ed.). London, UK: Oxford University Press.

McLaughlin, H. (2012). *Understanding social work research* (2nd ed.). Thousand Oaks, CA: Sage.

National Association of Social Workers. (2017). *Code of ethics*. Silver Spring, MD: Author Retrieved from https://www.socialworkers.org/about/ethics/code-of-ethics/code-of-ethics-english

Nugent, W. R. (1992). Psychometric characteristics of self-anchored scales in clinical application. *Journal of Social Service Research, 15*, 137–152. doi:10.1300/J079v15n03_08

Robinson, J. P., Shaver, P. R., & Wrightsman, L. S. (1991). *Measures of personality and social psychological attitudes*. San Diego, CA: Academies Press.

Rossi, P. H., Lipsey, M. W., & Freeman, H. E. (2003). *Evaluation: A systematic approach* (6th ed.). Thousand Oaks, CA: Sage.

Royse, D., Thyer, B. A., & Padgett, D. K. (2016). *Program evaluation: An introduction to an evidence-based approach* (6th ed.). Boston, MA: Cengage.

Rubin, A., & Bellamy, J. (2012). *Practitioner's guide to using research for evidence-based practice* (2nd ed.). Hoboken, NJ: John Wiley & Sons.

Samson, P. L. (2015). Practice wisdom: The art and science of social work. *Journal of Social Work Practice, 29*(2), 119–131. doi:10.1080/02650533.2014.922058

Seaburg, J. R., & Gillespie, D. F. (1977). Goal attainment scaling: A critique. *Social Work Research and Abstracts, 13*, 43–56. doi:10.1093/swra/13.2.4

Szuchman, L. T., & Thomlison, B. (2011). *Writing with style: APA style for social work* (4th ed.). Belmont, CA: Brooks/Cole.

Worsley, A., Smith, R. S., & Hardwick, L. (2016). *Innovations in social work research: Using methods creatively*. London, UK: Jessica Kingsley Publishing.

Yegidis, B. L., Weinbach, R. W., & Myers, L. L. (2018). *Research methods for social workers* (8th ed.). New York, NY: Pearson.

CHAPTER 10

Engaging in Policy Practice in Your Field Placement

CASE VIGNETTE

Reggie was a first-year MSW student doing his placement at a homeless shelter. He typically had a caseload of approximately 20 to 25 clients. Reggie assisted clients with going through their orientation to the shelter, scheduling medical and dental appointments, obtaining referrals to other community resources providers, and arranging transportation to those providers.

After about 2 months at the shelter, Reggie began to notice some themes in his work within his caseload. First, he noticed that within the field of social work, individuals who are experiencing homelessness are often "lumped together." However, his experience indicates that the needs of his clients differ significantly. Some need only connection to resources to be self-sufficient again. Others are lacking important skills needed for employment, facing addiction or mental health problems, or facing other serious challenges.

This reflection left Reggie with some questions. How do we get community members, agencies, funders, and others to see that approaches cannot be "one size fits all"? How can we develop a new model of service? Once developed, what needs to happen next? Community support, political will, and funding initiatives were all ideas Reggie had to move forward.

LEARNING OBJECTIVES

This chapter focuses on Competency 5: Engage in Policy Practice. It begins with a brief introduction of the ways in which the field of social work is inherently political, when viewed through the lens of the National Association of Social Worker's (NASW's) *Code of Ethics*. This is followed by an overview of organizational policies, theories, and perspectives; how they look within field; and where they fall within the political framework. The chapter then moves on to social welfare policy and its relevance to the field of social work. Finally, it looks at advocacy in practice and the unique ways that advocacy is supported by the NASW's *Code of Ethics*. By the end of this chapter, you will be able to

(continued)

LEARNING OBJECTIVES *(continued)*

- Recognize the importance of policy practice in the field of social work.
- Recognize the ways in which social work and political work are intertwined through the lens of the NASW's *Code of Ethics*.
- Engage in organizational policy field practice.
- Engage in advocacy practices.

SOCIAL WORK VALUES

The NASW's *Code of Ethics* (2017) states that social workers should:

> engage in social and political action that seeks to ensure that all people have equal access to the resources, employment, services, and opportunities they require to meet their basic human needs and to develop fully. Social workers should be aware of the impact of the political arena on practice and should advocate for changes in policy and legislation to improve social conditions to meet basic human needs and promote social justice. (p. 30)

Unique and essential to the field of social work is the dual emphasis on not only individuals but also their corresponding environments. An important characteristic of the social work lens is the understanding that, within the helping relationship, it is sometimes necessary to focus on social conditions and oppression within the individual's environment, which may be the root cause or a factor intensifying the individual's problems. This dual focus is emphasized within the NASW's *Code of Ethics* (2017).

When people think of social work, what often comes to mind are the micro-level roles that social workers fill—often lost is social work's emphasis on working in the political arena to promote a variety of important social causes and to champion disadvantaged client populations. In fact, this role has been engrained in the fabric of social work since the beginning of the profession. As Ritter (2013) details, social workers have long worked to improve living conditions, and their efforts were part of the movements arising around settlement houses, child labor, women's suffrage, occupational safety, immigrant rights, the development of policies to address poverty during the Great Depression, and the fight for welfare rights and civil rights.

You may be feeling discomfort, or even fear, about being political within your work. You would not be alone in this discomfort (Harding, 2004). However,

Field Reflection Questions

What does the responsibility to social and political action, detailed in the NASW's *Code of Ethics*, mean to you for your future practice? What do you need to change to meet this obligation?

In your current field placement, have you had the opportunity to meet this responsibility? If not, how can you begin to implement this part of your role as a social worker?

social workers must come to terms with the fact that the work we do is fundamentally political—one cannot claim ownership in the pursuit of social justice without recognizing the ways in which policies, on all levels, disenfranchise and marginalize individuals and groups. If a social worker's mission is to simply help his or her clients adjust to their separate, disenfranchised, unequal living conditions—which may take the form of environmental hazards, subpar educational opportunities, lack of access to health care, and more—without any concern for organizing and advocating for social change, is the social worker not, in some way, complicit in the maintenance of the status quo?

POLICY PRACTICE

The Council on Social Work Education (CSWE, 2015) explains that one of the main components of policy practice is the ability to "analyze, formulate, and advocate for policies that advance human rights and social, economic, and environmental justice" (p. 8). Although often conceptualized as something that occurs within federal, state, and local political systems, policy practice occurs at multiple levels. Micro-level policy practice is the translation of mezzo- and macro-level policies into actual services for clients (Ritter, 2013). It is important to point out that micro-level workers are often the first to recognize patterns that call for change in policy, as was true in the case example that opened this chapter. Indeed, the direct-service social worker has the obligation to initiate change in organizations and communities by calling attention to these patterns.

Mezzo-level policy practice is the work done on administrative policy within organizations (Ritter, 2013). Organizational policy is integral to what actually happens on the ground. Who is allowed access to the services the organization provides? What services are provided? What interventions are used? The list of ways in which organizational policies impact service providers and clients is endless. This fact highlights why a practice orientation that recognizes how certain problems necessitate action to effect change at the organizational level is imperative.

Macro-level policy practice focuses on influencing policies at all levels of government and within the judicial system (Ritter, 2013). There are, again, endless ways in which legislation and policy affect the ways in which individuals and groups are able to go about their lives. These include foreign policy, labor policy, environmental policy, tax policy, health care policy, transportation policy, education policy, agriculture policy, energy policy, and the policy most often focused on within the field of social work and discussed later in this chapter—social welfare policy. These policies have such a drastic impact because they have the ability to create and improve social programming, determine and alter funding levels, determine the goals of specific policies, provide protection to vulnerable populations, and cause significant harm (Ritter, 2013).

Field Reflection Questions

Do you believe that all social work is inherently political? Why or why not? Can you give examples from your field placement to help articulate your stance?

Can you think of examples of policies that have helped vulnerable populations on the micro, mezzo, and/or macro levels? What about policies that have caused harm on those levels? Can you point to a policy within your field placement that you think does one or the other, or potentially both?

ORGANIZATIONAL POLICIES

Organizations, public and private, must continually obtain pertinent information and adjust their operations accordingly if they are going to continually provide effective service delivery in constantly changing circumstances. This ability to adapt will allow the organization to assess current client needs, develop projections so as to predict future needs, and brainstorm possible alternative service delivery strategies. These processes often result in a ripple effect of change, intentional or not. In practice, the result of this adaptability could have a variety of appearances: designing new programs, expanding the services offered, changing the client population served, obtaining new funding sources, implementing cutting-edge training programs for service providers, or developing new collaborators, to name a few. As discussed earlier in the chapter, organizations are required to develop and implement their own policies—with those policies often being greatly influenced by funding providers that specify certain guidelines for service delivery and population. Because of the contextual nature of the social problems that social workers are working against, they must continually examine and engage in organizational policy adjustment. Think of the complexities faced by the clients in your field placement—some may be experiencing substance use, violence, poverty, lack of health care, homelessness, and more. Regardless of the situation they are in, a multitude of organizations have been established for the purpose of providing services that attempt to address the needs of individuals in their communities. If you think about it, you can really identify the major impacts that organizations have on people's lives. This section acquaints you with the practice of assessing policies, the process of updating policies, and dissemination of organization policies in your work.

ASSESSING POLICIES

During the assessment process, it is important that the social worker identify whether the phenomenon he or she is considering has been formally recognized as a problem or unmet need by the organization, as this recognition impacts how the social worker will need to begin his or her efforts. In the assessment process, one of the main goals is the acknowledgment of the problem or unmet need, if that has not already happened, so as to advocate for formal resources to be dedicated to updating problematic policies or gaps (Netting, Kettner, McMurtry, & Thomas, 2017).

The assessment of policies often requires substantial information gathering, which can take many forms. Becoming familiar with the policies that are connected to the issue, conducting interviews with people within the organization, researching the professional knowledge base, locating data and information about the problem or unmet need, and obtaining information about the organization's receptiveness to policy change are some of the ways that social workers engage in the assessment of organizational policies. After gathering as much information as possible to gain a better understanding of both the problem or unmet need and the specific population, through both the existing knowledge base and the information collected for sources within the organization, a profile should begin to emerge. This profile will assist in better understanding potential responses to the problem or need, and allow the social worker to develop a hypothesis about how the policy or policies need to be updated to address the problem or unmet need. Exhibit 10.1 lists the three major steps for assessing organizational policies.

EXHIBIT 10.1	
Steps for Assessing Organizational Policies	
Step 1: Identify problem or unmet need	• Continually evaluate work for themes around problematic policies and/or unmet needs

Step 2: Gather information	• Gather information about:
	  • The organization's recognition that the problem exists
	  • Organizational history and receptiveness to policy change
	  • Experience of individuals within the organization
	  • Data and information about the problem or unmet need and population served
	  • Policies that may be impacting the problem or unmet need

Step 3: Develop hypothesis for policy change	• State the problem or unmet need • Share profile that emerged through the research • Develop a hypothesis for policy change

UPDATING AND DISSEMINATING POLICIES

The updating of policies often indicates the hand-off of responsibility from the social worker to those persons with decision-making authority within the organization. Kirst-Ashman and Hull (2001) developed an organizational assessment called "PREPARE: An Assessment of Organization Change Potential." Although designed specifically for macro practitioners, it also applies to the process of updating problematic or outdated organizational policies. The seven-step process of PREPARE is as follows:

- Step 1: Identify problems to be addressed.
- Step 2: Review your macro and personal reality.
- Step 3: Establish primary goals.
- Step 4: Identify relevant people of influence.
- Step 5: Assess potential financial costs and potential benefits to consumers and the organization.
- Step 6: Review professional and personal risks.
- Step 7: Evaluate the potential success of the macro change process.

Steps 1 to 3 were completed in the assessment process covered in the previous section. Step 4 focuses on identifying key change agents within the organization. The social worker who originally identified the problem or need would need to answer the following questions: Who has decision-making power in this process? Who may be able to assist in moving this policy change forward? Who may be potentially resistant to this policy update, and why? How will you address the concerns for those who are resistant?

Step 5 is the process by which the organization evaluates the financial costs and benefits. This often happens after the social worker has presented his or her assessment, and the need has been recognized formally or informally as a problem or gap. Note that this is often one of the first steps in updating policy if the potential problem or service gap was identified by those with decision-making authority. Also reviewed by the organization are the risks in implementing the policy change (step 6). Will implementing this policy update place the organization in violation of any funding agreements? How will the policy update be perceived by recipients of services, collaborating organizations, current and potential funders, employees, community members, and others? Which stakeholders have not been consulted that may be impacted by this change? Finally, those with decision-making authority will decide whether this policy change is worth the resources it will take to implement it, and if so, when that change should take place. In addition, organizations should decide how they will evaluate whether the policy change resulted in the intended outcome of solving the identified problem or service gap—all components of step 7.

What the dissemination of organizational policies looks like will depend on the scope of the policy change. Minor policy changes may need to be disseminated only to those internal to the organization who are impacted by that particular change. An example may be a change in intake procedure that will save time for both the organization and the client. This policy change may affect only intake staff. Something as small as a memo, or perhaps something more involved, such as a training, will suffice for disseminating this kind of change. However, for more far-reaching policy changes, wider dissemination may be necessary. Some examples of dissemination methods include publishing program or policy briefs via news release; presentations of the policy change to local community groups, agencies, and other local stakeholders; creating and distributing program materials, such as flyers or pamphlets, that detail how the policy change impacts programming; creating training materials and curricula for internal and external stakeholders; sharing vital information through social media or on the organization's website; hosting informational events at community functions; and publicizing new or altered services.

SOCIAL WELFARE POLICY

The social welfare system of the United States is made up of a highly complex set of programs, services, and agencies that are designed to address the multitude of needs that citizens have. These include, but are not limited to, health care needs, economic needs, educational needs, and others. Examples of social welfare programs include Temporary Assistance for Needy Families (TANF), Medicare, Medicaid, public education, Social Security, Supplemental Nutrition Assistance Program (SNAP), Head Start, unemployment compensation, college financial aid, public housing, and others. Nonprofit organizations, for-profit organizations, and faith-based organizations are private entities that are similarly designed to meet individual and community needs around social welfare; some of them also receive government funding to deliver services through grants and other funding sources.

The legislation, laws, rules, and regulations that direct social welfare systems in the United States make up social welfare policy. DiNitto (2011) points out that social welfare policy includes whatever the government of the United States decides to do or not do, which has an impact on citizens' quality of life. This is an important viewpoint because it highlights that quality of life can be greatly affected by governmental inaction, not just governmental action. In the United States, we have an ongoing debate about how much of a role, if any, and in what capacity, government should play in providing for the general welfare of the country's citizens (Ritter, 2013).

The ways in which the field of social work is impacted by social welfare policy are endless. Policy related to mental health, poverty, homelessness, child welfare, criminal justice, and many, many more subjects all impact clients' and communities' quality of life through access—or lack thereof—to services and resources, experiences of discrimination, unequal application of policy (e.g., sentencing of individuals convicted of a crime), and other ways. This is why social workers should be involved in political advocacy on behalf of the clients and communities they serve: If they ignore that role, they are missing out on the potential to make immense positive changes in their clients' lives.

So far, we have largely focused on social welfare policy as a force for positive change. We would be remiss if did not also mention the ways in which social welfare policy has also been used throughout the U.S. history to harm groups of people. The United States has a long history of using policy as a way to alienate, discriminate, marginalize, and inflict violence on oppressed communities. Some examples include the Indian Removal Act, Jim Crow laws, legalized slavery, executive order 9066 (which forced Japanese Americans into internment camps during World War II), withholding the right to vote from all except White men, and laws that made same-sex marriage illegal and barred same-sex couples from adopting children, among other harmful policies.

ADVOCACY

When Schneider and Lester (2001) analyzed the literature, they found more than 90 distinct definitions of advocacy. Schneider, Lester, and Ochieng (2013) point out that because of the multiple meanings and lack of common understanding, the field of social work has neglected to refine its skill set around advocacy practice. Herbert and Mould (1992) have suggested that this neglect prompted many social workers to believe that advocacy was something done primarily individually with a client by arranging services, not by partisan intervention when necessary.

Schneider and Lester (2001) defined social work advocacy as "the exclusive and mutual representation of a client(s) or a cause in a forum, attempting to systematically influence decision-making in an unjust or unresponsive system(s)" (p. 64). The benefit of this specific definition is that it includes the action piece of advocacy, not just the outcome of advocacy. Also, this definition is useful because it can be applied to micro, mezzo, and macro social work roles in a variety of settings. More recently, Schneider, Lester, and Ochieng (2013) have honed in on specific language within the definition to explain some of the ways in which social workers act out advocacy. These tactics include communicating concerns of the client, standing up for another person of group, and/or serving as an agent or proxy for another.

As Ritter (2013) points out, advocacy allows social workers to impact the lives of vulnerable populations by effecting large-scale social or political change. Social workers have unique, direct experience working with individuals, communities, and families, and, as such, should use that expertise to weigh in on proposed legislation through advocacy efforts.

PROMOTING SOCIAL JUSTICE

Advocacy and the promotion of social justice are linked in the Preamble of the NASW's *Code of Ethics* (2017). Social justice is a broad concept that encompasses fair and unbiased treatment of all individuals, eradication of discriminatory practices and institutionalized oppression, and establishment of equality for members of historically marginalized and oppressed groups: it is achieved through the establishment of truly equal opportunity and access to resources (Barsky, 2010; Reisch, 2002; Young, 2001). The CSWE addresses the social justice mandate by stating that "social work's purpose is actualized through its quest for social justice, the prevention of conditions that limit human rights, the elimination of poverty, and the enhancement of the quality of life for all persons" (2015, p. 5). It specifically calls upon all social workers to "understand the global interconnections of oppression and human rights violations; advocate for human rights [...]; and engage in practices that advance social, economic, and environmental justice" (2015, p. 8).

What does promoting social justice look like in practice? Although often thought of by social workers as a mezzo- or macro-level intervention only, the knowledge base of the field has theorized the promotion of social justice in all levels of social work; thus, clinical social workers need not feel disempowered to incorporate social justice practices into their daily work (Aldarondo, 2007; Johnson, 1999; Mitchell & Lynch, 2003; Parker, 2003; Stuart, 1999; Van Wormer, 2004). It can take many forms (Birkenmaier, 2003; Finn & Jacobson, 2008):

- Advocacy
- Empowerment of clients through consciousness raising, skill building, and resource development
- Community education and organizing
- Legislative and media activism
- Social movement participation
- Policy analysis and development
- Violence intervention
- Diversity promotion
- Program development and evaluation

Social workers must be prepared to become part of a values-driven and -applied profession (Havig, 2013). For many social workers in field, there is a lack of specific attention to social justice practices—this is a disservice to the social workers' efforts in building their efficacy in this realm (De Maria, 1992). As Havig (2013) aptly points out, to move toward the promotion of social justice within social work education, and specifically in field placements, the social work student must be purposeful and proactive in seeking out opportunities to engage and obtain those skills. Seeking out these opportunities is truly parallel to the challenging of social injustices and oppression in society, as both require intentional effort on behalf of the social worker (Havig, 2013).

ENGAGING IN ADVOCACY EFFORTS

Most agree that being actively engaged in issues of public concerns leads to stronger communities; however, most Americans feel that civic engagement is a choice, not a responsibility (Ritter, 2013). Although that may be the opinion of many Americans, social workers know that we are truly obligated to undertake advocacy, as discussed earlier in this chapter. Our profession is the only one in the United States that has a mission of social justice (Ritter,

2013). Indeed, social workers are uniquely positioned to work toward social justice through advocacy efforts. Much like the clinical skills needed in social work direct practice, advocacy requires commitment, determination, patience, energy, support, the use of research, and evaluation and assessment skills (Schneider & Lester, 2001). Also useful are political skills and knowledge of government and those involved in it (Schneider & Lester, 2001).

Schneider et al. (2013) argue that the ultimate goal of advocacy is to influence the modification, change, initiation, or altering of decisions by individuals or groups with authority or power over policies or resources that, in some way, impact others. Some advocacy activities include establishing coalitions; forming client groups; educating community members and groups; reaching out to legislators or other decision makers through letters, emails, phone calls, or individual meetings; providing testimony; and petitioning review boards (Hepworth, Rooney, Dewberry-Rooney, Strom-Gottfried, & Larsen, 2006). Similar to policy practice in organizations, the steps in this process allow for a more effective advocacy process (Schneider & Lester, 2001, pp. 116–147):

1. Identify the issues and set goals.

2. Get the facts.

3. Plan strategies and tactics.

4. Supply leadership.

5. Get to know decision makers and their staff.

6. Broaden the base of support.

7. Be persistent.

8. Evaluate your advocacy effort.

Ritter (2013) encourages social workers to advocate on issues they are already passionate about, reach out to those already working in that arena, and find out how they can be helpful to the cause. Ritter (2013) suggests multiple ways that social workers can become engaged in advocacy efforts:

- Joining an organization that is focused on passion issue or issues, such as the National Alliance on Mental Illness (NAMI) or Court Appointed Special Advocates (CASA).

- Joining in on electoral work, on behalf of either a specific issue (e.g., Medicaid expansion) or candidate(s) who support your issue(s); fundraising on behalf of a specific organization.

- Influencing legislation by speaking directly with legislators, especially on local issues impacting clients.

- Grassroots lobbying—that is, lobbying that occurs on behalf of an organization or campaign to inform decision makers, such as legislators, about specific legislation that you and the organization either support or oppose.

- Seeking media coverage of the specific issue you are focused on—this can be achieved by writing an opinion editorial (op-ed) or letters to the editor of local newspapers, using social media, or participating in action-oriented activities (e.g., rallies, protests, marches) with the intention of bringing media attention to the cause.

- Bringing together groups of people who are focused on the same issue to gain power in numbers and the pooling of resources, also known as coalition building (e.g., environmentalist groups and outdoor sporting groups joining forces on protecting public lands).

- Providing testimony in legislative committee hearings to share powerful stories that are related to specific issues (always remember to obtain the client's consent before sharing his or her story when testifying, and always protect the client's confidentiality even when permission is granted).

- Providing education outreach about your specific issue.

- Using civil disobedience or political dissent—that is, going "outside" the system to participate in sit-ins, pickets, and other forms of protests that attract visibility. Civil disobedience takes special consideration and a full understanding of its potential ramifications (e.g., arrest, ticketing).

EMPOWERING CLIENTS TO ADVOCATE FOR THEMSELVES

In micro practice, we focus on the strengths perspective and the empowerment approach—this focus goes beyond the individual work with clients. Social workers are asked to involve clients and community members in evaluating collective strengths and identifying opportunities for change (Long, Tice, & Morrison, 2006). The social worker does this by assisting in the formation of community-based groups. These groups are designed to fulfill multiple roles: provide support for community members, assess the collective's resources, and find ways to advocate for policies and practices designed to improve the community's collective condition. Social workers should seek to establish spaces, electronic and in person, that encourage open and productive dialogue among members.

> **Field Reflection Questions**
>
> What is an issue you are passionate about? What are you already doing in this arena? Which of the listed ways would you be more comfortable using to advocate for that issue? What would be the one you would be least comfortable using?
>
> What organizations are associated with the issue that you identified as being passionate about? Would you want to join forces with an organization or would you prefer to advocate on your own?

Social workers need to be careful not to restrict the empowerment of community members, and to ensure others do not as well. Action, intentional or not, that compromises the community members' ability to be active participants in advocating for specific policies and programs is to be avoided. Including community members in the advocacy process is vital. When working with others who are not community members, but perhaps leaders or professionals who are also passionate about the issue, the social worker may have to encourage a reorientation of how community members are perceived. These individuals must acknowledge community members as rightful stakeholders and decision makers during the advocacy process (Long et al., 2006).

Principles have been identified to help ensure that inclusion of community members is successful and beneficial for the community members. It is the social worker's responsibility to create opportunities for nonintrusive collaboration; establish mutual trust and respect; encourage a common analysis of strengths and issues; promote a commitment to solidarity; emphasize equality in relationships; focus on the process; recognize the importance of promoting inclusive and collegial language; and lay a foundation that allows strengths to emerge. Thinking back to Chapter 7, we know the importance of honoring community members' role as the experts on themselves and their communities—it is our role to also remind others of this fact when working together to advocate for common interests.

When possible, clients and community members should be encouraged to engage in any of the advocacy practices listed in the previous section—from joining organizations to lobbying, to using media, and more. However, we as social workers know that the ability to carry out these tasks requires a substantial amount of resources. As such, there are a multitude of reasons why this may not be possible: The client may be too intimidated to testify in front of professionals or legislators, he or she may be unwilling to share his or her marginalized status out of fear of retribution (e.g., violent, discrimination, deportation), he or she may be unable to attend such activities because of transportation issues or work responsibilities, and so on. In these circumstances, it is appropriate to advocate on behalf of the client or community member—working in close concert with him or her to carefully craft the message, sharing only the information that he or she has granted you permission to share, and always doing so anonymously.

APPLICATION TO FIELD PLACEMENT

The CSWE (2018) instituted the "Policy Practice in Field Initiative" in an effort to create opportunities for social work students to develop skills around policy practice and deepen their knowledge related to the intersection of race, ethnicity, and poverty. It is safe to assume that this initiative is the response to an identified gap in the skill building of social workers around policy practice within their field placements. This probably is not a surprise to many of you reading this chapter. While reading about the different ways in which to engage in policy practice, it may feel as though you do not have the time or authority to engage in policy practice within your current placement.

Policy practice can occur at any level and can occur regardless of placement. Some ways that you can engage in policy practice in your field placement include identifying existing policies that are relevant to your agency or client population, identifying publicly available data sources, identifying legislators who are involved in advocacy pertaining to your field area or client population, and identifying federal, state, and local organizations that are working on key issues related to your work. Similarly, getting involved in legislative advocacy that pertains to your work in your field placement—including contacting legislators to address key barriers your clients are facing—is an exceptionally useful way of applying policy practice to your work. Also, signing up for listservs and clearinghouses to keep you up-to-date on pertinent information pertaining to your field placement is a very easy and helpful way to stay involved and get ongoing invitations to different advocacy events. Share the information you obtain through these activities with your field supervisor. Perhaps the two of you can brainstorm ways of further engaging in policy within your practice and mobilize others within the agency to get involved as well.

SUMMARY

This chapter focused on different concepts related to policy practice. Social workers are encouraged to acknowledge the importance of policy practice and its connection to the NASW's *Code of Ethics*. Although policy making is often considered only something that macro-level social workers engage in, this chapter highlighted the ways in which policy practice can be achieved in multiple settings, regardless of whether your role is at micro, mezzo, or macro level.

Policy practice requires skills around analyzing, formulating, and advocating for policies that advance human rights and social, economic, and environmental justice. Micro-level policy practice is the translation of mezzo- and macro-level policies into actual services for clients (Ritter, 2013). Mezzo-level policy practice is the work done on administrative policy within organizations (Ritter, 2013). Macro-level policy practice focuses on impacting policies at all levels of government and within the judicial system (Ritter, 2013). All of these levels of policy practice are important because they all contribute significantly to the quality of life of clients and communities.

Social services organizations need to be willing and able to adapt in an effort to meet client needs, make projections so as to predict future needs, and brainstorm possible alternative service delivery strategies. Social workers will need to be able to recognize themes in regard to problematic policies or policy gaps and assess policies accordingly. The process of policy assessment includes information gathering, developing a profile on the basis of information gathered, and developing a hypothesis on how the policy or policies need to be updated. Updating and disseminating policies comes next, with examples of dissemination including publishing information, presentations, creation of program materials and/or training materials, sharing information on social media or on an organization's website, hosting informational events, and publicizing services.

The chapter also covered the social welfare system of the United States, and policy related to it. Social welfare is a highly complex topic, and many different organizations work to meet a variety of citizen needs. These include both public and private organizations, such as nonprofit, for-profit, and religious organizations. The legislation, laws, rules, and regulations that direct this complex system are considered social welfare policy. This can include policies that are implemented as well as those that are not implemented. In the United States, there is an ongoing debate about how much of a role the government should play in meeting its citizens' general welfare needs. The field of social work is greatly impacted by social welfare policy. Social welfare policy has resulted in both significant gains and significant harms to different groups of people.

The chapter also explored the role of advocacy in social work. Advocacy is the exclusive and mutual representation of a client(s) or a cause in a forum, attempting to systematically influence decision making in an unjust or unresponsive system(s); it can be applied to micro, mezzo, and macro social work roles in a variety of settings (Schneider & Lester, 2001). It is through advocacy that social workers promote social justice, and such engagement by all social workers is called for by the NASW's *Code of Ethics*. Social justice encompasses fair and unbiased treatment of all individuals, eradication of discriminatory practices and institutionalized oppression, and establishment of equality for members of historically marginalized and oppressed groups; it is achieved through the establishment of truly equal opportunity and access to resources (Barsky, 2010; Reisch, 2002; Young, 2001). Social justice in practice was also explored.

The skills necessary for engaging in advocacy include commitment, determination, patience, energy, support, the use of research, evaluation and assessment skills, political skills, and knowledge of government and those involved in it (Schneider & Lester, 2001). Different advocacy activities and steps in the advocacy process were explored in the chapter, and the skills necessary for empowering clients to advocate for themselves were discussed. The importance of recognizing clients and community members as the experts on the issues impacting them was highlighted. Finally, a section devoted to applying this information to your field placement was included.

CRITICAL THINKING QUESTIONS

Competency 5 focuses on engaging in policy practice. Social workers must recognize the importance of policy practice at all levels—micro, mezzo, and macro. One of the defining characteristics of the field of social work is our mission of advancing human rights and social, economic, and environmental justice. Because of this, social workers have the obligation to engage in advocacy efforts on some level. In addition, you are expected to empower your clients to advocate for policies and practices that benefit themselves and their communities. You may advocate alongside those individuals and communities, or speak on their behalf if they are unable or unwilling to do so. Social workers have the understanding that it is sometimes necessary to focus on social conditions and oppression within the individual's environment, which may be the root cause or a factor intensifying the individual's problems; social workers do not always, simply focus on individuals themselves. The following questions deal with engaging in policy practice:

1. Elizabeth is a social worker who is working with the National Coalition Against Domestic Violence. She has been discussing with a long-term client the potential of testifying in favor of legislation that provides additional resources for victims of domestic violence. Elizabeth had been working with the client for several weeks crafting her testimony—it was a powerful and heartbreaking account of her experience with domestic violence, and how much she would have benefited from the additional resources that may become available through this legislation. Two days before testimony was set to begin, the client called Elizabeth to say she just could not go through with a public testimony. The pain of recounting her story in front of so many people would be more than she could handle. What are some potential options for Elizabeth and the client? Discuss how you would approach this scenario. Reflect upon and describe your affective reaction to this scenario.

2. Think about your current field placement. What issue would you be able to advocate for on behalf of the clients you serve in your field placement? How could you envision yourself doing so within the agency? How would you envision advocating for your clients outside of the organization? Identify what skills you possess that would help you during your advocacy effort. What skills would you like to improve?

3. Engaging in advocacy efforts requires an attention to diversity and difference, Competency 2. You must recognize the client and community members as the expert on their experience about the social issue targeted, much as you do while engaging in a helping relationship beyond difference. What skills can you use to engage your clients in a helping relationship beyond difference that would also be useful in advocacy work?

4. In reflecting upon your work with clients in your field placement, identify a time when a client discussed an issue that reflected a social issue more than a personal

issue. Reflect upon and describe which social issue came up. Describe how you could potentially empower the client to advocate toward improving this specific social issue. If you are unsure, how might you go about finding out potential options?

COMPETENCY 5: ENGAGE IN POLICY PRACTICE

Social workers understand that human rights and social justice, as well as social welfare and services, are mediated by policy and its implementation at the federal, state, and local levels. They understand the history and current structures of social policies and services, the role of policy in service delivery, and the role of practice in policy development. Social workers understand their role in policy development and implementation within their practice settings at the micro, mezzo, and macro levels, and they actively engage in policy practice to effect change within those settings. They recognize and understand the historical, social, cultural, economic, organizational, environmental, and global influences that affect social policy. They are also knowledgeable about policy formulation, analysis, implementation, and evaluation. Social workers:

- Identify social policy at the local, state, and federal levels that impacts well-being, service delivery, and access to social services.

- Assess how social welfare and economic policies impact the delivery of and access to social services.

- Apply critical thinking to analyze, formulate, and advocate for policies that advance human rights and social, economic, and environmental justice.

CASE SUMMARY—"BUT I AM CLINICAL"

PRACTICE SETTING DESCRIPTION

My name is Rita and I am a second-year MSW student completing an internship at a community counseling center in the Northwest. The agency provides individual and family counseling services on a sliding fee scale to members of the surrounding community, most of whom are refugees from African countries, as our community is a resettlement area for incoming refugees. I work with clients on a variety of issues—mostly depression, anxiety, and posttraumatic stress disorder (PTSD). My role at the agency has thus far been entirely clinical, which I am fine with because I want to become a clinical social worker and obtain my license as a Clinical Social Worker.

PRESENTING PROBLEM

A new law has been proposed in my state with a stated goal of saving taxpayers money. This proposed law does two different things:

1. *Address a perceived problem of encouraging dependency on the government by reducing the amount of time refugees would qualify for specific social welfare services. Currently, the state augments federal funding to allow refugees access to certain social welfare services such as cash assistance, subsidized housing, day care, Medicaid, counseling services, and translation*

and interpretation services for eight months to one year. The proposed bill would take away all state funding and drastically reduce refugees' ability to receive support while adjusting to the expectations of living in the United States and looking for employment.

2. *The proposed legislation would deny the children of refugees access to state-funded social services.*

This issue has been receiving an increased amount of media attention in recent years. People in our community are highly polarized over the issue. Racial tensions are also rising as a result of the increased attention and the proposed legislation. Recently, an anti-refugee group has begun a social media campaign stoking racial tensions and spreading inaccurate information about the cost of these services to taxpayers, unemployment rates in the area, and incidents of violence perpetrated by refugees. This campaign is implying that refugees are increasing the crime rate and "stealing" jobs, neither of which has been shown to be true in the crime or employment data.

My clients are sharing increased incidences of hate-filled and racist interactions in the community, and many are scared for their safety and the safety of their children. They are becoming stressed about what they will do if their cash assistance and child care are cut off before the original termination date, and most are too afraid to reach out to the legislators in our area, as they are the ones who proposed the legislation.

CASE PROCESS SUMMARY

I am very upset about the proposed legislation, the anti-refugee campaign, and how many people in the community are falling for their lies. My clients are already experiencing the negative ramifications of this legislation, and it has not even been passed into a law. The thought of going to speak to my legislator is terrifying to me, because I know he and I are in disagreement on these issues. And somewhat selfishly, I am wondering if it is appropriate for me to use field placement time to look into how to potentially do something about this bill when my title is clinical social work intern.

Rita, clinical MSW student intern

DISCUSSION QUESTIONS

- Think about your own values. Think about the values of the profession of social work. How does this legislation fit within those values? Do you agree with the proposed legislation personally? What about professionally?

- Evaluate what you know about the proposed legislation through the lens of the NASW's *Code of Ethics*. Do you believe that this legislation would be harmful to Rita's clients? If so, what aspects of the NASW's *Code of Ethics* would come into play?

- What actions should Rita take? If you were in the same situation as Rita, how would you feel about the potential for taking on the actions you detailed for her?

- Do you believe that action on this legislation is Rita's role as a clinical social work intern? Why or why not?

ELECTRONIC COMPETENCY RESOURCES

WEBSITE LINKS

Advocacy—National Association of Social Workers
www.socialworkers.org/Advocacy

Education Resources—Council on Social Work Education
www.cswe.org/Education-Resources.aspx

Advocacy Handbook for Social Workers—Dan Beerman
http://c.ymcdn.com/sites/naswnc.site-ym.com/resource/resmgr/Advocacy/
Advocacyhandbook.pdf

VIDEO LINKS

Labor Movement Leader—Dolores Huerta
www.youtube.com/watch?v=eyEkOzYFf20

The Role of the Social Worker—Steve Perry
www.c-span.org/video/?320179-1/discussion-role-social-workers

David Sant Testimony in Support of HB 2307—NASW Oregon
www.youtube.com/watch?v=mg_Zcb27tR8

Community Organizers Share Experiences—Silberman School of Social Work at Hunter
College
www.youtube.com/watch?v=fmKFSjp9CI0

Environmental Justice—Peggy Shepard at TEDxHarlem
www.youtube.com/watch?v=zJX_MXaXbJA

A Brief History of Social Work—Maria Beatriz Alvarez, & Michael Bettencourt
www.youtube.com/watch?v=CxctzJg-p-g

REFERENCES

Aldarondo, E. (Ed.). (2007). *Advancing social justice through clinical practice.* Mahwah, NJ: Routledge.
Barsky, A. E. (2010). *Ethics and values in social work: An integrated approach for a comprehensive curriculum.* New York, NY: Oxford University Press.
Birkenmaier, J. (2003). On becoming a social justice practitioner. *Social Thought: Journal of Religion in the Social Services, 22*(2-3), 41–54. doi:10.1080/15426432.2003.9960340
Council on Social Work Education. (2015). *Council on Social Work Education curriculum policy statements.* Alexandria, VA: Author.
Council on Social Work Education. (2018). Policy practice in field education initiative. Retrieved from https://www.cswe.org/Centers-Initiatives/Initiatives/Policy-Practice-in-Field-Education-Initiative
De Maria, W. (1992). Alive on the street, dead in the classroom: The return of radical social work and the manufacture of activism. *Journal of Sociology and Social Welfare, 19*(3), 137–158. Retrieved from https://scholarworks.wmich.edu/cgi/viewcontent.cgi?article=2036&context=jssw
DiNitto, D. M. (2011). *Social welfare: Politics and public policy* (7th ed.). Boston, MA: Pearson.

Finn, J. L., & Jacobson, M. (2008). *Just practice: A social justice approach to social work* (2nd ed.). Peosta, IA: Eddie Bowers Publishing.

Harding, S. (2004). The sound of silence: Social work, the academy, and Iraq. *Journal of Sociology & Social Welfare, 31,* 179–197.

Havig, K. (2013, October). Empowering students to promote social justice: A qualitative study of field instructors' perceptions and strategies. *Field Educator, 3.2.* Retrieved from http://fieldeducator.simmons.edu/article/empowering-students-to-promote-social-justice-a-qualitative-study-of-field-instructors-perceptions-and-strategies/

Hepworth, D. H., Rooney, R. H., Dewberry-Rooney, G., Strom-Gottfried, K., & Larsen, J. A. (2006). *Direct social work practice: Theory and skills* (7th ed.). Pacific Grove, CA: Brooks/Cole.

Herbert, M. D., & Mould, J. W. (1992). The advocacy role in public child welfare. *Child Welfare, 71,* 114–130.

Johnson, Y. M. (1999). Indirect work: Social work's uncelebrated strength. *Social Work, 44*(4), 323–334. doi:10.1093/sw/44.4.323

Kirst-Ashman, K. K., & Hull, G. H., Jr. (2001). *Macro skills workbook: A generalist approach.* Pacific Grove, CA: Brooks/Cole.

Long, D. D., Tice, C. J., & Morrison, J. D. (2006). *Macro social work practice: A strengths perspective.* Monterey, CA: Brooks/Cole.

Mitchell, J., & Lynch, R. S. (2003). Beyond the rhetoric of social and economic justice: Redeeming the social work advocacy role. *Race, Gender, and Class, 10*(2), 8–26.

National Association of Social Workers. (2017). *Code of ethics of the National Association of Social Workers.* Washington, DC: Author.

Netting, F. E., Kettner, P. M., McMurtry, S. L., & Thomas, L. (2017). *Social work macro practice* (6th ed.). Boston, MA: Pearson Allyn & Bacon.

Parker, L. (2003). A social justice model for clinical social work practice. *Affilia, 18*(3), 272–288. doi:10.1177/0886109903254586

Reisch, M. (2002). Defining social justice in a socially unjust world. *Families in Society: The Journal of Contemporary Social Services, 83,* 343–354. doi:10.1606/1044-3894.17

Ritter, J. A. (2013). *Social work policy practice: Changing our community, our nation, and the world.* Boston, MA: Pearson.

Schneider, R. L., & Lester, L. (2001). *Social work advocacy: A new framework for action.* Belmont, CA: Wadsworth/Thomson Learning.

Schneider, R. L., Lester, L., & Ochieng, J. (2013). Advocacy. *Encyclopedia of Social Work.* NASW Press & Oxford University Press. Retrieved from http://socialwork.oxfordre.com/view/10.1093/acrefore/9780199975839.001.0001/acrefore-9780199975839-e-10

Stuart, P. H. (1999). Linking clients and policy: Social work's distinctive contribution. *Social Work, 44*(4), 335–347. doi:10.1093/sw/44.4.335

Van Wormer, K. S. (2004). *Confronting oppression, restoring justice: From policy analysis to social action.* Alexandria, VA: CSWE Press.

Young, I. M. (2001). Equality of whom? Social groups and judgments of injustice. *Journal of Political Philosophy, 9*(1), 1–18. doi:10.1111/1467-9760.00115

Micro Assessment: Individuals, Families, and Groups

CASE VIGNETTE

Julie is a first-year MSW student who was placed in a unit of a drug and alcohol center. She is assigned to the intake unit. Typically, Julie has two interviews with her clients prior to admission into the outpatient recovery program. The first focuses on conducting a biopsychosocial assessment and the second focuses on developing the clients' treatment goals.

Before she entered the MSW program, Julie worked for 2 years in a foster care agency that served children who were in long-term placement. She spent a lot of time with her clients, and she felt that she got to know them and developed strong helping relationships with them. In contrast, her work at the rehabilitation center is fast paced and short term. She has to complete the assessment and treatment goals after two brief client contacts.

By the end of her third week of placement, Julie was concerned about the effectiveness of her work. She felt that her approach was too task focused and that she was not truly understanding her clients' strengths and challenges. She felt that she did not really understand who they were. Instead, she was getting information as quickly as possible, filling out a form, and telling the clients about their treatment goals and the outpatient program. It felt rote and dehumanizing to her. She wondered what she could do to make the experience more positive for her clients and for herself. Julie felt that she needed a better understanding of her clients to develop realistic and appropriate treatment goals. How can she complete her biopsychosocial assessments and get the information the agency requires, while gaining a beginning understanding of her clients' strengths, challenges, and life experiences to develop meaningful treatment goals?

LEARNING OBJECTIVES

This chapter focuses on Competency 7: Assess Individuals, Families, Groups, Organizations, and Communities. It covers assessment of the three micro-level client systems: individuals, families, and groups. The chapter begins with a brief review of the process of critical thinking,

(continued)

© Springer Publishing Company DOI: 10.1891/9780826175533.0011

LEARNING OBJECTIVES *(continued)*

which is one of the keys to conducting successful client system assessments. This is followed by a brief review of a strengths-based approach to conducting collaborative assessments. The chapter then reviews the assessments with three micro-client systems. It ends with a section containing various micro-level assessment tools. By the end of this chapter, you will be able to

- Apply critical thinking skills in conducting assessments with individuals, families, and groups.
- Describe the strengths perspective and its six key principles.
- Conduct individual client system assessments.
- Conduct assessments of individual group members and the group as a whole.
- Use a range of microsystem assessment tools.

■ CRITICAL THINKING

Critical thinking is more than a rational step-by-step problem-solving process (Gibbons & Gray, 2004). It involves an intuitive process as well as disciplined evaluation and analysis. Thinking critically includes the synthesis, comparison, and evaluation of ideas from a variety of sources, such as texts, direct observation and experience, and social dialogue (Gibbons & Gray, 2004). A critically thinking social worker attempts to understand the client systems' perception of their reality and how their perceptions inform their work together. Critical thinking in social work assessment is the process of figuring out what is going on with your client, including what to believe or not believe about a situation. Social work is, by definition, a process in which there is no definitive answer. There are often multiple pathways to address a situation or reach a targeted goal. Effective social work assessment requires critical thinking. A key component of the assessment process is formulating hypotheses and critically assessing them to better understand the client system. Practice interventions and/or strategies flow out of our understanding of the client's perception of his or her situation and social reality. Critical thinking is the open-minded search for understanding.

Associated with critical thinking is the process of considering evidence when making decisions (Gambrill, 2013). Walker, Briggs, Koroloff, and Friesen (2007) point out that there are two kinds of evidence that social workers must balance in making informed decisions about their work with clients. The first is "empirically based knowledge generated through the scientific method" (p. 361). The second is "knowledge that is acquired through relationships with unique individuals (or unique groups like families, communities and organizations)" (pp. 361–362). Balancing empirical knowledge and practice wisdom allows social workers to

Field Reflection Questions

In your field placement, what do you need to do to strengthen your critical thinking skills in relation to your cognitive processing, affective reactions, and professional judgments?

What clues can you give yourself to remember to self-reflect upon your affective reactions while in the moment with your clients at your field placement?

move forward and make assessments with "reasonable confidence while also acknowl-edging uncertainty" (Walker et al., 2007, p. 362).

STRENGTHS PERSPECTIVE

The idea of building on clients' strengths has received a lot of attention in social work. Most social work agencies now claim adherence to "the strengths perspective." A strengths-based assessment is very different from approaches that focus on client problems and history taking (Hepworth, Rooney, Rooney, & Strom-Gottfried, 2017). Social work has a long history of help-ing disadvantaged clients overcome individual problems and problem situations. Clients come to us with problems, and there is a natural tendency to attempt to resolve the problems and to view the clients from a deficit perspective. Often social workers' perceptions differ from their clients' self-perceptions. The clients may view themselves as proactive, autonomous human beings who are using counseling services to enhance their functioning and competence. Unfortunately, in the past, social workers tended to underestimate clients' strengths, focusing on their problems, underlying weaknesses, and limited potential.

When social workers focus on problems, they tend to perceive clients in essentially neg-ative terms, as a collection of problems and diagnostic labels. This negative perception may lower expectations for positive change. More likely than not, clients are seen as diagnostic categories or their presenting problems, or both. These labels may create distance between clients and helpers (Saleebey, 2013). They also create pessimism in both parties. Negative labels and expectations obscure the unique capabilities of clients. The social worker's ability to recognize and promote a client's potential for change is markedly reduced. The focus is on what is wrong and the client's inability to cope with his or her life situation. Saleebey (2013) suggests that instead of focusing on problems, we should focus on possibilities.

The pathological problem approach searches the past for causes. How did the client get into this situation? Why is the client experiencing these difficulties? The search for causes and rational explanations assumes a direct link between cause, disease, and cure (Saleebey, 2013). Human experience is rarely that simple. More often than not, it is uncertain and tremendously complex. In addition, looking to the past diverts attention away from exploring the present.

The shift from problems to strengths moves the focus from the past to the present and future. Strengths-oriented social workers seek to discover the resources clients currently have that can be used to change their futures. The past cannot be completely dismissed, because it provides a context for the present. However, in strengths-based practice, the focus is on the present and the future. Rather than focusing on why clients are having problems, social workers who have adopted a strengths perspective focus on what clients want, what they need, and how they have managed to survive (Saleebey, 2013). These and similar questions will help you and your clients identify, use, build, and reinforce clients' strengths, resources, and abilities.

PRINCIPLES OF STRENGTHS-BASED ASSESSMENT

Six principles guide strengths-based generalist practice (Saleebey, 2013). They also link the strengths perspective to the core values of the profession. Social work practice is not only about whether and how to intervene or about skills and techniques, but also about our profession's core values.

PRINCIPLE 1: EVERY INDIVIDUAL, GROUP, FAMILY, AND COMMUNITY HAS STRENGTHS

Regardless of the situation, every person, family, and community possesses assets, resources, wisdom, and knowledge that you need to discover (Saleebey, 2013). To become aware of these strengths, you need to be genuinely interested in your clients and respectful of their perceptions of their own experiences. The ultimate key to identifying client strengths is your belief in the clients and their possibilities. Adopting a strengths perspective requires you to view your clients as underused sources of knowledge and untapped resources.

PRINCIPLE 2: TRAUMA, ABUSE, ILLNESS, AND STRUGGLE MAY BE INJURIOUS, BUT THEY MAY ALSO BE SOURCES OF CHALLENGE AND OPPORTUNITY

Dwelling on clients' pasts and hardships promotes an image of clients as helpless. Focusing on past hurts and deficits leads to discouragement and pessimism. What is more extraordinary is that your clients have survived and that they are working with you to bring about changes in their lives. There is dignity and affirmation in having prevailed over trauma, abuse, illness, and other difficult situations. Posttraumatic growth illustrates the capacity for resilience and growth despite previous adversity. The strength of having survived and coped with numerous obstacles is often lost on clients who are struggling to meet life's daily challenges. A strengths approach recognizes clients' inherent competencies, resilience, and resourcefulness in having survived past difficulties as well as their current motivation for growth and development.

> **Field Reflection Questions**
>
> After reviewing the six strengths principles, which principle do you feel you have the most difficulty applying in your field placement work?
>
> Which principle is the easiest for you to apply? What makes one harder to incorporate into your practice than the other?

PRINCIPLE 3: ASSUME THAT YOU DO NOT KNOW THE UPPER LIMITS OF THE CAPACITY TO GROW AND CHANGE, AND TAKE INDIVIDUAL, GROUP, AND COMMUNITY ASPIRATIONS SERIOUSLY

Simply put, this principle means that you should set high expectations for your clients and help expand their hopes, visions, and aspirations. The strengths perspective is the perspective of hope and possibilities. Believe in clients' capacities for change, growth, and self-actualization. If you do not believe in their abilities and motivation, you really do not believe in the possibility of change. Creating hope where there is little to hope for, strengthening belief when there is little to believe in, and creating aspirations where there are none are the essence of social work practice from a strengths perspective.

PRINCIPLE 4: WE BEST SERVE CLIENTS BY COLLABORATING WITH THEM

The strengths perspective calls for a partnership characterized by reciprocity and mutual respect between you and your client. There should be a sharing of knowledge and resources. You are not the sole expert or the only one with specialized information; your clients are experts who know more about coping with their situations than you do (Saleebey, 2013).

Take advantage of the wisdom, insights, and understanding your clients bring to the helping process by entering into a collaborative partnership with them. The strengths approach to social work practice requires it. Work with your clients in partnership. Do not presume to work on your clients or to do the work for them.

No matter how deprived a client's community, neighborhood, or family system, each has an abundance of untapped resources. In every environment, there are individuals, associations, groups, and institutions that have something to give (Saleebey, 2013). Looking to these untapped resources does not negate our responsibility to work for social and economic justice, and it does not mean that we accept the notion that a disadvantaged person should assume sole responsibility for his or her situation and its amelioration. It does mean, however, that the possibilities for identifying and arranging needed resources for clients from within their own environment are more numerous than you would expect.

PRINCIPLE 5: EVERY ENVIRONMENT IS FULL OF RESOURCES

No matter how deprived a client's community, neighborhood, or family system, each has an abundance of untapped resources. In every environment, there are individuals, associations, groups, and institutions who have something that can help. (Saleebey, 2013). Looking to these untapped resources does not negate our responsibility to work for social and economic justice, and it does not mean that we accept the notion that a disadvantaged person should assume sole responsibility for his or her situation and its amelioration. It does mean, however, that the possibilities for identifying and arranging needed resources for clients from within their own environment are more numerous than you would expect.

PRINCIPLE 6: CARING, CARE TAKING, AND CONTEXT ARE IMPORTANT

Caring for others and being cared for is a basic human right. Families can assist in caring for their members (Saleebey, 2013). Caring strengthens our social web, our interconnectedness. Social work is a caring profession, and the strengths perspective recognizes and embraces our dependence on others for our well-being.

ASSESSING INDIVIDUALS

Most students in a generalist field placement will at some point be asked to conduct an assessment of an individual client. The process and the assessment tools used are determined by the field placement agency and will vary from agency to agency. As a social work intern, you are required to follow the protocols and procedures of your placement agency. The content in this section focuses on information that would apply to any individual assessment regardless of agency expectations and requirements. Our aim is to help

EXHIBIT
11.1

Individual Client Subsystems

Demographics	Personal Characteristics
Gender Race Age Socioeconomic status	Responsibility Commitment Motivation Coping skills Resourcefulness
Ethnicity and culture Values and beliefs Spirituality and religion	**Life experiences** Relationships Support networks Life-cycle stage Mental health status Health status

you prepare for conducting biopsychosocial assessments of an individual client using best practices in terms of use of self during the assessment process.

An individual client system consists of four major subsystems: demographic characteristics, ethnicity and culture, personal characteristics, and life experiences. These four subsystems and the specific characteristics associated with each of them are shown in Exhibit 11.1.

DEMOGRAPHIC CHARACTERISTICS

Demographic characteristics—such as gender, race, age, and socioeconomic status—potentially affect the helping relationship and the identified target problem. Although demographic characteristics might directly influence the helping relationship, their primary influence is through transactions with the worker system. Workers and clients need to explore the effects of clients' demographic characteristics on their work together. For example, there are often significant age discrepancies between workers and their clients. Social workers who are significantly younger than their clients should raise the issue of age for discussion. If it is not a concern for the client, no harm has been done, and it opens the door for a discussion of other factors. If it is a concern, it can be addressed.

Another sensitive demographic factor is race. In the United States, race is a highly charged issue for most people. Race may be an issue when there are racial differences between workers and clients. It may also be an issue when both the worker and the client have minority status. Being willing to explore the potential effect of race on the helping relationship communicates sensitivity and a willingness to enter into a partnership.

ETHNICITY AND CULTURE

The second category of client characteristics that affects the helping relationship is ethnicity and culture. This broad category includes personal ideologies and cultural values and beliefs. Assessment of this group of factors requires introspection. You have to understand your value system and how values influence your perceptions of yourself and others. Only after developing an awareness of your own value system can you explore value differences with clients.

You need to be sensitive to areas of disagreement and agreement when exploring personal beliefs, cultural traditions, and value positions with clients. It is important to explicitly recognize both. Identifying differences in values and beliefs allows recognition and acceptance of the differences and development of strategies for dealing with them. Identifying areas of agreement strengthens the connection between you and the client. It is important to limit mutual exploration of values and beliefs to areas that potentially affect the helping relationship and your work together. It is not possible or appropriate to explore all aspects of the belief systems of you and your client. However, the more that each understands what the other holds dear, the more likely it is that a strong helping relationship will develop.

PERSONAL CHARACTERISTICS

Three primary characteristics influence a client's ability to benefit from a helping relationship: responsibility, commitment, and motivation. A number of factors influence a person's ability or willingness to make a commitment and assume responsibility for creating change. Responsibility and commitment profoundly affect the helping relationship and are critical to the success of the helping process. Social workers help clients help themselves. Success requires a commitment to the change process.

It is unrealistic to expect all clients to assume responsibility for change and to be committed to the helping process at the outset. Clients need to develop commitment to the helping process and self-help through the ongoing helping relationship.

Many clients seeking social work services have difficulty taking responsibility for their actions and sustaining their commitment to improve their life situations. Thus, the interaction between you and the client is critical. You must use your interpersonal qualities and clinical skills to address the client's level of commitment and responsibility. You and the client need to explore experiences and feelings related to taking responsibility and making a commitment to change. You have to motivate clients to take responsibility for their actions and support their commitment to the process.

Two additional personal characteristics that should be assessed are the client's coping skills and resourcefulness. Identifying past ways of coping with problem situations is an important aspect of the assessment. The strengths perspective emphasizes client capacity and previous success in coping with the target problem. Clients often are unaware of their resourcefulness and past successes. Exploring past experiences and providing ideas about additional ways of coping empowers the client and enhances the helping relationship.

> **Field Reflection Questions**
> Which of the individual client subsystems do you feel most comfortable with while obtaining assessment information with your field placement clients? Why?
>
> Which subsystem do you feel least comfortable with? Why and what can you do to increase your comfort level in obtaining this type of assessment data?

LIFE EXPERIENCES

The broad category of life experiences refers to the client's history, including experiences with family and interpersonal relationships, support networks, developmental life stages, and mental health and health status. These are the traditional topics of biopsychosocial assessment. You need to explore the client's life story. You need to understand the client's self-perceptions, worldview, and prior experiences, and the way these experiences may potentially influence the helping relationship.

ASSESSING CLIENT STRENGTHS

Strengths-based assessments enhance the individualization of clients. The focus is on what is unique about each client in terms of interests, abilities, and ways of coping with the problem situation. The work should focus on what the client has achieved and what resources are currently available to the client. Give preeminence to the client's understanding of the facts and figure out what the client wants. Above all, avoid blame and blaming. Join with your clients in a collaborative effort to understand their reality and their strengths.

Adherence to these concepts will help ensure that your assessment interviews are collaborative and that the process will identify client strengths. The tendency to focus on pathological symptoms and dysfunction will be minimized. Identifying client strengths is not always easy. Clients are often unable to name specific strengths they have used in coping with a problem situation. They often indicate that they do not have any strengths, or they respond in very general terms. The challenge is to help clients recognize how they have taken steps, summoned up resources, and coped (Saleebey, 2013).

Using a strengths perspective does not negate the very real problems that clients face. The problems that cause clients to seek professional help cannot be disregarded or ignored. The assessment process must attend to both the obstacles and the strengths that potentially affect the resolution of the problem and the helping process. Much of the assessment that takes place in social work is focused on client problems and deficits (Saleebey, 2013). The strengths approach seeks to provide a balance between client obstacles and strengths.

Cowger (1997) proposed an assessment axis to help attain this balance. It has two coordinates: the environmental–personal continuum and the strengths–obstacles continuum. There are four quadrants: environmental strengths, personal strengths, environmental obstacles, and personal obstacles. The quadrants for personal strengths and obstacles include both psychological and physiological components. Attention to all four quadrants helps ensure a comprehensive assessment that is balanced in terms of individual and environmental strengths and obstacles.

USE OF SELF

Most social work assessments explore the presenting problem, the client's history and experiences, family dynamics, and community resources. All have potential impacts on the client's identified target problem. Most assessments, however, do not take into account the impact the worker has on the client's environmental system. The interactions between you and your client are important data for your assessment. In exploring the client's reality, it is important for you to be aware of your own biases and beliefs, which may influence your clinical perceptions. You need to be able to differentiate between your interpretations and those of your client. Also, remember that by exploring your client's subjective reality, you become part of that reality. That is, you become part of the client's person-in-environment system. Thus, you can influence a client's subjective perceptions of self and of experiences. Care must be taken, however, to allow the client's subjective reality to emerge.

Conducting a person-in-environment assessment is immensely complex and difficult. Even so, it is critical to the success of the work. Assessment is an ongoing task in the helping process and should not be limited to the beginning assessment phase. It requires mutual exploration and evaluation of the client's person-in-environment system throughout the helping relationship.

In conducting a client assessment, it is important that you factor in your relationship and interactions with your client. Critically assess how they might affect your assessment of your client's strengths, challenges, and service needs. This is where practice wisdom comes into play. Use your experiences and interactions with your client to help guide your assessment. Your agency's assessment forms, more likely than not, will include questions about the client's ecological system. We encourage you to include yourself and your interaction with your clients into the assessment process. This process is not about asking questions and filling out the assessment form. Instead, it is about you critically assessing all of the information, forming an understanding of your client, and making an informed assessment on the basis of the empirical and subjective data.

> **Field Reflection Questions**
>
> Describe how you will incorporate your experiences and interactions with your clients into your client assessments.
>
> In what ways does your use of self impact your client assessments?

The key to conducting an assessment in which you begin to truly understand your client is to use your social work interviewing skills. Your agency will have an assessment form with many questions that need to be answered. But asking the questions on the form is not enough: You need to be able to get the whole story to understand your client's unique situation. This requires your ability to engage your clients in a helping relationship in which trust is built and sensitive information shared, and in which your clients are willing to expose their vulnerability. This is not easy to accomplish. You must use your social work interviewing skills to make this happen. More than anything, we believe that clients need to feel heard and understood. Active listening, empathic responding, reaching for feelings, elaboration skills, and summarizing are all key skills when conducting assessments. Remember, your task is to understand your client and provide a professional assessment. This requires skill and compassion. It is not just about filling out the form.

ASSESSING FAMILIES (CRANE, 2010)

Creating an empowering assessment process with families is similar to doing strengths-based assessment with individuals. The main difference, and the biggest challenge, is to focus your attention and efforts on the family as a whole as well as on each individual member. Assessment must be a collaborative process in which concerns are heard, strengths are recognized, and understanding, empathy, and hope are communicated. Together you will explore the family members' perceptions of their situation and work to create goals. Think of doing assessment *with* a family, rather than *of* a family. In this way, the assessment process becomes an educative tool, in that the family comes to understand itself better as a functioning unit.

Assessment emphasizes the identification of family strengths as well as the strengths of each individual family member. Families have power from within to bring about positive change. The strengths perspective, however, may have to come from you. Although all families have strengths, family members may not always recognize or be aware of them. By adopting the attitude that strengths exist and that they can be used to help the family resolve the problem situation, you can help the family recognize their individual and collective strengths. Focus on strengths. Look for the ways the family and its members have coped with problem situations and concerns. Help them recognize past successes as well as resources and abilities they can draw on in the helping process.

A collaborative approach to family assessment empowers families by allowing their expertise in functioning and their concerns to emerge. Strive to empower the family as well as each individual member. Begin by asking the family and its members about their perceptions of their needs and their goals. Do not force your analysis and assessment of their problems, interpersonal relationships, or individual dysfunction on them, even if you believe that numerous problems exist. Engage in a collaborative exchange, sharing your insights and perceptions, and exploring those of family members. Become a partner with the family by sharing responsibility and decision making.

Assessment is the key to the helping process. To be able to effectively help families, you need to develop a shared understanding of their concerns, their strengths, potential resources, and the challenges they face. The assessment process provides an opportunity for families to tell their stories. It is more about listening than asking questions. Strengths-based assessments focus on clients' perceptions of their situation and their goals, rather than on diagnostic labels. Ideally, the process should lead to increased family empowerment and create a sense of hopefulness. Focusing on strengths rather than deficits helps create expectations about the possibilities of change.

Assessment of a family system can include review of six major family subsystems: (a) structure, (b) life-cycle stage, (c) ethnicity and culture, (d) communication patterns, (e) emotional climate, and (f) boundaries. These subsystems, as shown in Exhibit 11.2, are highly interrelated, interdependent entities. Taken as a whole, they provide a comprehensive

EXHIBIT 11.2

Family Client System: Assessment Subsystems

Structure
    Number and ages of family
        members
    Informal rules for interaction
    Relationship subsystems
	Ethnicity and culture
	    Values and beliefs
	    Rules
	    Myths
		Life-cycle stage
		    Developmental stage
		    Transitions

Emotional climate
    Affective tone
    Involvement
	Communication patterns
	    Verbal
	    Nonverbal
	    Contextual
		Boundaries
		    Open/closed
		    Rigid/diffuse
		    Enmeshed/detached

idea of the internal structure and functioning of a family system, an overall picture of how the family relates and functions as a unit.

There is no one right way to walk through this type of assessment with a family because the subsystems are so interrelated. You might briefly explain each area, and then encourage the family to choose which topic they want to talk about first. Then facilitate the discussion as an exercise in self-understanding. Any one of these areas, or looking at them in combination, may turn out to have major explanatory value for the family, that "Aha" moment when they might say, "Oh, that's what's going on with us." For example, let us imagine that an elderly grandparent has recently moved into a daughter's home. Looking at how this life-cycle transition is affecting their family structure and the way they communicate may help them understand why there is less closeness and more conflict, and why some family members may be more detached.

ASSESSING GROUPS

Like assessing families, assessing small groups is similar to assessing individuals. Again, the main difference is that you focus your attention and efforts on the group as a whole as well as on each individual member. The use of groups in generalist social work practice is very prevalent in almost all fields of practice. The chances of you being asked to facilitate or cofacilitate a group in your field placement are very high. Facilitating a group can be very scary, especially if you do not have prior experiences in group work. When groups are working well together, it can be a very powerful and rewarding experience for both the participants and the facilitator. When groups are not working well, the opposite is true. Case Example 11.1 describes a group that is not functioning well, and Case Example 11.2 presents a successful group.

CASE EXAMPLE 11.1: A GROUP THAT IS NOT FUNCTIONING WELL TOGETHER (BAROL, 2010)

Gwen has been involved on a team to address the quality concerns in her agency. There are 10 people on the team. They are positive and productive supervisors and administrators across the agency. Their goal is to review a policy or a procedure each time they meet. Most of the time, they "wordsmith" it and set up a new deadline for project completion. Work assignments are given to group members between meetings. However, members rarely complete the assignments. The meetings are often interrupted as members step out to answer cell phone calls, come in late, or leave early. Members jump at any excuse not to attend meetings, citing work obligations that Gwen knows are not so urgent that they could not be addressed after the meeting time. In addition, no matter how far in advance the meetings are scheduled, members plan their compensatory day and vacations days for the days the meetings are scheduled. Gwen is under the impression that members of the team would rather be anywhere else than in this group. She feels that trying to manage the team is like "herding cats." It has become a waste of time for everyone, including Gwen.

Gwen dislikes attending these meetings. They ruin her day. She feels like a failure with respect to this project. She is worried that her reputation as a competent worker is at stake. She has tried being more strict and authoritative around attendance and compliance with assignments, but the harder she works, the less the group members cooperate. It seems that they expect her to do all of the work so that they can just criticize and shoot down her efforts.

CASE EXAMPLE 11.2: A GROUP THAT IS WORKING WELL TOGETHER (BAROL, 2010)

Andrea is responsible for a team in her agency whose mission is to address quality within the agency. She is excited by the assignment. She enjoys working with this group of focused, productive, and positive supervisors from across the agency. The time that they meet together seems to fly by. They are usually on the same wavelength with what they are doing, and they have healthy discussions and occasional friendly arguments when they work on issues that represent their different vantage points. However, even when there is a disagreement with some tension attached to it, the group members are issue focused rather than person focused. After working through the tension and issues, they always seem to find common ground. Members know and respect each other and are not worried that a disagreement within the meeting will have a negative effect on their relationships on the team and their reputation outside of the meeting time. Team members are creative and excited in this work and strive to include all members of the agency in parallel processes. In fact, people think that it is an honor to be on this team and are excited when they are chosen to participate.

ASSESSING INDIVIDUAL GROUP MEMBERS

Facilitating or cofacilitating a group requires you to monitor the functioning of each member of the group. You have to be sensitive to each group member's participation, nonverbal communication, emotional responses, and behaviors. Your assessment of the individual members is done primarily by observation. Your observations and your knowledge of the client are the data you will use to assess the individual members in your group. This information, combined with your critical thinking skills, will provide you with hypotheses about what might be going on with individual members in terms of their functioning in the group. You then must make a professional judgment as to whether you should address a possible concern in the group or handle it individually with the group member. This is never an easy decision, especially when you have limited experience in facilitating groups. Adding to the difficulty is the fact that you have to make the decision in the moment and while you are also attending to the needs of the group as a whole. Nevertheless, your ongoing assessment of each participant in the group is a critical component of effective group facilitation (see Case Examples 11.3 and 11.4).

CASE EXAMPLE 11.3: IN THE MOMENT (BAROL, 2010)

Alex is placed in a program that provides residential and treatment services to male sex offenders. As a first-year MSW student, Alex cofacilitates a weekly treatment group with her field instructor. The group has eight participants who are required to attend. Each week focuses on a different topic and the participants are encouraged to share their stories related to the topic.

The topic during week 5 was on dating and building trusting relationships; Alex was tasked with leading the session. During the beginning of checking-in portion of the meeting,

Alex noticed that Juan seemed very withdrawn and disengaged. This was unusual for him. Most of the time, he was an active and engaged participant. Alex used nonverbal cues to check in with Juan. He was nonresponsive and avoided eye contact. Alex asked whether he was having a bad day, and Juan shook his head no and slouched further into his chair.

On the basis of previous group meetings and information in his case, Alex knew that (a) Juan is 22 years old, (b) was convicted of molesting his 12-year-old male cousin, (c) has never had a sexual relationship with a female, and (d) has just begun a dating relationship with a 21-year-old female, which is his first ever heterosexual relationship. Alex hypothesized that Juan was anxious about his sexuality and possibly embarrassed about being judged by his peers in the group about his inexperience with intimate relationships. She was unsure what to do. Should she just ignore Juan and pass her observations on to his therapist? Should she ask Juan to share with the group? Neither seemed to feel right. Her gut feeling (affective reaction) was that the group was not yet a safe space for Juan to share details about his intimate relationships or the lack of them. On the basis of the data available and her cognitive and affective analysis of the situation, Alex decided to shift the discussion to new dating relationships and asked the group members to share their experiences, if they felt comfortable doing so. As the group discussion proceeded, Juan appeared to relax as he listened to the other group members. Alex invited Juan to share when he was ready or just listen, and either would be okay. At that point, Juan stated that he had a new girlfriend and that he was nervous when they went on dates. He got some encouragement from the other members, but he never shared that she was the first female he had dated.

Alex felt that she had made the correct decision. If she had taken the issue head on, Juan probably would have shut down completely. By not doing so and by giving him the choice to join in the discussion, she made it easy for him to share his feelings with his therapist and/or with group in the future when he was ready. Alex also decided that because other group members did not share Juan's issue, bringing it to the group for discussion would not serve the overall group and would put Juan in an isolated and vulnerable position. Alex exercised her professional judgment in the moment— during the group session—on the basis of her analysis of the data available and her critical thinking skills. After the session, Alex processed the interaction and her decision with her field instructor, who supported her approach. They also discussed Alex's affective reaction about the group being a safe space and decided that Alex would do an assessment of the functioning of the group.

ASSESSING THE GROUP AS A WHOLE

Concerns about group functioning may arise from the group, or you may raise them. In this respect, group assessment differs from individual and family system assessment. Individuals and families usually seek professional help for a problem they are aware of and want to correct. Problems in group functioning, however, are not always apparent to individual members or to the group as a whole, and groups usually do not seek professional help. An important part of your job as the group leader is to identify potential issues and concerns and to bring them to the attention of the group.

Field Reflection Questions

Reflect upon your experiences in facilitating groups. Were there any signs of dysfunction that could have been accessed? What do you think was going on in terms of group process? What might you have done differently?

What areas of group functioning do you find most challenging to access in the moment? What can you do to be better prepared to access and respond in the moment?

As shown in Exhibit 11.3, there are five major subsystems within the group-in-environment system that have potential relevance for the assessment process: purpose, structure, life-cycle stage, culture, and alliances. Like family subsystems, group subsystems are highly interrelated. Taken as a whole, they provide a comprehensive picture of the internal structure and functioning of a group system. An ecosystem assessment requires the social worker and the group to mutually and continually assess the effect the various subsystems have on one another and on the functioning of the group.

Purpose

Every formed group has a purpose. The purpose varies according to the type of group. Because in many respects, the type defines a group's purpose, assessment of purpose is an excellent first step in assessing group functioning. Many groups fail because of a lack of understanding of their purpose (Barol, 2010). The group's purpose should be clearly stated and agreed on by group members. It is from the purpose that all other aspects of a group evolve. Is the identified problem or concern related to confusion or disagreement about the purpose of the group? Is the purpose clear and unambiguous? Is there agreement about the purpose of the group? Does the group have more than one purpose? If so, are the different purposes in conflict?

Structure

Structure is the composition of the group, its size, whether the group is time limited or ongoing, and whether the group is open to new members or closed. Problems in group functioning can often be traced back to structural issues. Examination of a group's structure and the effect that the structural dimensions are having on the area of concern is an important aspect of group assessment. The four dimensions are group composition, size of the group, how long the group stays together, and open versus closed group membership. All of these factors can influence group functioning and need to be considered in conducting an assessment of the group.

EXHIBIT 11.3

Group Assessment Subsystems

Purpose (type)
- Therapy
- Support
- Education
- Growth
- Project
- Administrative
- Professional
- Citizen

Structure
- Membership composition
- Size
- Duration
- Open/closed

Life-cycle stage
- Developmental stage

Culture
- Traditions
- Values
- Norms

Alliances
- Communication patterns
- Interpersonal attraction
- Power
- Leadership

Life-Cycle Stages

This aspect of group functioning deals with group development. Groups go through a number of developmental stages. They change and evolve as they mature. Like individual humans, groups have a pattern of development. Various typologies of group development have been suggested that range from three stages (Schwartz, 1986) to nine stages (Beck, 1983), although there is considerable overlap in the labels applied to the stages and in their conceptualization. One widely used conceptualization is Tuckman's (1965) four-stage model of group development: forming, storming, norming, and performing. Magen (1995) added a fifth stage, adjourning, to Tuckman's model.

Forming

The initial stage of the group, forming, is when members come together for the first time. In most groups, especially client groups, this is an exciting and anxious time for both the members and the leader. The participants are anxious about what will happen, what their experience in the group will be, and how they will perform. At this point, the group is a collection of individuals with individual concerns. Dependency on the worker is common in the early stages (Barol, 2010). Group members look to the leader for answers and direction. Interactions among members are superficial and guarded. Members do not have a strong commitment to the group and have not developed an identification with the group as a whole.

Storming

The second developmental stage is characterized by conflict among the members and with the leader. The emotional climate is characterized by tension. Members exhibit hostility toward one another and frustration with the group. The worker's leadership is challenged, and the purpose, structure, and operation of the group are often questioned. Conflict is an expression of the group's emerging identity and group members' efforts to obtain power and control of the group. Group members challenge, attack, or withdraw. Through this process, the group begins to develop a collective identity and a sense of togetherness. Although this stage of group development is difficult for the worker, it presents an opportunity to model behavior for the group. In the face of often unpleasant challenges, you need to stay calm, nondefensive, and open to criticism, and you should demonstrate a willingness to share power and control with the group.

Norming

The third stage is the period during which group identity is solidified and the various roles, norms, and boundaries of the group emerge. Guidelines for group functioning are agreed on during this stage of development; they are the product of the group's coming together and developing a sense of itself. Guidelines are not just the leader's vision of what the group should do and how they should do it; they are the group's guidelines. At this point, the group has established ownership, and a collective sense of purpose and expected behavior has emerged.

Performing

The fourth stage is the action phase of the group's life cycle, the time when the group has worked out its leadership issues, structural concerns, and behavioral expectations. The performing stage is characterized by solidarity, cohesion, and commitment. Patterns of communication have become more predictable, and the members are more comfortable with one another. Exchanges are open and honest, and differences are less likely to lead to conflict. The group has worked out mechanisms for managing and resolving conflict. There is a sense of cohesiveness among the members. They are now a group, and they are ready to work on and accomplish the tasks at hand.

Adjourning

This is the ending phase or termination stage of the group's development. A wide range of feelings among the members often characterizes it. If the group has developed a sense of closeness characteristic of the performing stage, the adjourning phase can be difficult for group members and the leader. Feelings of loss and abandonment are common. There is often regression on the part of some members. They revert to earlier stages in an attempt to keep the group going. Reasons for continuing are put forth. Groups may go through a grieving process similar to that of individuals: denial, rage and anger, bargaining, depression, and acceptance. Group members have a variety of feelings and emotions about ending. The worker needs to help each member examine his or her responses to ending.

Assessment of the group's stage of development is an important aspect of understanding group functioning. Groups develop at different rates and progress in their development differently. What might seem like a problem in group functioning may be a normal stage of the group's development. To what extent is the behavior being exhibited by group members related to the group's developmental stage? How far has the group progressed developmentally?

Culture

The traditions, beliefs, and norms developed by the group constitute the cultural components of group functioning. Traditions, beliefs, and norms are highly interrelated. An examination of a group's culture and the effect it has on an identified area of concern is an important aspect of group assessment. All groups develop *traditions,* which are ritualized activities, such as ceremonies, prayers, and songs, that are incorporated into group meetings. A group's traditions are influenced by members' ethnic, racial, and cultural backgrounds (Seabury, Seabury, & Garvin, 2011). They are important symbols for group members, strengthening group identification and helping members feel closer to the group. They also help define the uniqueness of a group. Members who violate group traditions are not viewed favorably by fellow members. Violations can lead to reprimand and rejection by the group. To avoid this, you should learn their traditions as quickly as possible (Seabury et al., 2011).

Group **norms** are the understandings group members have about behaviors. They define what members should and should not do within the group (Hepworth et al., 2017; Seabury et al., 2011). All groups develop unwritten rules that govern the behavior of the members. Norms may have a positive or negative influence on group functioning. Regular attendance at meetings, treating one another with respect, and communicating concerns directly to the group are examples of norms that have a positive effect on groups. Norms that have a negative or dysfunctional effect on the group include encouraging discussion of topics not related to the purpose of the meeting, letting a few members dominate the group, and avoiding talking about group problems. Group norms are not explicitly expressed, but rather are implicit rules of behavior. Norms are discerned by observing the behavior of members and reactions to it. Sanctions and social disapproval are given for violating a norm; praise and social approval are given for compliance (Toseland & Rivas, 2012).

Groups also develop *values* or beliefs that are held in common by all or most group members. Values are what group members believe to be true. They are the shared belief system of the members. The values held by a group can have a positive or negative influence on group functioning. As with norms, values can be inferred only through observation. They are not written down, nor are they usually stated explicitly.

Assessment of a group's culture is an important function of the group leader. Cultural influences can have either positive or negative effects on a concern or problem. To be able to effectively assess a group's culture, you need to be aware of the traditions, values, and norms that have developed. This is an ongoing process. How does group culture affect the target problem? What are its positive influences? What are its negative influences?

Alliances

There are four dimensions of alliance: communication patterns, interpersonal attractions, power, and leadership. These four dimensions are highly interrelated. Taken together, they provide a comprehensive overview of the alliance component of group functioning.

Communication patterns

Communication patterns involve who talks to whom and about what (Seabury et al., 2011). They represent the structure of the interactions among members. An analysis of communication patterns will indicate who dominates group discussions, whether some members are isolated, and who the informal leaders are. It also provides insight into subgroup formation and the effect of the various subgroups on the functioning of the group. Subgroups do not necessarily adversely affect a group. In fact, the formation of subgroups helps members form closer attachments to other members and to the group as a whole. Subgroups negatively affect the group when they become exclusive or when power struggles between subgroups interfere with member support for the larger group (Hepworth et al., 2017).

Interpersonal attractions

As members get better acquainted, some members are attracted to others and some are not. *Interpersonal attraction* is influenced by race, culture, and gender as well as by physical appearance, personality, and interests, among other factors (Seabury et al., 2011). Members with similar backgrounds and interests are more likely to be attracted to each other than those who are very different from one another.

Power

Power is the ability of one individual to influence another in a specific way. There are five types of power:

1. **Reward power** is the ability to influence others by providing them with something that they value. A group member may offer friendship, support, praise, or other goods and services.

2. **Coercive power** is the ability to influence others by the use of punishment. A group member may use coercive power by criticizing, insulting, or physically threatening another group member.

3. **Legitimate power** is the ability to influence others by virtue of one's position in the group. The social work leader may exercise legitimate power on the basis of his or her assigned role.

4. **Referent power** is the ability to influence others by being liked or respected. A group member may have referent power on the basis of his or her personality or attractiveness.

5. **Expert power** is the ability to influence others because of specialized knowledge or skills. A member may exercise expert power by virtue of his or her special training (Seabury et al., 2011).

Both the sources of power and the locus of power within the group may vary. Power does not itself negatively affect group functioning. Problems arise when there are power struggles within the group. Groups, in fact, sometimes fall apart because of unresolved power issues (Hepworth et al., 2017). The issue in group assessment is not so much who has the power, but rather the group's ability to share power and to find resolutions to power conflicts that do not result in some members feeling that they have been forced to give up too much.

Leadership

In simple terms, leadership is the capacity to mobilize group members into action. Leadership is a process that grows out of interactions among group members related to the attainment of goals (Seabury et al., 2011). *Task leadership* occurs when the individual helps the group move toward defining and achieving group goals. *Social-emotional leadership* occurs when the member positively affects the interaction among group members by, for example, reducing conflicts and facilitating the expression of positive feelings (Seabury et al., 2011).

The alliance component has powerful influences on group functioning. A comprehensive assessment needs to carefully evaluate the effect of these processes on an identified problem area or concern. As the social worker involved with the group, part of your leadership task is to become aware of the alliance structure of the group. This requires ongoing observation of group behavior. Before you can assess the impact the processes have on the group, you need to understand how the group functions. Once you have a clear understanding of communication patterns, interpersonal alliances, power, and leadership within the group, you can assess their effect on a specific area of concern.

STRENGTHS-BASED GROUP ASSESSMENT

Group assessment is a collaborative process that the leader and members of the group undertake to change conditions that impede the group from achieving its purpose or improving its functioning. An empowering approach to group assessment involves the members in the analysis of group functioning and the problem situation. You may raise an issue or concern, but the entire group explores it and its effect on the group. The group decides whether it is a problem, what contributes to the concern, and what should be done to help correct the situation. The group and its members are the experts. Your starting point is their perceptions of the problem situation. Do not force your analysis and assessment of the group's problems, interpersonal relationships, or individual dysfunctions on the group. Engage in a collaborative exchange with the group, share your insights and perceptions, and explore the perceptions of the members. You guide the assessment process, but the group members actually conduct the assessment. Ensure that each member's perception of the situation is acknowledged and validated. There is no single correct view; instead, there are always multiple perceptions of reality. Each member's perception of the situation is accurate from his or her perspective. Seek consensus about the target problem. If that is not possible, seek agreement about the need to address the concern. The group has the power to set the agenda. It has ownership of the problem as well as the potential solutions.

A strengths-based assessment emphasizes the identification of group strengths as well as strengths of each individual member. Group members have individual and collective power to bring about positive change. Incorporating a strengths perspective in the assessment process, however, is the professional leader's responsibility. Regardless of the type of group, emphasizing strengths requires a conscious effort on your part. All groups, regardless of the level of functioning of individual members, have strengths. Do not expect group members to recognize or be aware of their individual and collective strengths. Instead, adopt the attitude that strengths exist and that they can be used to help the group resolve the problem situation.

CASE EXAMPLE 11.4: WHAT IS GOING ON WITH THE GROUP? (BAROL, 2010)

Alex's field instructor suggested that she conduct a preliminary assessment of their treatment group for male sex offenders. During the last session, Alex felt that the group probably did not feel like a safe space for some of the members, including Juan, with whom Alex is also assigned to work with individually. Prior to the next weekly group meeting, Alex reviewed the five dimensions and subdimensions of group functioning—purpose, structure, life-cycle stage, culture, and alliances. Alex and her field instructor agreed that during the next group session, her field instructor would be the lead facilitator and she would observe the group functioning and prepare an assessment for review in supervision.

In the group meeting, Alex noticed a couple of factors that might be hindering the life-cycle development of the group. Her first observation was that the group was still in the forming stage. They appeared to be a collection of individuals with individual concerns. The group members all looked to either her or her field instructor for answers and direction. The communication patterns tended to be back and forth between the facilitator and a group member, and then the same thing with another group member. During these exchanges, the other group members appeared bored and distracted. They were not engaged. This communication pattern and member behavior suggested that the purpose of the group was probably not clear to the members and that clear norms for participating in the group had not been established.

Alex also observed that three of the group members appeared to be in denial about their sex offenses and the need for treatment. These members tended to make jokes on the side when others were talking, pointing again to the need to establish norms of behavior for the group. The side joking appeared to be a significant contributor to Alex's feeling that the group probably was not a safe space to share sensitive information.

In supervision, Alex and her field instructor reviewed her assessment and identified some interventions. They agreed that the first step was to go back and review the purpose of the group and to have the group members identify rules for the group. They felt that it was important for the members to come up with the rules and that they would write them down on poster paper and always bring the rules to future group meetings. The also decided to do their best to change the communication patterns so that there would be less facilitator/individual member interactions and more facilitator/group interactions.

MICROSYSTEM ASSESSMENT TOOLS

Generalist social workers practice in a multitude of settings. The types of assessment tools they use are as varied as the settings. Agencies adopt or develop assessment procedures on the basis of the kinds of information they need and the types of services they provide. Most assessment tools are variations of the generic biopsychosocial assessment that has been taught in schools of social work for many years. Typically, these instruments are used to collect information on client problems and past behaviors and experiences. Little or no attention is given to client strengths. Tools that focus on client strengths are now emerging, and strengths-based assessments are beginning to be incorporated into agency-based practice.

STRENGTHS-BASED ASSESSMENT WORKSHEET

Form 11.1 found in the chapter appendix and available in the Student Toolbox on Springer Publishing Company's website (www.springerpub.com/fieldwrk) is a strengths-based worksheet that was developed to help social workers and clients identify clients' strengths as well as the obstacles they face in resolving problem situations. The strengths and obstacles worksheet helps you and your clients summarize areas of concern and priorities, identify strengths and obstacles, and analyze the effects of the obstacles and strengths on the target problem.

You should try to complete as much of the worksheet as possible between your first and second meetings with the client. During the second meeting, review your initial assessment findings and then, with the client, revise and finish the worksheet. Be sure to review the completed worksheet with your client and make any needed adjustments. Ensuring your clients have a clear picture of their strengths and obstacles is as important as you having an understanding of the client's situation.

BIOPSYCHOSOCIAL ASSESSMENT FORM

Strengths-based worksheets integrate ecosystems and strengths perspectives. They focus on the present—the here and now. To complete the picture, some understanding of past experiences is also needed (Sheafor & Horejsi, 2014). Biopsychosocial assessments incorporate an ecosystems perspective and are widely used in agency settings. Typically, these assessments focus on the biological, psychological, and social functioning and the histories of individual clients. A description of a biopsychosocial assessment and a sample assessment can be found in Chapter 6 and an electronic copy of a Biopsychosocial Assessment Form is available in the Student Toolbox at www.springerpub.com/fieldwrk.

MENTAL STATUS EVALUATION

Another type of assessment frequently used in mental health and family services agencies is a mental status evaluation (Lukas, 1993). Its purpose is to assess the quality and range of perception, thinking, feeling, and psychomotor activity of an individual client. The examination is usually organized around different categories of client functioning, including appearance, attitude, speech, emotions, thought process, sensory perceptions, and mental capacities. A Mental Status Evaluation can be found in the appendix of this chapter or in the Student Toolbox at www.springerpub.com/fieldwrk.

Appearance

The individual's physical appearance includes dress, posture, body movements, and attitude. What is the overall impression of the client's appearance? Are there any unusual aspects of the client's appearance, posture, movements, or demeanor?

Speech

Is there anything unusual about an individual's speech? Does he or she speak unusually fast or slow? Is the volume appropriate? How are the tone and pattern of the client's speech? Are there any noticeable speech problems?

Emotions

Emotions or feelings encompass two dimensions: affect and mood. *Affect* "refers to the way the client shows his emotions while he is with you, and it may or may not coincide with the internal state the client describes himself as feeling over time" (Lukas, 1993, p. 19). Is the client's affect flat or blunted, expressing little emotion? Does the client experience rapid shifts in affect? Is the affect appropriate given the subject matter? *Mood* refers to how the client is feeling most of the time (Lukas, 1993, p. 8). Is the client happy, sad, or angry? Do the client's feelings appear to be appropriate given his or her situation? Are they understandable given the topic and the context?

Thought Process

The thought process represents the client's judgment about the content of speech and thought. *Process* concerns how the client thinks. Is there a logical flow? Are the client's thoughts all jumbled together? Is there a coherent stream of ideas? Does the client have difficulty getting to the point in responding to your questions? Does the client keep repeating certain words or phrases? Does the client have difficulty connecting ideas?

   Content refers to what the client says. Do the client's thoughts appear to be delusional? Does the client have thoughts that he or she believes to be true that you know absolutely to be untrue? Does the client have reoccurring thoughts that have an obsessive or compulsive quality?

Sensory Perceptions

Sensory perceptions concern indications of illusions or hallucinations. "*Illusions* refer to normal sensory events that are misperceived" (Lukas, 1993, p. 25). *Hallucinations* are sensory experiences unrelated to external stimuli (Lukas, 1993). Are there clear distortions in the client's view of reality? If so, when and under what conditions do they occur?

Mental Capacity

Mental capacity refers to orientation, intelligence, concentration, and memory. *Orientation* concerns time, place, and person. Does the client know the approximate time of day, day of the week, and year? Does the client know where he or she is and what his or her name is?

   What is the client's overall level of intelligence? Does the client appear to possess average, above-average, or below-average intelligence (Lukas, 1993)? Can the client concentrate and focus on what you are discussing? Is the client easily distracted? Is the client able to remember recent events? How is the client's long-term memory? Can the client remember events from his or her past?

Attitude

What kind of attitude does the client project toward his or her problem, the interview, and you? Is the client cooperative and forthcoming, or uncooperative and withholding? Is the client overly aggressive or submissive? If disturbed, how aware is the individual of his or her disturbance?

Case Example 11.5 provides a sample mental status evaluation for the same client introduced in the biopsychosocial assessment shown earlier. A Mental Status Form can be found in the appendix of this chapter (Form 11.2) and in the Student Toolbox at www.springerpub.com/fieldwrk.

CASE EXAMPLE 11.5: SAMPLE MENTAL STATUS EVALUATION

Theodore J. is an 82-year-old Caucasian male. He was well groomed and very well dressed in appropriate, immaculate, casual attire that had been carefully coordinated. He sat in a slouched position, legs crossed, leaning to the left of his chair. He had swollen eyes and a washed-out complexion. His attitude was one of concern, and he appeared to be worried, as exhibited by his facial expression and verbal presentation.

The volume of Mr. J.'s speech was low. His pace of speech was slow, and he presented slight psychomotor retardation. Mr. J. had difficulty recalling words to finish his thoughts and sentences but was able to formulate complete sentences.

Mr. J. was engaging but appeared to lack a positive self-image. His mood and affect were depressed. His perception of his problem, content of thought, and associations were appropriate.

The patient denied any hearing deficits, and none were noted. He denied having visual or auditory hallucinations. His eyesight had significantly declined over the past 2 years, and this appeared to be of major concern to him. He wore glasses.

Mr. J. was oriented to person but could not recall the name of the program he was in, the floor he was on, or the date. There were apparent deficits in his immediate memory. He appeared to be of average intelligence and had the ability to concentrate on the subject being discussed. However, he was not able to count backward by threes. Mr. J.'s short-term memory appeared somewhat intact in relation to recent events. He was able to recall facts from his past, but was not able to recall or trace a timeline. He remembered that he had undergone surgery, but he could not remember if it was 2 or 3 years ago. His insight and judgment did not appear to be impaired.

Although depressed, Mr. J. was polite and cooperative. He was easy to relate to and appeared capable of developing a helping relationship. Mr. J. appeared motivated to participate in the partial hospitalization program and to get help with his depression and memory loss.

ECOMAPS

Ecomaps graphically display the person-in-environment perspective. They focus on the relationships between the client and the major systems in the client's environment. The major systems vary by client. Typically, they include kin and friendship relationships;

work, school, community, and neighborhood organizations; and the social worker, agency, and other social services and health care organizations. An ecomap shows the relevant systems, whether the relationships are positive or negative and strong or weak, and the direction or flow of energy and resources between the client and the systems. A dashed arrow indicates a weak relationship, a solid arrow indicates a strong relationship, and a dashed line indicates the absence of a relationship between the client and the subsystem. A plus sign (+) or a minus sign (–) indicates whether the relationship is positive or negative. The direction of the arrowhead indicates the direction of the energy or resource flow (Hepworth et al., 2017).

Ecomaps are constructed in collaboration with the client. The worker begins by placing the client in the middle of the ecomap, and then identifies the various personal and environmental systems with which the client interacts. The social worker reviews the relationships with the client using open-ended questions and elaboration techniques. Together, the worker and the client complete the ecomap. The worker and the client review and analyze the completed ecomap. This process encourages collaboration in the worker–client relationship. Ecomaps can be very useful tools in helping clients understand their person-in-environment systems and the effects the various relationships or absence of relationships have on the presenting problem. They also help the worker and the client identify areas of strength and resources.

Figure 11.1 is a completed ecomap for an individual client. The client is a 55-year-old African American male named Harry M. He is divorced, has two adult children, lives alone, and is currently unemployed. He attends a partial hospitalization program for adults with mental health problems.

The ecomap indicates that Mr. M. has strong, mutually supportive relationships with the partial program, the social worker, his mother, and his next-door neighbor. He also receives support from his church and his belief in God, and from his job. Mr. M. has a weak but supportive relationship with his son and weak stressful relationships with his sister and daughter. His relationship with his ex-wife is completely dissolved. He does not have any romantic or friendship relationships or other connections with neighbors or the community.

Overall, Mr. M.'s person-in-environment assessment reveals a number of strengths and sources of support. He receives a great deal of support from formal associations, such as the partial program, his social worker, and his church. His informal support network appears to be limited to his mother and a next-door neighbor. His relationships with his ex-wife, children, sister, friends, and lovers are either weak or nonexistent.

Figure 11.2 is a completed ecomap for a family client system. The family consists of a single mother and her two daughters, ages 11 and 15. The mother has requested help from a family services agency for problems she is having with the 11-year-old daughter. She reports that the younger daughter is having problems in school and is acting out at home by not obeying her. She is disrespectful and defiant.

The ecomap shows that the mother has a stressful relationship with her younger daughter and a positive relationship with her older daughter, and that the two girls have a conflicted relationship. The father does not live with the family. He and the mother have no contact or ongoing relationship. The older daughter has a stressful relationship with her father, and the younger daughter feels close to him.

The identified patient is the 11-year-old daughter. She is having problems in school and in her relationships with her mother and sister. Her mother is also concerned about the girl's friends. She believes that they are a negative influence on her daughter. On the positive side, the daughter is active in clubs and sports. She has a supportive relationship with her father.

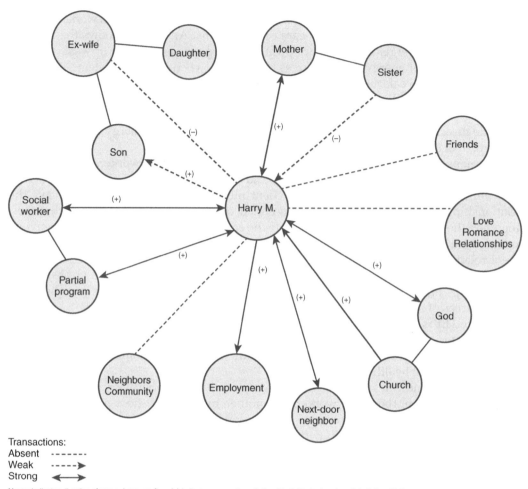

Transactions:
Absent ------
Weak ----->
Strong <----->

[Arrow indicates direction of energy/resource flow; (+) indicates supportive relationship; (−) indicates stressful relationship.]

FIGURE 11.1 Ecomap for individual client.

The older sister is close to her mother, does well in school, and gets a great deal of satisfaction from her musical pursuits. On the negative side, she does not have any close friends, and her relationships with her father and sister are strained.

The mother has a supportive extended family network and derives a great deal of support from church-related activities. She also has a neighbor who is a source of support. Other than her neighbor, she does not have close friends, nor is she involved in the community beyond her church activities. Her relationship with the social worker and the family services agency at the time of the interview was weak but supportive, whereas her job was viewed as moderately stressful.

GENOGRAMS

Genograms graphically display information about family members over at least three generations (Pope & Lee, 2015). They are commonly used in assessments of family client systems. Basic types of information included in genograms are birth, gender, marriages,

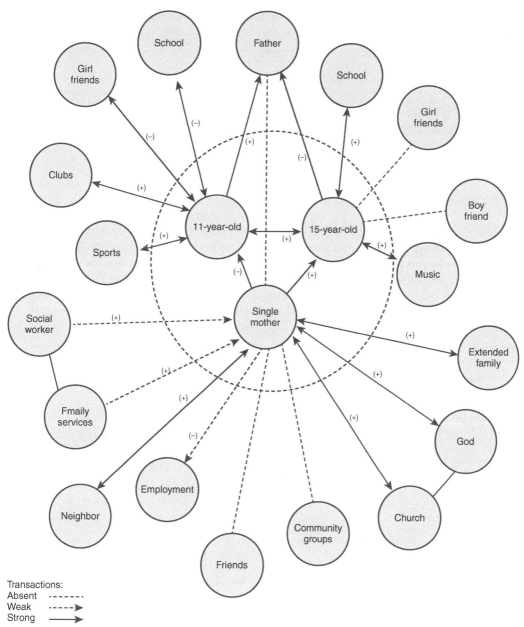

Transactions:
Absent   - - - - - -
Weak   - - - - ▸
Strong   ⟶

[Arrow indicates direction of energy/resource flow; (+) indicates supportive relationship; (–) indicates stressful relationship.]

FIGURE 11.2 Ecomap for family client.

offspring, death, and household composition. Genograms aid our understanding of relationship patterns, transitional issues, and life-cycle changes (Miley, O'Melia, & DuBois, 2013). They are used to highlight cultural information about a family and patterns of family strengths.

Genograms should be constructed in collaboration with family members. Gathering family information and constructing the genogram should be part of the more general task of joining and helping the family. McGoldrick, Gerson, and Petry (2008) suggest gathering information by casting the "information net" into wider and wider circles, moving from:

- The presenting problem to the larger context of the problem
- The immediate household to the extended family and broader social systems
- The present family situation to a historical chronology of family events
- Easy, nonthreatening inquiries to difficult, anxiety-provoking questions
- Obvious facts to judgments about functioning
- Relationships to hypothesized family patterns

The genogram shown in Figure 11.3 indicates that the family client system is composed of a husband and wife and two children. It is the second marriage for the wife, who has a 5-year-old son from her first marriage, which ended in divorce because of domestic abuse. The couple's son is 1 year old. The wife's mother divorced her first and second husbands and is currently in a long-standing relationship. The husband's mother died in a car accident, in which his younger brother also died. His father remarried and had three daughters with his second wife.

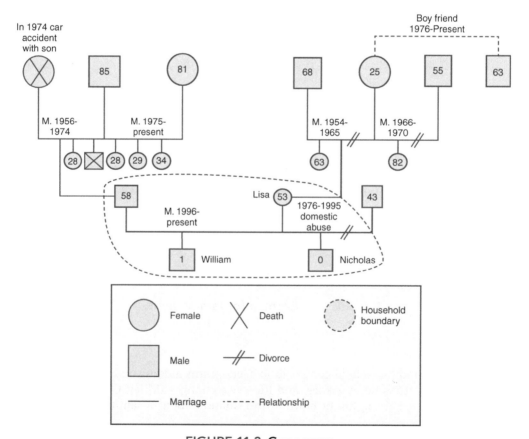

FIGURE 11.3 Genogram.

GROUP FUNCTIONING ASSESSMENT WORKSHEET

Form 11.3, which can be found in the appendix of this chapter and in the Student Toolbox available on Springer Publishing Company's website (www.springerpub.com/fieldwrk), can be used to assess group functioning. It covers the five dimensions of group functioning. We suggest that you do your group assessment in two steps. The first step is to complete the form on the basis of your observations of group functioning, critical thinking, and affective reactions before meeting with the group. This will give you a starting point for conducting the assessment with the group members in step 2. The goal is to have all the members of the group understand how they are functioning as a group and having a voice in determining possible solutions. If that occurs, the problem areas will be corrected, and group functioning should improve. It will take time and the agreed-upon solutions will need to be reinforced periodically and revisited by the group as a whole.

> **Field Reflection Questions**
>
> In what ways could you use any of the micro assessment tools in your field placement? What would you need to do to incorporate any into your field placement practice?
>
> What do you see as a benefit of using an assessment tool? What are the challenges for you in using assessment tools in your field placement?

SOCIOGRAMS

A group sociogram is similar to an ecomap. The ecomap describes a person-in-environment system; the sociogram describes the relationships among members of the group. Hartford's (1971) approach to sociogram construction examines attraction and repulsion between members of the group. It is a graphic representation of the alliances within a group. Usually, a worker constructs a sociogram on the basis of observations of the group interactions. You include yourself in the sociogram. Doing so recognizes that you are part of the group-in-environment system and forces you to objectively analyze your relationships with each member of the group. Seabury et al. (2011) point out that discussion of alliances within groups can create anxiety and concerns about rejection. Therefore, sharing a sociogram with the group should be approached with caution. However, a sociogram can be an effective tool for helping group members understand the dynamics of the group and the effect of group alliances on a problem area or concern.

The sociogram shown in Figure 11.4 consists of six members, three males and three females, and the social worker. It shows that the social worker has strong positive relationships with members 3 and 5; weak positive relationships with members 1, 4, and 6; and a strong negative relationship with member 2. Members 3 and 6 are somewhat isolated. Each has a strong relationship with only one other member. Member 2 appears to be the informal leader of the group. She has strong positive relationships with members 1, 5, 3, and 4. She also appears to be in competition for leadership with the social worker, with whom she has a strong negative relationship.

SUMMARY

This chapter focused on micro-client system assessment. Mezzo-client system assessment is covered in Chapter 12. The chapter began with a review of critical thinking and how it is used in conducting client assessments. We then reviewed the strengths

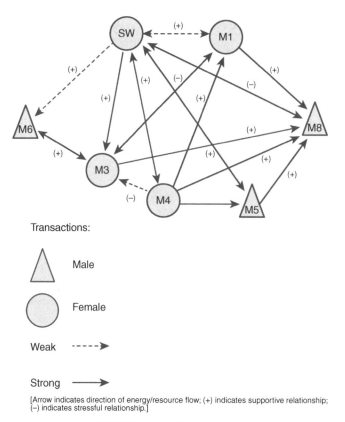

Transactions:

△   Male

◯   Female

Weak   ----->

Strong   ——>

[Arrow indicates direction of energy/resource flow; (+) indicates supportive relationship; (–) indicates stressful relationship.]

FIGURE 11.4 Sociogram.

perspective and its six major principles. We believe that generalist social work practice and microsystem assessments should be approached from a strengths perspective as well as with an assessment of the client's problems and concerns; the two go hand in hand. We then reviewed assessment of individuals, assessment of families, and group assessment. Each client system was reviewed in terms of subsystems that need to be assessed and incorporating a strengths approach to the assessment process. The chapter concluded with brief descriptions of several micro-client system assessment tools and a concluding case summary tied to Competency 7: Assess Individuals, Families, Groups, Organizations, and Communities.

CRITICAL THINKING QUESTIONS

Competency 7 focuses on client system assessment. You are expected to understand that assessment is an ongoing component of the dynamic and interactive process. You should be able to critically evaluate and apply your knowledge in the assessment of diverse clients and constituencies. You are also expected to demonstrate how your personal experiences and affective reactions affect your assessments and professional judgments.

Competency 6 focuses on engagement. You are expected to understand that engagement is an ongoing component of the dynamic and interactive process of social work practice. You should understand how your personal experiences and affective reactions may impact your ability to effectively engage with diverse clients and constituencies. As a social worker, you should value principles of relationship building and use empathy, reflection, and interpersonal skills to effectively engage with your clients. The following discussion questions focus on assessment competency and the interrelationship between engagement (Competency 6) and assessment (Competency 7):

1. Alex completed, with her field instructor, an initial assessment of their treatment group's functioning as a group. They identified some issues that might be interfering with the functioning of the group. A major issue of concern is that a couple of the group members seem to dislike another member, and that person is getting scape-goated by the group. It appears that the other group members are joining in on the scapegoating. Alex is unsure how to approach this sensitive topic with the group and how to engage the group in the assessment process. Identify at least three possible pitfalls that could occur when broaching this topic with the group. Describe how you would minimize the pitfalls. Discuss how you would conduct your group-as-a-whole assessment around this potential issue. Describe your affective reaction to your proposed plan.

2. In the previously mentioned example, what engagement skills would you use to conduct your in-group assessment? What engagement skills are you most confi-dent using? What skills are you less sure about? What would you do to prepare and strengthen your engagement skills to conduct a more effective assessment?

3. What is the relationship between the skills of engagement and assessment? How does one affect the other in the helping process? Can you effectively assess a client without engagement? How can assessment strengthen client engagement?

4. Assessment involves critical thinking, self-reflection on your affective reactions, and the rendering of your professional judgment. It also involves your ability to engage your clients in a helping relationship. In reflecting upon your work with clients in your field placement, describe an experience in which your engagement skills were in conflict with your ability to conduct a strengths-based client assessment. What was the conflict? Upon reflection, how could you have more effectively dealt with the conflict?

COMPETENCY 7: ASSESS INDIVIDUALS, FAMILIES, GROUPS, ORGANIZATIONS, AND COMMUNITIES

Social workers understand that assessment is an ongoing component of the dynamic and interactive process of social work practice with, and on behalf of, diverse individuals, families, groups, organizations, and communities. They understand theories of human behavior and the social environment, and critically evaluate and apply this knowledge in the assessment of diverse clients and constituencies, including individuals, families, groups, organizations, and communities. Social workers understand methods of assess-ment with diverse clients and constituencies and use them to advance their practice effectiveness. They recognize the implications of the larger practice context in the assess-ment process, and they appreciate the importance of interprofessional collaboration in this process. Social workers understand how their personal experiences and affective reactions may affect their assessment and decision making. Social workers:

- Collect and organize data, and apply critical thinking to interpret information from clients and constituencies.

- Apply knowledge of human behavior and the social environment, person-in-environment, and other multidisciplinary theoretical frameworks in the analysis of assessment data from clients and constituencies.

- Develop mutually agreed-on intervention goals and objectives on the basis of the critical assessment of strengths, needs, and challenges within clients and constituencies.

- Select appropriate intervention strategies on the basis of the assessment, research knowledge, and values and preferences of clients and constituencies.

CASE SUMMARY—"ADJUSTING TO LIFE WITHOUT MOM"

PRACTICE SETTING DESCRIPTION

My name is Janson and I am a first-year MSW student completing an internship at a family services agency in a medium-sized city in the Midwest. The agency provides individual and family counseling services on a sliding fee scale. The agency also runs a number of educational and treatment groups. My field instructor assigned me to work with the K. family, who are seeking help in dealing with the accidental death of the wife and mother in a car crash.

IDENTIFYING DATA

The K. family consists of the father, Bob, and three children, Sharon, Chad, and Jason. Ellen, Bob's wife and the children's mother, passed away 8 months ago as a result of injuries she sustained in an automobile accident. Bob is 45 years old, Caucasian, and works in the banking industry. Sharon is 18 years old and a senior in high school. Chad is 17 years old and is currently a junior in high school. Jason is 15 years old and in the ninth grade. Bob has steady employment as a salesman with adequate income to support his family. Ellen worked part-time in retail sales, and her income was used primarily for family vacations and family outings.

PRESENTING PROBLEM

Chad has taken the death of his mother especially hard. This past year, he has been receiving failing grades in school and has been involved in numerous fights. He also has begun to experiment with drugs and alcohol. Ellen had been a constant source of support for Chad and the other children. However, the children describe Bob as not being supportive of them, and as having an especially stressful relationship with Chad.

In addition to the previously mentioned problems, the family seems to not have allowed outsiders, even extended family members, to help them deal with their grief and loss. Family traditions ended with Ellen's death, as did involvement with the church and other organizations. The family's emotional climate has become tense, and the family's communication patterns have been greatly altered since Ellen's death.

ASSESSMENT

The greatest obstacle facing the K. family is Ellen's absence. It is clear that she maintained the closest relationships with the children, led family traditions, was the mediator between Bob and the children, kept communication open, and allowed family boundaries to remain open to the outside world. Ellen was involved with the schools her children attended, the church she and the rest of the family attended weekly, and numerous community-wide events. Ellen also kept the lines of communication open between extended family members, including Bob's mother, siblings, and cousins.

Upon Ellen's death, the K. family seemed to completely "shut down." Although Sharon's and Jason's performance at school has not changed as drastically as Chad's, the two children reported not feeling as good about themselves as they once did and also reported not wanting to continue participating in extracurricular activities.

Chad's sudden change in behavior and school performance is directly related to the death of his mother. His recent experimentation with drugs and alcohol is related to his mother's death and to the fact that alcoholism is prevalent in Ellen's family history. Ellen's father and brother are both recovering alcoholics. Chad, like the rest of his family, is dealing with Ellen's death in an unhealthy manner.

The weak relationships between Bob and his children had an effect before Ellen's death and are now greatly affecting the family's identified problem situation. Another obstacle the family faces is the fact that Bob never learned effective coping or parenting skills.

However, the K. family does have several strengths. All family members realize that there are definite obstacles and that no one has been dealing with Ellen's death in a healthy fashion. Chad appears to want to stop using drugs and alcohol and to change his recent behavior patterns at school. The children have expressed interest in maintaining strong and supportive relationships with their father. Bob has admitted that he never had a strong relationship with any of his children or with his own father.

Another major strength is that the family wants to return to family traditions, change their emotional climate, open communication patterns, reset the family's boundaries, and use family resources. In addition, the children seem to have strong and supportive relationships among themselves, and extended family members have expressed an interest in being active participants in the lives of Bob, Sharon, Chad, and Jason. External strengths include a sincere desire by all family members to again become a part of their church, the community, and other associations.

CASE PROCESS SUMMARY

Bob and the children all recognize that, first and foremost, they need to deal with the sudden death of Ellen. They also acknowledge the need to deal with the strained relationship between Chad and his father and the need to strengthen Sharon's and Jason's relationships with their father. Chad has also agreed to receive help for his academic and behavioral problems at school. I feel that I have made excellent progress in assessing the families' strengths and challenges. After discussing my family assessment with my field instructor, we decided that the next step would be for me to share my preliminary assessment with the family and to engage the family in completing a family ecomap to help identify supports and areas that need work.

Jason, MSW student intern

DISCUSSION QUESTIONS

- Critique the family assessment on the K. family. What are the strengths of the assessment? What areas need to be strengthened? What additional information is needed to better understand the functioning of this family?

- On the basis of the information provided in the case summary, identify at least three individual and/or family issues that you think need to be addressed and discuss why and how the issues impact family functioning.

- Jason's case summary did not include any of his affective reactions to the family's situation or their interactions together. If this family was assigned to you, reflect upon what your emotional response to the family and its members would be. How would their circumstances affect you emotionally? Is there anyone in the family you probably would feel a close identification with? Anyone you who might bring up negative feelings? What are some possible countertransference feelings you should watch out for?

- The fourth social work competency focuses on practice-informed research and research-informed practice. If you were in Jason's shoes, what would you do to bring research-informed practice into your work with the family? What knowledge areas would you need to strengthen? What evidence-based interventions might be appropriate for this family?

ELECTRONIC COMPETENCY RESOURCES

WEBSITE LINKS

Strengths-Based Assessment in Social Work—Social Care Institute for Excellence
www.scie.org.uk/care-act-2014/assessment-and-eligibility/practice-examples/strenghts-based-approach-in-assessment.asp

Family Assessment Tools slideshow—Aileen Pascual
www.slideshare.net/abpascual/tools-in-family-assessment

Group Work Process slideshow—Bimal Antony
www.slideshare.net/BimalAntony/group-work-process-23990034

VIDEO LINKS

Assessment Process video—Oregon Department of Human Services
www.youtube.com/watch?v=kagGIylgAnw

Social Work Assessment video—Rebecca French
www.youtube.com/watch?v=N-h83Ev_s5w

Family Assessment video—Austen Riggs
www.youtube.com/watch?v=khWzUzfvtLg

Stages of Group Development video—Analyze Grabowski
www.youtube.com/watch?v=T_gptRmpFyk

Group dynamics and the initial phase in social group work slideshow—JFM Lohith Shetty
www.slideshare.net/Lohith_hrd/group-work-practice-iii?qid=2d473104-ce2b-4aa9
-87ef-dd8f368189c8&v=&b=&from_search=15

REFERENCES

Barol, B. (2010). Generalist practice with groups. In J. Poulin (Ed.), *Strengths-based generalist practice: A collaborative approach* (pp. 219–253). Belmont, CA: Cengage.

Beck, A. (1983). A process analysis of group development. *Group, 7*, 19–28. doi:10.1007/BF01456476

Cowger, C. (1997). Assessing client strengths: Assessment for client empowerment. In D. Saleebey (Ed.), *The strengths perspective in social work practice* (2nd ed., pp. 59–73). New York, NY: Longman.

Crane, B. (2010). Generalist practice with families. In J. Poulin (Ed.), *Strengths-based generalist practice: A collaborative approach* (pp. 184–218). Belmont, CA: Cengage.

Gambrill, E. (2013). *Social work practice. A critical thinker's guide* (3rd ed.). Oxford, UK: Oxford University Press.

Gibbons, J., & Gray, M. (2004). Critical thinking as integral to social work practice. *Journal of Teaching in Social Work, 24*, 19–38. doi:10.1300/J067v24n01_02

Hartford, M. (1971). *Groups in social work*. New York, NY: Columbia University Press.

Hepworth, D. H., Rooney, R. H., Rooney, G. D., & Strom-Gottfried, K. (2017). *Direct social work practice: Theory and skills* (10th ed.). Boston, MA: Cengage.

Lukas, S. R. (1993). *Where to start and what to ask: An assessment handbook*. New York, NY: W. W. Norton.

Magen, R. (1995). Practice with groups. In C. Meyer & M. A. Mattaini (Eds.), *The foundations of social work practice* (pp. 156–175). Washington, DC: NASW Press.

McGoldrick, M., Gerson, R., & Petry, S. (2008). *Genograms: Assessment and intervention* (3rd ed.). New York, NY: W. W. Norton.

Miley, K. K., O'Melia, M. W., & DuBois, B. L. (2013). *Generalist social work practice: An empowering approach* (7th ed.). Boston, MA: Pearson.

Pope, N. D., & Lee, J. (2015). A picture is worth a thousand words. *The New Social Worker*. Retrieved from http://www.socialworker.com/feature-articles/practice/a-picture-is-worth-a-thousand-words-genograms-social-work-practice

Saleebey, D. (2013). *The strengths perspective in social work practice* (6th ed.). London, UK: Pearson.

Schwartz, W. (1986). The group work tradition and social work practice. *Social Work With Groups, 8*, 7–28. doi:10.1300/J009v08n04_03

Seabury, B., Seabury, B., & Garvin, C. D. (2011). *Interpersonal practice in social work: Promoting competence and social justice* (3rd ed.). Thousand Oaks, CA: Sage.

Sheafor, B. W., & Horejsi, C. R. (2014). *Techniques and guidelines for social work practice* (10th ed.). London, UK: Pearson.

Toseland, R. W., & Rivas, R. F. (2012). *An introduction to group work practice* (7th ed.). Boston, MA: Allyn & Bacon.

Tuckman, B. W. (1965). Developmental sequence in small groups. *Psychological Bulletin, 63*, 384–399. doi:10.1037/h0022100

Walker, J., Briggs, H., Koroloff, N., & Friesen, B. (2007). Implementing and sustaining evidence-based practice in social work. *Journal of Social Work Education, 43*, 361–375. doi:10.5175/JSWE.2007.334832007

APPENDIX

FORM 11.1. INDIVIDUAL AND FAMILY STRENGTHS AND OBSTACLES WORKSHEET

Client: _____ Worker: _____ Date: _____/_____/_____

Instructions: Briefly describe to the best of your knowledge as many items on the worksheet as possible. Base your assessment on information you have obtained directly from your client, indirectly by your observations, case records, contacts with collaterals, and any other sources of information. The first page focuses on a description of the clients' concerns/problem situation. The remaining pages comprise an assessment of personal, family, and environmental factors. For each relevant factor, describe potential obstacles, strengths, and its impact on the problem situation.

CONCERNS/PROBLEM SITUATION

Briefly summarize client concerns and/or problems that the client wants to address

List concerns or problems in order of priority from highest to lowest.

(continued)

FORM 11.1. INDIVIDUAL AND FAMILY STRENGTHS AND OBSTACLES WORKSHEET *(continued)*

Individual Factors			
Subsystem	**Obstacles**	**Strengths**	**Impact Problem**
Motivation and Commitment			
Coping and Resourcefulness			
Values and Beliefs			
Developmental Life Stage			
Mental Health Status			
Health Status			
Employment/Economic Status			
Interpersonal Relationships			
Family Factors			
Subsystem	**Obstacles**	**Strengths**	**Impact Problem**
Family Structure			
Power and Authority			
Family Life-Cycle Stage			
Family Values and Beliefs			
Family Rules and Myths			
Emotional Climate			
Communication Patterns			
Boundaries			
Environmental Factors			
Subsystem	**Obstacles**	**Strengths**	**Impact Problem**
Work/School			
Clubs, Churches, and Associations			
Community/Neighborhood			
Service Organizations			
Other Factors and Considerations			

FORM 11.2. MENTAL STATUS FORM

Client: _____ Worker: _____ Date: ____/____/____
(Be specific; if no problem exists in an area, indicate NA)

Appearance (Dress, posture, body movement, attitude)

Speech (Speed, volume, pattern, tone)

Emotions (Affect, mood)

Thought Process (Content, perception, associations)

Sensory Perceptions (Hearing, sight, hallucinations)

Orientation (Person, place, time)

Intellectual Functioning (Intelligence, concentration, insight, judgment, memory)

FORM 11.3: GROUP FUNCTIONING ASSESSMENT WORKSHEET

Group Name: _____ Worker: _____ Date: ____/____/____

Instructions: Briefly describe to the best of your knowledge as many items on the worksheet as possible. Base your assessment on information you have obtained by your observations, case records, contacts with collaterals, and any other sources of information. For each dimension of group functioning, describe your observations, assess the impact on group functioning, and identify potential interventions or solutions.

Dimension	Observations	Assessment	Possible Interventions
Group Purpose			
Structure (composition, duration, size, open/closed)			
Life Stage (forming, storming, norming, performing, adjourning)			
Culture (traditions, values, norms)			
Alliances (communication patterns, interpersonal attractions, power, leadership)			

CHAPTER 12

Mezzo Assessment: Organizations and Communities

STEPHEN KAUFFMAN ■ MARINA BARNETT

CASE VIGNETTE

Lucy could not have been happier about her first-year MSW field placement. She had her "dream placement" with the perfect location, type of clients, and learning opportunities she was looking for. And perhaps most importantly, the agency had an outstanding reputation in its field of practice.

But from the very first week at the agency, things seemed strained. Case files for her new caseload were incomplete or missing, and no one seemed to have any idea where they might be. Furthermore, many of her coworkers, although quite kind and helpful to her, often appeared distracted or "edgy." And to top things off, her field instructor, whom Lucy had looked forward to working with and learning from, quit on Lucy's third day.

Over the next 2 weeks, things got only more difficult. Staff increasingly stayed in their offices with their doors closed, making it very hard for Lucy to ask for guidance. And her new supervisor, a long-term employee of the agency, also quit during her fourth week of placement. Even the clients seemed to be more and more stressed out, with angry outbursts in the halls and growing numbers of missed appointments.

Increasingly, Lucy began to question whether this was really her dream placement after all. As a new intern, she did not feel she had the power to bring these issues to the attention of the administration— after all, she was not an employee. Reflecting back on one of her social work classes, she worried that maybe the whole problem was with the administration. If it was, what could she do? What questions, and whom, could she ask? And then, after finding out the answers, what could she do?

LEARNING OBJECTIVES

This chapter focuses on Competency 7. Assess Individuals, Families, Groups, Organizations, and Communities. The chapter reviews assessment of the two mezzo-level client systems: organizations and communities. It begins with a brief review of the three major components of

(continued)

organizations. This is followed by a brief review of organizational assessment methods. The chapter then reviews two approaches to community assessment: community needs assessment and asset assessment. By the end of this chapter, you will be able to

- Describe the three major organizational dimensions of your field placement agency.
- Develop a proposal to conduct an organizational assessment of your field placement agency.
- Design a community needs assessment for your field placement agency.
- Conduct a community asset assessment of your field placement agency's local community.

ASSESSING ORGANIZATIONS

As organizations so readily serve as the intermediary between citizens and need fulfillment, concern with organizational function becomes all the more important. The key to a good assessment is knowing what represents optimal functioning of the organization. Yet, at the same time, there is no "one best way" to construct an organization to meet all desired ends. Organizations may be structured in any one of a number of ways, each of which may be effective at achieving the goals of the organization under some conditions, but at the same time may be problematic at other times. Various groups or "constituencies" make up an organization. These may variously include line staff, supervisors, support staff, administration, clients, and external collaborators. Each typically has their own set of needs and perceptions about the organization, and thus each will have something valuable to contribute to the assessment (Kauffman, 2010).

Your field placement agency, like all organizations, has different dimensions or components. These components can be classified into three domains: organizational identity, internal characteristics, and environmental characteristics. Within each of these groupings are found many elements that strengthen and support the organization, or act as stressors or obstacles to optimal functioning. Each domain contributes to organizational functioning and is an important component of an organizational assessment.

UNDERSTANDING YOUR ORGANIZATION

ORGANIZATIONAL IDENTITY

Organizational identity refers to all of the elements of organizations that are commonly used to classify or describe organizations. Some of these are straightforward and easy to understand. Among them are the following: (a) *size*, meaning the number of staff, customers, or transactions; (b) *age*, or how long the organization has been in operation; (c) *location*;

(d) auspice as *governmental versus nongovernmental*—commonly referred to as a nongovernmental organization (NGO); or (e) *religious affiliation*.

INTERNAL ORGANIZATIONAL CONSIDERATIONS

Beyond the issues of identity, a large number of elements are associated with the internal characteristics of the organization that need to be included in an assessment. These characteristics can be placed into three groupings: foundation policies, internal structure, and internal processes. Elements from each grouping must be examined for their possible usefulness as strengths to the organization or their possibility as serving as an obstacle or stressor to the organization (Kauffman, 2010).

> **Field Reflection Questions**
>
> How would you describe the organizational identity of your field placement agency?
>
> What is your field placement agency's mission? How is its mission reflected in its programs and services? Its treatment of staff?

Foundation Policies

Foundation policies refer to the documents and guidelines (generally written) that give meaning and guidance to the agency. Organizations exist for a purpose, and these policies express both this purpose and a description of the overarching structure and processes of the organization. At the same time, simply because something is written does not mean it is followed; it may be that this disconnect between what is written and what is real is causing some of the organization's difficulties. The most important types of foundation policies are the constitution and by-laws, vision, mission, goals, and strategic plans.

Organizational Mission

Organizations are guided by a set of principles outlined in their mission. Mission statements specify the fundamental purpose of the organization. The mission documents the needs that the organization seeks to address (purpose), specifies how the organization addresses those needs (business), and states the principles or beliefs (values) of the organization. According to Kettner et al. (2017), the mission statement "should focus on what lies ahead for its clients and or consumers if the agency is successful in addressing their problems and meeting their needs" (p. 110).

Organizational Vision

Organizations also have vision statements. The vision statement is a statement of the future. They are statements about what the organizations hopes to become. The values and philosophy of the organization determine the priorities of the mission and the design and implementation of programs and activities. The organization's mission and vision statements set the stage to identify its clients, programs, and activities.

Organizational Goals and Objectives

Much of what has been stated about micro-system client goals and the goal-setting process applies to mezzo systems as well. Organizational goals are the statements of the desired qualities in human and social conditions. Goals suggest intended outcomes, provide organizational direction, and provide standards of criteria for evaluation and legitimacy (Coley & Scheinberg, 2017). Goals are broad, nonmeasurable statements that describe a "desired state."

Goals are often confused with objectives, but these are not interchangeable concepts. Although goals provide the direction for the organization's focus, **objectives** establish precise expectations of what the organization is attempting to achieve, including a time frame (Kettner, et al., 2017). Objectives are the means by which the goals are achieved. Although goals are broad statements of what we would like to see, objectives should be specific, measurable, achievable, realistic, and time-bound. The Centers for Disease Control and Prevention (CDC, 2017) offers the following checklist to make sure that your objectives are written correctly:

1. Is the objective SMART?

   - **S**pecific: Who (the target population and people doing the activity) and what (the action or activity)

   - **M**easurable: How much change is expected

   - **A**chievable: Can be accomplished given current resources and constraints

   - **R**ealistic: Addresses the scope of the health program and proposes reasonable programmatic steps

   - **T**ime-phased: Provides a timeline indicating when the objective will be met

2. Does it relate to a single result?

3. Is it written clearly?

   Examples of SMART objectives include the following:

Non-SMART objective 1: Schools will be trained on the selected scientifically based sun-safety health education curriculum.

This objective is not SMART because it is not specific, measurable, or time-phased. It can be made SMART by specifically indicating who is responsible for training the schools, how many people will be trained, who they are, and by when the training will be conducted.

SMART objective 1: By year 2 of the project, the Division of Cancer will have trained 75% of elementary schools in districts 1, 3, and 6 on the selected scientifically based sun-safety health education curriculum. (CDC, 2017)

The client interventions (at all levels) take place within programs or activities of the organization. Ideally, these interventions are defined by the mission, goals, and objectives of the organization. In identifying goals and specifying objectives, organizations prioritize interventions on the basis of client needs and concerns identified during the assessment process. The social worker will need to include clients, staff, administrators, and other stakeholders in the assessment to ensure that a diversity of voices and concerns are represented in the identification of priorities. Exhibit 12.1 provides samples of vision and mission statements and goals and objectives.

EXHIBIT 12.1

Vision, Mission, Goals, and Objectives of a Community Substance Abuse Treatment Agency

VISION
The community we see is one in which all persons are free and empowered to make their own life choices, supported by caring families, neighbors, institutions, and government. All people are able to make these choices in part because they are free from the pain of addiction or unhealthy forms of dependence, but able to receive the care and treatment they need, without fear of punishment, stigma, or discrimination should life's pathways lead them in other directions.

MISSION
It is the mission of Seven Arrows to provide effective, compassionate, ethically sound, and stigma-free substance abuse treatment to all persons who suffer from the pain of addiction or unhealthy forms of dependence. We seek to provide our services to all persons in need, without regard to age, gender, race/ethnicity, sexual orientation, or past experience. We also seek a variety of funding sources so that no person will be turned away from treatment because of inability to pay.

GOALS AND OBJECTIVES
Goal 1: Seven Arrows will provide a variety of effective, evidence-based substance abuse treatment services, both inpatient and outpatient, to all persons in need in the North Hills region.
    Objective 1.1: To provide inpatient, residential treatment services to a minimum of 250 clients per year
    Objective 1.2: To provide methadone maintenance services for a maximum of 500 clients per year
    Objective 1.3: To provide outpatient counseling services for a maximum of 1,000 clients per year

Goal 2: Seven Arrows will achieve the highest standards of quality through support of staff, nondiscriminatory practices, and community involvement.
    Objective 2.1: Seven Arrows will provide a minimum of 100 hours of advanced training to each staff member each year.
    Objective 2.2: Staff satisfaction will be maximized by establishing a benefits package, customized for each employee, that will include health and dental care, retirement plans, and rotating sabbaticals for all full-time employees.
    Objective 2.3: A Community Advisory Board will be established to assist the agency in developing policies that help the agency better meet community needs.

Internal Structure

The structure of an organization varies dramatically depending on the purposes of the organization, but there are some commonalities that cross-cut most types. Simply stated, these are the administration, frontline workers, and a large variety of support staff. The central questions that an assessment should focus on here relate to the qualifications and skill of each of the positions in these structural components, as well as how staff are supported and how the work responsibilities create burdens for the staff (Kauffman, 2010).

Most social workers are in administration, middle-line, or frontline positions. These are the workers who are most concerned with the primary tasks of the organization, whatever they may be. Generally, administrators are concerned with the overall functioning of the organization. This often includes policy development, planning, personnel, resource development and acquisition, compliance with external (and legal) requirements, as well as leadership and setting the tone of the organization. In other words, the administration sets the informal climate of the organization. A climate where workers feel supported can go a long way toward overcoming the stress that is created by clients or the environment that the organization rests. Conversely, a climate that feels oppressive and uncaring may make even pleasant work tasks feel stressful.

Supervisors (the middle line) serve as intermediaries between the administration and the front line. Their task in the human services organization is to translate policies from the administration to the front lines, communicate information both up and down the chain of command, oversee job functions, and provide guidance to frontline workers. The quality with which these functions are carried out may be a source of either serious problems for the organization or its greatest successes. The assumption is that the supervisor understands both the needs and the problems of the frontline workers, while also understanding the work requirements of the administration.

Finally, the front line comprises those employees who are most responsible for carrying out the primary tasks of the organization. In social services agency settings, these tasks usually require working with people in some form. The tasks of the frontline staff are vastly different depending on the agency's function, so it is somewhat difficult to state any generalities. It is, however, critical to consider their training, education, preparedness, and support. The quality of their work is a function of their ability, resources, and workload.

Internal Processes

How the staff and structure operate—that is, the organization's processes—represent the final element of the internal organizational considerations. How they function often proves to be the most problematic concerns for an organization. Among the various aspects of internal processes, the most well known are power (and its manifestations as authority and leadership) and information (and its manifestation as communication).

Every organization demonstrates some degree of applied power. It is this applied power that ensures that the right work is done in the right amount at the right time. This form of power is what people refer to as authority, or the degree and type of control exerted within the organization.

How this authority is applied, in what settings, and to what degree need to be considered. Authority that is used correctly and judiciously will be a positive for the organization, while that incorrectly applied may damage or hurt the organization.

Most particularly, authority is necessary to motivate staff to move the organization in the desired direction. This is a function of leadership. Staff may work to achieve organizational goals without some form of external authority, but the odds of success are greatly improved in the presence of an effective leader. Organizational assessments very often find that the problems that exist in the social services agency are closely connected to the quality of the leadership provided, and how well the leader manages the agency. Thus, a good assessment will spend time examining the quality of leadership.

> **Field Reflection Questions**
>
> How does informal communication take place in your field placement?
>
> How effective are the formal and informal communication processes in your field placement agency?

Along with authority, a second internal process is obtaining and communicating information. An organization cannot function without the free flow of information both up and down the structure. A number of obstacles can affect the flow of communication, and as with leadership, a major focus of an organizational assessment should be on communication.

ORGANIZATION ENVIRONMENTAL CONSIDERATIONS

A number of direct variables might be included in an assessment of an organization. For example, a major potential barrier to effectiveness for any organization is access to resources. Resources for different organizations may mean different things—people, technology, and information are some examples. But few, if any, social services organizations can continue to exist for very long without one critically important resource—money.

The methods and degree of success with which the agency is able to fund its services affect almost all aspects of the agency, from the quality of services provided to levels of employee satisfaction. The key questions relating to resources are simple enough: Is funding adequate, has there been a change in the funding source, and is the method effective? In any case, funding shortages or even the possibility of changes in funding can be enough to cause significant fear among both workers and clients and to disrupt the agency's functioning.

Technology has and continues to change at impressive rates. In brief, technology is how the organization does what it does. It may be counseling, methadone maintenance, community organization, or use of computers. The big issue associated with technology that any assessment should consider is its effectiveness.

ORGANIZATIONAL ASSESSMENT: HOW TO ASSESS AND WHAT TOOLS TO USE

Organizational assessment allows an agency to evaluate whether it is meeting its mission and its goals. This is a planned systematic review of an organization's processes, work environment, and organizational structure within the constant-changing work environment; there is a periodic need to review how jobs are defined, departments organized, processes structured, and problems managed. Awareness of the variables that affect the agency, its workers, services, and climate is only part of the process of assessment. Deciding how to assess and what tools to use is also very important. The first consideration is often the methodology, and almost any research methodology can be used. Following are a few of the more common organizational assessment methods.

Focus Groups

Focus groups are a wonderfully flexible method that may be used to obtain a large amount of data quickly under almost any set of conditions—except in case of a constituency that is unable to carry on a conversation. At its most general, a focus group is a group of 6 to 15 (usually) similar persons who are led through discussion of a series of open-ended questions with the purpose of finding consensus answers. Focus groups are very helpful in understanding the *why* question. A major limitation of this method is the lack of representativeness of the findings. Another limitation is the inability to provide descriptive data about the magnitude and scope of the issue being assessed.

Observational Performance Ratings

A second approach in assessment involves observation of the functioning of the organization, and then rating what is seen. A large number of organizational assessment tools can be used for this purpose. Many of them either are in the public domain or may be used with the permission of the persons who hold the copyright. A sample organizational assessment tool (Form 12.1) can be found in the Appendix of this chapter

Field Reflection Questions

What aspects of your field placement agency's organizational functioning need to be strengthened?

How would you assess that component of your field placement agency's organizational functioning?

Some useful examples of these types of tools include the Checklist of Nonprofit Organizational Indicators (Greater Twin Cities United Way, 1995) developed by Minneapolis United Way to help clarify organizational strengths and weaknesses. The rating is a very simple choice of "Needs Work," "Met," or "Not Met" in several areas, including performance indicators for legal issues, governance, human resources, planning, financial, and fundraising (Greater Twin Cities United Way, 1995). The form can even be completed online (www.surveymonkey.com/s.asp?u=3754722401) for free.

ASSESSING COMMUNITIES

An empowerment approach to assessing community needs focuses on building relationships with community members. With this approach, the community is known to be capable of identifying and addressing its own issues. As a social worker, you are a partner in the assessment process. You provide technical assistance and support to the community members and constituent groups. The following section describes the steps in conducting a community needs assessment (Barnett, 2010).

COMMUNITY NEEDS ASSESSMENTS

Community assessments help to empower community residents to create services and programs that respond to their challenges, concerns, and opportunities. Such an assessment is a systematic way to identify the resources and needs of residents by gathering data, soliciting the perspectives of residents and leaders, and surveying service providers and other community resources (Samuels, Ahsan, & Garcia, 1995, p. 8).

The social worker and the community partners develop a community profile that incorporates data obtained through the use of quantitative statistics, demographic indicators, focus groups, and key informant interviews that provide information about political and sociocultural factors. Needs assessments can be used to:

1. Determine whether an intervention exists in a community.

2. Determine whether there are enough clients with a particular problem to justify creating a new program.

3. Determine whether existing interventions are known or recognized by potential clients.

4. Determine what barriers prevent clients from accessing existing services.

5. Document the existence of an ongoing or exacerbating social problem (Royse, Thyer, Padgett, & Logan, 2005, p. 53).

Regardless of how the needs assessment will be used, the process entails the identification and documentation of issues identified by the community that represent an issue, problem, or gap in services that needs to be addressed. The following discussion outlines the steps in completing a needs assessment and the activities associated with each stage (Philadelphia Health Management Corporation, 1997).

Stages and Activities in Conducting Needs Assessments

Step 1: Define the Goal

When conducting a needs assessment, it is important to understand how you want to use it. Generalist social workers use needs assessments to provide information to mobilize for social action, identify potential partners, and develop "buy-in" for the community. The key to conducting an assessment from the empowerment perspective is to for the community to define the needs, rather than the social worker.

Step 2: Define the Community

As stated earlier, communities encompass various geographic localities, interests, and a diversity of people. It is necessary to define the boundaries of the community in which you are working. Examples of community definitions may include physical boundaries (e.g., counties, zip codes, neighborhoods where the agency provides services) or a specific population (e.g., immigrants from Vietnam, Spanish-speaking residents). It is important to involve the community members in the needs assessment process. Often indigenous residents are able to uncover issues that may not be known to the professional community.

Step 3: Identify and Collect Existing Data

In documenting the needs of a community, multiple sources of information and a variety of research methodologies are available to you. A mixed methods approach to analyzing needs will allow for a balanced presentation of the information that not only describes phenomena in a community but also may provide information about the history of the phenomena and potential explanations of causes or contributing factors. You can find information about a social problem in a variety of places. A good place to start is with your clients and professionals in the field who may know something about the existence of the problem that you are trying to address. You will also need to obtain data from the research literature as well as from existing sources of secondary data.

Effective needs assessments must be grounded in the research literature. In conducting analyses of the literature, we want to consider the following questions: What do we know about the causes and consequences of the problem? What are the magnitude and scope of the problem? What has worked? What has not worked? How does the target community or population vary from those reported in the literature? Answers to these and other questions place your needs assessment within a context and provide a basis for comparing the significance of the problem being studied and the relevance of the proposed solution with the problem in general and in other communities.

Multiple population-based and resource-based sources of information are needed to provide a demographic assessment of the community. Population-based information includes census data, public health vital statistics data, and results of community surveys conducted by either professionals or community residents. These data are generally available from government agencies at the federal, state, and local levels. Census data are available online at www.census.gov and can be analyzed by state, county, municipality, and census tracts. Numerous types of population and neighborhood data are contained within the census data. In addition to federal data, "every state maintains a wealth of useful data for planners and evaluators" (Royse et al., 2005, p. 59). Most states have databases of crime and arrest statistics, health indicators, teen pregnancy rates, educational statistics, and many other kinds of information that can be helpful in conducting needs assessments. Other types of government data from over 70 federal government agencies can be accessed on the Internet (https://fedstats.gov).

Resource data also include government reports that are available on a specific topic. In addition, data from published reports and from private foundations can be used to document need. Secondary data sources are excellent resources for needs assessments. These reports are available from service providers or private vendors, if available; are relatively cheap to access; and provide a wealth of quantitative and qualitative data about many social and community problems. Examples of resource data are the National Survey of Children's Health (http://childhealthdata.org/learn/NSCH) and the Philadelphia Safe and Sound Community Report Card, 2006 (www.phila.gov/pdfs/reportcard2006.pdf).

Exhibit 12.2 provides a sample listing of Internet sites where you can access demographic data and reports. "Research Navigator Guide: The Helping Professions" is an excellent reference for social workers (Kjosness, Barr, & Rettman, 2004). You might also check with the reference librarian at your university. Often academic departments have designated library liaisons who create specialized reference listings of discipline-specific resources on the Internet. The categories are usually listed on the library website. Programs such as PolicyMap use the U.S. Census data to compile relevant data into a complete report. PolicyMap offers easy-to-use online mapping with data about demographics, real estate, health, jobs, and more in communities across the United States (Policymap.com, 2018).

Conducting an assessment of the population and resource data will provide you with information about age, race, ethnicity, educational attainment, population size, marital status, morbidity and mortality, income inequality and socioeconomic status, wages, population mobility, employment trends, and community and academic definitions of social problems and previous attempts to address them.

Step 4: Analyze Data

Once you have collected the appropriate data, you can prepare a profile of the community that describes the population (e.g., socioeconomic, demographic, health, crime).

EXHIBIT 12.2

Sample Data Resources Internet Sites

- Child Trends (www.childtrends.org)
- Children Now (www.childrennow.org)
- Children's Defense Fund 2007 Annual Report (www.childrensdefense.org/site/DocServer/CDF_annual_report_07.pdf?docID=8421)
- ChildStats.gov (www.childstats.gov)
- Child Welfare Information Gateway—Statistics and Research (www.childwelfare.gov/topics/can)
- CSU Long Beach Social Work Statistics by Topic (www.csulb.edu/library/subj/swork/sworkjournals.html)
- Data.gov (www.data.gov)
- Institute for Research on Poverty (www.ssc.wisc.edu/irp)
- KIDS COUNT Data Center (www.kidscount.org/datacenter)
- National Data Archive on Child Abuse and Neglect (www.ndacan.cornell.edu)
- National Sexual Violence Resource Center (www.nsvrc.org)
- State and Local Government on the Net (www.statelocalgov.net/index.cfm)
- State of the World's Children (www.unicef.org/sowc05/english/sowc05.pdf)
- University of Michigan Statistical Resources on the Web/Sociology (www.lib.umich.edu/govdocs/stsoc.html)
- World Health Organization Project Atlas: Resources for Mental Health and Neurological Disorders (www.who.int/globalatlas/default.asp)

At this point, you have conducted an assessment of who lives in the community, what it looks like, and what some of the health or economic issues that may need to be addressed are.

Step 5: Identify Data Needs

The quantitative analyses tell us what the conditions are, but not necessarily what caused the conditions or why they continue to exist. The analysis may also not give us an accurate picture of the composition of the community. In many communities, disenfranchised populations do not necessarily show up in census data. Many minorities go undercounted and unnoticed. Accurate measures of, say, the number of gay or lesbian Spanish-speaking residents in a community is not likely to be documented in a report or on the web. This information can often be discovered only through discussion with community partners. In Step 5, it is necessary to determine what information you still need to collect to accomplish your needs assessment goals.

Step 6: Collect New Data

There are many ways to collect the data that you need for your community assessment. Observation, surveys, and focus groups provide three options. **Observation data** focus on documenting behavior as it occurs. The observation may be conducted independently from the group being observed or as a participant. Observation includes going out into the community, walking the streets, interacting with community members, or attending meetings. It allows you to get to know the people and the environment.

Survey data use questionnaires and/or interview schedules. Both tools are excellent ways of "collecting information that you hope represents the views of the whole community or group in which you are interested" (Center for Community Health and Development at the University of Kansas, n.d.). When developing a community survey, it is important to consult with community partners to understand the purpose for conducting the survey. Reaffirm the need or problem that they seek to address. What information do they want to know in the end? How will the information be used? Who are the best people to interview? How can interviewing these people help the community to achieve its goals? What is your time frame for completing the analysis? The three most common types of community assessment surveys are key informant surveys, community surveys, and client satisfaction surveys.

Key informant surveys obtain data from those who are informed about a given problem because of training or work experience—usually because they are involved in some sort of service with that population (Royse et al., 2005). Typically, they are the community residents, block captains, organizational leaders, local politicians, ward leaders, local business owners, law enforcement officers, school officials, and human services professionals who work with the client population whose need is being assessed.

Snowball sampling techniques are often used to generate a list of key informants. The person developing the survey begins with a few key informants and asks them to identify other persons knowledgeable about the problem or population being studied. Depending on the size of the key informant list, the key informants can be interviewed by telephone, in person, or by a mailed questionnaire. The interview or questionnaire obtains their perceptions of the community issue being studied as well as information about possible solutions.

Survey research methods are used to construct the questionnaire and to conduct the data analysis. Key informant surveys are a relatively inexpensive and convenient way to obtain subjective (expert opinion) needs assessment data.

Community surveys of households or community residents are another approach for assessing needs. Typically, these types of surveys are more expensive and require a high level of survey research expertise to carry out. Community surveys can provide information about residents' perceptions of their needs and community conditions as well as empirical data that can be extrapolated to the community or population being investigated. The benefit of a well-executed community survey is that the findings are representative and can be generalized with a specified degree of confidence to the community or population being studied. The downside is cost and difficulties in carrying them out.

Client satisfaction surveys are similar to community surveys except that current or past recipients of a service or program are queried instead of community residents in general. Obtaining a sample of former or current clients tends to be easier than conducting a community survey because the study population is known, defined, and more limited. Client satisfaction studies can provide useful information for needs assessments. Clients are in a unique position to provide feedback on how well the service or program is meeting their needs, additional unmet needs, and the operation of the service or program.

Focus groups, described earlier, are another approach to documenting needs using key informants, community members, or clients. The social worker facilitating the focus group uses open-ended questioning and elaboration skills to obtain in-depth information about the topic under investigation. Focus group participants are selected on the basis of their knowledge of the problem as well as how representative they are of the population group.

Step 7: Identify Needs

The needs statement should define the issues and problems that face the community. This includes, but is not be limited to, home, school, work, services, businesses, neighborhoods/ streets, psychosocial, and recreational activities.

The needs statement should be supported by evidence gathered from your community assessment, including the following: your own experience, quantitative data/statistics, and qualitative data from persons or organizations that are knowledgeable about the community. The statement should be related to the goals articulated by the community, clear and concise, and stated in terms of those who will benefit in the community rather than the needs or problems faced by your organization.

Step 8: Inventory Resources

One of the functions of social workers is that we often act as resource managers. To provide adequate services to our clients, we must be knowledgeable about what resources, assets, or opportunities exist in our community. Resource mapping requires us to leave our offices to look around the community to see what is out there and available to our clients. There are various sources of resource data, including personal observation, existing resource manuals, and the Internet. Useful tools for identifying resources include the individual capacity assessment and the organizational assessment. A more detailed explanation of these tools appears in the section "Asset Assessment."

Step 9: Identify Gaps in Services

This step involves the use of critical analysis skills to compare problems and needs that have been identified to existing resources. Here it is necessary to determine whether you have the resources available in the community to actually address the social problem. Social workers engage community members in a discussion to decide which problems they would like to address first. This is not an easy process. We all have our own opinions about which problem is the most important. Addressing the problems is a collaborative process that will involve all of the community partners. The challenge is to encourage buy-in and to keep partners engaged throughout.

Step 10: Plan Interventions

Program planning is the development, expansion, and coordination of social services and social policies. It involves activities that "address the development and coordination of community agencies and services to meet community functions and responsibilities and to provide for its members" (Hardcastle, Powers, & Wenocur, 2004, p. 2). Program planning can be conducted at the individual agency level, by a consortium of human services agencies, or by regional or state human services planning agencies (Weil & Gamble, 1995). Generalist social workers typically become involved in program planning activities that seek to improve the operation of existing services and programs and to develop new services and programs at the agency and community levels by working with agency task forces, professional task forces, or community coalitions.

Field Reflection Questions

What are some of the needs of the community that your field placement agency serves? In what ways could your field placement agency better serve the community in addressing those needs?

How would you determine what the community thinks about its needs? How might the perceptions between the professionals and community members differ?

ASSET ASSESSMENT

Asset assessment is the process of determining the amount of social capital within the community. The solutions to community challenges are seen as residing within the community residents themselves. Community assets, as defined by Kretzmann, McKnight, Dobrowolski, and Puntenney (2005), refer to those strengths that exist in a community. They include individual, economic, institutional, and organizational resources that are available to community residents. In addition, a strengths-based assessment reveals the existing opportunities for residents to both access needed resources and contribute their individual "gifts" toward the betterment of the communities in which they live. Components of an asset assessment may include the following:

1. Local residents—their skills, experiences, passions, capacities, and willingness to contribute to the project (special attention is paid to residents who are sometimes "marginalized")

2. Local voluntary associations, clubs, and networks—for example, all of the athletic, cultural, social, and faith-based groups powered by volunteer members—that might contribute to the project

3. Local institutions—for example, public institutions such as schools, libraries, parks, and police stations, along with local businesses and nonprofit organizations—that might contribute to the project

4. Physical assets—for example, land, buildings, infrastructure, and transportation— that might contribute to the project

5. Economic assets—for example, what people produce and consume, businesses, informal economic exchanges, and barter relationships

An excellent resource for organizers seeking to understand asset-based community development is the Asset-Based Community Development (ABCD) Institute at Northwestern University (www.sesp.northwestern.edu/abcd). The three basic steps of ABCD are the following: (a) discovering the strengths in the community, (b) connecting with each other and with the community, and (c) coming together to build on knowledge and skills. The ABCD website provides a detailed description of asset-based community development, tools and instruments for conducting assessments, and case examples of the use of ABCD.

ASSET MAPPING

A useful community assessment tool is the development of an asset map. Asset maps are visual representations of a community's resources. Organizers use capacity assessment instruments to determine the strengths and skills of individual residents (individual capacity assessment) and the opportunities and resources available to residents through the provision of social services programs offered by agencies or organizations (organizational capacity assessment). Once information is collected regarding community resources, community social workers use geographic information system (GIS) mapping to depict the special relationships between the existing resources and the community residents. Simple asset maps can be created by conducting a community resources assessment and plotting the addresses of the resources found on a map. The community resources assessment allows the social worker to identify potential assets and resources that are available to the client.

Although some resources can be found by conducting a simple Internet search, many resources in low-income communities may not be documented. To uncover hidden assets, walk the neighborhood in which your agency resides. Often services exist in faith-based organizations, in hospitals, within fraternal and sorority organizations, or even in recreation centers. Social workers can develop a helpful resource for their agencies and their clients by collecting this information and geographically plotting it on a map. These asset maps allow clients to see where resources exist and how far they are from their homes, as well as identify gaps or under-resourced areas.

Programs that use GIS software are available at ESRI.com. Mapping for 200 or fewer addresses can be plotted using free programs such as Batchgeo.com. Both of these programs interface with Excel spreadsheets. Be sure to read licensing agreements to determine the charges for your organization's or personal use of such software.

Community Members Capacity Assessment

This type of assessment is designed to measure the skills of individual residents in the community and to determine what resources they have available to address a particular social problem. Community members respond to questions that assess their vocational, interpersonal, and associational capacities. The goal is not only to ascertain the individual's personal assets, but also to determine the amount of interaction that a person has in the community. Often community members belong to or have connections with organizations or associations that can be helpful in addressing a problem. The inventory also asks residents to identify skills they would like to learn or that they could teach. An individual capacity assessment tool can be found in the appendix of this chapter.

Resource Mapping

Resource mapping is a visual representation of the data that allows you to see where the resources in a community are in relation to your client population. Data can be mapped using a variety of tools that are available either through purchase or by using free resources on the Internet. Programs such as Microsoft MapPoint are relatively inexpensive and are fairly easy to learn. It is necessary to develop a database of information to categorize your resource findings prior to mapping.

SUMMARY

This chapter focused on the assessment of organizations and communities. It began with a review of the three domains of any organization or agency: organizational identity, internal characteristics, and environmental characteristics. Each domain contributes to the functioning of your field placement agency. An organizational assessment could include any of the domains or all of them and their subcomponents. We also reviewed organizational assessment methods and tools.

The second half of the chapter focused on assessing communities. The problem-solving approach was contrasted with an empowerment approach. Approaches to conducting community needs assessments were reviewed, and a 10-step model for conducting community needs assessments was presented. The chapter concluded with a review of assets assessment that included asset mapping and resource mapping.

CRITICAL THINKING QUESTIONS

Competency 7 focuses on client system assessment. You are expected to understand that assessment is an ongoing component of the dynamic and interactive process and be able to critically evaluate and apply your knowledge in the assessment of diverse clients and constituencies. You are also expected to demonstrate how your personal experiences and affective reactions influence your assessments and professional judgments.

1. All organizations have function-related issues that could be improved. What is an organizational issue that you have noticed in your field placement? How would you assess this issue to obtain data to present to the administration and/or board?

2. How does the communication pattern between the administration and profes-sional staff in your field placement affect client services and/or staff morale? How would you go about assessing communication and its impact on clients and staff? What are the strengthens of your proposed assessment? What are some of its limitations?

3. Describe the local physical and professional communities of which your field place-ment agency is a member. How does your agency impact those communities, and how is your agency impacted by them? What could your agency do to strengthen its impact on its local community? What could your agency do to strengthen its impact on its professional community?

COMPETENCY 7: ASSESS INDIVIDUALS, FAMILIES, GROUPS, ORGANIZATIONS, AND COMMUNITIES

Social workers understand that assessment is an ongoing component of the dynamic and interactive process of social work practice with, and on behalf of, diverse individuals, families, groups, organizations, and communities. They understand theories of human behavior and the social environment, and critically evaluate and apply this knowledge in the assessment of diverse clients and constituencies, includ-ing individuals, families, groups, organizations, and communities. Social workers understand methods of assessment used with diverse clients and constituencies to advance practice effectiveness. They recognize the implications of the larger practice context in the assessment process, and they appreciate the importance of interprofes-sional collaboration in this process. Social workers understand how their personal experiences and affective reactions may affect their assessment and decision making. Social workers:

● Collect and organize data, and apply critical thinking to interpret information from clients and constituencies.

● Apply knowledge of human behavior and the social environment, person-in-environment, and other multidisciplinary theoretical frameworks in the analysis of assessment data from clients and constituencies.

● Develop mutually agreed-on intervention goals and objectives on the basis of the critical assessment of strengths, needs, and challenges within clients and constituencies.

● Select appropriate intervention strategies on the basis of the assessment, research knowledge, and values and preferences of clients and constituencies.

CASE SUMMARY—"PRESCRIPTION DRUG COVERAGE?"

PRACTICE SETTING DESCRIPTION

My name is Rachel and I am a graduate social work student doing my first-year field placement at County Services for the Aging (COSA). COSA provides a wide range of free and low-cost services to seniors in the county. I am assigned to the Towers, a residential facility for seniors and disabled community members run by the local housing authority. My assignment is to provide case management services to the residents.

Sandra, my field instructor, is the director of communication and community services at the agency. One of her tasks is to conduct information sessions with seniors and assist them in signing up for the prescription drug plan that best meet their needs. I was asked to assist Sandra in developing and implementing a plan for informing residents about their options and to answer any questions that they had about their coverage and participation. As part of the planning process, I was asked to conduct a community assessment of the residents' information needs and participation in prescription drug plans. In supervision, Sandra and I discussed possible ways I could conduct the community assessment.

IDENTIFYING DATA

There are 125 residents living in the Towers. Ninety-eight are seniors age 65 or older, and 27 are disabled adults. All of the residents are low-income individuals. Almost all of the residents receive Supplemental Security Income (SSI) and either Medicare or Medicaid for their health insurance coverage. Approximately 90% of the residents are African Americans, and all are single, divorced, or widowed. Only about 15% of the residents have completed high school and none attended college. In terms of health status, it appears that almost all have some health issues and very few would be characterized as being in good to excellent health. In sum, the Towers residents are for the most part, African American elderly or disabled persons with very low incomes, limited education, and poor heath. who live alone.

PRESENTING PROBLEM

The presenting problem is that the social work staff serving the Towers residents do not know if the community members have prescription drug coverage and if they do, whether it is the best option available. Because all the residents have very low incomes and numerous health issues, it is quite possible that they are spending more for their medications than they can afford or need to. This is a community-wide problem, not just a problem for individual residents.

ASSESSMENT

I was charged with conducting a community assessment of the Towers residents to gather data about their prescription drug coverage and information needs regarding their prescription drug coverage options. After conferring with Sandra, my field instructor, I decided to conduct a series of focus groups with the community members. We eliminated a pen- and-paper survey approach because of the overall low educational level of the residents. We also eliminated conducting personal interviews because of the large number of residents and time constraints. We both felt that the focus group approach would work best with the Towers population. The focus group approach would be manageable in terms of the time constraint, and it would be a comfortable format for the residents, who enjoy talking with one another. We decided that holding the focus groups with between 8 and 10 participants would give us enough information about the community residents to plan for informational and advocacy sessions. We decided to randomly invite 36 residents to participate in one of three focus groups. We also decided that I would personally invite each person selected to explain the purpose of the focus group, answer questions, and obtain informed consent. As an incentive to participate, each focus group participant would be entered into a drawing for a food basket.

CASE PROCESS SUMMARY

I conducted three focus groups. One group had 10 participants, one had eight, and the other group had five participants. I used open-ended questions to obtain information about the participants' prescription drug plans, how much they were spending on medications, and their knowledge of the different coverage options. Conducting the focus groups was challenging. The community residents were much more interested in talking with one another and had a hard time staying on the topic of prescription drugs. They seemed to really enjoy socializing and being in a group. In each group, someone asked if they could meet again to talk about something else or just get together.

I compiled the findings and presented them to Sandra. I concluded that most of the residents are not sure what prescription drug plan they are using and that almost all felt that they spend too much of their limited incomes on medications. Their knowledge of different options was very limited to nonexistent. I also concluded that thinking about the complicated topics such as drug insurance and co-pays appeared to be too difficult for many of the residents.

Rachel, MSW student intern

DISCUSSION QUESTIONS

- On the basis of this case summary, discuss whether the decision to use focus groups for the community assessment was appropriate. If you were tasked with conducting the community assessment, what would you have done differently?

- Given Rachel's findings from her focus groups, describe how you would approach Sandra's task of implementing a plan for informing residents about their prescription drug plan options. Describe the intervention you would use to provide the information and help the residents enroll in insurance plans that work best for them.

- In thinking about Rachel's experience in conducting the focus groups, what types of services or programs would you propose to your field instructor to better serve the needs of the Towers residents? Describe the reasons for your proposed programs.

- Rachel conducted an assessment of a 125-person residential community of low-income elderly and disabled adults. Describe at least one macro implication of her findings. What macro-policy changes do you think need to be addressed?

■ ELECTRONIC COMPETENCY RESOURCES

WEBSITE LINKS

Organizational Assessment Tool—Adelphi University, Center for Nonprofit Leadership
http://nonprofit.adelphi.edu/resources/organizational-assessment

Community Needs Assessments—Child Welfare Information Gateway
www.childwelfare.gov/topics/systemwide/assessment/community

Asset Mapping—Vista Campus
www.vistacampus.gov/what-asset-mapping

Resource Mapping—National Center on Secondary Education and Transition
www.ncset.org/publications/essentialtools/mapping/overview.asp

VIDEO LINKS

Organizational Assessment—Method Corporation
www.youtube.com/watch?v=SfSiYDID888

Organizational Culture—Denison Consulting
www.youtube.com/watch?v=Rd0kf3wd120

Creating Organizational Culture—TEDx Talks
www.youtube.com/watch?v=BlhM7vALtUM

Community Needs Assessment Part 1—CHOP Program Planning and Evaluation
www.youtube.com/watch?v=624PSllFWsA

Community Needs Assessment Part 2—CHOP Program Planning and Evaluation
www.youtube.com/watch?v=CziB8X_4T7U

Asset Mapping—Service Resources
www.youtube.com/watch?v=mJ7pSoJ25Hc

REFERENCES

Barnett, M. (2010). Generalist practice with communities. In J. Poulin (Ed.), *Strengths-based generalist practice: A collaborative approach* (pp. 322–371). Belmont, CA: Cengage.

Center for Community Health and Development at the University of Kansas. (n.d.). *Community tool box.* Retrieved from https://ctb.ku.edu/en

Centers for Disease Control and Prevention (2017). How to write SMART objectives. Retrieved from https://www.cdc.gov/cancer/dcpc/pdf/dp17-1701-smart-objectives.pdf

Coley, S. M., & Scheinberg, C. A. (2017). *Proposal writing effective grantsmanship for funding* (5th ed.). Thousand Oaks, CA: Sage.

Data Resource Center for Child & Adolescent Health. (n.d.). National Survey of Children's Health. Retrieved from http://childhealthdata.org/learn/NSCH

Greater Twin Cities United Way. (1995). Checklist of nonprofit organizational indicators. Retrieved from http://www.managementhelp.org/org_eval/uw_list.htm#anchor149020

Hardcastle, D. A., Powers, P. R., & Wenocur, S. (2004). *Community practice: Theories and skills for social workers.* New York, NY: Oxford University Press.

Kauffman, S. (2010). Generalist practice with organizations. In J. Poulin (Ed.), *Strengths-based generalist practice: A collaborative approach* (pp. 254–321). Belmont, CA: Cengage.

Kettner, P. M., Moroney, R. M., & Martin, L. (2017). *Designing and managing programs: An effectiveness-based approach* (5th ed). Thousand Oaks, CA: Sage.

Kjosness, J., Barr, L. R., & Rettman, S. (2004). *Research navigator guide: The helping professions*. Boston, MA: Allyn & Bacon.

Kretzmann, J. P., McKnight, J. L., Dobrowolski, S., & Puntenney, D. (2005). *Discovering community power: A guide to mobilizing local assets and your organization's capacity*. Retrieved from http://www.sesp.northwestern.edu/images/kelloggabcd.pdf

Philadelphia Health Management Corporation. (1997). *Doing the right thing: Community-based program planning and evaluation*. A Community Health Database Seminar for the William Penn Youth Violence Prevention Grant Program.

Royse, D., Thyer, B. A., Padgett, D. K., & Logan, T. K. (2005). *Program evaluation: An introduction* (4th ed.). Stamford, CT: Brooks Cole.

Samuels, B., Ahsan, N., & Garcia, J. (1995). *Know your community: A step-by-step guide to community needs and resources assessment* (2nd ed.). Family Resource Coalition. Retrieved from http://eric.ed.gov/ERICDocs/data/ericdocs2sql/content_storage_01/0000019b/80/15/c3/fc.pdf

Weil, M., & Gamble, D. (1995). Community practice models. In R. Edwards (Ed.), *Encyclopedia of social work* (19th ed.). Silver Spring, MD: NASW Press.

APPENDIX

FORM 12.1: ORGANIZATIONAL CAPACITY ASSESSMENT

Agency Name: _____ **Assessor:** _____

Location of Agency	Address 1	Address 2	
	State	Zip	Phone
	E-mail	Fax	
	Contact person		

Is the agency for-profit or nonprofit?	For profit	Nonprofit		
Is the agency governmental or nongovern-mental?	Governmental	Nongovernmental	Level of government	
Is the agency faith-based?	Faith-based	Non faith-based	Religious affiliation (Type or denomination)	

Programs (Name of program)	**Description**	**Number of Staff**	**Number of Clients**	**Year Service Started**	**Annual Budget**
1					
2					
3					

Groups Interviewed for Assessment	**Number of Persons Interviewed**	**Primary Expressed Concerns**
Administration		
Supervisors		
Direct care staff, type I		
Direct care staff, type II		
Support Staff		
Clients		
Community members		
Other (describe)		
Other (describe)		

(continued)

Part I: *In the Score column, identify each asset as a Strong Strength, Weak Strength, Neutral, Weak Challenge, or Strong Challenge. Provide comments where relevant.*

Internal Organizational Considerations	Strong Strength	Weak Strength	Neutral	Weak Challenge	Strong Challenge
Foundation Policies					
Vision					
Mission					
Goals					
Objectives					
Constitutions and by-laws					
Strategic plans					

Internal Organizational Considerations		Strong Strength	Weak Strength	Neutral	Weak Challenge	Strong Challenge
Internal Structure and Processes						
Administration— Board of trustees						
		Quality of policy development, planning tasks				
		Quality of resource development and acquisition tasks				
		Quality of compliance with external (and legal) requirements tasks				
		Quality of networking tasks				
		Attention to long-term sustainability				
Administration— Executive Director						
		Quality of policy development, planning tasks				

(continued)

Internal Organizational Considerations		Strong Strength	Weak Strength	Neutral	Weak Challenge	Strong Challenge
Internal Structure and Processes (Cont.)						
		Quality of resource development and acquisition tasks				
		Quality of compliance with external (and legal) requirements tasks				
		Quality of networking tasks				
		Quality of support for subordinate staff				
		Appropriateness of use of authority				
		Quality of leadership tasks				
Supervisors						
		Quality of policy translation tasks				
		Quality of communication tasks				
		Quality of support for frontline workers				
		Quality of guidance/ education for frontline workers				
Frontline Staff						
		Perception of workload size				
		Level of training and skills				
		Perception of work-task clarity				
		Quality of primary work-task outcomes				

(continued)

Internal Organizational Considerations		Strong Strength	Weak Strength	Neutral	Weak Challenge	Strong Challenge
Level of conflict						
Adequacy of resources to complete work tasks						
External Organizational Considerations		Strong Strength	Weak Strength	Neutral	Weak Challenge	Strong Challenge
Level of support from community, community groups						
Perception of legal and policy environment						

Comments on areas of concern. Identification of source of problem _____

_____
_____
_____
_____
_____
_____
_____
_____
_____
_____

Comments on conflict (if relevant)

- What are the causes of conflict?
  - Is there a history, or is this a new event? _____
  - Are the causes concrete, or are they ideological? _____
  - Are there motivations that support the conflict? _____
  - What forces sustain/reduce the conflict?_____

(continued)

- Who are the participants?
  - Is it between individuals or groups? _____
  - What are the power differences between participants? _____
- What possible solutions exist?
  - Are there common points of agreement among the participants? _____
  - Are there individuals or groups that both sides trust, and that may be called upon to help reduce the conflict? _____

CHAPTER 13

Micro Interventions: Individuals, Families, and Groups

CASE VIGNETTE

Chelsea is an MSW student completing her first-year internship at a public child welfare agency. She had worked at the same agency for 4 years as a child protective services worker conducting investigations and assessments of reports of abuse and neglect. Although Chelsea had learned a great deal while doing her job, she was very happy to have been selected by her agency to pursue her MSW degree under the agency's education leave program.

In the 4 years that Chelsea had been a child welfare caseworker, she had felt both challenged and gratified by her job. She felt challenged by the extraordinary unmet needs of the children and families with whom she worked, but also gratified by the many opportunities she found to make a big difference in their lives by helping them to access resources and making sure that children were safe. Chelsea was aware that she had relied on her "gut feelings" and innate empathy to guide her in her work. With MSW education, Chelsea looked forward to learning the theories, techniques, and skills to make more informed assessments and decisions. She was also eager to learn about new methods that might provide more effective services for the children and families she had encountered.

When Chelsea arrived at her internship on Monday morning, she could feel the tension in the air. She soon learned from coworkers that over the weekend, 14-year-old Daniella Patrick had died as a result of dehydration and malnutrition. Although the girl was living with her mother and three younger siblings at the time of her death, the family had been known to the agency for over 3 years as a result of repeated reports from family and friends alleging neglect and abuse of Daniella and her siblings. A protective services worker, assigned to the family when the initial reports were received, was responsible for assessing the safety of the Patrick children and making recommendations regarding needed services.

The family had also been referred for services from a private provider agency under contract with Chelsea's agency. The role of the provider agency was to deliver intensive supervision and supportive services for the Patrick family in their home. It was routine practice to assign a public agency caseworker to monitor the provision of services by private provider agencies to make sure that appropriate support was available to the family. Accordingly, a second caseworker from Chelsea's agency was responsible for visiting the family monthly to evaluate the situation and to review the reports of the provider agency regarding the family's status.

© Springer Publishing Company DOI: 10.1891/9780826175533.0013

CASE VIGNETTE *(continued)*

Chelsea was horrified, and the mood among the staff at the agency was one of depression and anxiety. The media and the public already viewed child welfare workers negatively. This would just make that perception worse. Two agencies—one public and one private—were responsible for ensuring the welfare and safety of Daniella. Three caseworkers had been involved in and charged with the responsibility of making sure that Daniella was safe. Yet she was found dead in her home, a victim of extreme neglect. How could this happen?

Chelsea already knew that her job required her to make decisions about the safety of vulnerable children in potentially high-risk situations. She was working with several families who could be considered "high risk." Could one of the children on her caseload die? Was she assessing safety and risk accurately? Was she using effective interventions in working with the parents or caregivers of the children for whom she was responsible? Were the current policies in place sufficient for protecting children from maltreatment and supporting families? If not, what changes in policies should be considered to prevent something like this from happening again? Should she reconsider the field of practice in which she had chosen to specialize?

LEARNING OBJECTIVES

This chapter addresses Competency 8: Intervene With Individuals, Families, Groups, Organizations, and Communities. It focuses on micro interventions with individuals, families, and groups. By the end of this chapter, you will be able to

- Define generalist social work practice.
- Understand the difference between micro, mezzo, and macro social work practice.
- Describe the role that goals play in an intervention plan.
- Identify micro social work practice interventions.
- Describe different case management interventions.

DEFINITION OF GENERALIST PRACTICE

Generalist social work practitioners work with individuals, families, groups, communities, and organizations in a variety of social work and host settings. Generalist practitioners view clients and client systems from a strengths perspective to recognize, support, and build upon the innate capabilities of all human beings. They engage, assess, broker services, advocate, counsel, educate, and organize with and on behalf of clients and client systems. In addition, generalist practitioners engage in community and organizational development. Finally, generalist practitioners evaluate service outcomes to continually improve the provision and quality of services most appropriate to the client's needs (Poulin, 2010).

Generalist social work practice is guided by the National Association of Social Workers' *Code of Ethics* (NASW, 2017) and is committed to improving the well-being of individuals, families, groups, communities, and organizations and to furthering the goals of social justice (Association of Baccalaureate Program Directors, 2017). The Council on Social Work Education (CSWE) states that:

> Generalist practice is grounded in the liberal arts and the person-in-environment framework. To promote human and social well-being, generalist practitioners use a range of prevention and intervention methods in their practice with diverse individuals, families, groups, organizations, and communities based on scientific inquiry and best practices. The generalist practitioner identifies with the social work profession and applies ethical principles and critical thinking in practice at the micro, mezzo, and macro levels. Generalist practitioners engage diversity in their practice and advocate for human rights and social and economic justice. They recognize, support, and build on the strengths and resiliency of all human beings. They engage in research-informed practice and are proactive in responding to the impact of context on professional practice. (2015, p. 11)

■ TYPES OF GENERALIST SOCIAL WORK INTERVENTIONS

A classification of generalist social work practice interventions is shown in Exhibit 13.1. In this conceptualization, intervention tasks are categorized by practice level (micro, mezzo, and macro) and system level (individual, family, group, organization, or community). Generalist practice often requires simultaneous interventions on multiple levels. In any case situation or practice setting, you might be involved in a number of interventions on different practice and systems levels.

As Exhibit 13.1 indicates, generalist social work practice entails change activities at the micro, mezzo, and macro levels. *Micro social work practice* is interventions with individuals, couples, and families (Hepworth, Rooney, Rooney, & Strom-Gottfried, 2017). Practice with these client systems is also referred to as *direct practice* or *interpersonal practice* (Seabury, Seabury, & Garvin, 2011). Some authors classify social work practice with small groups as *mezzo-level interventions* (Miley, O'Melia, & DuBois, 2013) and others as *micro-level direct practice* (Hepworth et al., 2017; Shulman, 2009). Because helping relationships with individual, family, and small group client systems share common purposes, this book treats social work practice with small groups as a form of micro practice. Regardless of the client system, the purpose of micro-level practice is to enhance functioning and empower the client. *Mezzo-level practice* involves interventions with organizations and communities or neighborhoods. The purpose of mezzo-level practice is to improve organizational functioning and service delivery and community well-being for vulnerable populations. *Macro-level practice* involves change efforts at the municipality, county, state, national, or international level, whereas the purpose of macro-level practice is to help vulnerable populations indirectly through policy change, program development, and advocacy.

Generalist social workers engage in a wide range of client system change activities with individuals, families, and small groups. Micro interventions commonly used by generalist

Field Reflection Questions

In your field placement, what practice level will be the primary focus of your work?

What levels of practice will need special efforts to ensure learning opportunities?

EXHIBIT
13.1

Generalist Practice Interventions

System Level	Client System	Generalist Interventions

Micro
Individual
Family
Group
	Individuals
	Families/couples
	Small groups
		Counseling
		  Assessment
		  Supportive counseling
		  Education and training
		
		Case management
		  Service linkage
		  Service coordination
		  Service negotiation
		  Resource mobilization
		  Client advocacy

Mezzo Organization Community/ neighborhood	Administrators Task forces Committees Advisory boards Community groups Professional task forces Community coalitions Neighborhood groups	Education and training Strategic planning Program development and grant writing Program evaluation Needs assessments Policy analysis Community organizing Community development Cause advocacy Resource coordination
Macro Municipality County State National International	Governmental bodies Advocacy groups Professional organizations Policy think tanks Foundations Research institutes Intergovernmental organizations	Policy analysis Policy proposals Advocacy Basic research Program evaluation Needs assessments

social workers are divided into two broad groups: counseling and case management (Exhibit 13.1). Counseling interventions include supportive counseling as well as education and training. Case management includes service linkage, service coordination, service negotiation, resource mobilization, and client advocacy.

Mezzo-level interventions focus on organizational and community change. As shown in Exhibit 13.1, typical client systems at the organizational level are organizational leaders, task forces, and committees. The system level is the organization, and the client systems that the social worker engages are the decision makers and decision-making structures of the organization. The worker usually participates in formally organized work groups, such as agency task forces or committees, often to develop new services or improve existing services. The client system might also be the organization's decision makers—that is, administrators and supervisors. Thus, a generalist social worker seeking to change an organization may view the decision makers or the decision-making structures as the client system when trying to improve how decisions are made or how the organization communicates about decisions, activities, or services. Addressing these client systems is often of the greatest importance, because micro systems (individual clients) tend to turn to these organizations for help. An organization that does not function well may not serve its clients or even the very staff who work within those organizations. Thus, at the organizational level, the purpose of macro-level practice is to improve the functioning of the organization, improve services and service delivery, or develop new services through program development and/or grant writing. All three purposes involve change of the organization or agency. Generalist social workers tend to be agency based and work within an organizational framework.

Typical client systems at the community level are professional task forces, community coalitions, and neighborhood or community citizens' groups. Often, the purpose of community practice is to improve community or neighborhood conditions, empower residents, develop resources, increase community awareness of social and economic problems, and mobilize people to advocate for needed resources and changes. Generalist social workers engaged in community change usually work with professional or community groups. Some groups have both professional and citizen members. Social workers engaged in community practice may view the group they are working with as the client system. In other words, the client system may be the professional task force, neighborhood group, or community coalition that is seeking to change or improve the community. Alternatively, the client system may be the residents of the community as a whole.

Macro-level generalist social work practice focuses on larger system change. As shown in Exhibit 13.1, macro-level client systems typically include governmental bodies, advocacy groups, intergovernmental organizations, professional organizations, and other entities focused on larger system change to improve the well-being of individuals, families, and communities. Macro interventions include policy analysis, development of policy proposals, cause advocacy, basic research, program evaluations, and needs assessments. There are even roles for international collaboration. In recent years, more and more social problems have begun to cross borders. Such issues as globalization, immigration, and climate change often require social workers to dialogue and work with international partners.

Importantly, all of the micro-level skills generalist social workers develop may well be needed when working with mezzo- and macro-level client systems. Effective communication, goal setting, and sensitivity to the needs of individuals in some ways become even more important when working with the (often) large and complex client systems that are found at the organizational, community, and national levels Case example 13.1 illustrates the variety of roles played by generalist social workers.

CASE EXAMPLE 13.1: PROFILE OF A GENERALIST SOCIAL WORK INTERN

Gina had her first-year MSW field placement at Social Work Consultation Services (SWCS), an innovative agency developed by her graduate school of social work and a community-based agency. SWCS provided generalist social work learning experiences for social work students and capacity-building services for the residents and organizations of an economically disadvantaged community.

At SWCS, Gina undertook a range of generalist social work tasks and activities. As a member of the senior services team, she provided micro-level counseling and case management services for elderly residents of a senior housing facility. Gina met with her senior clients weekly. For some, she provided supportive counseling addressing a variety of concerns, such as family relationships, isolation, depression, and a host of loss issues. For other clients, she served as a case manager. She referred clients to other service providers (service linkage), negotiated on their behalf with other service providers (service negotiation), obtained resources for them (resource mobilization), and advocated for them in any way she could (client advocacy).

Gina's work on the senior team also entailed a number of mezzo-level practice activities. Gina and two of the senior team interns established a 1-day-a-week drop-in center at the senior housing facility (program planning) and began holding monthly meetings with local providers who served elderly clients to share information, reduce service duplication, and increase coordination (resource coordination). Gina helped develop programs and monthly group activities for residents and organized two ongoing support groups (program planning). In addition, Gina and her team organized a community service day that targeted elderly community residents (community development). The student volunteers provided cleaning and chore services for 125 elderly people. Gina also wrote a grant proposal (program planning) for additional funding for the SWCS program, helped conduct a program evaluation (program planning), and conducted a series of training workshops for another agency's case managers (education and training).

Gina engaged in mezzo-level practice by organizing a 3-day community event designed to promote community awareness of violence against women (education and advocacy). Gina and two other student interns planned, organized, obtained funding for, and implemented the city-wide event. Approximately 200 community residents, students, faculty, and staff participated in the program.

Gina, MSW Intern

MICRO-LEVEL INTERVENTIONS

GOALS

Client goals are derived directly from client problems and concerns. The assessment process focuses on identifying the areas of concern that clients want to address in the helping process. It also identifies client system strengths and resources. The contracting process follows up on this work by focusing on what the client system hopes to accomplish. Problems are negative statements about the client's current situation, whereas goals are positive statements about what the client's situation will be after the identified problem has been resolved or ameliorated.

One of the major purposes of goals is to set the direction for the work. Specifying goals ensures that you and your client are in agreement about what is expected. Without specific goals, you may have different expectations about what needs to be accomplished. Goals also help facilitate the development of your intervention plan by identifying tasks and activities that will be undertaken to address the identified target problems and concerns. Finally, goals provide benchmarks for monitoring

Field Reflection Questions

In your field placement, how do you set goals with your clients?

How do you incorporate client goals into your practice?

client progress. Without clear and specific goals, it is impossible for you or your client to determine whether progress is being made and whether a desired end has been attained. In summary, goals provide direction for the helping process, ensure agreement between you and your client about what you hope to achieve, facilitate the development of your intervention plan, and provide a benchmark for judging progress.

INTERVENTION PLAN

The intervention plan specifies what will be done by whom to achieve the identified goals. It is the plan of action for the helping relationship. This action plan is essentially a contract between you and your client about how you will collaboratively work toward the identified goals.

Several considerations are involved in developing the intervention plan. The contract is an evolving entity and continues throughout the entire course of the helping process (Hepworth et al., 2017). The intervention plan should not be viewed as fixed once it is developed. The nature of social work practice is such that priorities, goals, and plans change and are modified as the helping process unfolds. Consequently, the contract evolves and is modified to reflect the changing nature of the work.

You and your client decide whether the contract will be verbal or written (Locke, Garrison, & Winship, 1998). The disadvantage of verbal contracts is that they rely on memory. As time passes, it becomes increasingly difficult to keep the specifics of the contract clear and in focus. Another disadvantage of a verbal contract is that there is a greater chance of miscommunication and misunderstanding between you and your client. Because of these potential problems, a written contract should be used whenever possible. The act of putting words on paper forces you and your client to come to terms with the specifics of the contract.

The intervention plan developed by you and your client is a collaborative undertaking. Your task is to provide guidance and technical support. Your client's task is to create the substance of the plan. Regardless of the client's level of functioning, it is imperative that the client participate in creating the action plan. The plan should belong to the client, not to you or anyone else. It should specify who will do what within what time frame to achieve each of the identified goals. For each goal, specify the tasks and activities that will be undertaken. The time frame for accomplishing each task also should be specified in the plan.

INDIVIDUAL AND FAMILY INTERVENTIONS

Most interventions are usually done in collaboration with your client. Sometimes you provide an intervention on behalf of your client. The two micro interventions usually undertaken by generalist social workers are supportive counseling and case management. Within each of these broad categories, there are a variety of more specific intervention tasks and activities. This section describes a number of micro interventions used by generalist social workers. The ones selected for inclusion here are the most common generalist interventions; they do not represent the full range of intervention strategies and approaches.

Counseling

Supportive counseling and education and training are two traditional direct service interventions that are frequently used by generalist social workers. Both are counseling-type interventions.

CASE EXAMPLE 13.2: SUPPORTIVE COUNSELING INTERVENTION

Jim is a 15-year-old sophomore previously diagnosed as having a moderate learning disability. He takes regular college preparation courses and has managed to maintain a "B" average. He receives tutoring in math and science and uses the writing center at the school to help him write all of his papers. Although he struggles academically, he has been relatively successful in school.

Jim has no close friends and very few friendly acquaintances. His peers view him as odd and as a "loser." His attempts to fit in and make friends have met with rejection and ridicule, and he has withdrawn socially and makes no attempt to interact with classmates. Jim spends all of his free time at home watching television and playing computer games.

While at home, Jim appears to take out his frustration on his family. He is very demanding of his parents and causes many disturbances within the family. He gets angry quickly and lashes out at his parents over little things. He constantly picks on his younger sister, puts her down in front of her friends, criticizes her looks and abilities, and treats her with general disrespect. When Jim gets into "one of his moods" or is "on the warpath," the tension in the family gets very high. During these times, everyone seems to be mad at everyone else. His parents start fighting, and the general mood in the family is tense and hostile.

Jim's parents are concerned about his lack of peer relationships and his behavior at home. They contacted the school social worker to inquire about help for their son. To his family's surprise, Jim agreed to meet regularly with the school social worker, and together they developed an intervention plan.

Supportive Counseling

In supportive counseling, the social worker takes the enabler role in the helping relationship (Hepworth et al., 2017). The social worker and the client agree to meet for a specified time period and engage in a collaborative therapeutic or counseling process. The purpose of the intervention is to help the client resolve concerns and challenges, enhance coping, and improve functioning.

The example in Case Example 13.2 illustrates a supportive counseling intervention. In this case example, supportive counseling was one of the agreed-upon interventions. Jim recognized his difficulties with peer and family relationships, and he wanted to do something to improve the situation. Jim and the school social worker met once a week to help him improve his relationships. The social worker provided supportive counseling to help Jim gain insight into the problem and to help him develop coping strategies that would increase his effectiveness with peers and family members. Jim also used the counseling sessions to deal with his feelings of low self-worth and the hurt and anger he felt toward his classmates.

Within the supportive counseling framework, the social worker and the client can engage in a variety of therapeutic modalities. The choice of a specific modality is determined, in part, by the focus of the work and the identified concerns. Walsh (2015) provides an excellent review of the theories behind many specialized interventions. It is beyond the scope of this book to review the various specialized individual and family interventions that might be used in your field placements, but Exhibit 13.2 provides a brief description of some of the more widely used individual and family interventions and website links to obtain more detailed descriptions for each. All of the interventions listed in the following text are evidence-based programs that have been researched, tested empirically, and shown to be effective interventions.

EXHIBIT
13.2

Specialized Interventions for Individuals and Families

Name	Brief Description	Website Links
Individual Interventions		
Cognitive Behavioral Therapy (CBT)	CBT is a time-sensitive, structured, present-oriented psychotherapy directed toward solving current problems and teaching clients skills to modify dysfunctional thinking and behavior.	Beck Institute https://beckinstitute. org/get-informed/ what-is-cognitive-therapy
Solution-Focused Brief Therapy (SFBT)	SFBT is future focused, goal directed, and oriented toward solutions, rather than the problems that brought clients to seek therapy. With SFBT, the conversation is directed toward developing and achieving the client's vision of solutions by exploring previous solutions, exceptions, the present and future, and the miracle question.	Institute for Solution-Focused Therapy https://solutionfocused. net/what-is-solution-focused-therapy
Motivational Interviewing (MI)	MI is a clinical approach that helps people with mental health and substance use disorders and other chronic conditions such as diabetes, cardiovascular conditions, and asthma make positive behavioral changes. The approach focuses on the following: expressing empathy and avoiding arguing, developing discrepancy, rolling with resistance, and supporting self-efficacy (the client's belief that she or he can successfully make a change).	SAMHSA-HRSA Center for Integrated Health Solutions www.integration. samhsa.gov/ clinical-practice/ motivational-interviewing
Narrative Therapy (NT)	NT is an empowering and collaborative approach that recognizes people possess natural competencies, skills, and expertise that can help guide change in their lives. People are viewed as separate from their problems; in this way, a therapist can help externalize sensitive issues. This helps clients be more open to change or a new, healthier narrative.	Dulwich Center https://dulwichcentre. com.au
Task Center Practice (TCP)	TCP involves a four-step process to establish distinct and achievable goals on the basis of an agreed-upon presenting problem, usually called the target problem. The social worker and the client cocreate a contract that contains the target problem, tasks to be implemented by both client and practitioner to address the target problem, and overall goals of the treatment. The client's priorities and strengths are interwoven into the entire TCP process. Most TCP involves working briefly with clients, typically in 8 to 12 sessions over the course of a 6-month period.	Encyclopedia of Social Work http://socialwork. oxfordre.com/ view/10.1093/ acrefore/ 9780199975839.001. 0001/acrefore-9780199975839-e-388

(continued)

**EXHIBIT
13.2**

Specialized Interventions for Individuals and Families (*continued*)

Name	Brief Description	Website Links
Family Interventions		
Functional Family Therapy (FFT)	FFT is a short-term, intervention program that involves an average of 12 to 14 sessions over 3 to 5 months. It works primarily with 11- to 18-year-old youth who have been referred for behavioral or emotional problems. FFT uses a strengths-based model built on a foundation of acceptance and respect. The focus is on assessment and intervention to address risk and protective factors within and outside of the family. FFT consists of five major components: engagement, motivation, relational assessment, behavior change, and generalization.	Functional Family Therapy, LLC www.fftllc.com/about-fft-training/clinical-model.html
Multisystemic Therapy (MST)	MST is an intensive family- and community-based treatment that addresses the multiple causes of serious antisocial behavior across key settings, or systems within which youth are embedded (family, peers, school, and neighborhood). Because MST emphasizes promoting behavior change in the youth's natural environment, the program aims to empower parents with the skills and resources needed to independently address the behavioral problems. Initial therapy sessions identify the strengths and weaknesses of the adolescent, the family, and their transactions with extrafamilial systems (e.g., peers, friends, school, parental workplace). Problems identified by both family members and the therapist are explicitly targeted for change by using the strengths in each system to facilitate such change.	Blueprints for Healthy Youth Development www.blueprintsprograms.com/factsheet/multisystemic-therapy-problem-sexual-behavior-mst-psb
Brief Structural Family Therapy (BSFT)	BSFT is a short-term, problem-focused therapeutic intervention, targeting children and adolescents 6 to 17 years old, that improves youth behavior by eliminating or reducing drug use and its associated behavior problems, and that changes family members' behaviors that are linked to both risk and protective factors related to substance abuse. The therapeutic process uses techniques such as the following: • Joining: Forming a therapeutic alliance with all family members • Diagnosis: Identifying interactional patterns that allow or encourage problematic youth behavior • Restructuring: Changing family interactions that are directly related to problem behaviors	SAMHSA Model Programs https://minorityhealth.hhs.gov/npa/materials/briefstrategyfamily-therapy.pdf

(continued)

EXHIBIT
13.2

Specialized Interventions for Individuals and Families (*continued*)

Name	Brief Description	Website Links
Families and Schools Together (FAST)	FAST is an 8-week program that brings multiple families together once a week after school. In each 2.5-hour session, the trained FAST t eam guides families through a scientifically structured agenda of evidence-based activities that enhance parenting skills and reduce family stress while encouraging family bonding. Each FAST ession includes group activities as well as one-on-one parent–child interaction and parent group time.	FAST: Families and School Together www.familiesand-schools.org

Education and Training

Education and training is a micro intervention used frequently by generalist social workers (Miley et al., 2013). It involves helping individuals, families, and groups learn new concepts and skills. Many clients do not have the skills needed to meet the demands and expectations of their environment (Seabury et al., 2011). Generalist social workers empower these clients through an exchange of information. This kind of information exchange occurs as a normal part of most social work interventions. However, when it is a primary goal of the interaction, it becomes an intervention.

When functioning as an educator or trainer with any client, especially with a disadvantaged and oppressed client, it is important to be mindful of power differences between you and your client. You have the knowledge and power, and it is easy to assume the role of expert. You can minimize this power differential by taking an empowering strengths-based approach and beginning with the capacities of your clients. Have them share their knowledge of the topic. Create a learning partnership in which you and your client are colearners (Miley et al., 2013). An educational intervention may involve helping clients learn new skills, such as parenting, disciplining children, life care, budgeting, time management, and/or shopping. Case Example 13.3 illustrates an educational intervention.

CASE EXAMPLE 13.3: EDUCATIONAL INTERVENTION

Time Out for Tots is a parenting program for teenage mothers. The program consists of 15 two-hour sessions. The young mothers attend a weekly mother-only group session, during which information about child development and parenting is presented by the social worker. Group members also share their personal experiences and challenges. The second component of the program involves both the mothers and the children in a weekly group play session. During these sessions, the social worker models appropriate parent–child interactions and supports the mothers' use of the concepts and techniques covered in the group sessions.

Case Management

Many micro generalist interventions fall within the broad category of case management. Typically, a social worker provides one or more of the following case management interventions: service linkage, service coordination, service negotiation, resource mobilization, and advocacy.

Service Linkage

Service linkage is a traditional direct service function performed by social workers (Seabury et al., 2011). The social worker takes the broker role in the helping relationship (Hepworth et al., 2017), referring a client to another agency for service. The process is more than just making a referral, though: Service linkage creates a new link between the client system and an existing service. This is a major function of generalist social workers, especially because many clients who are referred to agencies for service do not follow through on the referral or, if they do, are not accepted for service.

One important aspect of successful referrals is the worker's ability to develop contacts and cultivate relationships with other workers and professionals in community resources (Seabury et al., 2011). Having relationships with key contact people throughout the professional community will help you get your client accepted for service. Often, the client does not exactly fit the eligibility criteria, or there may be a limited number of service slots available. In these situations, your relationship with the agency contact person can help smooth the way so that the client is accepted for service. The importance of knowing someone in the system cannot be overstated. Becoming familiar with existing services within the community as well as developing relationships with professional colleagues is an important aspect of the broker role in generalist social work practice.

In the case of Jim (Case Example 13.2), service linkage was one of the agreed-upon interventions. Jim and his social worker, in consultation with Jim's parents, decided that a referral to an agency that provides family treatment was appropriate. The school social worker acknowledged that she had limited training and experience in family therapy and that family relationship problems could be more effectively addressed by a social worker who specialized in family treatment. The social worker also referred Jim to the social worker at the neighborhood teen center in an effort to get him involved in after-school activities with other teenagers. Both referrals and her follow-up efforts were part of a service linkage intervention.

Service Coordination

Many clients have multiple problems and often need more than one service. In service coordination, you as the social worker coordinate the various services and professionals to ensure that they are integrated and working toward common goals. This involves monitoring the current status of your client, the services delivered, and your client's progress (Woodside & McClam, 1998).

In the case of Jim (Case Example 13.2), a service coordination intervention was not used. Although the social worker stayed in contact with the social worker providing family therapy and the worker at the teen center, she did not coordinate the unrelated services. No effort was made to ensure that the services were integrated. If Jim's social worker and the family therapist had developed an integrated treatment plan for Jim and the family, and if Jim's social worker had assumed responsibility for coordinating their efforts, a service coordination type of intervention would have taken place.

Service Negotiation

Service negotiation involves helping individuals and families overcome difficulties they have encountered with service delivery systems. This function is also referred to as mediation (Seabury et al., 2011) and the expediter role (Woodside & McClam, 1998). Service negotiation focuses on helping the client resolve problems and difficulties with existing service linkages. As a social worker, you take a position between your client and the service provider to improve linkage and resolve conflicts. You help your client negotiate with system providers to address duplication of services, ineligibility, and poor service quality. Your primary task is to facilitate communication between your client and service representatives so that they can reach an agreement.

Service negotiation was not used in Jim's case (Case Example 13.2). However, later in her work with Jim, the social worker helped the family negotiate with the school system. Jim's parents asked the school to run a full battery of psychological and diagnostic tests to assess Jim's learning difficulties. The school system's first response was that he could not be tested until the start of the following school year, a delay of more than 9 months. Jim's parents asked the school social worker to intervene. She helped the family negotiate a much earlier testing date by assisting them in presenting relevant information about Jim's functioning at home and his social isolation at school at a meeting she set up with the school psychologist. Thus, the school social worker provided a service negotiation intervention for the family by facilitating better communication between the school psychologist and the family.

Resource Mobilization

Resource mobilization involves helping the client obtain needed resources, such as housing, clothing, food, furniture, financial support, or health care (Hepworth et al., 2017). The distinction between resource mobilization and service linkage is a very small. Resource mobilization is the acquisition of needed services, whereas service linkage is helping clients obtain such services. Both are concerned with helping the client system gain access to needed services, both require knowledge of service networks, and both involve a referral process. The difference lies in the type of service: Resource mobilization focuses on helping clients obtain resources needed to meet basic human needs, whereas service linkage helps them obtain social, psychological, and health care services. Case Example 13.4 illustrates a resource mobilization type of intervention by a generalist social worker.

CASE EXAMPLE 13.4: RESOURCE MOBILIZATION INTERVENTION

Joanne is a first-year MSW student with a field placement at Catholic Social Services (CSS), where she is assigned to a case management unit that works primarily with low-income mothers who receive public assistance. One of her clients is a 20-year-old mother, Nicole B., who was referred to CSS by her welfare caseworker. Nicole had been evicted from her apartment and had no food for her two children, no money, and very few clothes for herself and her children suitable for the approaching winter. Joanne met with her client to assess her needs. Together they developed a list of Nicole's short-term and long-term resource needs.

Joanne helped her client locate an emergency shelter in which she could live until she found an apartment, obtained clothing from the Salvation Army, and secured a one-time emergency *cash payment of $100 from her own agency. Joanne continued to work with Nicole during her stay in the shelter. Together they found a one-bedroom apartment, modestly furnished it, and filled the pantry with nonperishable food. After Nicole moved into the apartment, Joanne helped her learn to budget, learn more about child development and parenting, and enroll in a General Education Development (GED) program.*

Client Advocacy

"Advocacy is speaking on behalf of clients when they are unable to do so, or when they speak and no one listens" (Woodside & McClam, 1998, p. 63). There are two types of client advocacy: case advocacy and class advocacy. In case advocacy, the client system is an individual, family, or group (Seabury et al., 2011). In class advocacy, the client system is a large collective or group of people defined by some demographic characteristic. Class advocacy is also referred to as cause advocacy (Miley et al., 2013).

Advocacy has a long tradition in social work and is defined as a professional responsibility of social workers (NASW, 2017). Unlike the interventions described earlier, client advocacy requires the social worker to take a strong position on behalf of the client system (Seabury et al., 2011).

Empowering practice involves the client system in the advocacy process. It is generally better to work with clients to advocate for rights, services, or resources than to advocate on their behalf without their participation in the process.

> **Field Reflection Questions**
>
> What micro interventions are used in your field placement agency?
>
> What micro interventions are you most comfortable preforming? What micro interventions are you least comfortable using?

Client advocacy involves educating clients about their rights, teaching advocacy skills to clients, and applying pressure to make agencies and resources respond to client needs.

GROUP INTERVENTIONS

Generalist social workers are involved with many different types of groups. At the broadest level, there are two categories of groups: treatment groups and task groups (Toseland & Rivas, 2012). Within these two categories, there are several subtypes. Toseland and Rivas (2012) have identified four types of treatment groups: educational, growth, remedial, and socialization groups. Seabury et al. (2011) have identified five types of individual change groups (therapy, support, self-help, educational, and peer groups) and four types of task groups (community professional, community resident, agency task, and policy groups).

The primary purposes of treatment groups are to increase members' coping abilities and help them resolve sociopsychological needs. The primary purposes of task groups, by comparison, are to accomplish a specific undertaking, produce a product, or carry out a mandate (Hepworth et al., 2017). The distinction between treatment and task groups, however, should be made loosely rather than rigidly (Seabury et al., 2011). In actual practice, groups often overlap in terms of function and objectives (Toseland & Rivas, 2012). For example, individuals who belong to a treatment group for substance abuse problems may become involved in a community education task group aimed at informing teenagers about the dangers of substance abuse. Exhibit 13.3 lists the types of groups that are common in micro-level generalist social work practice.

EXHIBIT
13.3

Types of Micro-Level Practice Groups

Client Groups	Description
Therapy	Groups that focus on the remediation or rehabilitation of members' intrapsychic or interpersonal problems, such as groups for depression, anger management, and substance abuse.
Support	Groups established to provide support to members and help them cope with an issue that is common to all the members of the group, such as a parent bereavement group.
Educational	Groups that have an educational objective and use educational techniques, such as parent training groups and teen leadership groups.
Growth	Groups that focus on self-improvement and personal growth of the members, such as consciousness raising groups and empowerment groups.

SUMMARY

In this chapter, we focused on intervening with micro-level clients. We began with a review of the definition of generalist social work practice and the different levels of social work interventions. At the micro level, we reviewed supportive counseling, education and training, and case management interventions for individual and family client systems. The types of group interventions generalist social workers facilitate in their micro-level practice were reviewed.

CRITICAL THINKING QUESTIONS

Competency 8 focuses on intervening with client systems. You are expected to understand that intervention is an ongoing component of the dynamic and interactive process of social work practice with, and on behalf of, diverse individuals, families, groups, organizations, and communities. You are also expected to critically choose and implement interventions to achieve practice goals and enhance capacities of clients and constituencies as well as negotiate, mediate, and advocate with and on behalf of diverse clients and constituencies.

1. In your work with clients in your field placement, how do the diversity and differences found among your clients impact how you intervene with them? What are your challenges in integrating the diversity competency with your ability to intervene with your clients who have values and beliefs that differ from your own?

2. In your field placement, what are the micro-level interventions that you use to intervene with your clients? How effective are those interventions? What makes them effective? What keeps them from being effective? How does diversity impact the effectiveness?

3. Describe the intersection between intervening with your individual and/or family clients and the diversity competency. How does your addressing diversity and difference affect how you intervene with your clients? What do you need to do to strengthen your cultural competence in your work with individual or family clients?

4. How have your field placement clients' life experiences with oppression, poverty, and/or marginalization informed your effort to provide micro-level social work services?

COMPETENCY 8: INTERVENE WITH INDIVIDUALS, FAMILIES, GROUPS, ORGANIZATIONS, AND COMMUNITIES

Social workers understand that intervention is an ongoing component of the dynamic and interactive process of social work practice with, and on behalf of, diverse individuals, families, groups, organizations, and communities. They are knowledgeable about evidence-informed interventions to achieve the goals of clients and constituencies, including individuals, families, groups, organizations, and communities. Social workers understand theories of human behavior and the social environment, and critically evaluate and apply this knowledge to effectively intervene with clients and constituencies. They understand methods of identifying, analyzing, and implementing evidence-informed interventions to achieve client and constituency goals. Social workers value the importance of interprofessional teamwork and communication in interventions, recognizing that beneficial outcomes may require interdisciplinary, interprofessional, and interorganizational collaboration. Social workers:

- Critically choose and implement interventions to achieve practice goals and enhance capacities of clients and constituencies.

- Apply knowledge of human behavior and the social environment, person-in-environment, and other multidisciplinary theoretical frameworks in interventions with clients and constituencies.

- Use interprofessional collaboration as appropriate to achieve beneficial practice outcomes.

- Negotiate, mediate, and advocate with and on behalf of diverse clients and constituencies.

- Facilitate effective transitions and endings that advance mutually agreed-on goals.

CASE SUMMARY—"BUT I AM NOT READY TO LEAVE"

PRACTICE SETTING DESCRIPTION

The Senior Care Center is a 16-week partial hospitalization program for individuals age 65 and older who are experiencing a mental illness. The majority of clients are experiencing depression, often following the onset of a medical condition (e.g., Parkinson's disease, cancer, a stroke) and/or following the loss of a spouse or loved one. Some clients have a long history of mental illness, including major depression, bipolar disorder, schizophrenia, and so forth. Many of the clients of the center are either coming out of psychiatric hospitalization or placed in this program to prevent hospitalization. Others are referred by their outpatient psychiatrist or primary physician, or make a self-referral.

The Senior Care Center provides individual and group therapy. The groups consist of psychoeducation, music and art therapy, discharge planning, relapse prevention, and more intense psychotherapy groups. Clients also meet weekly with their social worker for supportive counseling. In addition, the social worker oversees the treatment plan and is responsible for developing the discharge plan.

IDENTIFYING DATA

Mrs. K. is a 77-year-old White woman with a 43-year history of depressive episodes. She and been diagnosed with both major depressive disorder and bipolar disorder. In late 1994, Mrs. K. was diagnosed with Parkinson's disease. Shortly after that, she was admitted to the hospital's inpatient psychiatric ward where she received electroconvulsive therapy (ECT). Following her discharge from the hospital, Mrs. K. was referred to the Senior Care Center for continued mental health treatment and therapy.

PRESENTING PROBLEM

After attending the Senior Care Center for more than 3 years, Mrs. K. was told several weeks ago that she is being discharged at the end of March. When she entered the program, there was no set time limit on how long a client could stay in the program. Recently, the center was informed by the managed care company that the maximum length of stay would be approximately 16 weeks per client.

Mrs. K.'s biggest obstacle is her physical health. Her Parkinson's disease has limited her ability to function independently, and it has also started to impair her cognitive abilities, including her memory. In addition, she is suffering from depression. With her medication and the benefits of the Senior Care Center, Mrs. K. has been coping with her depression very well. The concern is that she will fall back into her depression once she is no longer attending the center.

ASSESSMENT

Mrs. K. needs to improve her ability to be assertive regarding her needs and wishes. She acknowledges this in her individual sessions with her social worker and realizes that she especially needs to work on this around the time of her discharge.

Fortunately, Mrs. K. also has many strengths. She is a genuinely caring and optimistic person; she is intelligent and has a wonderful sense of humor. In addition, Mrs. K. is determined to stay active and fight the effects of Parkinson's disease. She rarely misses her scheduled days at the center and states that she cannot stand to sit around the house and do nothing. Mrs. K. has a caring, supportive husband and son.

CASE PROCESS SUMMARY

Given her current level of functioning, the treatment team does not feel that her continued participation in the program is justified given the new reimbursement guidelines and policies. Mrs. K., her husband, and their son are upset about her pending discharge. All of them feel that she benefits from the treatment she receives at the Senior Care Center and that after more than 3 years the center has become an important part of her life.

I explored with Mrs. K. her feelings about termination. She was very clear that she did not want to stop coming to the center every day. She was very fearful of getting depressed again and also fearful about her health deteriorating. I acknowledged her feelings about the termination. Although I could not justify keeping Mrs. K. in the program based on the new guidelines, I felt that Mrs. K. needed the support and stability the program offered. Together we developed the following termination plan:

- *Mrs. K., in coordination with her case manager, will enroll in the aftercare group at the hospital and attend outpatient therapy at the center.*
- *Leslie will investigate the possibility of Mrs. K. receiving physical and/or occupational therapy for Parkinson's disease through the hospital.*
- *Mrs. K. will begin attending a Senior Activities Center once a week.*
- *Mrs. K. will continue to verbalize feelings about being discharged during individual counseling with Leslie and at home with her family members.*
- *Mrs. K. will verbalize her needs and wishes regarding her discharge to the Senior Care Center staff and her family members.*

DISCUSSION QUESTIONS

- Discuss the ethics of discharging Mrs. K. and whether Leslie is facing an ethical dilemma. What benefits do you see in having Mrs. K. stay in the program? What are the benefits of termination? What are the negatives of staying and leaving? What would you do if you were Leslie?

- Critique Mrs. K.'s discharge plan. What additional aftercare services need to be added to the plan?

- List the types of activities you perform in your field placement. For each activity, identify the client system level and client systems. What client systems are relevant to this case?

- What social work values appear to have a bearing on this case? Are there any ethical dilemmas that you would want to address? If so, how would you resolve them?

ELECTRONIC COMPETENCY RESOURCES

WEBSITE LINKS

International Association for Social Work With Groups
   www.iaswg.org

American Association for Marriage and Family Therapy
   www.aamft.org/iMIS15/AAMFT

Clinical Social Work Association
   www.clinicalsocialworkassociation.org

VIDEO LINKS

Developing Treatment Plans—The Social Work Podcast
   http://socialworkpodcast.blogspot.com/2007/03/developing-treatment-plans-basics.
   html

Evidence-Based Practice—USC Suzanne Dworak-Peck School of Social Work
   www.youtube.com/watch?v=BPqv9K-IZUI

Ben Furman—Solution-Focused Therapy
   www.youtube.com/watch?v=OlGQDq2j6Gw

George Kalarritis—Functional Family Therapy
   www.youtube.com/watch?v=72YRyNlYNfw

REFERENCES

Association of Baccalaureate Program Directors. (2017). Generalist social work practice. Retrieved from http://www
   .bpdonline.org/BPDMEMBER/Resources/Definitions/BPDMEMBER/Resources/Definitions.aspx?hkey=
   f1b36a02-5142-4776-b401-49eb2ae40657
Council on Social Work Education (CSWE). (2015). Educational policy and accreditation standards for bac-
   calaureate and master's social work programs. Retrieved from https://www.cswe.org/Accreditation/
   Standards-and-Policies/2015-EPAS
Hepworth, D. H., Rooney, R. H., Rooney, G. D., & Strom-Gottfried, K. (2017). *Direct social work practice: Theory and skills*
   (10th ed.). Boston, MA: Cengage.
Locke, B., Garrison, R. J., & Winship, J. (1998). *Generalist social work practice: Context, story, and partnerships*. Pacific Grove,
   CA: Brooks/Cole.
Miley, K. K., O'Melia, M. W., & DuBois, B. L. (2013). *Generalist social work practice: An empowering approach* (7th ed.).
   Boston, MA: Pearson.
National Association of Social Workers (NASW). (2017). *Code of ethics*. Silver Spring, MD: Author. Retrieved from
   https://www.socialworkers.org/About/Ethics/Code-of-Ethics/Code-of-Ethics-English
Poulin, J. (2010). *Strengths-based generalist practice: A collaborative approach* (3rd ed.). Belmont, CA: Cengage.
Seabury, B. A., Seabury, B. H., & Garvin, C. D. (2011). *Interpersonal practice in social work: Promoting competence and social
   justice* (3rd ed.). Thousand Oaks, CA: Sage.
Shulman, L. (2009). *The skills of helping individuals, families, groups and organizations* (6th ed.). Belmont, CA: Cengage.
Toseland, R. W., & Rivas, R. F. (2012). *An introduction to group work practice* (7th ed.). Boston, MA: Allyn & Bacon.
Walsh, J. (2015). *Theories for direct social work practice* (3rd ed.). Belmont: CA: Cengage.
Woodside, M. R., & McClam, T. (1998). *Generalist case management: A method of human service delivery*. Pacific Grove, CA:
   Brooks/Cole.

CHAPTER 14

Mezzo Interventions: Organizations and Communities

STEPHEN KAUFFMAN ■ MARINA BARNETT

CASE VIGNETTE

Kelly is a first-year MSW student placed in a community-based program that provides consultation services to grassroots human services programs in an economically disadvantaged community with numerous social problems. The agency's mission is to increase the number of services available to community residents as well as to strengthen the capacities of the local service organizations. Kelly is developing a collaborative program with the local legal aid clinic. The clinic provides legal services to the low-income residents, many of whom also need social work and case management services. The objective is to develop a program that will provide social work and case management services to the legal aid clients.

Kelly is excited but also feeling overwhelmed about helping develop a new service for the residents that would also strengthen an existing community agency. She knows that her first step is to learn all she can about the community and the experiences of the low-income residents who will use the new program. What is it like to be a member of a disadvantaged community? What is it like to be poor? What kinds of services and assistance do the potential clients need? How is working with disadvantaged communities and citizens different than working with other client populations? In what ways is it similar? What professional and community groups need to be involved in the planning process?

LEARNING OBJECTIVES

This chapter addresses Competency 8: Intervene With Individuals, Families, Groups, Organizations, and Communities. It focuses on micro interventions with organizations and communities. By the end of this chapter, you will be able to

- Understand the purposes of mezzo social work practice.
- Identify mezzo social work practice interventions.

306 ■ The Social Work Field Placement

ROLE OF ORGANIZATIONS AND COMMUNITIES IN GENERALIST PRACTICE

As you read in Chapter 13, generalist social work practitioners work with individuals, families, groups, communities, and organizations in a variety of social work and host settings. Although many generalist practitioners find work with micro systems very important, it is often quickly found that many of the problems that clients experience are rooted in the larger systems of organizations, communities, national policy, and even global policy. Likewise, many of the strengths and resources individuals and families may draw upon are the result of larger social systems. Consider something as "simple" as finding a place to live. The overall availability of housing for purchase or rent properties is affected by choices that realtors, banks, developers, communities, and even national governments have made. The options any given person has are affected by the knowledge and skills of organizations such as realtors or housing authorities. Also, an individual's or family's ability to pay for their home is affected by employment, mortgage rates, and/or assistance with housing vouchers—each of which is strongly influenced by community or national policy actions.

NASW'S *CODE OF ETHICS* AND ORGANIZATIONS AND COMMUNITIES

As discussed in Chapter 1, generalist social work practice is guided by the National Association of Social Workers' (NASW's) *Code of Ethics* (NASW, 2017). What all of this means to the generalist social worker is that many of the skills addressed in Chapters 5 and 13 can be called upon to build the strengths and innate capabilities of all human beings. The primary difference is the target. It is not only individuals, families, and groups for which the social worker seeks to engage, assess, broker services, advocate, counsel, educate, or organize, but also the organizations and communities where micro systems exist. The context for the change process occurs at the organizational or community level. Furthermore, generalist practitioners will need to engage in community and organizational development, as well as to evaluate service outcomes so as to continually improve the provision and quality of services most appropriate to their clients' needs (Poulin, 2010). The *Code of Ethics* details important concepts and ideas affecting work with the mezzo systems of organizations and communities. Exhibit 14.1 provides just a few examples from the *Code* that are most salient for mezzo systems.

MEZZO GENERALIST PRACTICE

Mezzo-level practice is interventions with organizations and communities or neighborhoods. The purpose of mezzo-level practice is to improve organizational functioning and service delivery and community well-being for vulnerable populations. The purpose of macro-level practice is to help vulnerable populations indirectly through policy change, program development, and advocacy.

Exhibit 14.1 lists generalist social work practice interventions related to organizations and communities. In this conceptualization, intervention tasks are categorized by practice

<table>
<tr><td colspan="2">EXHIBIT
14.1</td></tr>
</table>

Ethical Issues Common to Generalist Practice
With Organizations and Communities

Value	Ethical Principle	Statement
Social justice	Social workers challenge social injustice.	Social workers' social change efforts are focused primarily on issues of poverty, unemployment, discrimination, and other forms of social injustice. These activities seek to promote sensitivity to and knowledge about oppression and cultural and ethnic diversity. Social workers strive to ensure access to needed information, services, and resources; equality of opportunity; and meaningful participation in decision making for all people.
Importance of human relationships	Social workers recognize the central importance of human relationships.	Social workers understand that relationships between and among people are an important vehicle for change. Social workers engage people as partners in the helping process. Social workers seek to strengthen relationships among people in a purposeful effort to promote, restore, maintain, and enhance the well-being of individuals, families, social groups, organizations, and communities.
Integrity	Social workers behave in a trustworthy manner.	Social workers are continually aware of the profession's mission, values, ethical principles, and ethical standards and practice in a manner consistent with them. Social workers act honestly and responsibly and promote ethical practices on the part of the organizations with which they are affiliated.

mezzo system level (organizations and communities) and client systems. Generalist practice often requires simultaneous interventions on multiple levels. In any case, situation, or practice setting, you might be involved in a number of interventions on different practice and systems levels.

Mezzo-level interventions focus on organizational and community change. As shown in Exhibit 14.1, typical client systems at the organizational level are organizational leaders, task forces, and committees. The system level is the organization, and the client systems that the social worker engages are the decision makers and decision-making structures of the organization. The worker usually participates in formally organized work groups, such as agency task forces or committees, often to develop new services or improve existing services. The client system might also be the organization's decision makers—that is, administrators and supervisors. Thus, a generalist social worker seeking to change an organization may view the decision makers or the decision-making structures as the client system to improve how decisions are made or how the organization communicates about decisions, activities, or services. Addressing these client systems is often of the greatest importance, because micro systems (individual clients) typically turn to organizations for help. An organization that does not function well may not serve its clients or even the very staff who work within those organizations. Thus, at the organizational level, the purpose of mezzo-level practice is to improve the functioning of the organization, improve services and service delivery, or develop new services through program development and/or grant writing. All three purposes involve changes within the organization or agency. Generalist social workers tend to be agency based and work within an organizational framework.

Field Reflection Questions

In your field placement, what practice level will be the primary focus of your work?

What levels of practice will need special efforts to ensure learning opportunities?

Typical client systems at the community level are professional task forces, community coalitions, and neighborhood or community citizens' groups. Often, the purpose of community practice is to improve community or neighborhood conditions, empower residents, develop resources, increase community awareness of social and economic problems, and mobilize people to advocate for needed resources and changes. Generalist social workers engaged in community change usually work with professional or community groups. Some groups have both professional and citizen members. Social workers engaged in community practice may view the group they are working with as the client system. In other words, the client system is the professional task force, neighborhood group, or community coalition that is seeking to change or improve the community. Alternatively, the client system may be the residents of the community as a whole as the client system.

Importantly, all of the micro-level skills that generalist social workers develop may well be needed when working with mezzo- and macro-level client systems. Effective communication, goal setting, and sensitivity to the needs of individuals in some ways become even more important when working with the (often) large and complex client systems that are found at the organizational and community levels.

MEZZO INTERVENTIONS

It is beyond the scope of this book to review all of the organization and community interventions listed in Exhibit 14.2. In this section, we review the mezzo interventions that social work field placement students are more likely to encounter in their internships. When thinking about mezzo interventions, remember that micro-level skills are almost always needed when working with mezzo- and macro-level client systems. In many cases, basic social work practices, such as simply opening up lines of communication with others, being respectful, or being sensitive to differences, will be critical and essential to ensuring effective outcomes. Social workers at the organizational level intervene using education and training, planning and program development, grant writing, and coalition building.

Education and Training

According to the NASW's *Code of Ethics* (2017, Ethical Standard 1.04a, 1.04b, and 1.04c):

(a) Social workers should provide services and represent themselves as competent only within the boundaries of their education, training, license, certification, consultation received, supervised experience, or other relevant professional experience.

(b) Social workers should provide services in substantive areas or use intervention techniques or approaches that are new to them only after engaging in

EXHIBIT
14.2

**Mezzo Generalist Practice Interventions With
Organizations and Communities**

System Level	Client System	Generalist Interventions
Organization	• Administrators • Task forces • Committees • Advisory boards • Community groups	• Education and training • Strategic planning • Program development and grant writing • Program evaluation • Needs assessments • Policy analysis • Community organizing • Community development • Cause advocacy • Resource coordination
Community/ neighborhood	• Professional task forces • Community coalitions • Neighborhood groups	• Policy analysis • Community organizing • Community development • Cause advocacy • Resource coordination

appropriate study, training, consultation, and supervision from people who are competent in those interventions or techniques.

(c) When generally recognized standards do not exist with respect to an emerging area of practice, social workers should exercise careful judgment and take responsible steps (including appropriate education, research, training, consultation, and supervision) to ensure the competence of their work and to protect clients from harm.

The generalist social worker will often encounter situations where client systems will benefit from education and training. Education involves assisting the client system to develop or improve knowledge, skills, values, and/or ways of thinking (cognitive processes) about problems, clients, and the environmental contexts that affect people's lives. For the intervention to be effective, education must always be targeted to the specific audience, with literacy, preexisting knowledge, and cultural sensitivities being taken into consideration. The concepts used in a training process may require greater time to explain than is expected.

One widely used application of education as a mezzo intervention is structured trainings, often conducted through workshops. Trainings may be designed to be short and narrowly targeted events, or they may be designed to take place over a longer period of time and address a large variety of issues. Among the kinds of issues that many social workers confront and about which trainings may be useful are improving productivity and using technology.

Trainings to Enhance Productivity and Technology Use

One common issue that social workers confront is how to improve a group's productivity. Productivity refers to the output of work relative to the effort involved. Often, a group may be expected "to do more with less." Indeed, groups and organizations may be otherwise effective, yet service demands exceed the resources necessary to address those demands. In these situations, the problems of the group or organization may be improved by enhancing or correcting the procedures already in place (Brody, 2014)—in other words, work to improve the productivity of the group by focusing on the strengths of the group. Rarely are organizations so lost that everything must be changed. More commonly, only some element of reform or enhancement is necessary.

Technology, for example, is a commonly used tool for enhancing productivity. The NASW's *Code of Ethics* provides some guidance in the use of technology in the provision of social work services (NASW, 2017, Ethical Standards 1.04d and 1.04e):

> **(d)** Social workers who use technology in the provision of social work services should ensure that they have the necessary knowledge and skills to provide such services in a competent manner. This includes an understanding of the special communication challenges when using technology and the ability to implement strategies to address these challenges.

> **(e)** Social workers who use technology in providing social work services should comply with the laws governing technology and social work practice in the jurisdiction in which they are regulated and located and, as applicable, in the jurisdiction in which the client is located.

In recent years, a variety of technological applications have become available that have aided everything from communication to diagnosis to service provision. Consider, for a moment, the difficulties associated with agency paperwork. With the development and application of some simple programs and perhaps an intranet, many routine tasks such as case notes, internal communication, and even diagnosis may be improved. A generalist social worker can convene or coordinate work groups to help choose and then train group members to use the proper technology.

The problem of group communication processes also serves as a case in point. It is not that difficult to greatly enhance communication through very simple processes. These may include selecting a better method of communication through matching the needs and purposes of the communication with the technique (Brody, 2014). Meetings, important as they are, do not need to be held if information can be more effectively passed on through individual contacts or electronic means.

Technology resources such as videoconferencing, online scheduling, and cloud document management can increase collaboration and productivity in organizations. These resources make more time available to staff, while reducing some complexity for administrators and clients. Again, the generalist social worker can convene or coordinate work groups to help select the appropriate solution, and then train group members in how to use it.

Trainings to Improve Group Skills

Trainings may also be used to enhance other needed skills. Many of us, for example, have benefited from trainings to address issues as broad as diversity and culture, or more narrow topics such as the application of a particular counseling technique. The question to address in planning for this kind of intervention is whether the need may be addressed in a single event, or if the need is for a multievent, long-term set of trainings. The generalist social worker can do the trainings, or can convene or coordinate planning for the trainings.

CASE EXAMPLE 14.1: EARLY STEPS IN STAFF WORKSHOP DEVELOPMENT

Christiana, Laurie, and Pat all were graduate social work students doing their second-year field placements at Social Work Consultation Services (SWCS). SWCS provided generalist social work learning experiences for student interns and social work and capacity-building services for residents and organizations of an economically disadvantaged community. The Director of Adult Probation in the county contacted SWCS about conducting a staff development workshop for her probation officers. Christiana, Laurie, and Pat took on the project under the supervision of a school faculty member.

The training team scheduled a meeting with the Director of Adult Probation to get a better understanding of the agency's needs and her expectations about the purpose and objectives of the workshop. The director felt that her staff could benefit from a workshop on relationship-building skills and on how to engage reluctant, resistant, or hostile clients in a collaborative working relationship. She felt that many of the probation officers were showing signs of burnout and a lot of frustration with their clients and the legal system. Many seemed to have given up trying to make a difference in their clients' lives and were not making any efforts to connect with them. The team left the meeting with a clear understanding of what the director wanted. They felt it was something that they would be able to put together and deliver effectively.

With the approval of the director, the training team scheduled a pre-workshop meeting with the probation officers who would be attending the workshop. The purpose of the meeting was to get an understanding of their training needs and interests. The meeting did not go as expected. The probation officers had absolutely no interest in learning "soft" relationship skills and were totally against the idea of having to attend a workshop on how to connect with reluctant or hostile clients. They felt that such training would be a total waste of time. They used the meeting to vent their feelings about the system and working with clients who lied and were manipulative.

The team struggled to find some common ground between the director's and staff's perceived needs. Because the probation officers were so clear about the frustrations of their job, Pat asked whether they would be interested in a workshop that focused on coping strategies and burnout prevention. This, too, was rejected as a waste of time. Most of the group members claimed not to have any problems in that area and said they could take care of themselves just fine.

Having struck out making suggestions to this group, Christiana asked them what would be helpful. After quite a bit of back-and-forth discussion among the probation officers, it was decided that a workshop on the link between mental health and substance abuse would be helpful. All of their clients were substance abusers, and the workers felt that for many, mental health issues compounded their difficulties with substance abuse and the law. The team agreed to the proposed focus, pending approval by the probation officers' director.

Case Example 14.1 illustrates the beginning steps in developing a staff workshop. This example illustrates the importance of getting input from members of the target group before implementing a training program. The probation officers' perceptions of what they were interested in were very different from their director's perceptions. The workshop turned out to be a success and was well received by the probation officers, even though it was not exactly what the director originally envisioned. If the training team had proceeded without any input from the participants, it would most likely have been less well received. The workshop would have been a trying experience for both the training team and the participants.

Trainings to Enhance Leadership

Social workers are called upon to be leaders in the fight against social injustice. Leadership development is a critical component that may require focus in training activities. Many people mistakenly consider leadership to be of concern only to managers or administrators. In reality, everyone can benefit from enhanced leadership skills. Indeed, it is very difficult for any mezzo-level group to function well without effective leadership.

Although leadership has been widely studied, recent studies have resulted in a number of important breakthroughs in understanding the concept. Research by Elpers and Westhuis (2008) found that organizational performance in the human services is enhanced by using a transformational leadership style accompanied by participatory decision making (Fuller, Morrison, Jones, Bridger, & Brown, 1999; Gellis, 2001). Transformational leaders are proactive and positive, and are able to motivate and influence others. Participatory leadership styles allow employees to engage in the problem-solving process. All members of the organization are viewed as having individual skills, abilities, and talents that can enhance the functioning of the organization or the community.

Emotional intelligence—the ability to accurately interpret emotional states and needs—is also a critical element of leadership (Ovans, 2015). It consists of such attributes as self-awareness, self-regulation, empathy, and solid social skills (Goleman, 1998; Goleman & Boyatzis, 2017), with the idea being that a leader who understands people will help improve many workplace conditions. Emotional intelligence can be improved through training.

Trainings to Address Organizational and Group Trauma

In recent years, the concept of "trauma" has taken root as an effective way to understand the causes and consequences of problems within group, organizational, and community systems. The problem of how to address trauma in groups can be addressed through trainings developing knowledge and skills as related to trauma. Why? Trauma implies disruption, and how well the system can cope with disruption should be of major concern to any system. For example, trauma affects communication, power and empowerment, emotions, conflict, and cognitions—all of which are closely linked to trust and the capacity to form and support human bonds and relationships.

Trauma may create disruption in a variety of ways. Clients may come to the agency with personal trauma. Workers can experience vicarious trauma by working closely with such clients. But sometimes the organizations may, in fact, be trauma-producing themselves! Because of ongoing issues of under-resourcing, poor (or traumatized) leadership, or stressful environments, the organization may be maladaptive. Indeed, many social services organizations are functioning as trauma-organized systems (Bloom, 2010). Consequences include authoritarian and punitive administrators, and workers who become more aggressive and display passive-aggressive behavior. The entire organizational environment may become progressively more dysfunctional and unjust (Bloom, 2010).

Community Education

The value of education and training does not stop with small groups and organizations. Often, larger mezzo groups, such as communities, can benefit from education and training activities. In recent years, for example, generalist social workers have created or partici-pated in community education programs to address issues as disparate as prevention of sexually transmitted infections (STIs), violence reduction, health education, cultural sensi-tivity, and environmental concerns.

Developing the appropriate education program is often complex. Issues as broad-ranging as how to choose the best model and how to effectively communicate in a small group have to be taken into consideration. Furthermore, social media provide useful tools for both identifying and contacting potential target groups, as well as actually distribut-ing informational content.

Ideally, community education seeks to empower and build internal capacity among the members or residents. As with organizational training and education, it is important for the members of the target community to be involved in the definition of the problems and the structuring of interventions.

PLANNING AND PROGRAM DEVELOPMENT

Generalist social workers may also find planning and program development to be a neces-sary mezzo-level intervention. Many of the problems identified by the target system may best be addressed by creating new programs and services. Sometimes an organization may choose to provide a new service, but communities may also benefit from programs that target the entire community. Planning, like education and training, has many dimen-sions and considerations. Nevertheless, two broad types can be distinguished: strategic planning and planning for program development.

Strategic Planning

Strategic planning focuses on giving the client system longer-term direction and identifies the steps to achieve the identified outcomes. Both organizations and communities may benefit from the development of strategic plans. Such plans can help identify concerns, assess and identify group values, create and operationalize goals, articulate specific steps, and characterize challenges and opportunities. Furthermore, external funding may be enhanced through strategic planning. Often, funders require strategic plans. The funder may see the plans as evidence that the group has adequately examined the need for certain programs, as well as the strengths and weaknesses of the system. Showing alignment between a strategic plan and a grant proposal will greatly improve the system being funded.

Although what specifically goes into a strategic plan should be dictated by the group's needs, such a plan usually describes the goals, needs, problems, and tasks for the group over the intermediate to longer-term future. Although it makes total sense that having a plan is a critical element for an organization or community, it is often the case that plans are old, outdated, and no longer relevant to the realities in which a group may find itself. A generalist social worker can help in the development or updating of a strategic plan.

In some ways, the strategic plan should be a priority concern for an organization or community. As such, it can become not just a guide but also a real review of what is rele-vant and what is not. Brody (2014) presents a series of steps and questions that can guide the strategic planning process (p. 35):

1. Carefully examine the purposes for the plan.

2. Determine the level of commitment of major constituencies.

3. Establish a committee to oversee the effort.

4. Assess the problems, opportunities, and strengths of the organization.

5. Analyze and/or recreate the organizational vision.

6. Examine/revise and/or draft a mission statement.

7. Prioritize the challenges to the organization.

8. Develop mid- and long-term goals.

9. Submit a draft of the plan for multiple reviews by different constituencies.

10. Implement the plan.

11. Update the plan annually.

SWOT ANALYSIS

One model to assist in this process is called a SWOT analysis. SWOT stands for strengths, weaknesses, opportunities, and threats. The results of the data analysis are organized into a four-component framework, which is divided into two internal analysis components (strengths and weaknesses) and two external components (opportunities and threats). Strengths and opportunities are helpful to the organization, whereas weaknesses and threats are those things that may be harmful to the organization. This perspective is shown in Exhibit 14.3.

PROGRAM DEVELOPMENT AND GRANT WRITING

Program development is not only a strategic activity, but also a necessary activity at the level of the program. The "program" is one of the central organizing units of social work practice. A program is defined as a coordinated service or set of services, often with its own set of resources, workers, and administrators. It is here that planning often connects with the issue of resources for the system. Resources and money are often the source of a group's problems. At the very least, creating new programs may require newly developed funds. As such, identifying and/or developing resources is often an essential concern of the social worker.

There are many ways a program may enhance its resources. A description of each type of funding is provided in Exhibit 14.4, along with a short description of the considerations needed for each.

Grant Writing

Although having knowledge of all these areas is often necessary, the one resource development skill set that all generalist social workers should develop is grant writing. Many organizations supplement or expand their resources through grant writing—and it is easy to see why. Americans have a long history of giving, and between federal, state, and local governmental sources, and the vast number of grant-making foundations, there are literally thousands of sources with billions of dollars. Indeed, in 2016, statistics show that Americans' total charitable contributions exceeded $390 billion (Indiana University Lilly Family School of Philanthropy, 2017). Although most of this funding (71%) came from

**EXHIBIT
14.3**

SWOT Analysis

Strengths	Weaknesses
• What do we do best? • What unique knowledge, talent, or resources do we have? • What advantages do we have? • What do other people say we do well? • What resources do we have available? • What is our greatest achievement?	• What could we improve? • What knowledge, talent, skills , and/or resources are we lacking? • What disadvantages do we have? • What do other people say we do not do well? • In what areas do we need more training? • What complaints have we had about our service?
Opportunities	**Threats**
• How can we turn our strengths into opportunities? • How can we turn our weaknesses into opportunities? • Is there a need in our agency that no one is meeting? • What could we do today that is not being done? • How is our field changing? How can we take advantage of those changes? • Whom could we support? How could we support them?	• What obstacles do we face? • Could any of our weaknesses prevent our unit from meeting our goals? • Who and/or what might cause us problems in the future? How? • Are there any standards, policies, and/or legislation changing that might negatively impact us? • Are we competing with others to provide service? • Are there changes in our field or in technology that could threaten our success?

Source: Louisiana Department of State Civil Service. (2015). SWOT analysis: Questions for conducting an analysis with your team. Retrieved from https://www.civilservice.louisiana.gov/files/divisions/Training/Job%20Aid/Supervisor%20Toolbox/Questions%20for%20Professional%20SWOT.pdf

individuals, 68 foundations donated more than $75 million each in 2013 (Philanthropy Roundtable, 2018) and many dozens more gave $1 million or more. Berlin (2017) reports that in 2016, the U.S. government allocated approximately $666 billion in federal grants to support state and local programs.

The process of writing a grant can range from an endeavor that is very short and simple—typically for small, community grants—to one that is complex and exhaustive. But in general, the process of applying for and organizing most grant proposals is more or less done the same way. The general steps are the following: (a) develop a clear project or problem; (b) select the grant source; and (c) write the proposal. Each of these steps is described in detail in the following subsections.

Step 1: Develop a Clear Project or Problem

This part of the process is not really very different from planning for any intervention, with perhaps two important differences. First, in many cases, the focus of the project may expand beyond the needs of a specific agency to possibly include other system client needs. Often, effective interventions will be strongest if many "partners" are a part of the

EXHIBIT
14.4

Methods of Program Funding

Funding Method	Description	Issues
Fee for service	Client pays for service provided.	Requires enough clients who have disposable income to support the agency. Client numbers change, making planning difficult.
Third-party payments, insurance reimbursements	Payments made by insurer for services.	Limited types of services covered. Requires certification/licensure. Services may require preauthorization by an insurance company.
Loans—commercial source	Loans provided at market rates.	Market rates fluctuate—rates are based on the agency's credit rating.
Loans—government or noncommercial source	Loans provided at nonmarket rates, often by government agencies.	Eligibility is often linked to specific policy/problem areas.
Contract with governmental source	Governmental source (federal, state, county) preselects types of services/clients, and chooses and contracts with the agency to provide services.	Dependent on political and legislative action. Agency must meet eligibility criteria. Contracts are competitive and time limited. Applies only to limited types of services or clients.
Grants—governmental source	Agency writes a grant proposal for funds to underwrite a program. Government source evaluates and chooses among submitting agencies.	Dependent on political and legislative action. Requires grant-writing expertise. Long application period with no guarantee of funding. Time-limited funding. Many limits on use of funds.
Grants—foundation source	Agency writes a grant proposal for funds to underwrite a program. Foundation source evaluates and chooses among submitting agencies.	Dependent on foundation attention to the problem area. Requires grant-writing expertise. Long application period with no guarantee of funding. Time-limited funding. Most funding sources are small. Many limits on use of funds.
Grants—general source (United Way, Walmart)	Agency writes a grant proposal for funds to underwrite a program. Foundation source evaluates and chooses among submitting agencies.	Dependent on foundation attention to the problem area. Requires grant-writing expertise. Long application period with no guarantee of funding. Time-limited funding. Many limits on use of funds.
Direct solicitation fundraising	Bake sales, direct mail requests, employee contributions.	Unless the organization is well known or "in the public spotlight," contributions tend to be small. Usually very undependable.

process. Although you might consider seeking funding for what is known as "capacity building," referring to enhancement of skills or agency infrastructure, you might also consider writing a grant to address an unmet client need through partnerships with other organizations. With this approach, the funding may be of value in addressing the organization's needs at the same time as it is helping the clients.

A second difference that may apply here is that most successful grants depend on a grounding in the literature. An empirical basis for any project, as drawn from the literature of social work, sociology, psychology, or similar fields, will have a much greater chance of success than one that is based on anecdotes or practice wisdom alone. Funders, especially for larger grants, want to provide money to projects that are likely to succeed. And the empirical basis may provide the evidence needed to support that sense. Many government agencies maintain databases of evidence-based practices (see Exhibit 14.5).

Overall, you can think about projects or problems as being one of several types. You will want to identify the type that is closest to your intent. Doing so will make searching for grants a bit easier and will improve the chances of being selected for funding. The various types of projects and problems include the following:

- Research or planning projects/problems: Projects designed to help the agency examine a problem and/or plan for new services

- Demonstration projects: Projects designed to implement new or untested services

- Operating expenses and services support: Projects designed to raise funds for existing services

- Endowment development: Projects designed to help build the endowment and long-term assets of the agency

- Construction projects: Projects designed to help the agency build a new structure or renovate the existing physical plant

- Capacity building: Projects designed to enhance the skills or knowledge of the staff, or to improve the agency's infrastructure

Although there are grants available for all of these types of projects, some are more readily available than others. Typically, funding will be somewhat more available for research or planning, demonstration projects, or capacity building than for construction or endowment development. Operating expenses and services support, which are commonly ongoing needs in any organization, are fairly easy to find funding for, but rarely in large amounts or in the amounts necessary to do anything more than partially support a major project. To put this another way, funding is an ongoing activity, and grant writing, while of unquestionable value, is also an ongoing process.

Step 2: Select the Grant Source

To begin, you must find out who (what organization) is providing funding. This is, at least "on paper," actually fairly easy, as organizations that give away money must notify the public that funds are available, although finding the right source might be more difficult. The notifications you will be seeking are variously known as an RFP (Request

Evidence-Based Programs

• **Blueprints for Healthy Youth Development** *Hosted by the CSPV, University of Colorado Boulder*	• www.blueprintsprograms.org
• **Community Health Online Resource Center** *DCH, CDC*	• https://nccd.cdc.gov/DCH_CHORC
• **CrimeSolutions.gov** *OJP, DOJ*	• www.crimesolutions.gov
• **Effective Interventions—HIV Prevention That Works** *CDC*	• https://effectiveinterventions.cdc.gov/en
• **ePSS** *AHRQ*	• https://epss.ahrq.gov/PDA/index.jsp
• **Evidence-Based Practices Resource Center** *SAMHSA*	• www.samhsa.gov/ebp-resource-center
• *Healthy People 2020* **Evidence-Based Resources** *ODPHP, DHHS*	• www.healthypeople.gov/2020/tools-resources/Evidence-Based-Resources
• **Prevention Strategies—CDC's Winnable Battles** *PRC, CDC*	• www.cdc.gov/WinnableBattles/index.html
• **Teen Pregnancy Prevention Resource Center: Evidence-Based Programs Database** *OAH, DHHS*	• www.hhs.gov/ash/oah/grant-programs/teen-pregnancy-prevention-program-tpp/evidence-based-programs/index.html
• **WWC** *IES, ED*	• https://ies.ed.gov/ncee/wwc

AHRQ, Agency for Healthcare Research and Quality; CDC, Centers for Disease Control and Prevention; CSPV, Center for the Study and Prevention of Violence; DCH, Division of Community Health; DHHS, Department of Health and Human Services; DOJ, Department of Justice; ED, Department of Education; ePSS, Electronic Preventive Services Selector; IES, Institute of Education Sciences; NREPP, National Registry of Evidence-Based Programs and Practices; OAH, Office of Adolescent Health; ODPHP, Office of Disease Prevention and Health Promotion; OJP, Office of Justice Programs; PRC, Prevention Research Center; SAMHSA, Substance Abuse and Mental Health Services Administration; WWC, What Works Clearinghouse.

for Proposals), NOFA (Notice of Funding Availability), FOA (Funding Opportunity Announcement), or SUPER NOFA (groups of NOFAs). Exhibit 14.6 shows the content that RFPs typically describe.

Make sure you review these sections carefully. Many grant sources receive hundreds of applications, so you must prepare the right proposal for the right source. Although individuals may provide grant funds, most conceptualizations of grant funding sources focus on a government level (federal, state, local) or a foundation. There are advantages and

**EXHIBIT
14.6**

Components of a Request for Proposals (RFP)

Section	Information Provided
Information about funder	Name of program Name of organization and auspice
Funding amounts and time frames	Minimum, maximum, and average grant size Duration of grant (typically 1–3 years, sometimes renewable) Expected match amount

Selection criteria—what may be funded	This could involve the following:
	    Discipline(s)
	    Problem area(s)
	    Client characteristics
	    Geography
	    Intervention approach, methods, or activities

Selection criteria—what may not be funded	Commonly seen are the following:
	    Limitations on overhead (indirect costs), administration, travel, and so on
	    Construction, lobbying, endowments

Application process	Due dates Contact information Where to get application forms (if necessary) Grant/technical assistance advisor

disadvantages to the different grant sources. Government sources are often considered to be more prestigious and to offer high-dollar amounts, but their grants are very competitive, restrictive, and extremely complex to write. Foundations are more varied. With literally thousands of different sources, it is possible to find everything from large, high-dollar, complex grants to small, essentially noncompetitive microgrants.

Where does one find an RFP, or learn about grant sources? With the federal government, the *Catalog of Domestic Federal Assistance* was the standard source of such information until the Internet arose and offered new opportunities. Now, almost every government agency provides information about sources on its website. And even easier access is available with www.grants.gov, which collects information across agencies.

Comprehensive information for foundations is harder to find simply because of the large number of foundations that exist. Yet again, several websites exist that can help, although they are often fee or subscription based. Some useful sites for government and foundational supports are given in Exhibit 14.7.

Step 3: Write the Proposal

Writing the proposal may seem complex, but in many ways it just involves pulling together information that may already exist, although that information must be put together

Grant Search Engine Websites

www.grants.gov	Grants Learning Center: Your gateway to the federal grants world. The Grants Learning Center is where you can learn more about the federal grants life cycle, policies on grants management, and profiles on grant making.
www.foundationcenter.org	The Foundation Center is the leading source of information about philanthropy worldwide. It maintains a comprehensive database of U.S. and global grants.
www.grantspace.org	A database maintained by the Foundation Center, GrantSpace provides easy-to-use, self-service tools and resources to help nonprofits worldwide become more viable grant applicants and build strong, sustainable organizations.
https://grantwatch.com	Website for international, Canada, and U.S. federal, state, local, foundation, and corporation grants.

in a clear, concise, and logical way. Although every proposal MUST be specific to the RFP, and MUST follow all of the directions perfectly, it is also the case that the components of most proposals are similar. These components are shown in Exhibit 14.8 (Coley & Scheinberg, 2008, p. 4).

Each of these sections should be logically connected to the others. This means that every section of the proposal builds on what has gone before and prepares for what comes after. Although this might seem evident and obvious, a lack of logical connections is a common flaw in many grant applications. One way to avoid this problem is to remember that the strongest proposals will have a clear relationship between indicators of need, your outcome objectives, and the degree of change in outcomes you seek to demonstrate in your evaluation. Do not identify and measure a need one way, while focusing your objectives and evaluation criteria somewhere else.

One tool that is commonly used as part of the grant development process is a logic model (also see Chapter 9 for a discussion of logic models). The logic model serves a number of useful purposes, both for the organization that is submitting it and for the funders, who are increasingly requiring logic models with grant submissions. A logic model presents a picture of how your effort or initiative is supposed to work. It explains why your strategy is a good solution to the problem at hand. Effective logic models make an explicit, often visual, statement of the activities that will bring about change and the results you expect to see for the community and its people. A logic model keeps participants in the effort moving in the same direction by providing a common language and point of reference (Center for Community Health and Development at the University of Kansas, n.d.-a).

Although there are a number of useful models for what is included in a logic model and for everything else related to grant development, you should follow the explicit directions given by a potential funder. The Community Tool Box (https://ctb.ku.edu/en) is a

**EXHIBIT
14.8**

Typical Grant Proposal Sections

Grant Section	Information Provided
Title or cover page	Often supplied by funder. Includes contact information for the submitting organization.
Abstract	Short overview of the proposal. Typically, 100 to 150 words.
Introduction/ summary	One- to three-page summary of the project. Introduces the project and the agency to the funder. Includes the mission and vision of the agency.
Needs statement (problem statement)	Describes the problem/issue that the grant wants to address. Typically includes a problem definition, statistics describing the community setting, the size of the problem, and some evidence about the seriousness of the problem (such as statistics comparing the target group with other groups).
Project description	Identifies the project's goals and objectives and provides details about the implementation plan, including the timeline to complete project activities. This section often includes a scope of work grid of the project delivery plan.
Evaluation plan	Explains the measurement procedures that will be used to determine whether the goals and objectives have been met.
Budget request	Itemizes the expenditures of the project and includes a rationale or budget justification for the expenses.
Applicant capability	Demonstrates the applicant's past performance and ability to accomplish the proposed project. Often includes an organizational chart.
Organizational sustainability	Indicates the plan to continue the project beyond the requested funding period.
Letters of support	Letters reflecting support for the proposed project from program recipients, community leaders, partnering agencies, coalitions, religious organizations, universities, or political leaders.
Memoranda of understanding	A written agreement from each of the partners or coapplicant agencies on how they will cooperate to implement the grant.
Appendix materials	May include an audited financial statement, insurance documentation, or any other documentation required by the funder.

useful reference in the development of logic models. A logic model typically provides a table that describes the following:

- **Purpose**, or mission. What motivates the need for change? This can also be expressed as the problems or opportunities that the program is addressing.

- **Context**, or conditions. What is the climate in which change will take place? (How will new policies and programs be aligned with existing ones? What trends compete with the effort to engage youth in positive activities? What is the political and economic climate for investing in youth development?)

- **Inputs**, or resources or infrastructure. What raw materials will be used to conduct the effort or initiative? Inputs can also include constraints on the program, such as regulations or funding gaps, which are barriers to your objectives.

- **Activities**, or interventions. What will the initiative do with its resources to direct the course of change? (In our example, the program will train volunteer mentors and refer young people who might benefit from a mentor.) Your intervention, and thus your logic model, should be guided by a clear analysis of risk and protective factors.

- **Outputs**. What evidence is there that the activities were performed as planned? (Indicators for our example program might include the number of mentors trained and youth referred, and the frequency, type, duration, and intensity of mentoring contacts.)

- **Effects**, or results, consequences, outcomes, or impacts. What kinds of changes came about as a direct or indirect effect of the activities? (Two examples for our program are bonding between adult mentors and youth and increased self-esteem among youth.)

COMMUNITY DEVELOPMENT

Community development involves the participation of community members in developing a capacity and consensus in identifying and solving their own problems (Fellin, 2001). Social work interventions are often aimed at improving community conditions and empowering residents to seek community change. Community development also has a social action component, which includes activities aimed at challenging inequalities, confronting decision makers, and empowering people to change unjust conditions (Rubin & Rubin, 2008; Zastrow, 2010; Zastrow & Kirst-Ashman, 2010). Recognizing that power/

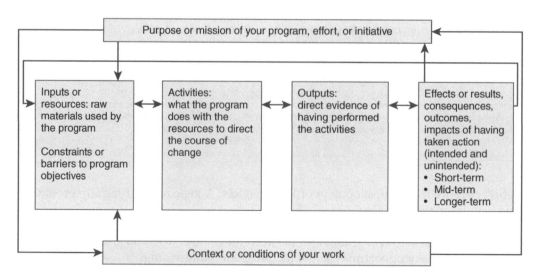

FIGURE 14.1 Logic Model Process

Source: Center for Community Health and Development. at University of Kansas. (n.d.-a). *Community tool box, Chapter 2: Section 1: Developing a logic model or theory of change.* Retrieved from https://ctb.ku.edu/en/table-of-contents/overview/models-for-community-health-and-development/logic-model-development/main

disempowerment is often at the core of many social problems, social action focuses on social, political, and economic justice for the disadvantaged and disenfranchised (Weil & Gamble, 1995; Zastrow, 2010; Zastrow & Kirst-Ashman, 2010).

Community development strategies seek to improve community conditions, empower residents, develop resources, and mobilize citizen groups. To achieve these purposes, the generalist social worker organizes constituent groups, builds community coalitions, conducts community needs assessments, lobbies political and government leaders, and advocates on behalf of constituent groups. Community development activities may also involve economic development projects, installation of public facilities, establishment of community centers, recruitment of new businesses, code enforcement, and developing homeowner assistance programs.

To achieve the varying ends of community development, almost every social work generalist skill is necessary. Social workers involved in organizing constituent groups often take responsibility for convening and facilitating meetings. They do the planning and the legwork to get participants to attend. This requires skill in managing groups and conducting meetings. An empowering approach to the process focuses on having community residents assume control and leadership of the development effort. The social worker helps get the process started, but ultimate responsibility for the ongoing effort rests with participants and indigenous leadership.

COALITION BUILDING

Both an independent activity and a component of community development, coalition building occurs when representatives of diverse community groups join forces to influence external institutions on one or more issues affecting their constituencies (Mizrahi & Rosenthal, 2001). The process may be intended to be short or long term, but the idea is that there is strength in numbers. Often, the problems to be addressed are larger and more intractable than a single individual or group can effectively address—in other words, a "common goal" exists (Center for Community Health and Development at the University of Kansas, n.d.-b). A coalition, then, has its goal is to build a power base sufficient to influence decision making and the allocation of resources (Weil & Gamble, 1995).

> **Field Reflection Questions**
>
> What mezzo interventions are used in your field placement agency?
>
> What mezzo intervention are you most comfortable performing? What mezzo intervention are you least comfortable using?

Unfortunately, coalitions are difficult to create and hold together. Often, there is inherent tension between the coalition members' interest in maintaining the autonomy and power of their constituent groups and the need to share power and resources to make the coalition successful. In addition, a number of barriers often exist to a successful coalition. These may include issues of turf ownership, history, attempted dominance by one group or professionals over the larger public, inadequate leadership, or real or perceived costs (Center for Community Health and Development at the University of Kansas, n.d.-b). To deal with such difficulties, all of a social worker's micro and mezzo skills may be needed. Social workers need well-developed mediation and negotiation skills to effectively build coalitions, as well as skills in interorganizational relations and planning (Gamble & Weil, 2010).

COMMUNITY EDUCATION AND TRAINING

As discussed earlier, education and training at the community level tend to focus on increasing community awareness and understanding of social issues and community problems (DuBois & Miley, 2008). Generalist social workers make formal presentations at community meetings, serve as panelists at public forums, and conduct community workshops and seminars. Examples 1 and 2 in Case Example 14.2 illustrate how generalist social workers may use education and training as a mezzo-level practice intervention.

CASE EXAMPLE 14.2: EDUCATION AND TRAINING INTERVENTIONS

MARCUS W.

Marcus W. is the social worker with the Chester Community Improvement Project, a grant-funded agency that provides community residents with information to assist them in achieving home ownership. The project seeks to address the needs of families through its rehabilitation project, new housing construction project, mortgage counseling, and job training for youth. Marcus designed a series of workshops for the local residents that were designed to educate them about financial literacy, saving for a first home, and understanding mortgages. Marcus discussed the current condition of the local neighborhood and cited statistics showing that the neighborhood could be stabilized by increasing home ownership among the residents.

SHARON D.

Sharon D. is a second-year student placed with the local charter school. This past year, the school was in jeopardy of not making the Annual Yearly Progress benchmarks. Significant numbers of students scored below grade level in reading and math.

In consultation with parents, students, and staff, Sharon and a staff member from the school developed a homework after-school project for parents. The program is designed to tutor parents in upper-level math and science so that they will be able to provide assistance to their children. In addition to the classes, Sharon has developed a monthly newsletter to communicate to parents about school events and provide tips on subjects such as time management and reducing stress.

SUMMARY

In this chapter, we focused on intervening with mezzo-level clients. We began with a review of the definition of generalist social work practice and the different levels of social work interventions. At the mezzo level, we reviewed a number of organizational and community-level interventions.

CRITICAL THINKING QUESTIONS

Competency 8 focuses on intervening with client systems. You are expected to understand that intervention is an ongoing component of the dynamic and interactive process of social work practice with, and on behalf of, diverse individuals, families, groups, organizations, and communities. You are also expected to critically choose and implement interventions to achieve practice goals and enhance the capacities of clients and constituencies, as well as to negotiate, mediate, and advocate with and on behalf of diverse clients and constituencies.

1. In your field placement, what are the mezzo-level interventions you use? How effective are those interventions? What makes them effective? What keeps them from being effective? How does diversity impact the effectiveness?

2. How does the diversity competency intersect with intervening with organizations and communities competency? How do diversity and difference impact your field placement agency? How do they impact the relationship between your field placement agency and the local community?

3. How have your field placement clients' life experiences with oppression and poverty impacted your agency's efforts to provide mezzo-level social work services? What does your field placement agency do to address its client populations' life experiences with oppression, poverty, and/or marginalization?

COMPETENCY 8: INTERVENE WITH INDIVIDUALS, FAMILIES, GROUPS, ORGANIZATIONS, AND COMMUNITIES

Social workers understand that intervention is an ongoing component of the dynamic and interactive process of social work practice with, and on behalf of, diverse individuals, families, groups, organizations, and communities. They are knowledgeable about evidence-informed interventions to achieve the goals of clients and constituencies, including individuals, families, groups, organizations, and communities. Social workers understand theories of human behavior and the social environment, and they critically evaluate and apply this knowledge to effectively intervene with clients and constituencies. They understand methods of identifying, analyzing, and implementing evidence-informed interventions to achieve client and constituency goals. Social workers value the importance of interprofessional teamwork and communication in interventions, recognizing that beneficial outcomes may require interdisciplinary, interprofessional, and interorganizational collaboration. Social workers:

● Critically choose and implement interventions to achieve practice goals and enhance capacities of clients and constituencies.

● Apply knowledge of human behavior and the social environment, person-in-environment, and other multidisciplinary theoretical frameworks in interventions with clients and constituencies.

● Use interprofessional collaboration as appropriate to achieve beneficial practice outcomes.

- Negotiate, mediate, and advocate with and on behalf of diverse clients and constituencies.

- Facilitate effective transitions and endings that advance mutually agreed-on goals.

CASE SUMMARY—"WE LOST EVERYTHING"

PRACTICE SETTING DESCRIPTION

My name is Shanna and I am a first-year MSW student completing an internship at a family services agency in a rural county near the Mississippi River. The agency provides individual and family counseling services as well as relief services and trauma services after emergencies and natural disasters. In the spring of my second semester of placement, the entire region was hit with a devastating flood during heavy rains. Everyone in the agency was dispatched to the surrounding communities to coordinate with Federal Emergency Management Agency (FEMA) officials and provide emergency relief services to flood victims as directed.

IDENTIFYING DATA

The W. family, Gloria and Henry, own 10 acres of land that they farm. They also have a small motel on their property and rent rooms to people who come during the hunting seasons every year. Gloria mentioned that Henry had just finished renovating the eight-room motel 3 weeks before the flood. Gloria and Henry have two grown children. Their son recently moved to New York City for a new job, and their daughter and her husband live in a nearby community in a small apartment with their two young children. Gloria also has a sister living in Georgia.

PRESENTING PROBLEM

The FEMA official assigned the W. family to our agency, and the case was assigned to my field instructor, Norman. Norman and I drove to the W. farm community and discovered that their home was surrounded by water. A community resident took us to the house by boat.

Gloria W. told us that she and her husband had not evacuated because her husband would not leave the home. He was staying in his room and refused to go to the city. In the 4 days since the flood began, Gloria and Henry had not left their house. Their daughter had brought some food by boat and registered her parents with FEMA. Gloria told me that the water covered their small motel next door and that most of the furniture had been destroyed. She indicated that her greatest concern was that the family would not receive compensation from FEMA because they did not have flood insurance.

Gloria indicated that she wanted to leave the house and move to the city shelter like every-one else, but she did not want to leave her husband alone. She was extremely worried about her husband. He was not sleeping or eating. She thought he might be suicidal. "I sometimes want to go and apply for loans or emergency assistance like everybody else, but I'm also afraid that if I leave him, he would hurt himself. I told him that we can't stay here by ourselves because we don't have a boat, and it does not seem that the water will go away soon." When I asked about her immediate need, she said, "I know we need food and stuff, but the most important thing is to leave and go where everybody is."

Gloria believed that her husband was traumatized by the experience. He had fought in Vietnam and still had dreams about the war. Since the flood, he had refused to take his blood pressure medicine, and she saw him crying the other day. She added, "We had a similar experience in the sixties, but the water didn't destroy everything. We helped each other, and the water receded three days after the flood." When we asked her what she thought would help her this time, she said, "I know we live in a floodplain area. We didn't buy insurance because the county decided to withdraw from the plan, but we have our will and many people are helping us. The thing that is difficult to accept is the flood. I try to work with the difficult circumstances, but my husband has a difficult time accepting that."

ASSESSMENT

Mr. and Mrs. W. had different perceptions of the situation. Henry was traumatized by the loss. Water covered their house, farm, and business. Henry felt isolated from his neighbors and immediate family. Gloria understood that living in a floodplain meant a high probability of flooding. She accepted the fact that the flood happened. Although she did not accept victimization, she struggled with their losses.

When we asked Gloria to assess the family's needs, she indicated that the most important thing was to move to temporary housing with the other survivors. She wanted to apply for assistance, communicate with people, and find out what resources were available. She also wanted to establish contact with her son, and her sister in Georgia. She asked for help in convincing her husband to leave and in getting him medical and professional assistance to help him deal with his feelings of loss and depression. By the end of the first interview, Gloria and I agreed on the following needs:

- Help Gloria convince her husband to move to a new place (she suggested asking Tom J., an old friend of her husband, to help convince Henry).

- Obtain information about possible places to move.

- Obtain copies of and review the application procedures of emergency relief programs and loans.

- Arrange for Henry to visit their family doctor.

- Make arrangements with someone who has a boat to take Gloria grocery shopping.

Gloria seemed highly motivated and willing to pursue solutions.

CASE PROCESS SUMMARY

I visited the W. family the next day. Prior to the visit, I contacted FEMA and found out that the agency has an apartment available only 15 miles away from their farm. During my visit, I gave Gloria the application forms for compensation and emergency funds. I shared that many families from the community had withdrawn from the flood insurance plan and were also not eligible to receive compensation for their damaged homes. I told them that I would be meeting with a FEMA representative in 3 days to advocate on their behalf and I would share the results with them. Gloria *was happy when I told her I had arranged a doctor's appointment for Henry and that Bob P., her neighbor, would take them to the appointment in his boat.*

I talked about applications for emergency assistance and loans. By the end of the visit, Gloria had convinced Henry that they had to move. He agreed to begin working on the process. We agreed to meet on my next field placement day at the emergency center to fill out the forms and applications.

When I met the couple at the center, Henry looked better and engaged in conversation. I helped them fill out applications for small loans and for the apartment. I drove them to look at the apartment and visit with their daughter. Henry's spirit got a boost from visiting his daughter and seeing his grandchildren. The process of moving to the new place was easier than they thought it would be. Gloria was glad that the temporary apartment was close to her daughter's apartment.

Four days later, Gloria called me from their new apartment. She asked me to refer Henry to the community mental health center for help with his depression. I did so, and Henry had his first counseling session with a mental health therapist the following week. The W.'s support network began to take shape. Their son came from New York and spent 4 days with his parents. Neighbors and friends surrounded the family. They began to attend church services.

I worked with FEMA, the county administrator, state emergency officials, and a state representative to set up a community meeting at which residents expressed their anger and frustration with the local community leaders who had withdrawn from the National Flood Insurance Program 3 years before. Following a heated discussion, a FEMA representative announced that FEMA would meet with survivors to discuss their requests for assistance.

Some of the needs were for food and furniture. I contacted the local church and helped open a food pantry there. I also found a way to transport food and supplies that were donated by people in other states. I spend the rest of my field placement working with individuals, families, local organizations, and community groups involved in helping with the recovery efforts.

Shanna, MSW student intern

DISCUSSION QUESTIONS

- How does social work practice in disaster relief differ from generalist practice with other client populations? How is it the same?
- Describe the micro practice interventions used by Shanna in the case example. What mezzo practice interventions did she use? How are the micro and mezzo interventions used in the case example interrelated? In what ways are they separate?
- This case example focused on the micro and mezzo interventions Shanna used in helping the W. family and their community. How does the social and economic justice competency impact the interventions provided by Shanna and her field instructor? What macro practice policies and interventions would help the community members and the community itself? Why?

■ ELECTRONIC COMPETENCY RESOURCES

WEBSITE LINKS

Association for Community Organization and Social Administration
www.acosa.org/joomla/about-acosa/acosapurpose

Network for Social Work Management
https://socialworkmanager.org

VIDEO LINKS

Community Organizing for Social Change—TEDx Talks, Dara Frimmer
www.youtube.com/watch?v=-DtILpmsCcA

Urban Indian Health Institute at Seattle Indian Health Board—Webinar on Centers for
Disease Control and Prevention's *Logic Models for Planning and Evaluation*
www.youtube.com/watch?v=0Vfc2uX6ciI

"How to Write a Grant Proposal: Step by Step"—Will Fanene
www.youtube.com/watch?v=ByQRri_LTUE

■ REFERENCES

Berlin, L. (2017). Money on the Table: Why Cities Aren't Fully Spending Federal Grants. Retrieved at https://cdn2
.hubspot.net/hubfs/68523/money-on-the-table.pdf?t=1514489565409

Bloom, S. L., & Sreedhar, S. Y. (2008). The sanctuary model of trauma-informed organizational change. *Reclaiming
Children and Youth: From Trauma to Trust, 17*(3), 48–53.

Brody, R. (2014). *Effectively managing human service organizations* (4th ed.). Thousand Oaks, CA: Sage.

Center for Community Health and Development at the University of Kansas. (n.d.-a). Developing a logic model or theory of change. In *Community tool box* (Chapter 2, Section 1). Retrieved from https://ctb.ku.edu/en/table-of-contents/
overview/models-for-community-health-and-development/logic-model-development/main

Center for Community Health and Development at the University of Kansas. (n.d.-b). Coalition building I: Starting a
coalition. In *Community tool box* (Chapter 5, Section 5). Retrieved from https://ctb.ku.edu/en/table-of-contents/
assessment/promotion-strategies/start-a-coaltion/main

Coley, S. M., & Scheinberg, C. A. (2008). *Proposal writing: Effective grantsmanship*. (3rd. ed.) Thousand Oaks, CA: Sage.

DuBois, B., & Miley, K. K. (2008). *Social work: An empowering profession* (6th ed.). Boston, MA: Allyn & Bacon.

Elpers, K., & Westhuis, D. J. (2008). Organizational leadership and its impact on social workers' job satisfaction: A
national study. *Administration in Social Work, 32*(3), 26–43. doi:10.1080/03643100801922399

Fellin, P. (2001). *The community and the social worker* (3rd ed.). Belmont, CA: Brooks/Cole.

Fuller, J. B., Morrison, R., Jones, L., Bridger, D., & Brown, V. (1999). The effects of psychological empowerment
on transformational leadership and job satisfaction. *Journal of Social Psychology, 139*, 389–391. doi:10.1080/
00224549909598396

Gamble, D., & Weil, M. (2010). *Community practice skills: Local to global perspectives*. New York, NY: Columbia University
Press.

Gellis, Z. D. (2001). Social work perceptions of transformational and transactional leadership in health care. *Social Work
Research, 25*(1), 17–25. doi:10.1093/swr/25.1.17

Goleman, D. (1998). What makes a leader? *Harvard Business Review, 76*, 93–102.

Goleman, D., & Boyatzis, R. E. (2017, February 6). Emotional intelligence has 12 elements: Which do you need to work on?
Harvard Business Review. Retrieved from https://hbr.org/2017/02/emotional-intelligence-has-12-elements
-which-do-you-need-to-work-on

Indiana University Lilly Family School of Philanthropy. (2017). Giving USA 2017: Total charitable donations rise to new high of $390.05 billion. Retrieved from https://givingusa.org/giving-usa-2017-total-charitable-donations-rise-to-new-high-of-390-05-billion

Louisiana Department of State Civil Service. (2015). SWOT analysis: Questions for conducting an analysis with your team. Retrieved from https://www.civilservice.louisiana.gov/files/divisions/Training/Job%20Aid/Supervisor%20Toolbox/Questions%20for%20Professional%20SWOT.pdf

Mizrahi, T., & Rosenthal, B. B. (2001). Complexities of coalition building: Leaders' successes, strategies, struggles, and solutions. *Social Work*, 46(1), 63–78. doi:10.1093/sw/46.1.63

National Association of Social Workers. (2017). *Code of ethics*. Silver Spring, MD: Author. Retrieved from https://www.socialworkers.org/About/Ethics/Code-of-Ethics/Code-of-Ethics-English

Ovans, A. (2015). How emotional intelligence became a key leadership skill. *Harvard Business Review*. Retrieved from https://hbr.org/2015/04/how-emotional-intelligence-became-a-key-leadership-skill

Philanthropy Roundtable. (2018). Statistics. Retrieved from http://www.philanthropyroundtable.org/almanac/statistics#a

Poulin, J. (2010). *Strengths-based generalist practice: A collaborative approach* (3rd ed.). Belmont, CA: Cengage.

Rubin, H. J., & Rubin, I. S. (2008). *Community organizing and development* (4th ed.). Boston, MA: Pearson/Allyn & Bacon.

Zastrow, C. (2010). *The practice of social work: A comprehensive worktext* (9th ed.). Belmont, CA: Cengage.

Zastrow, C., & Kirst-Ashman, K. K. (2010). *Understanding human behavior and the social environment* (8th ed.). Belmont, CA: Cengage.

Index